Lecture Notes in Computer Science 3905

Commenced Publication in 1973
Founding and Former Series Editors:
Gerhard Goos, Juris Hartmanis, and Jan van Leeuwen

Pierre Collet   Marco Tomassini
Marc Ebner   Steven Gustafson
Anikó Ekárt (Eds.)

Genetic Programming

9th European Conference, EuroGP 2006
Budapest, Hungary, April 10-12, 2006
Proceedings

 Springer

Volume Editors

Pierre Collet
Université du Littoral Côte d'Opale, Laboratoire d'Informatique du Littoral
BP 719, 62100 Calais Cedex, France
E-mail: Pierre.Collet@Univ-Littoral.fr

Marco Tomassini
University of Lausanne, Information Systems Department
1015 Lausanne, Switzerland
E-mail: Marco.Tomassini@unil.ch

Marc Ebner
Universität Würzburg, Lehrstuhl für Informatik II
Am Hubland, 97074 Würzburg, Germany
E-mail: ebner@informatik.uni-wuerzburg.de

Steven Gustafson
GE Global Research, Computing and Decision Sciences
One Research Circle, Niskayuna, NY 12309, USA
E-mail: steven.gustafson@research.ge.com

Anikó Ekárt
Aston University, Computer Science
Aston Triangle, B4 7ET Birmingham, UK
E-mail: ekarta@aston.ac.uk
and
Hungarian Academy of Sciences
Computer and Automation Research Institute
1111 Budapest, Kende u. 13-17, Hungary

The cover illustration is the work of Pierre Grenier

Library of Congress Control Number: 2006922466

CR Subject Classification (1998): D.1, F.1, F.2, I.5, I.2, J.3

LNCS Sublibrary: SL 1 – Theoretical Computer Science and General Issues

ISSN   0302-9743
ISBN-10   3-540-33143-3 Springer Berlin Heidelberg New York
ISBN-13   978-3-540-33143-8 Springer Berlin Heidelberg New York

Springer is a part of Springer Science+Business Media

springer.com

© Springer-Verlag Berlin Heidelberg 2006
Printed in Germany

Typesetting: Camera-ready by author, data conversion by Scientific Publishing Services, Chennai, India
Printed on acid-free paper   SPIN: 11729976   06/3142   5 4 3 2 1 0

Preface

The present volume contains the contributions for the 9th European Conference on Genetic Programming (EuroGP 2006). The conference took place during April 10-12, 2006 in Budapest, Hungary. EuroGP is a well-established conference and the only one exclusively devoted to genetic programming worldwide. EuroGP began as a workshop in 1998 in Paris, and has been held annually since then, becoming a conference in Edinburgh in 2000. All previous proceedings have been published by Springer in the *Lecture Notes in Computer Science* series. More recently, EuroGP has been co-located with EvoCOP 2006, the 6th European Conference on Evolutionary Computation in Combinatorial Optimization, and the EvoWorkshops, focusing on applications of evolutionary computation, resulting in the largest combined event dedicated to evolutionary computation in Europe.

Genetic programming (GP) is evolutionary computation that solves complex problems or tasks by evolving and adapting a population of computer programs, using Darwinian evolution and Mendelian genetics as its sources of inspiration. The 32 papers included in these proceedings address fundamental and theoretical issues, along with a wide variety of papers dealing with different application areas, such as computer science, engineering, machine learning, Kolmogorov complexity, biology and computational design, showing that GP is a powerful and practical problem-solving paradigm.

A rigorous, double-blind, selection mechanism was applied to 59 submitted papers, that resulted in the acceptance of 21 plenary talks (36% acceptance rate) and 11 poster presentations (54% global acceptance rate for talks and posters). Each paper was reviewed by three members of the international Program Committee, each with post-doctoral experience and selected for expertise in their own field. Assignment was done manually, by trying to match as closely as possible each reviewer's domain of expertise to the topics covered by the paper. The results of this rigorous selection process are reflected in the quality of the contributions published within this volume.

We would like to express our sincere gratitude to the two internationally renowned invited speakers, who gave the keynote talks: Richard J. Terrile, astronomer, Director of the Center for Evolutionary Computation and Automated Design at NASA's Jet Propulsion Laboratory, and Stefan Voß, Chair and Director of the Institute of Information Systems at the Faculty of Hamburg.

The success of this conference results from the input of many people, to whom we would like to express our appreciation. Firstly, we thank the members of the Program Committee for their time and involvement. Their reviews were often very thorough and constructive, giving the authors valuable advice on how to improve their papers for the final publication. The local organizers and Judit Megyery have done an extraordinary job that was a key contribution to the success of this conference. Last but not least, the deep involvement of Jennifer

Willies and the School of Computing, Napier University, in the organization of this event was of paramount importance. Her professionalism and organizational qualities allowed for a smooth-running, enjoyable conference.

We thank the Artpool Art Research Center of Budapest, and especially György Galántai, for offering space and expertise without which the wonderful evolutionary art and music exhibition associated with the conference would not have been possible.

April 2006

Pierre Collet
Marco Tomassini
Marc Ebner
Steven Gustafson
Anikó Ekárt

Organization

EuroGP 2006 was organized by EvoGP, the EvoNet Working Group on Genetic Programming.

Organizing Committee

Program Co-chairs: Pierre Collet (Université du Littoral Côte d'Opale, France)
Marco Tomassini (University of Lausanne, Switzerland)
Publication Chair: Marc Ebner (Universität Würzburg, Germany)
Local Chair: Anikó Ekárt (Hungarian Academy of Sciences, Hungary, and Aston University, UK)
Publicity Chair: Steven Gustafson (GE Global Research, USA)

Program Committee

Abbass, Hussein. University of New South Wales, Australia
Aydin, Emin. London South Bank University, UK
Azad, Raja Muhammad Atif. University of Limerick, Ireland
Brabazon, Anthony. University College Dublin, Ireland
Bredeche, Nicolas. TAO/INRIA-LRI, France
Burke, Edmund. University of Nottingham, UK
Cagnoni, Stefano. University of Parma, Italy
Cheang, Sin Man. Hong Kong Institute of Vocational Education, China
Collard, Philippe. I3S laboratory (UNSA-CNRS), France
Collet, Pierre. Université du Littoral Côte d'Opale, France
Costa, Ernesto. University of Coimbra, Portugal
de Jong, Edwin. Utrecht University, The Netherlands
Defoin-Platel, Michael. Université de Nice Sophia-Antipolis, France
Divina, Federico. Tilburg University, The Netherlands
Ebner, Marc. Universität Würzburg, Germany
Ekárt, Anikó. Hungarian Academy of Sciences and Aston University, UK
Essam, Daryl. University of New South Wales, Australia
Fernández de Vega, Francisco. University of Extremadura, Spain
Folino, Gianluigi. University of Calabria, Italy
Fonlupt, Cyrll. Université du Littoral, France
Gagne, Christian. Université Paris Sud, France
Giacobini, Mario. University of Lausanne, Switzerland
Gustafson, Steven. GE Global Research, USA
Hao, Jin-Kao. University of Angers, France
Howard, Daniel. QinetiQ, UK
Johnson, Colin. University of Kent at Canterbury, UK

Table of Contents

Posters

802.11 De-authentication Attack Detection Using Genetic Programming

Patrick LaRoche and A. Nur Zincir-Heywood

Faculty of Computer Science, Dalhousie University,
Halifax, Nova Scotia, B3H 1W5, Canada
plaroche@cs.dal.ca
zincir@cs.dal.ca

Abstract. This paper presents a genetic programming approach to detect deauthentication attacks on wireless networks based on the 802.11
protocol. To do so we focus on developing an appropriate fitness function
and feature set. Results show that the intrusion system developed not
only performs incredibly well - 100 percent detection rate and 0.5 percent
false positive rate - but also developed a solution that is general enough
to detect similar attacks, such as disassociation attacks, that were not
present in the training data.

1 Introduction

As computer networks have become more prevalent, in varying forms, different
protocols are being developed in order to support alternative networking under
different environments. One such protocol is 802.11, where this describes a standard for communication over wireless connections. This protocol, also known as
WiFi, has been deployed in a growing number of locations resulting in a diversity
of purposes, from providing a household with a wireless network, to supporting
an entire office building. Due to this growing popularity and exposure, more and
more exploits are being discovered, undermining the use of the 802.11 network
protocol.

The very nature of a wireless network, no matter the protocol being used,
opens the network up to vulnerabilities not present in wired networks. These issues arise from the fact that data is being transfered over the air, where anyone
with the appropriate device can intercept. For this reason the 802.11 network
provides many security features, such as encryption and client verification. These
measures, as important as they are, have received the majority of emphasis. Unfortunately, they do not cover all the possible weaknesses in the 802.11 protocol.
In our work we look at the issue of maintaining the availability of the network
itself. That is to say there are well known exploits with the 802.11 protocol that
allow users of malicious intent to disrupt the use of the network, either for a
specific client or the entire network. This in return disrupts the availability of
the network for its users; whereas the availability and ease of use represent one
of the main reasons behind the widespread deployment of WiFi networks.

P. Collet et al. (Eds.): EuroGP 2006, LNCS 3905, pp. 1–12, 2006.

Traditionally, intrusion detection systems (IDSs) are used to detect attacks against the integrity, confidentiality and availability of computer networks [1]. In order to build effective IDSs and automate the detection process, various machine learning and artificial intelligence techniques have been proposed. These techniques include neural networks [2], data mining [3], decision trees [4], genetic algorithms (GA) [5, 6], and genetic programming (GP) [7, 8, 9]. In general, data mining techniques are introduced to identify key features and machine learning and AI techniques are introduced to automate the classification of normal and attack traffic / behavior on the network. To the best of authors' knowledge, works utilizing genetic algorithms and genetic programming were all based on the TCP/IP protocol stack. This corresponds to the third and fourth layers of the network stack. On a WiFi network running a TCP/IP protocol stack, however, their exist attacks based on vulnerabilities in the physical and data link layers, i.e. the first and second layers respectively.

Thus, past work applying evolutionary methods to network intrusion detection has focused on connection based attacks. In doing so, much progress has been made in providing an efficient and effective intrusion detection system (IDS) using genetic programming as the tool to create the rules in which to detect attacks [7]. This does not necessarily make a GP or GA based IDS effective in detecting network protocol specific attacks at layer one and two, such as in the case of WiFi networks.

In this paper we present our work towards developing a GP based IDS for WiFi networks. By using past research as a starting point, we aim to build on the past successes (quick training time, transparent solutions) while adapting to the challenges of intrusion detection on the 802.11 network. The remainder of this paper first details background information on 802.11 networks in Section 2, followed by a description of the GP that we have implemented in Section 3. In Section 4, we detail our approach for developing our GP based IDS, followed by Section 5, in which we list the performance of our GP based IDS, and concluding with Section 6 where we discuss our findings and how we will be proceeding with our work.

2   802.11 - WiFi Networks

The network protocol we focus on in our work is that of the 802.11b network (WiFi). WiFi networks have increased in popularity over the past few years, so much so that their use as a last mile solution for Internet connection has become common place, not only with homes but businesses alike. It has become so popular, that in the year 2001, the market for 802.11 based networks exceeded $1 Billion Dollars [10]. This wide spread (and growing) deployment of WiFi networks makes them a growing area for research, both in improvement of service, but also in security and reliance of the service they provide. In this section, we discuss the basics of WiFi networks, current security features and the known exploits of the WiFi protocol. This is not an exhaustive description of the WiFi protocol, as that is beyond the scope of this paper.

2.1   Management Frames

WiFi networks have a series of MAC frame types, as described in the IEEE 802.11 Standard (see [11]). Of concern for our work are the management frames. The management frame type allows clients to associate with (or conversely disassociate from) the network via an access point (AP), as well as maintaining a channel for communications to proceed. We focus on a subset of the management frame subtypes; *Association request* , *Deauthentication* and *Disassociation*. These subtypes allow clients to join, leave, and be told to leave WiFi networks.

In order for a client to establish a connection with an existing WiFi network, it first must associate with an AP. This *association* is established through searching for an access point on a specific BSSID (basic service set identification, an identifier of a specific WiFi network) on a given channel (usually on a range of channels). Once the client has found an access point on the desired BSSID and channel, the following procedure is used to establish a connection with the AP (simplified from [11]) :

1. The client can transmit an association request to an AP with which that client is authenticated.
2. If an Association Response frame is received with a status value of successful, the client is now associated with the AP.
3. If an Association Response frame is received with a status value other than successful or a timeout value passes, the client is not associated with the AP.

This procedure relies on a one-way trust, the client trusting the validity of the AP, not visa versa. This distinction is important. At no time does the client require that the AP prove that it is a valid AP.

A procedure exists for a client to *disassociate* itself from a network. As described in the IEEE 802.11 Standard ([11]), in order to disassociate, the client must send a disassociation subtype management frame. This frame type can be sent in either direction, from the client to the AP or from the AP to the client. The frame contains the hardware address of the client that is being disassociated (the broadcast address in the case of an AP disassociating with all associated clients). It also contains the hardware address of the AP with which the client is currently associated. [11]

Similarly, a client or AP can invalidate an active authenticated connection through the use of *de-authentication* subtype of the management frame type. This frame can again be sent from a client to an AP, an AP to a client, AP to AP, or even client to client. This frame subtype contains the same information as the disassociation subtype.

2.2   Known Exploits

The 802.11 MAC layer includes functionality that addresses issues specific to a wireless network [10]. For example, the ability to search for networks, broadcast networks, join and leave networks are all taken care of by MAC layer frames, specifically management frames. As mentioned earlier (and in other works [10]), there is an implicit trust in the ethernet address of the sender of a management frame. This implicit trust opens up the door to a group of Denial of Service (DoS) attacks on the 802.11 network. If a malicious client, or hacker, fakes its ethernet address (a trivial task with most operating systems and a small Internet search) it can then send management frames onto an 802.11 network with the network assuming the hardware address is valid. This can cause problems if the hardware address has been set to that of another valid client, or to that of a valid access point.

DoS attacks are not the only exploits or security weaknesses that exist on 802.11 networks. Much work has been done in addressing other security concerns. Papers such as [12] and [13] point out security weaknesses of the encryption algorithms implemented on 802.11 networks, and that is assuming the network administrators have even enabled encryption. This is not always a fair assumption given the wide spread adoption of 802.11 network for home networking, where the network administrator could be assumed to have no networking knowledge at all. This has resulted in a slew of acronyms, protocols and protocol extensions (WEP, WPA, RADIUS, 802.11g, 802.11i, 802.1X, etc) that have all tackled issues from speed to security concerns; however, to the best of our knowledge none of these deal with ensuring that the network remains *usable*. By this we mean that it is still possible to perform simple forms of DoS attacks even on the newest and latest protocol version of 802.11. For this purpose, we have chosen to focus on a specific subset of DoS attacks, described below.

2.3   De-authentication DoS Attacks

The DoS attack we focus on in this work is that caused by the attacker sending de-authentication frames onto the wireless network . An attacker chooses a target on the network (which has been gathered by actively monitoring the 802.11 network traffic using a tool such as kismet [14]) and then spoofs their ethernet address. At this point, the attacker then sends a de-authentication attack to the access point in which the target is associated. This causes the access point to send a de-authentication frame back at the target, removing the target from the network, preventing it from sending or receiving any further communications. The duration of which the target remains removed from the network depends on the frequency in which it attempts to regain network access.

This attack, simple in its implementation, is quite powerful for several reasons. The first being that the attacker can choose the scope of the attack, be it a single network client, several, or an entire network (by choosing the access point itself as the spoofed address). The result being that an attacker can completely disrupt all communications on a single network, no matter how many clients the network may have. Secondly, if the attacker has targeted a single client, once the client is removed from the network the attacker can then continue with several other attacks, such as a man in the middle attack [15].

3   GP Based Intrusion Detection Systems

In order for us to be able to detect attacks that exploit the above mentioned vulnerabilities in the 802.11 standard, we have applied a genetic programming based intrusion detection system (IDS). Due to previous success in application of GP based IDSs to wired networks [7], we have chosen to take the same approach in creating an IDS for 802.11 networks. In previous work, a page based linearly structured GP was employed [16] as well as the utilization of a RSS-DSS algorithm which scales GP to data sets consisting of hundred of thousands of exemplars [7]. For the work we present here, we have used a similar approach, but concentrated on the devopment of an appropriate fitness function and feature set. For this work, our goal is to not only to develop a machine learning technique to detect network intrusions on 802.11 networks with a high accuracy and low false positive rate, but to also be able to develop these solutions in a quick, transparent matter.

3.1   Linear Page Based Genetic Programming

Linear Page Based GPs (L-GP) consist of a sequence of integers that once decoded, form the basis of a program in which the output is taken from the best performing register, as defined by the fitness function. In order to decode this linear set of instructions, each integer is mapped to a valid instruction from the *a priori* defined instruction set. The instruction set consists of operands and either a source or destination register. The operands in our work are a set of register arithmetic functions, while the source and destinations are a set of valid general purpose registers. The decoding of a sequence then creates a program that consists of simple register level transformation [7]. Upon completion of execution of the program, the output is taken from the best performing register.

The sequence of integers are grouped in *pages*, each page consisting of the same number of integers (therefore the same number of instructions). The crossover operation performs a crossover on an entire page, preserving the total number of pages in an individual. The mutation operator selects one instruction with uniform probability and performs an Ex-OR operation between this and a bit sequence created with uniform probability. A second crossover operator performs a swap of two instructions within the same individual (selected again with uniform probability) [16]. The page size itself, which controls the number of instructions per individual, is dynamically modified depending on the fitness level of the population. If the fitness level has not changed for a specified window, the page size is increased. This pattern will continue until a maximum page size is reached, at which point the page size is dropped back down to the initial starting page size. This entire process is continued until the GP has reached either optimal fitness, or some sort of previously set stopping criteria. Results show that the dynamic page size algorithm is significantly more efficient then a fixed page size [16].

3.2   RSS-DSS Algorithm

The Random Subset Selection - Dynamic Subset Selection (RSS-DSS) algorithm mentioned   above   is   a   technique   implemented   in   order   to   reduce   the computational overhead (therefore time to train the GP) involved with applying GPs to large data sets. To do so, the RSS-DSS algorithm utilizes a hierarchical sampling of training exemplars, dividing the problem into two levels [7]. We present here a brief overview of how the algorithm functions for completeness, as we have implemented it in our GP, but it is not the focus of our work.

The first level of RSS-DSS divides the training set into blocks of equal size, the second level chooses (stochastically) a block and places it in memory (RSS). Level 2 performs the DSS step, as it dynamically selects a subset of the set in memory (the tournament selection). The dynamic selection is based on two metrics the GP maintains, the age of the exemplar and the apparent difficulty of the exemplar [17]. The tournament individuals are then trained on the current subset, genetic operators are applied, and then placed back in the subset. This DSS is continued until a maximum number of DSS iterations or a stoping criteria is met, then the algorithm returns to the RSS step, selecting another block to place in memory and repeats DSS. This entire process continues until a maximum number of RSS iterations or the stop criteria has been met.

The RSS-DSS algorithm removes the requirement to train on the entire data set, instead only uses a small subset of the data set that represents the more difficult or least recently encountered exemplars. This allows the GP to train more efficiently then standard techniques, with results being comparable or better than more common GP training techniques [7].

4   Approach

Due to the above mentioned ability of L-GP when applied to Intrusion Detection [7], we felt that this previous work would make for a strong foundation for applying GP techniques to WiFi Intrusion Detection. To this end, we have developed an appropriate fitness function and feature set for the detection of the de-authentication attack on 802.11b networks. As mentioned, this attack is both real and easily performed, and has damaging effects on network usability.

4.1   Data Set Creation

Our L-GP based IDS requires training and testing on labeled data sets. That is to say, we require data files that have a fixed number of input fields creating an exemplar, with an output field that indicates that it is either an attack (binary 1) or normal (binary 0). For this realm, each exemplar represents a management packet on a WiFi network. To the best of authors' knowledge, no known public database exists of wireless network traffic to use in training IDSs based on learning algorithms. To this end, we first set upon creating such a data set in order to train and test of our L-GP based IDS. Our approach to this task was both practical (to be feasible within our research facilities ability) as well as appropriate (large enough data set to be considered useful for training a learning algorithm).

A data set collection of 12 different network traffic dumps were collected on a real WiFi test network(performed using kismet [14] which dumps network traffic in a pcap format, a standard format for network traffic). These *dump files* were grouped into two different sets, the *large* and *small* sets, as six data sets were considerably larger then the other six. File statistics are shown in Table 1 (the original file size is equal to the normal packet count).

These data sets were assumed to have no attacks existing within them (a fair assumption given they were developed from load testing networks). From this, we developed a series of scripts that allowed us to inject simulated deauthentication attacks into the network stream. In order to create these attacks, we attacked our own small test network consisting of one client, one access point, a hacker laptop and a monitoring machine. The AP was the latest Apple Airport Base Station, the client a Mac Mini. The client connected to the AP via an 802.11b network on channel 6. The attack machine was an Intel based laptop running a Prism 2 based WiFi card running the Auditor Security Collection operating system. The monitoring machine was a Intel based Desktop computer running Debian and using Kismet for monitoring the wireless network of the AP.

Using this network we implemented a DoS attack directed at both the client and then the AP. The packet stream gathered via the monitoring machine indicated that the attack required a stream of management frames of subtype 12 (indicating a de-authentication frame) with the source and BSSID ethernet addresses to be that of the target, and the destination address to be that of the broadcast address (ff:ff:ff:ff:ff:ff). It is important to note that this attack can be performed with slight variations of this frame, but this format seemed the most effective. The frequency and duration of the transmission of the attack frames depended upon the desired persistence of the attacker, we found that continuous frame transmissions for a period of thirty frames (minimum) was required to have the desired DoS result on the target. Due to these findings, our injected de-authentication attacks vary in length between 30 and 100 attack frames at random locations within the provided network streams. Our test "injected" data sets then consisted of a varying number of actual attacks, with each attack varying in length. The statistics of these data sets are listed in Table 1.

Table 1. Injected Network Stream File Statistics

File	Normal Packets	Attack Packets	Total Packets	% Attack/Normal
1	155079	61959	217038	0.400
2	152759	126399	279158	0.827
3	156559	184159	340718	1.176
4	158399	241399	399798	1.524
5	153839	309079	462918	2.009
6	154679	364559	519238	2.357
7	44879	119	44998	0.003
8	44959	119	45078	0.003
9	44999	239	45238	0.005
10	45119	399	45518	0.009
11	45079	1759	46838	0.039
12	44999	3079	48078	0.068

A second pair of data sets were also created in order to validate the above approach. For these data sets, we implemented a small test network (the same as described as above, with 5 more clients added to the network, all generating web traffic) then attacked the network (using the techniques described above). Thus the result being two data sets of varying length, with two different attack placements and durations. These data sets are then used as a training testing pair, as they represent *live* network traffic with an inline attack (file statistics in Table 3).

4.2   Feature Selection

The data files listed in Table 1 are made up of management frame packets. A management frame on a 802.11 network consists of several fields. For our L-GP based IDS, we chose to train and test on the following features of the frame:

1. Frame Control - indicates the subtype of the frame
2. DA - destination address of the packet
3. SA - sender address of the packet
4. BSSID - ethernet address of the access point
5. Fragment Number - from the sequence control field
6. Sequence Number - from the sequence control field
7. Channel - the channel the transmission is occurring over

In total, this gives us seven inputs, and one output (attack label). This selection of features to select from each packet was chosen based on a priori knowledge of the attack type. Our work here is to see if the GP can use this information to then learn to detect the attack.

4.3   Fitness Function Selection

The fitness function (or cost function) we chose for our GP was based on our goals of having a high detection rate (DR), as well as low false positive (FP) and false negative (FN) rates, defined as follows;

$$DetectionRate = 1 - (\frac{\#FalseNegativeClassifications}{TotalNumberofAttackConnections}) \qquad (1)$$

$$FalsePositiveRate = (\frac{\#FalsePositiveClassifications}{TotalNumberofNormalConnections}) \qquad (2)$$

To this end, we define a switching fitness function that will punish the GP depending on whether the GP has had a false positive or a false negative result. Two different costs will be associated with the switch depending on the makeup of the data set itself. If the individual has resulted in a false positive, the individual is awarded a cost equal to the error over the number of normal packets in the data set (Equation 3). Similarly, if the individual has resulted in a false negative, it is awarded the cost of the error over the number of attack packets in the data set (Equation 4). A higher cost is deemed a poorer performance then a lower cost.

$$Performance of individual+ = \frac{Error}{TotalNumber of NormalConnections} \quad (3)$$

$$Performance of individual+ = \frac{Error}{TotalNumber of AttackConnections} \quad (4)$$

The result of this switching cost function is that an individual will get awarded costs that are proportional to how *easy* it is to achieve either a false positive or a false negative. For example, if the individual results in a false negative, and there are less normal packets then attack packets in the data set (say a ratio of 3 to 1), then the cost associated with this will be larger then if it were a false positive.

Table 2. Disassociation Injected Network Stream File Statistics

File	Normal Packets	Attack Packets	Total Packets	% Attack/Normal
1	45040	0	45040	0
2	44960	120	45080	0.003
3	45120	160	45280	0.004
4	45120	440	45560	0.010
5	45200	880	46080	0.019
6	45120	1800	46920	0.038
7	45320	2800	48120	0.058
8	45400	5840	51240	0.114

5   Results

We ran the GP over all 12 data sets (Table 1), using each data set as a training data set, as well as testing data sets. That is to say, we would run the GP on data set 1, then test on data sets 2-12, etc. This insured that the GP was being evaluated on an array of different data sets, with different ratios of attack to normal exemplars, different placements and durations of attacks, as well as the size of the data sets themselves. We then ran each one of the above experiments 10 times, with different random seeds used for the initial population creation. The parameters used during the running of the GP are shown in Table 6, the results are shown in Table 4.

As seen from the results, our L-GP based IDS performed incredibly well. Thus for verification purposes, two more experiments were conducted. The first being

Table 3. Live Network Data Set File Statistics

File	Normal Packets	Attack Packets	Total Packets	% Attack/Normal
Training	5890	450	5440	0.083
Testing	6370	130	6240	0.021

to create another 8 data sets (file statistics show in Table 2). This collection of data sets were injected with a similar attack to the de-authentication attack: the disassociation attack [10], which is different only in the type of frame that is sent by the attacker. We tested the previously trained GPs (trained with the de-authentication attack) on these newer data sets. The intent was to determine if the GP had over specified its training; if so, it would miss the very similar attack. The results, shown in Table 4, indicate that the GP had developed a solution that was general enough to detect this new (admittedly similar) attack.

The second additional experiment used the data set pair created with live network traffic and inline attacks (described in 4.1). These data sets represent a real WiFi network that had been attacked using the DoS attack, with the network traffic before, after and during the attack recorded and labeled for use in training and testing the L-GP based IDS. The goal of this experiment is to show that the response of the network to the attack (such as the rejoining of the clients to the network after being de-authenticated) would not cause difficulty to the IDS. The GP was run 40 times, using different initial seeds for the initial population generation, which resulted in two best performing solutions shown in Table 5. As shown, even on live network traffic, the L-GP based IDS performs incredibly well. The best solution with respect to the detection rate, maintains

Table 4. Results

Performance:	De-Authentication Attacks			Disassociation Attacks		
	Run Time	DR	FP Rate	Run Time	DR	FP Rate
1st Quartile	19.9983	100.00%	0.00	18.5455	100.00%	0.00
Median	23.5468	100.00%	0.00	26.145	100.00%	0.00
3rd Quartile	27.712	100.00%	0.00	33.9506	100.00%	0.00

Table 5. *Live* Network Resulting Solutions

Best Performer	with respect to DR	with respect to FP Rate
Time	44.098	40.838
Detection Rate	100.000%	86.154%
FP Rate	0.529%	0.000%

Table 6. Parameter Settings for Dynamic Page Based Linear GP

Parameter	Setting	Parameter	Setting
Population size	125	Number of registers	8
Maximim number of pages	32	Function set	$\{+,-,*,/\}$
Page size	8 instructions	Terminal set	$\{0, ..., 255\} \bigcup \{i_0, ...,i_{63}\}$
Maximum working page size	8 instructions	RSS subset size	5000
Crossover probability	0.9	DSS subset size	50
Mutation probability	0.5	RSS iteration	1000
Swap probability	0.9	DSS iteration	100
Tournament size	4		

a 100% DR, while still providing a very low FP rate, as well the best solution with respect to the false positive rate can achieve a 0% FP rate, with a high DR.

6 Discussion/Future Work

We have successfully shown that a L-GP based IDS can be applied to attacks that are unique to the realm of WiFi networks. Our results show that the GP can be trained on one of the most common attacks to 802.11 networks, with an outcome of 100% detection rate with a 0.529% false positive rate. We have also shown that the GP, even when trained on such a specific attack type, can provide a solution that is generalized enough to detect similar attacks.

We hypothesize that the original collection data sets did not simulate the real reaction of the network from the attack, thus providing the GP with a clean separation between the attack packets and the network background traffic. By then running our IDS on live network traffic during a DoS attack, and using this as our training and testing data sets, we have shown that we can still achieve such high DR and low FP rates. Our future work will explore larger live network data sets including both DoS attacks and more complicated attacks such as Man in the Middle Attacks.

Acknowledgments

This research is supported by the NSERC Discovery and the CFI New Opportunities grants. This work is conducted as part of the NIMS project at http://www.cs.dal.ca/projectx/.

References

1. Lundin, E., Jonsson, E.: Survey of intrusion detection research (2002)
2. Mukkamala, S. Sung, A.: A comparative study of techniques for intrusion detection, 15th ieee international conference on tools with artificial intelligence. 15th IEEE International Conference on Tools with Artificial Intelligence – ICTAI (2003) 570 – 577
3. Xia, T., Qu, G., Hariri, S., Yousif, M.: An efficient network intrusion detection method based on information theory and genetic algorithm. Performance, Computing, and Communications Conference, 2005. IPCCC 2005 (2005) 11 – 17
4. Sinclair, C., Pierce, L., Matzner, S.: An application of machine learning to network intrusion detection. In: Computer Security Applications Conference, ACSAC '00 (1999) 371–377
5. Ren Hui Gong; Zulkernine, M.; Abolmaesumi, P.: A software implementation of a genetic algorithm based approach to network intrusion detection. Sixth ACIS International Conference on Software Engineering, Artificial Intelligence, Networking, and Parallel/Distributed Computing - SNPD/SAWN 2005 (2005) 246 – 253
6. Li, W.: Using genetic algorithm for network intrusion detection, Kansas City, Kansas, United States Department of Energy Cyber Security Group 2004 Training Conference (2004)

 7. Song, D., Heywood, M.I., Zincir-Heywood, A.N.: Training genetic programming on half a million patterns: an example from anomaly detection. IEEE Transactions on Evolutionary Computation **9**(3) (2005) 225–239
 8. Lu, W., Traore, I.: Detecting new forms of network intrusion using genetic programming. In Sarker, R., Reynolds, R., Abbass, H., Tan, K.C., McKay, B., Essam, D., Gedeon, T., eds.: Proceedings of the 2003 Congress on Evolutionary Computation CEC2003, Canberra, IEEE Press (2003) 2165–2172
 9. Crosbie, M., Spafford, E.H.: Applying genetic programming to intrusion detection. In Siegel, E.V., Koza, J.R., eds.: Working Notes for the AAAI Symposium on Genetic Programming, MIT, Cambridge, MA, USA, AAAI (1995) 1–8
10. Bellardo, J., Savage, S.: 802.11 denial-of-service attacks: real vulnerabilities and practical solutions. In: USENIX Security Symposium. (2003) 15–28
11. IEEE-SA Standards Board: ANSI/IEEE Std 802.11, 1999 Edition (R2003). IEEE, New York, NY, USA (1999)
12. Fluhrer, S., Mantin, I., Shamir, A.: Weaknesses in the key scheduling algorithm of RC4. Lecture Notes in Computer Science **2259** (2001) 1–24
13. Borisov, N., Goldberg, I., Wagner, D.: Intercepting mobile communications: The insecurity of 802.11. `http://www.isaac.cs.berkeley.edu/isaac/wep-faq.html` (2001)
14. Kershaw, M.: Kismet http://www.kismetwireless.net/ (2005)
15. Schmoyer, T., Lim, Y.X., Owen, H.: Wireless Intrusion Detection and Response: A case study using the classic man-in-the-middle attack. In: IEEE Wireless Communications and Networking Conference, Atlanta Ga. (2004)
16. Heywood, M.I., Zincir-Heywood, A.N.: Dynamic page based crossover in linear genetic programming. IEEE Transactions on Systems, Man, and Cybernetics: Part B - Cybernetics **32**(3) (2002) 380–388
17. Gathercole, C., Ross, P.: Dynamic training subset selection for supervised learning in genetic programming. In Davidor, Y., Schwefel, H.P., Männer, R., eds.: Parallel Problem Solving from Nature III. Volume 866 of LNCS., Jerusalem, Springer-Verlag (1994) 312–321

A Divide & Conquer Strategy for Improving Efficiency and Probability of Success in Genetic Programming

Cyril Fillon and Alberto Bartoli

University of Trieste, P.le Europa, 1, 34127 Trieste, Italy
{cfillon, bartolia}@univ.trieste.it

Abstract. A common method for improving a genetic programming search on difficult problems is either multiplying the number of runs or increasing the population size.

In this paper we propose a new search strategy which attempts to obtain a higher probability of success with smaller amounts of computational resources. We call this model Divide & Conquer since our algorithm initially partitions the search space in smaller regions that are explored independently of each other. Then, our algorithm collects the most competitive individuals found in each partition and exploits them in order to get a solution. We benchmarked our proposal on three problem domains widely used in the literature. Our results show a significant improvement of the likelihood of success while requiring less computational resources than the standard algorithm.

1 Introduction

When one uses Genetic Programming to solve a problem, he has two expectancies: on the one hand, maximize the probability to obtain a solution, and on the other hand, minimize the amount of computational resources to get this solution.

Unfortunately performance on a given problem may be strongly dependent on a broad range of parameters, including the choice of the functions and terminals set, size and composition of the initial population, maximum number of generations and so on.

To overcome the difficulties of such problems a traditional method was to use a larger population and to increase the maximum number of generations [1][6]. Large populations were considered beneficial because they maintain diversity and may avoid premature convergence. However, more recent works advocate for different approaches, using either populations of moderate or variable size (e.g. [5][9]), or using multiple independent short runs (e.g. [8][2]) in order to outperform a long run.

Recent research [4] confirms that the composition of an initial population has a crucial influence on the probability of success for a problem. It is suggested that the initial population must contain a sufficient quantity of useful building blocks and that these blocks must be part of the fittest individuals. Moreover it

P. Collet et al. (Eds.): EuroGP 2006, LNCS 3905, pp. 13–23, 2006.

was shown in [3] that the building blocks used during the GP process are not dispersed throughout in the initial population, but is instead concentrated in a subset of individuals.

Thus the effectiveness of GP to solve a problem is conditioned by its ability to create potential good individuals in the initial population and identify the individuals which are most likely to provide building blocks useful to find the solution.

In this paper we build on these existing results and propose a new model attempting to meet these requirements. Our model works in two phases. During the first phase we partition the search space in smaller regions that are explored independently of each other. We do so by generating initial populations carefully tailored to maximize the coverage of each region. Then, in the second phase, we collect the most competitive individuals found in each region and explore the resulting search space. In other words, we attempt to generate individuals which maximize the coverage of the search space and then we attempt to exploit the most promising individuals. Our strategy aims to obtain a solution with a better probability of success for a lower computational cost.

The outline of the paper is as follows. In Section 2 we describe our strategy in detail. Section 3 presents the experimental procedure used to study the behavior of the new algorithm with various metrics. Section 4 discusses the results of our experiments. Section 5 concludes and anticipates on further evolutions of our strategy.

2   Divide & Conquer Strategy

Our proposal, that we call *Divide & Conquer*, is inspired by earlier models for coarse-grained parallelization of the genetic programming process [10][11]. These models build a net of subpopulations called "demes". Each deme evolves independently of one another during a sequence of consecutive generations. Then, demes may exchange information by migrating individuals between each other according to a predefined pattern. Our proposal uses the concept of demes but works differently.

2.1   Model Description

First of all, we apply a reduction and differentiation function on the functions set F_S, as follows. Let n denote the cardinality of F_S. We build all possible subsets of F_S composed of exactly p elements, where p is a parameter of the algorithm such that $p < n$. We may apply the same procedure also on the terminals set T_S, or on the union of both $T_S \cup F_S$. If the reduction and differentiation is applied on F_S then the elements of T_S are added to the new subsets, if it is applied on T_S we add the elements of F_S. We denote by f_{RD} the reduction and differentiation function and by RD_{SS}^i ($i \in [1, n]$) the subsets generated.

Each deme operates on one of the subsets generated by f_{RD}. It follows that each deme operates on a subset of functions and terminals different from the subset of any other deme. Subsets obtained from T_S must contain at least one element and those obtained from F_S must contain at least two elements or, two elements and one element respectively from T_S and F_S. Otherwise, the use of an evolutionary approach would be meaningless.

The number of demes must be the same as the number of the subsets generated by f_{RD}, that is $numOfDemes = C_n^p$. The algorithm analyzed in this paper use $p = n - 1$. It follows that, in our case it will be $numOfDemes = C_n^{n-1}$, hence $numOfDemes = n$.

At this point, the initial population of each deme is constructed based on the subset associated with that deme. Each deme evolves independently of each other deme, until either the problem is solved or a maximum number of generations $maxDemeGenNumber$ is reached.

If no solution is found, i.e., all demes reach the maximum number of generations, we merge all the demes and keep only the best individuals based on a ranking selection procedure. This new population then evolves as usual, i.e., either until the problem is solved or a maximum number of generation is reached.

Full details about our algorithm are given in Figure 2.

2.2   Model's Dynamics

An example of the algorithm's dynamics is shown in Figure 1 where the final population size is 500, the maximum number of generations is 95 and the maximum number of generations for a deme is 5. For this example we have chosen to reduce only the functions set. The algorithm initiates by creating 4 demes which evolve independently for 5 generations. Then, the individuals of the demes are ranked according to their fitness. The best 500 individuals are used to build up a new population. This population evolves until the problem is solved or until the maximum number of generations is reached.

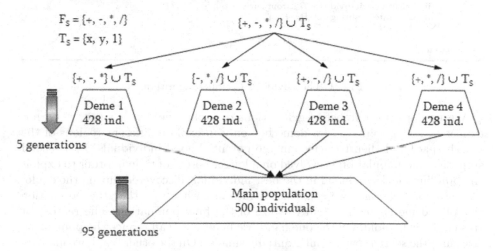

Fig. 1. Example of the Divide & Conquer strategy

$divideAndConquer(T_S, F_S, C_S, populationSize, maxGenNumber, maxDemeGenNumber)$

T_S	Terminals set
F_S	Functions set
C_S	the set chosen by the user where f_{RD} is applied either T_S, or F_S, or $T_S \cup F_S$
$populationSize$	Population size
$maxGenNumber$	Maximum number of generations
$maxDemeGenNumber$	Maximum number of generations for each deme

1. $n = |C_S|$
2. $numOfDemes = C_n^{n-1} = n$ // Number of demes
3. Generate subsets $RD_{SS}^1, RD_{SS}^2, \ldots, RD_{SS}^n$ by applying f_{RD} on C_S
4. **if** $C_S == F_S$ **then**
   Foreach $i \in [1, n]$, $RD_{SS}^i = T_S \cup RD_{SS}^i$
5. **else if** $C_S == T_S$ **then**
   Foreach $i \in [1, n]$, $RD_{SS}^i = F_S \cup RD_{SS}^i$
6. $demePopulationSize = floor\left(populationSize \frac{|T_S \cup F_S| - 1}{|T_S \cup F_S|}\right)$ // Population size for each deme
7. $j = 1$ // Deme counter
8. **while** problem is not solved **or** $j \leq numOfDemes$
   (a) Randomly initialize a deme population D_j from elements of RD_{SS}^j
   (b) $D_j = evolve(D_j, demePopulationSize, maxDemeGenNumber)$
   (c) Next deme: $j = j + 1$
9. Create a new population P composed of the best ranked individuals in $\bigcup_{k=1}^{numOfDemes} D_k$
10. $P = evolve(P, populationSize, maxGenNumber)$
11. Get the best individual from P

$evolve(population, populationSize, maxGenNumber) : finalPopulation$

$population$	Population to evolve
$populationSize$	Population size
$maxGenNumber$	Maximum number of generations
$finalPopulation$	the population returned after evolution

1. $i = 0$ // Initial Generation
2. $P_i = population$ // Population at a given generation i
3. **while** problem is not solved **or** $i < maxGenNumber$
   (a) Evaluate population P_i
   (b) Generate a new population P_{i+1} by reproduction, crossover, mutation of individuals
      i. Select genetic operation $O(O_r, O_c, O_m)$
      ii. Select best individuals B_S from current population (P_i)
      iii. Generate offspring (O, B_S, P_{i+1})
   (c) Next generation: $i = i + 1$
4. **return** P_i

Fig. 2. The Divide & Conquer algorithm

We used a little number of generations to evolve the demes since we do not expect to find a solution in a deme but only to explore different regions of the search space and then to make emerge potential good individuals. In a second step, the final population is evolved on a longer period of time in order to exploit the building blocks included in the best individuals discovered during the exploration step. Note that we construct demes in such a way that the population size of a deme is smaller than the size of the final population. The reason for this choice is twofold. On the one hand, we believe we can reduce the population size since the search space is substantially smaller. On the other hand, we increase the probability that the final population will include individuals from different demes, thereby increasing its diversity.

3   Experimental Procedure

We benchmarked our proposal on a range of standard test problems used in genetic programming research. We present them briefly here but a more detailed description can be found in [6].

Multiplexer 6 bits. The goal is to determine a boolean function which decodes a binary address and restores the value contained in the corresponding register of data. The training set consists of the 64 possible combinations of inputs-outputs. The fitness function evaluates the number of correct answers provided by the program considered on the whole set of training.

Santa Fe ant. An artificial ant tries to find some pieces of food which are arranged along a path on a two dimensional grid. The "Santa Fe Trail" is an irregular trail composed of 89 food pellets. The fitness function counts the number of pieces of food picked up by the ant.

Symbolic regression. The goal is to find a mathematical expression, in symbolic form, that fits a given sample of data points. Our training set is composed of 81 elements corresponding to all combinations of the integer values taken in the interval $[-4, 4]$ assigned to each combination of input's variables. The fitness function computes the sum of the errors on the training set i.e. the sum of the distances between the desired values and those obtained with the program considered.

We used a second degree polynomial function with two parameters:

$$2x^2 - 3y^2 + 5xy - 7x + 11y - 13$$

We indicate functions and terminals set for each problem in Table 1

Table 1. Terminals and functions set

	Multiplexer 6 bits	Santa Fe ant	Symbolic regression
Terminals set	$A0, A1, D0, D1, D2, D3$	Left, Right, Move	$1, x, y$
Functions set	And, Or, Not, If	IfFoodAhead, Progn2, Progn3	$+, -, /, \times$

For our experiments we used Sean Lukes Evolutionary Computation and Genetic Programming Research System (ECJ13) which is freely available on the web at http://cs.gmu.edu/ eclab/projects/ecj/. We developed a companion package which implements our Divide & Conquer model without any modification to the original API.

The first two problems are provided with the API, for the third we slightly modified the code of the multivalued regression example in order to implement our own function.

For each problem, we executed the following algorithms.

Classical GP. For comparison purpose, we used the standard GP algorithm with populations size 500, 1000, 1500 and 2000.

Divide & Conquer. For each problem we apply the Divide & Conquer strategy by reducing either the terminals set, or the functions set, or the union of both. The size of the final population, as resulting from merging the demes, was set to 500. We refer to these as follows:

$D\&C$ (F_S) when the reduction and differentiation function f_{RD} is applied only on F_S

$D\&C$ (T_S) when f_{RD} is applied only on T_S

$D\&C$ $(F_S \cup T_S)$ when f_{RD} is applied on $F_S \cup T_S$

Divide & Conquer naive. In order to evaluate the effectiveness of our reduction and differentiation procedure, we repeated the very same tests as those of the previous suite, but without applying f_{RD}. For example, we repeated the test $D\&C$ (F_S) with the same number of demes but without applying f_{RD} on F_S.

It can be seen that we executed 10 tests for each problem. Each test is the result of 100 independent executions. Each execution starts with a different seed for the random number generator. Moreover, we used the same seeds for each test.

We allocate the same maximum number of fitness evaluations for each test. That is, the generation at which that number of fitness evaluation is reached (200000 in our experiments) is the last generation. The parameters common to all tests are summarized in the Table 2.

Table 2. Parameter settings

Parameter	Setting
Selection	Tournament of size 7
Initialization method	Ramped Half-and-Half
Initialization depths	2-6 levels
Maximum depth	17
Internal node bias	90% internals, 10% terminals
Crossover rate	90%
Reproduction rate	10%
Number of runs	100
Max number of generations for a deme 5	

We focused on the following metrics:

Percentage of success, a run is considered successful if the algorithm finds an optimal solution.

Number of fitness evaluations performed on successful runs.

Time spent on successful runs. This index captures the fact that each evaluation has its own cost, depending for instance on the number of nodes or the complexity of each node in that evaluation. The previous index, in contrast, treats all evaluations as having the same cost.

Obviously, the absolute value of the "time" performance index is not very meaningful: while probability of success and number of evaluations describe properties that are intrinsic to the genetic programming process, time is related to the specific hardware and software platform used. However, as we shall see, the *normalized* value of the "time" performance index does provide important insights into the behavior of the algorithms.

4   Results

Figure 3 shows the percentage of success achieved by each test. We do not report the percentages of success for the *Multiplexer 6 bits* because almost all tests reach 100% (only the test based on the standard algorithm with a population size of 500 give a value sligtly lower with 97% of success).

We note that our proposal exhibits the best probability of success, provided the differentiation and reduction function is applied either on the function set F_S or on the union $F_S \cup T_S$. In particular, for the symbolic regression problem, the improvement with respect to the best result with the classical GP algorithm is 27% and 22%, respectively. For the ant problem the improvement is 20% and 19%, respectively. It can be seen that the Santa Fe ant problem benefits by our strategy whereas it is considered as a deceptive problem[7].

We also note that, with the classical GP algorithm and for a limited number of evaluations, use of a larger population may improve the probability of success but up to a certain upper bound. For example, in the ant problem, the performance

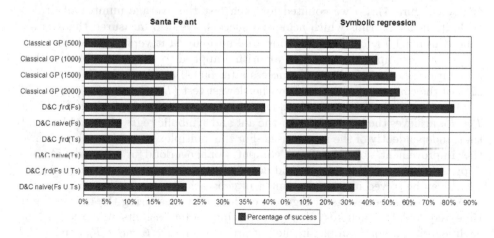

Fig. 3. Percentage of success (for the classical algorithm we indicate in parenthesis the population size)

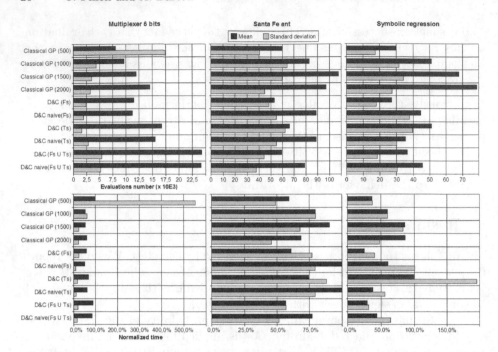

Fig. 4. The upper row of charts presents the average and standard deviation number of fitness evaluations and the lower row, the average and standard deviation of the normalized time

with initial population 2000 is worse than with initial population 1500. In the symbolic regression problem we have not reached the upper bound, however, the improvement from 1500 to 2000 is quite small.

The next suite of experiments is meant to assess the efficiency of the methods (cf. Figure 4). So we counted for each test the average number of fitness evaluations for all runs which achieve a success. We also measured the average time consumed Te for the same runs, and normalized it versus the slowest one $\frac{Te}{Te_{slow}}$. For example, the standard algorithm applied to the ant problem with a population size of 500 obtains a success after 60000 fitness evaluations or after 22% of the computing time used by the slowest test ($D\&C\ naive(F_S)$).

Once again, the Divide & Conquer strategy using f_{RD} applied on F_S or on $T_S \cup F_S$ achieves the best results for the ant and symbolic regression problem and that, independently of the metric used. For the multiplexer problem, there is neither improvement, nor a significant computational overload for our model. As our approach uses several demes, we did not expect to give any benefits to problems which can be solved in a small number of generations with small populations.

As an aside, the results in Figure 4 confirm that measuring the (normalized) time required for each test does provide important insights into the cost of each algorithm. For example, in the ant problem, the $D\&C\ naive(F_S)$ and $D\&C\ naive(T_S)$ are by far the most expensive tests, but this fact would be hidden if one assumed that all evaluations have the same cost.

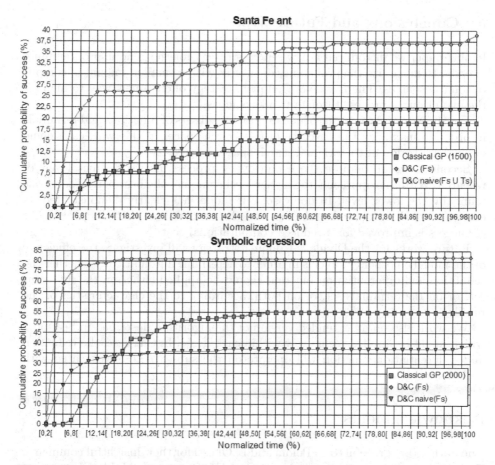

Fig. 5. Cumulative probability of success versus normalized time for the ant and symbolic regression problem

Finally, we evaluate the cumulative probability of success as a function of the computational cost (measured by the normalized time). For example, the standard algorithm applied to the ant problem gives a likelihood of success of 15% for a computing time ranging between 48 and 50% of the slowest test. For the sake of readability, we plotted only the tests that give the best probability of success for each model (*Classical GP, Divide & Conquer, Divide & Conquer naive*).

It appears clearly that *D&C* (F_S) maximizes the probability of success for a given computational cost. It is interesting to note that, in the symbolic regression problem, *D&C* (F_S) reaches its upper bound very quickly, that is, not only this method provides the best probability of success, it also reaches its best performance much faster (more than 10 times) than the two other best methods.

One can also note that for all the methods, increasing the number of generations and thus the computing time does not bring a significant improvement. Thus, for the problems considered our experiments confirm the fact that long runs are not useful.

5   Conclusions and Future Work

In this paper we introduced a new search strategy for the genetic programming in order to maximize the probability of success with a smaller amount of computational resources. The Divide & Conquer strategy offers a new way to manage the evolutionary process through two keys ideas.

Firstly, we use the concept of demes built on subsets of functions and terminals in order to maximize the coverage of the search space. In this way, each deme works on a region of the original search space.

Secondly, we decompose the evolutionary process in two distinct levels of research. With this approach, the higher level combines the best partial solutions found by the lower level. In doing so, our model has clearly demonstrated its efficiency on the proposed problems, and the results show that the probability of success is improved for a reduced computational cost.

Future works for the Divide & Conquer strategy will investigate the efficiency of the model on others problems in order to determine automatically whether the reduction and differentiation function should be applied either on the functions set, or on the terminals set, or on both, according to the characteristics of the problem.

We work also on an extended version of the algorithm described in Section 2 which might be applied recursively within each deme. In this case, the reduction and differentiation function will operate on the subset RD_{SS} associated with each deme.

Acknowledgments

The authors are grateful to C. Poloni and L. Onesti for their insightful comments. This work was supported by the Marie-Curie RTD network AI4IA, EU contract MEST-CT-2004-514510 (December 14th 2004).

References

1. Banzhaf, W., Nordin, P., Keller, R.E., Francone, F.D.: Genetic Programming - An Introduction; On the Automatic Evolution of Computer Programs and its Applications. (1998), Morgan Kaufmann, dpunkt.verlag
2. Cantu-Paz, E., Goldberg, D.E.: Are Multiple Runs of Genetic Algorithms Better than One? In Proceedings of the Genetic and Evolutionary Computation Conference GECCO'03, (2003), LNCS 2723, Springer-Verlag, 801-812
3. Daida, J.M., Samples, M.E., Byom, M.J.: Probing for Limits to Building Block Mixing with a Tunably-Difficult Problem for Genetic Programming. In Proceedings of the Genetic and Evolutionary Computation Conference GECCO'05, June 25-29, (2005)
4. Daida, J.M.: Towards Identifying Populations that Increase the Likelihood of Success in Genetic Programming. In Proceedings of the Genetic and Evolutionary Computation Conference GECCO'05, June 25-29, (2005)

5. Gathercole, C., Ross, P.: Small Populations Over Many Generations Can Beat Large Populations Over Few Generations in GP. In Koza, J.R. et al. eds GP, (1997), Morgan Kaufmann, 111–118
6. John R. Koza.: Genetic Programming: On the Programming of Computers by Means of Natural Selection. MIT Press (1992)
7. Langdon, W.B., Poli, R.: Why Ants are Hard. In Genetic Programming 1998: Proceedings of the Third Annual Conference (1998), Morgan Kaufmann publishers, 193–201
8. Luke, S.: When Short Runs Beat Long Runs. In Proceedings of the Genetic and Evolutionary Computation Conference GECCO'01, (2001), Morgan Kaufmann publishers, 74–80
9. Luke, S., Balan, G.C., Panait, L.: Population Implosion in Genetic Programming. In Proceedings of the Genetic and Evolutionary Computation Conference GECCO'03, (2003), LNCS 2724, Springer-Verlag, 1729–1739
10. Alba, E.; Tomassini, M.: Parallelism and Evolutionary Algorithms. Evolutionary Computation, IEEE Transactions on Volume **6**, Issue 5, (October 2002) 443–462
11. Van Veldhuizen, D.A., Zydallis, J.B., Lamont, G.B.: Considerations in Engineering Parallel Multiobjective Evolutionary Algorithms. Evolutionary Computation, IEEE Transactions on Volume **7**, Issue 2 (April 2003) 144–173

A Genetic Programming Approach to Solomonoff's Probabilistic Induction

Ivanoe De Falco[1], Antonio Della Cioppa[2],
Domenico Maisto[3], and Ernesto Tarantino[1]

[1] Institute of High Performance Computing and Networking,
National Research Council of Italy (ICAR–CNR),
Via P. Castellino 111, 80131 Naples, Italy
{ivanoe.defalco, ernesto.tarantino}@na.icar.cnr.it
[2] Natural Computation Lab – DIIIE, University of Salerno,
Via Ponte don Melillo 1, 84084 Fisciano (SA), Italy
adellacioppa@unisa.it
[3] Department of Physical Sciences, University of Naples "Federico II",
Via Cinthia , 80126 Naples, Italy
domenico.maisto@gmail.com

Abstract. In the context of Solomonoff's Inductive Inference theory, Induction operator plays a key role in modeling and correctly predicting the behavior of a given phenomenon. Unfortunately, this operator is not algorithmically computable. The present paper deals with a Genetic Programming approach to Inductive Inference, with reference to Solomonoff's algorithmic probability theory, that consists in evolving a population of mathematical expressions looking for the 'optimal' one that generates a collection of data and has a maximal *a priori* probability. Validation is performed on Coulomb's Law, on the Henon series and on the Arosa Ozone time series. The results show that the method is effective in obtaining the analytical expression of the first two problems, and in achieving a very good approximation and forecasting of the third.

1 Introduction

Given a symbolic string coding for a sequence of n values measured in an ongoing experiment, which will the $(n + 1)$–th string element be? Among all logical processes, Inductive Inference (II) is the best suited to face this question, because it can carry out forecast starting from some observed data. As an example, let us consider an alphabet $\mathcal{B}$; let $\Sigma = \mathcal{B}^{\infty}$ be the fundamental space composed by all the possible sequences of symbols from $\mathcal{B}$. With these premises, let us assume an *a priori* probability distribution P over Σ and let us denote by P(x) the probability that a sequence begins with the string x. Thus, given x, an II system must be able to extrapolate the sequence beginning with x by forecasting, one at a time, the symbols which follow in the composition of the string itself (incremental mode). In algorithmic words, this means to find the effective process which has generated the string x and which can continue it. More formally, if P(xa) is the probability associated to the hypothesis that the sequence x continues with a

P. Collet et al. (Eds.): EuroGP 2006, LNCS 3905, pp. 24–35, 2006.

given symbol $a \in \mathcal{B}$, by noting that $P(x|a) = 1, \forall a \in \mathcal{B}$, we can obtain from Bayes' rule that: $P(a|x) = P(xa)/P(x)$, which is the probability that, given the initial string x, the next string symbol is a. All is needed to evaluate this probability is just to find the *a priori* probability distribution $P(\cdot)$. The problem is that, for the most interesting cases, $P(\cdot)$ is either unknown or unknowable. As a consequence, in order to be the II an effective tool for scientific investigations, it is necessary to have for any considered case an estimate for P associated to it.

In early Sixties Solomonoff proposed a formal theory for II. Basic ingredients of the theory are the concepts of algorithmic probability and Kolmogorov Complexity (KC) [1]. By making use of a variant of the notion of KC called "prefix" [2], it is possible to define an *a priori universal probability distribution* such that the *a priori* universal probability for a string x is the sum over the probabilities of all the *self–delimiting* [1] programs which, whenever it is given as input to a universal Turing machine, compute x. It can be demonstrated that for the infinite and enumerable set of programs for x, the sum which defines the universal *a priori* probability behaves as $|\mathcal{B}|^{-K(x)}$, where $|\mathcal{B}|$ is the cardinality of the chosen alphabet $\mathcal{B}$ and $K(x)$ is the "prefix" complexity of the string x.

The universal *a priori* probability distribution shows important features [3]. Firstly, due to the use of KC which is a measure of the quantity of information for a string independent of the way used to describe it, it is an objective and absolute estimate for any computable probability distribution. Moreover, it can be shown that, by using the universal distribution as an estimate of the exact *a priori* probability, the square error made in forecasting the occurrence of the $(n + 1)$–th symbol converges to zero faster than $1/n$, where n is the number of previously forecasted elements. Hence, any *a priori* probability distribution can be approximated with extreme accuracy by directly using the universal distribution. Finally, the distribution introduced by Solomonoff allows to mathematically formulate the epistemic principle known as *Occam's razor*. In other words, *a priori*, 'simple' strings, i.e. strings with low algorithmic complexity, are more probable. Unfortunately it has been demonstrated that the universal *a priori* probability distribution is not computable. Nonetheless it exists a partial recursive function that, to the limit, approximates it from below. The problem is that an algorithmic procedure reaching the mentioned approximation requires infinite space and time resources, thus resulting unfeasible. Then, one can only provide himself with a procedure which in general does not terminate, yet computes intermediate results which represent more and more accurate estimates for the universal *a priori* probability.

Genetic Programming (GP) seems to be the best suited technique for the above goal. In fact, it generates a population of individuals, each representing a possible solution to the examined problem, and makes it evolve generation after generation so to obtain that these individuals get closer and closer to the solution looked for. Particularly, with the aim to help the evolution to explore

---

[1] A program of a string x is said self-delimiting if it is not the prefix of any other program describing x.

the most interesting parts of the solution space, it is needed to define a *fitness function* which can evaluate the effectiveness for the proposed solutions.

Our goal is to show that to model a forecast for the next results of an experiment, i.e. to solve induction problems by II method, it is possible to introduce, by premising some hypotheses to the model, a fitness function directly derived from the expression of the probability distribution of any possible result for the future experiments, as a function of those recorded in the previous n.

The confirmation of the made hypotheses is given by the set of results obtained from both symbolic regression trials and modeling and forecasting experiments conducted in the experimental validation phase.

In Section 2 we provide the roots of Solomonoff's theory on induction. The theoretical hypotheses and applicative solutions adopted are outlined in Section 3. The approach by GP is described in Section 4 while the experiments and the related results are shown in Section 5. Finally, we report the conclusions from our work and some possible ways for further improvements.

2   Solomonoff's View on Induction

During his research activity, Solomonoff has often considered the opportunity to develop a general method for probabilistic forecasting [3, 4]. One of the faced problems is the extrapolation on an unordered set of ordered couples of elements Q_i and A_i, which can be strings and/or numbers. In other words, given a new Q_j, this means to find a probability distribution for all the possible A_js. The i–th couple, hereinafter denoted by (Q_i, A_i), can be of very different kinds and cover a great variety of induction problems, i.e., grammar discovery identification and categorization problems, curve fitting and time series prediction.

A generic induction problem on an unordered set can be solved by defining an operator, which is able to satisfy the following request: let $[Q_i, A_i]$ be an unordered set of n couples (Q_i, A_i), $i = 1 \ldots n$. Given a new element Q_{n+1}, which is the function F such that $F(Q_i) = A_i$, for $i = 1, \ldots, n+1$, and with the highest *a priori* probability?

Once assigned a new element Q_{n+1}, let us start by determining the corresponding distribution probability for any possible A_{n+1}. From bayesian considerations, and by supposing that each couple (Q_i, A_i) is independent of the others, the distribution probability of A_{n+1} can be written as [3]:

$$P(A_{n+1}) = \sum_j a_0^j \, O^j(A_1 \ldots A_{n+1} | Q_1 \ldots Q_{n+1}) = \sum_j a_0^j \prod_{i=1}^{n+1} O^j(A_i | Q_i) \quad (1)$$

where $O^j(\cdot | \cdot)$ is the conditional probability distribution with respect to the function F^j such that $F^j(Q_i) = A_i$, and where a_0^j is the *a priori* probability associated to F^j. a_0^j approximately equals $2^{-l(F^j)}$, where $l(F^j)$ is the length in bits of the shortest description for F^j. The (1) can be written as follows:

$$P(A_{n+1}) = \sum_j a_n^j \, O^j(A_{n+1} | Q_{n+1}), \quad \text{with} \quad a_n^j = a_0^j \prod_{i=1}^{n} O^j(A_i | Q_i). \quad (2)$$

Solomonoff called the (2) **Induction Operator** (IO) [3]. From it, it can be deduced that the probability distribution $P(A_{n+1})$ is the sum of all the conditional probability distributions $O^j(A_{n+1}|Q_{n+1})$s associated to the functions F^js, weighted by the product of the respective *a priori* probabilities and of the probabilities of the previously observed data based on F^j. It is of course impossible to compute the infinite sum in (2) by using finite resources, yet it can be approximated by using a finite number of terms, i.e. those having a high value of a_n^j. The ideal case would be to include the terms with maximal weights among the a_n^js, but singling them out is tied to the problem of searching the highest *a priori* probabilities a_0^js, i.e. to the search of programs u whose length $l(u)$ is as small as possible. The problem is that no effective procedure exists able to carry out this search, since some among the u programs might not terminate, but this cannot be known *a priori*. Thus, the application of the IO consists in trying to find, in a preset time, a set of functions F^js such that the sum:

$$\sum_j a_n^j \tag{3}$$

be as high as possible. It is evident that for deterministic induction it is sufficient to find, in a finite time, the one among all the a_n^js which dominates (3). In the following, we shall consider only deterministic induction problems.

It should be noted that the approach followed is that of the bayesian inference method, so the better is the *a priori* estimate the more are consistent the forecasts. In this way, by using the (2), we are able to express the probability of an arbitrary A_{n+1} directly as a function of the set $[Q_i, A_i]$. We just need to decide which expressions to use for the $O^j(\cdot|\cdot)$ and for the a_0^j. We will face these two issues separately, respectively in next section and in Section 4.

3   Theoretical Hypotheses and Applicative Solutions

Let us start by estimating the conditional probability distribution $O^j(\cdot|\cdot)$ associated to the functions F^js. To this aim, we introduce in our model the hypothesis that any element A_i is given by a deterministic function F^j of Q_i plus an error, denoted by ε_j, which directly depends on the function F^j:

$$A_i = F^j(Q_i) + \varepsilon_j \tag{4}$$

Let us now assume that the ε_j has a normal distribution with zero mean value and with standard deviation σ independent of both Q_i and the index j:

$$p(\varepsilon_j) = (2\pi\sigma^2)^{-1/2} e^{-\frac{\varepsilon_j^2}{2\sigma^2}} \tag{5}$$

Substitution of the (4) in the (5) yields that the distribution probability, with respect to F^j, of the A_is conditioned by the Q_i, can be written as

$$O^j(A_i|Q_i) = (2\pi\sigma^2)^{-1/2} e^{-\frac{[F^j(Q_i)-A_i]^2}{2\sigma^2}} \tag{6}$$

Therefore, under the hypotheses (4) and (5), the $O^j(\cdot|\cdot)$s are distributions of gaussian probabilities with standard deviation σ. By substituting the (6) in the second of (2), it results:

$$a_n^j = a_0^j \, (2\pi\sigma^2)^{-1/2} e^{-\sum_{i=1}^{n} \frac{[F^j(Q_i) - A_i]^2}{2\sigma^2}} \tag{7}$$

This new expression for the a_n^j suggests a different way from the one proposed by Solomonoff [3]. Rather than maximizing the (3), we minimize, with respect to the functions F^js, the negative of the natural logarithm of its terms:

$$-\ln a_n^j = \frac{1}{2\sigma^2} \sum_{i=1}^{n} \left[F^j(Q_i) - A_i \right]^2 - \ln a_0^j + \ln \sigma + \frac{\ln(2\pi)}{2} \approx \tag{8}$$

$$\approx \frac{1}{2\sigma^2} \sum_{i=1}^{n} \left[F^j(Q_i) - A_i \right]^2 - \ln a_0^j \ . \tag{9}$$

In such a way, we will not only have linear functions of the a_n^j, which depend on F^j and on its *a priori* probabilities a_0^j, but we will also be able to write a less expensive procedure, in terms of exploited resources, which computes them.

It is worth noting an important feature of our approach. Actually, the ordering of the set on which the induction is effected is a property involved neither in the construction of the theoretical model adopted nor in the formulation of the (9). It is therefore sensible to suppose that the solutions found, in principle achieved in order to solve cases of II on unordered sets, can be expanded to inductive problems defined on ordered $[Q_i, A_i]$ sets. Such hypothesis, of course, must be verified in the experimental validation phase.

Finally, some computational considerations. We recall that the sum in the (2) should be computed on all the *recursive* functions, but, given that the set of those functions is not effectively enumerable, we will limit ourselves to take into account only the *partial* recursive functions. The best one can do is to use a procedure not terminating in general, yet providing as intermediate results a better and better approximations of the a_n^j, thus finding a term whose weight has the highest possible value, in an arbitrary amount of time.

4   Grammar–Based GP

The use of the Evolutionary Algorithms (EAs) seems to be a sensible approach to solve this problem [3]. In particular, among EAs, GP [5, 6] is definitely preferable when functional expressions are searched for, e.g., the F^j, which can interpolate all (Q_i, A_i) couples while maximizing their *a priori* probability. It should be noted, however that, differently from Solomonoff's incremental approach, in ours the data are presented to the II system grouped in sets (batch mode).

Particular attention must be paid to the genetic generation and preservation of valid programs in order to overcome the possible lack of closure property

GP is subject to. Whigham, as an example, created a GP based on Context–Free Grammars (CFGs) [7]. He used derivation trees of CFGs as genotypes, the phenotypes being the programs generated by those trees. The introduction of a CFG in the GP scheme yields noticeable advantages: among them we can recall the possibility of defining a structured language in which programs are strings, and an easy definition and modification of the genetic operators so that they can preserve program coherence and thus closure property. Whigham also showed that CFGs are an efficient approach to introduce a bias into the evolutionary process. In fact, by assigning weights to specific productions so to increase their probability of selection, they allow to introduce a *bias* in the search process, implicitly exploiting the *a priori* information about the specific problem tackled.

Following [7], our GP is based on an expression generator that provides the starting population with a set of programs differing in terms of size, shape and functionality. The expression generator is implemented by means of a CFG which ensures the syntactic correctness of the programs. Differently from Whigham, the choice of the production rules taking place in the derivation tree of any individual is effected by using a uniform distribution so to avoid favoring a rule. At start, the automaton calls upon the starting rule and then continues by applying, one at a time, other ones allowed in that situation. The automaton halts if no applicable rules exist in a given situation or if the program size exceeds a set limit. In this latter case the individual is discarded and a new one is generated. The result is a tree in which the nodes are nonterminal symbols, the branches are derivation steps and the fruit is the represented program.

The encoding for the programs, i.e. the phenotypes, as derivation trees for the adopted CFG, i.e. the genotypes, allows to implement the changes to the genotypic structures by the genetic operators used as simple operations on trees. It is also easy to respect closure condition: it is sufficient to act on internal tree nodes and substitute a production rule with another having in its left part the same nonterminal symbol. The operators implemented are crossover and mutation. Crossover works by randomly choosing in a first individual a nonterminal node and then selecting in a second individual a node representing the same symbol. Finally this operator swaps the respective subtrees thus obtaining two new individuals. Crossover has no effect if it is not possible to find in the second parent a node corresponding to the nonterminal symbol selected in the first parent. Mutation, instead, randomly acts on a nonterminal node of an individual by removing the related subtree and by substituting it with a new one having as its root the selected node. Two variants have been introduced for the mutation: macro–mutation works on terminal and nonterminal symbols at the same time, while micro–mutation acts only on a terminal symbol at a time.

4.1   Evaluation

The evaluation of an individual takes place in two steps: in the first the fruit of its derivation tree, i.e. the program, is extracted and executed on a set of sample data, thus attaining a sequence of values as output; in the second phase the obtained output is used to compute the fitness value to assign to the

Table 1. The grammar used

Rules	
S	$\rightarrow f(x) = E$
E	$\rightarrow f(x - N) \,|\, (EOE) \,|\, F(E) \,|\, R \,|\, x$
O	$\rightarrow + \,|\, - \,|\, * \,|\, /$
F	$\rightarrow sqr \,|\, cube \,|\, sqrt \,|\, cubert \,|\, log \,|\, exp \,|\, sin \,|\, cos$
N	$\rightarrow t \in \mathcal{S} \subseteq \mathbb{N}$
R	$\rightarrow c \in I_R \subseteq \mathbb{R}$

individual. The evaluated expressions are strings of the language defined by the chosen grammar. The evaluator implemented can interpret any expression belonging to the language described by the grammar in Table 1. The wish has arisen to verify the correctness and the effectiveness of the theoretical results achieved for induction problems defined on ordered and on unordered sets. This has conditioned the implementation of the evaluation process. For the study of inductive problems on unordered sets, the evaluator works on any program with the set of the *questions* of the couples (Q_i, A_i) – the empirical data. The data are randomly divided into three sets, i.e., *training* $(\mathcal{T})$, *validation* $(\mathcal{V})$ and *prediction* $(\mathcal{P})$. The program is actually evaluated on $\mathcal{T}$ and the values obtained in output are then compared to the *answers* A_i of the data, to compute the fitness. At the end of the inferential process, the best program is selected according to the values achieved on $\mathcal{V}$ and on which the inductive capabilities of the solutions are estimated. Finally, the "goodness" of the best induced solution is verified on $\mathcal{P}$. If, instead, an inductive problem defined on an ordered set $[Q_i, A_i]$ is examined, the ordering in the set $[Q_i, A_i]$ implies that the set of Q_is is an interval. In this case, $\mathcal{T}$ and $\mathcal{V}$ are mixed, while $\mathcal{P}$ is consecutive to them. Moreover, a further interval, i.e., *seed* $(\mathcal{S})$, has to be introduced. Such a set consists of the first values of the data, which are provided as seed to the program to be executed. Length of $\mathcal{S}$ can optionally be computed dynamically so that its length coincides with the maximal number of preceding values required by the program.

4.2 The Fitness Function

In section 2 it has been shown that an induction problem on a generic set $[Q_i, A_i]$ can be solved by finding a function F^j with respect to which (9) is as low as possible. Consequently to Solomonoff's theory and to the hypotheses made, we have adopt the following fitness function:

$$F(p) = \omega \cdot \left(\frac{1}{n} \frac{1}{\sigma^2} \sum_{Q_i \in \mathcal{Q}} |p(Q_i) - A_i|^2 \right) - \ln(a_0(p)) \qquad (10)$$

where p is the expression evaluated, σ is the standard deviation of the empirical data, $\mathcal{Q}$ is the set of the *questions* Q_i from which Π is made and n is their number, $p(Q_i)$ is the value of the program for the i–th *question*, A_i is the *answer* related to Q_i, ω is the weight associated to the error term. Finally $a_0(p)$ is the *a priori* probability of the program p.

The (10) is a functional expression of two terms, exactly matching those composing the (9). In fact, the first term is the product of a Mean Square Error (MSE) by a weight $\omega \in \mathbb{R}^+$, and evaluates the error made by the program p in the approximation of the problem under examination. The presence of the weight is justified because, due to the hypotheses (4) and (5) and due to the (6), the standard deviation for the noise ε is set while that of MSE depends on the particular solution considered and, in general, on the biases and parameters driving the evolutionary search. The second term, instead, depends on the *a priori* probability of the program p examined. To evaluate it, starting from the CFG, an algorithm computes the *a priori* probability $a_0(p)$ of the derivation tree which generates the expression p. It must be remarked that, although the (10) may resemble a particular form of parsimony pressure heuristically built, it derives expressly and as a whole from the theoretical results achieved above.

As mentioned before, $\mathcal{V}$ allows us to select the overall best expression discovered during the entire inference process. In fact, at each generation for all the individuals in the population the (10) is computed on the set $\mathcal{V}$. Hence, the result of a run is the individual with the best such value achieved in all the generations making up the run.

Computation of the *a priori* probability. The computation of the a_0s is carried out by means of the "Laplace's rule" for successive and independent events. Once specified the grammar, the probability α_{i_p} that a given production is present in the i–th node of the derivation tree of the program p is k/m, where k is the number of times in which the production has previously occurred in the definition of the tree and m is the total number of all the productions which are legal there, incremented by the number of times in which they have previously occurred in the definition of the tree. The product

$$a_0(p) = \prod_{i_p=1}^{q} \alpha_{i_p}, \qquad (11)$$

yields the *a priori* probability of the program p, i.e. of the fruit of the tree with q productions, related to the grammar chosen [3]. This procedure is in accordance with the results obtained by the theory of algorithmic probability, in the sense that, once set the reference grammar, it attributes higher probabilities to functions which have a lower descriptive complexity with reference to the grammar. So, between two different functions which represent two possible solutions to a given problem, the GP will choose the "simplest" one, thus causing an effective application of "Occam's razor".

5   Experimental Results

The system has been tested on three different problems, namely Coulomb's law as an example of II on unordered sets, the Henon series and the Ozone time series in Arosa (Switzerland), as examples of II on ordered sets. Any program execution is determined by a set of parameters, among which those related to the evolutionary process and, for the series, those specifying the widths of the intervals they are divided into. Another important parameter is the weight ω: it should be chosen so to favor evolution of simpler individuals, while also allowing creation of programs complex enough to adhere to the original function.

For any problem 10 runs with different random seeds have been carried out with the same parameters. We have used a population size of 200, a tournament selection mechanism with size of 5, a crossover operator taking place with a 30% probability and a mutation operator (with 100% probability) which distinguishes between macro– and micro–mutations, applying them with probabilities equal to 30% and 70% respectively. The maximum number of generations allowed for all the runs is set to 1000. After a preliminary tuning, ω has been set to 10^3. For any problems a maximum tree depth of 15 has been considered. Finally, we have set $I_R = [0, 10]$ for the first two problems and $I_R = [-1, 1]$ for the third one.

Coulomb's Law. As an example of a regression problem we have faced Coulomb's Law. Its expression is:

$$\boldsymbol{F}_{21} = \frac{1}{4\pi\varepsilon_0} \frac{q_1 q_2}{r^2} \hat{r}_{21} \ , \tag{12}$$

where r is the module of the position vector $\boldsymbol{r}_{21}$ of q_2 with respect to q_1 and $\hat{r}_{21}$ is its versor, q_1 and q_2 are two point charges and ε_0 is the dielectric constant of vacuum. We have computed $|\boldsymbol{F}|$ between an electron and a proton and added a normal error with a standard deviation of 1.0, thus obtaining 60 pairs (r_i, F_i) with r and F in nanometers and in 10^{-8}N respectively.

We have set sizes for $\mathcal{T}$, $\mathcal{V}$ and $\mathcal{P}$ to 40, 10 and 10 respectively. Since the problem concerns an unordered set, the production rule $E \rightarrow f(x - N)$ has been deactivated. In all the runs the (10), with *a priori* probability of 7.44E-6, has been found. In the best case, it has been achieved in 32 generations, and on average in 142.9. As in the most time–consuming run (Fig. 1 (right)), the evolution consists of two distinct phases. The former is characterized by search for an expression which better and better approximates (12). In this phase, larger and larger expressions are found which provide lower and lower errors on $\mathcal{T}$. This takes place until about generation 120. The latter phase, instead, begins when a solution equivalent to (12) emerges, and consists in achieving other solutions with higher *a priori* probabilities, thus shorter. At the end of this phase, at about generation 360, the optimal solution, i.e., (12), is reached. Even though this "simplification" is an effect of the evolution process, which tends to favor simpler solutions, it has a behavior very similar to that which could be obtained by a human one. In fact, in all the runs GP has been able to discover intermediate solutions equivalent to (12). Once such solutions have emerged, then GP has evolved them towards the optimal one.

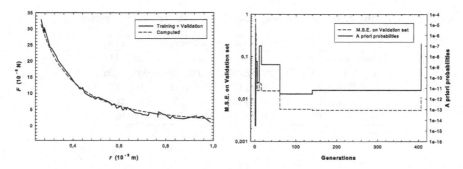

Fig. 1. Most time–consuming run for the Coulomb

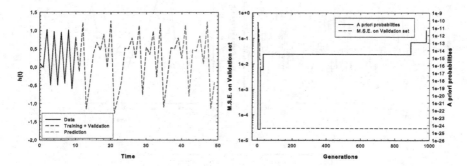

Fig. 2. Most time–consuming run for the Henon series

Henon series. It is a 2–D iterated map with chaotic solutions proposed by M. Henon (1976) [8] as a simplified model of the Poincarè map for the Lorenz model:

$$h(t) = 1 + b \cdot h(t - 2) - a \cdot h^2(t - 1) \ , \ \text{with } h(0) = 0.1 \text{ and } h(1) = 0 \qquad (13)$$

where a and b are positive bifurcation parameters, with b a measure of the rate of area contraction (dissipation). Henon series is the most general 2–D quadratic map and, for $b = 0$, it reduces to the quadratic map, which is linked to the Logistic series. Bounded solutions exist for this series over a range of a and b values, and some yield chaotic solutions. Evidence of chaotic behavior can be found for $a = 1.4$ and $b = 0.3$ and such values have been used for the experiments. Widths for $\mathcal{S}$, $\mathcal{T}$, $\mathcal{V}$ and $\mathcal{P}$ have been set to 10, 20, 10 and 10 respectively, while the CFG production rules with the symbol F have been deactivated.

Notwithstanding the Henon series strongly depends on the boundary conditions, in all the runs effected the canonical solution (13) has been obtained, apart from a possible swap between the terms. In the best case, the solution has been achieved in 153 generations, and on average in 289. The evolution evidences two phases as described for Coulomb's Law (see Fig.2 (right)).

Ozone time series. The last problem we have faced is the monthly time series of total ozone amounts at Arosa (Switzerland) from the beginning of the record in 1926 through 1972 [9]. The ozone measurements at Arosa show a strong seasonal cycle, with a range of about 100 Dobson Units.

Table 2. Results achieved on the Arosa Ozone time series

	Best	Average	St.Dev.
Generation	876	651.2	281.03
A priori probability	2.06E-25	2.08E-26	6.49E-26
M.S.E. on $\mathcal{T}$	0.2345	0.21609	0.0158
M.S.E. on $\mathcal{V}$	0.1956	0.2325	0.0315
M.S.E. on $\mathcal{P}$	0.2011	0.2525	0.0460

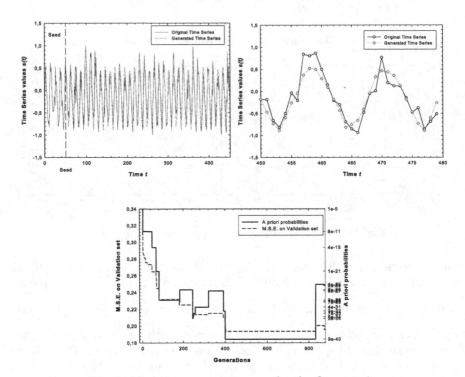

Fig. 3. Most time–consuming run for the Ozone series

The length for $\mathcal{S}$ has been set equal to 50, that for $\mathcal{T} + \mathcal{V}$ to 400, 30% of which to be used as $\mathcal{V}$, and that for $\mathcal{P}$ to 30.

With respect to the previous series, some complications take place here. The experimental results evidence that none of the runs achieves an error equal to zero on $\mathcal{T}$. However, in each run expressions with a good approximation of the series have been obtained. The program with the overall best expression obtained among all the 10 runs is the following:

$$f(t) = f(t-24) + \frac{((\cos(f(t-6) + e^{f(t-24)}))^2 - 0.41)^3}{e^{f(t-27)}} \tag{14}$$

Table 2 reports the results, while Fig. 3 shows the behavior on $\mathcal{T}$ and $\mathcal{V}$ (top left) and $\mathcal{P}$ (top right). A simple analysis of the solution evidences that, although the task difficulty, GP has been able to discover the underlying seasonal cycle. As regards the evolutionary behavior, it is evident from Fig. 3 (bottom) that the system dynamics shows that the scheme composed of two phases evidenced in the previous cases is repeated from generation 1 to 256, from 257 to 399 and, finally, from 400 to the end. We suppose that the more complex the problem is, the more frequent the repetition of such a scheme is.

6   Conclusions

The problem of Inductive Inference has been faced by taking into account Solomonoff's probabilistic induction theory. This implies to search for solutions which better approximate data while showing higher a priori probabilities. We have made use of a GP scheme based on Context Free Grammars.

Our system has found the exact expression of Coulomb's Law and the Henon series, while pursuing appealing computational strategies. As regards the Arosa Ozone time series, GP has been able to discover an expression that, making use of the seasonal period, provides a good approximation of the data. Moreover, the results evidence that our approach is effective also on ordered sets, thus confirming the hypotheses made in Section 3.

Further improvements could consist in implementing an II system based on Solomonoff's incremental mode and in using more accurate methods for the computation of the *a priori* probabilities assigned to F^js, e.g., the Monte Carlo method. In such a way, the search abilities of the system should be improved. In fact, from bayesian considerations it results that the more precise is the evaluation of the *a priori* probabilities, the more efficient is the search process.

References

1. Li, M., Vitànyi, P.: An introduction to Kolmogorov complexity and its applications. 2nd edn. Springer (1997)
2. Solomonoff, R.J.: Complexity–based induction systems: comparisons and convergence theorems. IEEE Trans. on Information Theory **IT–24** (1978) 422–432
3. Solomonoff, R.J.: Progress in incremental machine learning. In: NIPS Workshop on Universal Learning Algorithms and Optimal Search, Whistler, B.C. (2002)
4. Solomonoff, R.J.: A formal theory of inductive inference. Information and Control **7** (1964) 1–22, 224–254
5. Koza, J.R.: Genetic Programming: on the programming of computers by means of natural selection. MIT Press, Cambridge, Massachusetts (1992)
6. Cramer, N.L.: A representation for the adaptive generation of simple sequential programs. In Grefenstette, J.J., ed.: Int. Conf. on Genetic Algorithms and Their Applications, Lawrence Erlbaum Ass., Hillsdale, N.J. (1985) 183–187
7. Whigham, P.A.: Grammatical Bias for Evolutionary Learning. PhD thesis, School of Computer Science, University of New South Wales, Australia (1996)
8. Hénon, M.: A two–dimensional mapping with a strange attractor. Communications of Mathematical Physics **50** (1976) 69–77
9. Hipel, K.W., McLeod, A.I.: Time Series Modelling of Water Resources and Environmental Systems. Elsevier, Amsterdam, NL (1994)

A Less Destructive, Context-Aware Crossover Operator for GP

Hammad Majeed and Conor Ryan

Biocomputing and Developmental Systems,
Department of Computer Science & Information Systems,
University of Limerick, Ireland
{hammad.majeed, conor.ryan}@ul.ie

Abstract. Standard GP crossover is widely accepted as being a largely *destructive* operator, creating many poor offspring in the search for better ones. One of the major reasons for its destructiveness is its disrespect for the context of swapped subtrees in their respective parent trees when creating offspring. At times, this hampers GP's performance considerably, and results in populations with *low* average fitness values.

Many attempts have been made to make it a more constructive crossover, mostly by preserving the context of the selected subtree in the offspring. Although successful at preserving context, none of these methods provide the opportunity to discover new and better contexts for exchanged subtrees.

We introduce a *context-aware* crossover operator which operates by identifying all possible contexts for a subtree, and evaluating each of them. The context that produces the highest fitness is used to create a child which is then passed into the next generation.

We have tested its performance on many benchmark problems. It has shown better results than the standard GP crossover operator, using either the same number or fewer individual evaluations. Furthermore, the average fitness of populations using this scheme improves considerably, and programs produced in this way are much smaller than those produced using standard crossover.

1 Introduction

Crossover is considered to be the major driving force behind evolution in GP. A simple one point crossover operator generates an individual by selecting a subtree *randomly* from a parent tree and placing it *randomly* in some other selected parent tree. The randomness of this operator makes it *mostly* destructive (generates children inferior to their parents) [1]. To overcome this problem, many *context aware* crossover operators are introduced, that attempt to ensure that exchanged subtrees are used in at least a similar way by the offspring.

Most of the context aware crossover operators defined for GP work by *preserving* the context of a selected subtree in the produced child, so that it will be used in a similar way. We argue that these approaches are restrictive in nature as they only focus on preserving the context rather than finding a new and better one

P. Collet et al. (Eds.): EuroGP 2006, LNCS 3905, pp. 36–48, 2006.

in the child. Brood recombination [9] has solved this problem to some extent by generating multiple children. Unfortunately, this does not guarantee the use of the selected subtrees in the best possible contexts in the produced children. The probability of finding the best context is further reduced by selecting *different* subtrees for each crossover.

We introduce a context-aware crossover which tries to find the best context of the selected subtree during crossover. Because it uses the increase in fitness to determine this, it has the ability to find a totally different and better context, and we show that the computational cost of this method can be substantially lower than standard GP when used in conjunction with standard subtree crossover. One positive side effect of the crossover operator is the elimination of the dead code (nodes not contributing towards individual's fitness) which results in a dramatic reduction in *bloat*.

In the next section we will discuss different context aware crossover approaches known to GP community and their shortfalls. This is followed by a discussion on the importance of the context in GP and introduction to the context-aware crossover. Section 4 discusses our experimental setup and the brief description of each, while section 5 discusses the findings of the experiments. Followed by conclusions and our future plans.

2 Alternative Crossover Operators in GP

A lot of research has been conducted to make crossover more *constructive* and many new operators are put forward by researchers. Some of them are discussed below.

D'haeseleer [2] described a crossover operator which preserves the context in which subtrees appeared in the parent trees. He proposed a node coordinates system for rooted trees.

The system uniquely identifies every node of the tree by specifying the path to be followed from the root to that node. A node's position therefore can be represented by a n coordinates tuple $T = \{b_1, b_2, b_3, ..., bn\}$, where n is the depth of the node in the subtree and b_i indicates which branch of the tree to choose at depth i (counting left to right).

Using this coordinate system two new crossover operators were introduced, namely *strong context preserving crossover* (SCPC) and *weak context preserving crossover* (WCPC). SCPS only allows the crossover between the subtrees having identical coordinates in their parents. This operator is very restrictive in its implementation as the depth of a subtree cannot change between the parent and the newly generated child. To overcome this issue, the restrictions imposed were relaxed and WCPC was proposed. In this, two subtrees, $T1$ and $T2$, are selected as in SCPS, and then $T1$ and any subtree $T2' \subseteq T2$ ($T2$ inclusive) is a valid choice of subtrees for crossover. This allows the subtrees to change their depths.

Hengraprohm and Chongstitvatna [3] understood that, in standard GP crossover, a good solution can be destroyed by an inappropriate choice of crossover points. They introduced *selective crossover* for GP which identifies a good subtree by measuring its impact on the fitness of the container-tree (the individual) by removing it and replacing it with a randomly selected terminal from the terminal set. This way they were able to preserve the best subtrees in an individual.

Ito *et. al* [4] proposed that the subtree selection for crossover should be restricted to shallower nodes of the parent trees. This was to avoid the disruption of building blocks. Additionally, they put a restriction that only children better than their parents are allowed into the next generation.

Tackett [9], inspired by the fact that animal species produce far more children than are expected to live, designed a *brood recombination* operator. It functions by first selecting two parents from the population. Then N random crossovers are performed between the selected parents to generate $2 * N$ children. Then all the generated children are evaluated and sorted. Finally, the best two children are selected and considered as the children of the selected parents. Rest of the children are discarded.

Poli and Langdon [8] in their *uniform crossover*, aligned the two parents before crossover so that their root nodes are overlapped. Then they swapped the corresponding nodes of parent trees.

Selective crossover using gene dominance [11] integrates the idea of gene dominance [10] and uniform crossover evolving into a new crossover technique designed with the feature of adaptability to the problem being optimized. This operator works by first detecting subtrees which have a good impact during crossover on the candidate solution, and then uses the difference between the fitness of the parent and that of the child to discover beneficial alleles. Finally, it preserves alleles by keeping the more dominant subtrees with individuals with higher fitness.

Most of these techniques work by preserving the context of the subtree in the children. However, this caps the performance of the system, as for each selected subtree a different and better context can exist in the children. The crucial difference between previous work and that presented in this paper is that our method always determines the best context, and so preserves the context from parent to child when it is beneficial.

3   Importance of Context in GP

The importance of the context of a subtree in its respective parent tree is already discussed in detail [2][7]. As shown in [6] the significance of a subtree can be evaluated by calculating its fitness contribution towards the fitness of the tree containing it (the *container-tree*). A small change in the context or position (with the same context) of a subtree within its container-tree can have significant effect on the container-tree's fitness.By maximizing a subtree's fitness contribution, we can identify the best possible context of a subtree in a particular container-tree. It has also been shown that the significant subtrees (schemata) within a population tend to increase their size and fitness contributions towards their respective container-trees with time. Unfortunately, standard subtree crossover works *syntactically* and has no respect for the current context of the subtrees. This is the main reason for its destructive nature. To make it constructive we have to make it *context* (semantics) aware.

3.1   Context-Aware Crossover

During crossover, by incorporating a subtree in its best possible context we can make a crossover *least* destructive if not constructive. Using this idea, we have devised a context-aware crossover operator. It finds the best context (hence the best crossover point) of a subtree by examining all possible contexts in which the subtree can be used during crossover.

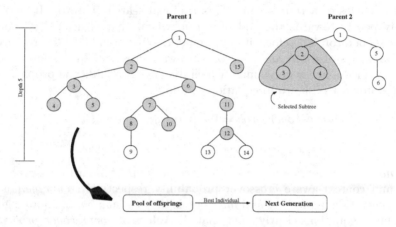

Fig. 1. Context aware crossover. Shaded nodes in parent-1 are possible crossover points where selected-subtree from parent-2 can go in. Maximum tree-depth is set to 5 in this example. Root node cannot be selected as a crossover point. All generated children are evaluated and the best one will go in the next generation. Same process is repeated for the selected-subtree from parent-1 (Not shown to make figure readable).

Fig. 1 shows the operation of this crossover. To make the figure more readable we have set tree-depth to five for this example. Two parents are selected for crossover using some selection scheme[1], and the root node (node 1 of each parent) cannot be selected as a crossover point. In the example, node 2 of parent 2 is selected *randomly* as a crossover point (the subtree is shown shaded in parent 2). In the next step, all possible crossover points producing *valid* offsprings are selected as crossover points in parent 1 (shaded nodes of parent 1). By valid offsprings we mean those individuals which fulfill the initial criteria laid down before the start of a run, such as maximum depth, node count and so on. The selection of all possible crossover points in parent 1 ensures the identification of the best context of the selected subtree of parent 2 in parent 1. The selection of the crossover points is followed by generation of a pool of offsprings

---

[1] The operator works indandantly of the selection scheme.

and their evaluation. The best individual among them is introduced in the next generation.

3.2 Context-Aware Crossover as a Refinement Operator

Context-aware crossover can be viewed as a local search operator, as it performs a brute force search for the best possible context for the selected subtree. Because the *best* context is chosen, as opposed to a random context as in standard GP crossover, smaller jumps in the search space tend to be made than with standard crossover, although context-aware crossover is more likely to make improvements in fitness.

In [1] it has been shown that standard GP crossover is most effective in the *initial* stages of a run, because it is a global search operator. It performs relatively poorly towards the end of a run, when what is needed is more of *refinement* operator. Therefore, it is reasonable to use standard GP crossover in the initial stages of a run and use context-aware crossover in the later stages. We have defined a linear polynomial which dynamically shifts the probability of these operators. It is shown in equations 1 and 2.

$$norm\_xover\_prob = 1 - (curr\_gen/max\_gen) \tag{1}$$

$$context\_aware\_prob = 1 - norm\_xover\_prob \tag{2}$$

Where *norm_xover_prob* and *context_aware_prob* are standard crossover probability and context-aware crossover probability respectively. *curr_gen* is the current generation in progress and *max_gen* is the max number of allowed generations. These equations clearly show that the values of *norm_xover_prob* varies from one to zero, whereas the value of *context_aware_prob* varies from zero to one as evolution progresses. No effort has been made to optimize the rate at which the proportions change.

4 Experimental Setup

The proposed crossover operator was tested on different set of problems. These problems include Koza's Quartic Polynomial Symbolic Regression problem, the 11-bit multiplexer problem, the Lawnmower problem, the Santa-Fe Ant Trail, and the Two-Boxes problem. Due to space constraints we will only discuss the first three. These problems were chosen because they represent a broad selection of problem types and difficulties.

The symbolic regression problem is representative of possibly the most commonly examined problem in GP, the 11-bit multiplexer is a very difficult problem without ADFs, and the Lawnmower problem is a useful scalable problem.

To facilitate data collection, all experiments were allowed to complete the maximum number of generations. The initial population was generated using the ramped half and half method, with initial tree depths varying from two to six, and the maximum depth of the trees was set to 17. All results were averaged over 100 runs. Two sets of experiments were conducted for each problem, one using standard GP crossover and the other using context-aware crossover.

Context-aware crossover is inherently more expensive than standard crossover, as each pair of parents selected for crossover can result in multiple individuals being evaluated. However, to make a fair comparison, the experiments that employ context-aware crossover use smaller populations, so that the total number of evaluations is kept lower than those required by the experiments using standard crossover.

When using standard crossover, the probabilities of cross and reproduction employed were 0.9 and 0.1 respectively. For the context-aware crossover, the reproduction operator was replaced by the context-aware crossover, as it is an inherently preservative operator. As mentioned above, the two crossover operators were employed with varying probabilities, and the same polynomials were used in all experiments.

At the end of experiments four types of graphs were plotted. A brief description of each is as follows.

The *Performance Graph* shows the comparison of the fitness improvements over generations. The average, best and worst fitness values of each generation are plotted for each crossover.

The *Running Evaluation Count graph* keeps track of the cumulative sum of individual-evaluations done during each generation. This graph along with performance graph helps to calculate *average computational effort* required by each crossover to attain certain fitness value.

The *Evaluations per generation graph* shows the cost of each crossover per generation. The count of the number of evaluations done per generation by a crossover is noted at the end of each generation. These values are used to plot the running evaluation count graphs.

The *Program size graph* shows the amount of bloat generated by each crossover operator. The program size of an individual effects, considerably, the computational effort required for its evaluation. Compact programs (fewer nodes) need less computation effort for their evaluations.

4.1   Quartic Polynomial Symbolic Regression

To show the performance of the context-aware crossover on the symbolic regression domain we attempted to solve Koza's quartic polynomial ($x^4 + x^3 + x^2 + x$) problem. Our experimental setup details are similar to Koza's implementation. For standard subtree crossover, a population size of 4500 was evolved for 100 generations. For the context-aware crossover, the population size was reduced to 200. Fitness proportionate selection was used for selecting parents. The results for the experiment are shown in Fig. 2.

Fig. 2 (Top-Left) shows the performance comparison of the two operators. The overall performance (the best and average curves) of the context-aware crossover is better than the standard subtree crossover.

After 40 generations, the best fitness curve for the context-aware crossover passes that of the standard crossover, while after 90 generations the *average*

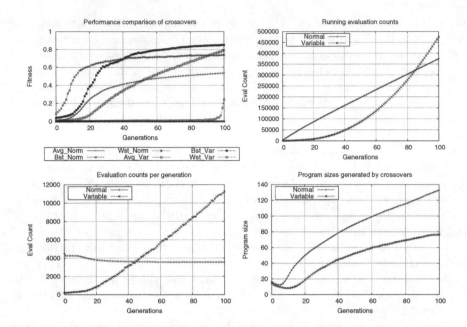

Fig. 2. Top-Left: Performance comparison of standard and context-aware crossovers. *Avg_Norm, Bst_Norm, Wst_Norm* are the average, best and worst fitness values respectively using standard crossover. Similarly, *Avg_Var, Bst_Var, Wst_Var* are the average, best and worst fitness values respectively using context-aware crossover. **Top-Right:** Running sum of the evaluations for each crossover. **Bottom-Left:** Evaluation counts per generation for each crossover. **Bottom-Right:** Program sizes (node count) of the individuals in a population.

fitness curve for the context-aware crossover passes it. Initially, the system using standard subtree crossover shows a faster increase in fitness, but this plateaus relatively early.

Fig. 2 (Top-Right) indicates that the context-aware crossover needs substantially fewer individual evaluations to achieve the same fitness values as achieved by standard subtree crossover. For example, at generation 40, the performance of both the crossovers is exactly the same. The context-aware crossover needs *three times* fewer evaluations to achieve this fitness value as compared to its counterpart.

Fig. 2 (Bottom-Left) shows the count of the evaluations at the end of each generation. The evaluations count is smaller for the context-aware crossover in the initial generations due to the smaller probability of the use of the context-aware crossover.

In Fig. 2 (Bottom-Right) we see that the size of the individuals generated by each crossover. Clearly, throughout the evolution, the context-aware crossover generates smaller programs, while standard subtree crossover generates very bloated individuals, especially in the latter stages of the run. The curve for the context-aware crossover has become increasingly more flat over time without effecting the fitness adversely. We argue that the reduction in the individual-sizes is due to the elimination of the dead code from the individual trees.

4.2 Boolean 11-Multiplexer

The multiplexer problem was implemented to observe the performance of the context-aware crossover on the hard problems; standard GP cannot solve the 6-bit or higher multiplexer problems. For this reason, ADFs were introduced to this problem and helped to solve it. Our aim here is not to solve the problem, however, but to compare the performance of standard subtree crossover and the context-aware crossover in the *identical* environments, therefore we tried to solve this problem with the conventional non-ADF setup. For standard subtree crossover a population of 2000 was allowed to evolve for 50 generations. For the context-aware crossover experiments, the population size was reduced to 50, and both sets of experiments employed fitness proportionate selection. The results are shown in Fig. 3.

Fig. 3 (Top-Left) shows the performance comparison of the two crossover operators. As expected, the standard GP setup found it difficult to evolve good

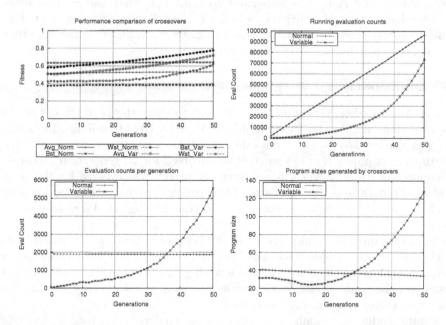

Fig. 3. Top-Left: Performance comparison of standard and context-aware crossovers. *Avg_Norm, Bst_Norm, Wst_Norm* are the average, best and worst fitness values respectively using standard crossover. Similarly, *Avg_Var, Bst_Var, Wst_Var* are the average, best and worst fitness values respectively using context-aware crossover. **Top-Right:** Running sum of the evaluations for each crossover. **Bottom-Left:** Evaluation counts per generation for each crossover. **Bottom-Right:** Program sizes (node count) of the individuals in a population.

individuals throughout the evolution and was stuck at a constant fitness value throughout the run. On the other hand the context-aware crossover started with lower fitness values (due to the smaller population used) than standard subtree crossover but, showed improvement in all the three fitness values throughout the run, particularly towards the end. Recall that towards the end of the run the context-aware crossover is the major crossover operator due to the use of variable crossover rates.

In Fig. 3 (Top-Right) we see that the evaluations count for the context-aware crossover remains quite lower than the subtree crossover evaluations throughout the run. It is a very encouraging result because not only the context-aware crossover is able to improve the fitness, but does so by evaluating substantially fewer individuals.

Fig. 3 (Bottom-Left) shows the evaluations per generation for each crossover. For the context-aware crossover it is increasing with time due to change in the individual sizes and depths.

Fig. 3 (Bottom-Right) shows that beyond the 30th generation the context-aware crossover has generated substantially larger trees than standard subtree crossover. One possible reason is the inability of standard crossover to improve fitness during the run. It is important to note here that the context-aware crossover has generated individuals smaller in size than the ones generated by standard subtree crossover prior to the 30th generation, and that not only they are smaller in size but are *better* in performance.

4.3   Lawnmower

As mentioned earlier, this problem is selected to show the performance of the proposed crossover on ADF based problems. We have tried to use the same setup that was employed by Koza [5] in his implementation. For the standard crossover experiments, a population of size 2000 was evolved for 20 generations, whereas for context-aware crossover a population size of 100 was evolved for the same number of generations. For both sets of experiments, tournament selection with size 7 was used. We employed the same function and terminal sets as used by Koza.

Fig. 4 contains the results, with Fig. 4 (Top-Left) showing the fitness plots for the two crossover operators. The best fitness curves for both the crossover operators are almost the same, but there is a big gap between the average fitness curves. For the context-aware crossover it is as high as 0.9 whereas for standard subtree crossover is under 0.2 and quite flat.

Despite producing a number of high performing individuals, albeit more slowly than the context-aware crossover, standard crossover has a considerably lower average fitness measure. This low fitness value is a consequence of the destructive nature of the crossover. The context-free crossover, on the other hand, has improved the population by placing the subtrees of the individuals of a population in their best context.

Fig. 4 (Top-Right) shows the cumulative sum of the evaluations done per generation by each crossover. By inspecting this graph along with the fitness

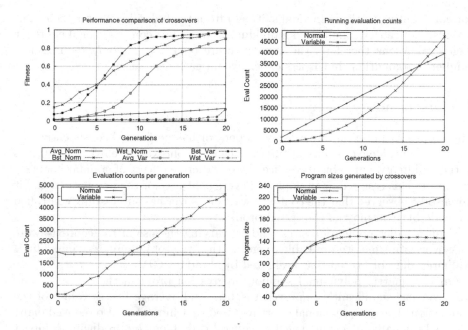

Fig. 4. Top-Left: Performance comparison of standard and context-aware crossovers. *Avg_Norm, Bst_Norm, Wst_Norm* are the average, best and worst fitness values respectively using standard crossover. Similarly, *Avg_Var, Bst_Var, Wst_Var* are the average, best and worst fitness values respectively using context-aware crossover. **Top-Right:** Running sum of the evaluations for each crossover. **Bottom-Left:** Evaluation counts per generation for each crossover. **Bottom-Right:** Program sizes (node count) of the individuals in a population.

performance graph (Top-Left) we can estimate the speed of the convergence of each crossover operator. For the context-aware crossover, the best fitness value (which is very close to the perfect value) is attained in the 12th generation, whereas standard subtree crossover needs 20 generations to attain the same fitness value. The context-aware crossover needs 17,000 evaluations (Top-Right generation 12) to attain this fitness value as compared to standard subtree crossover's 40,000 evaluations (Top-Right generation 20).

Fig. 4 (Bottom-Left) is the comparison of the evaluations done per generation by each crossover operator. As expected, the evaluations count of standard subtree crossover remains constant to the population size whereas it increases linearly for the context-aware crossover.

Fig. 4 (Bottom-Right) shows the amount of bloat produced by each crossover. In the case of standard subtree crossover the trees are constantly increasing (bloating) but for the context-aware crossover their size remains constant to a lower value after the 9th generation. This is a clear indication of the fact that the context-aware crossover has attained the maximum fitness value *quickly* by evaluating *substantially fewer, smaller* individuals than standard subtree crossover. The main reason behind this bloat control is the elimination of dead code(nodes not contributing to the individual's fitness) from the individuals after their evaluations. Notice that small-sized individuals require less computational effort for their evaluations therefore, the context-aware operator not only requires less number of evaluations but is less expensive on each evaluation.

5   Discussion

The proposed context-aware crossover operator has performed consistently well on different problem domains. By finding the best context of the selected subtrees in the children we are able to reduce the destructive effects of standard subtree crossover. This resulted in an improved average fitness for the population, and it can also be observed that the context-aware crossover has successfully controlled the code bloat in most of the tested problems.

Using smaller population sizes, and by varying the use of the context-aware crossover with time, we were able to ensure that the total number of individuals evaluated did not exceed that evaluated by standard GP.

On the quartic polynomial symbolic regression problem the context-aware crossover has significantly improved the best and average fitness values of the population. The computational effort required to achieve it is also reduced many fold. Additionally, it has managed to control code bloat by producing compact programs unlike standard subtree crossover.

On the 11-bit multiplexer problem the context-aware crossover has shown improved fitness in the later generations. Notice that standard subtree crossover is unable to show any fitness improvement throughout the run. As in the symbolic regression problem, in this problem too the context-aware crossover has achieved *better* performance using *less* computational effort than standard subtree crossover.

Finally, on the lawnmower problem the context-aware crossover resulted in the rapid increase in the fitness without becoming expensive. For this problem the size of the generated programs was almost constant without adversely effecting the performance of the system in the later generations.

6   Conclusions

We have introduced a new context-aware crossover operator which has been successfully tested on several different problem domains. The results shown are promising on all the problems used.

It has the ability to find better and different crossover points for a given subtree in different parent trees. This is accomplished by placing the subtree in various positions in the parent tree and then calculating the effect on the parent tree's fitness.

The use of the proposed method has produced improvements in both mean best fitness and mean average fitness, reduced bloat in most of the tested problems, and has produced significantly smaller individuals in most cases.

Although each context-aware crossover can result in multiple evaluations, we have found that in all of the problems examined, it produced fitter individuals with fewer evaluations than standard crossover. This is because context-aware crossover permits the use of much smaller populations, and that the probability of its use is varied linearly with time.

6.1 Future Work

Currently, only one offspring from each crossover enters the next generation. Future work will look at how to increase this without the population converging too quickly. We believe this will help us to reduce the evaluations count per generation.

We will also examine the possibility of use of some method other than random selection to choose the subtree to be swapped in the first place. It may be possible to maintain a history of improvements by all subtrees to bias selection towards them.

Finally, the application of the operator is currently varied linearly over time. There may be some benefit is being more selective about its application, possibly based on the rate of improvement of the population.

References

1. Wolfgang Banzhaf, Peter Nordin, Robert E. Keller, and Frank D. Francone. *Genetic Programming – An Introduction; On the Automatic Evolution of Computer Programs and its Applications*. Morgan Kaufmann, dpunkt.verlag, January 1998.
2. Patrik D'haeseleer. Context preserving crossover in genetic programming. In *Proceedings of the 1994 IEEE World Congress on Computational Intelligence*, volume 1, pages 256–261, Orlando, Florida, USA, 27-29 June 1994. IEEE Press.
3. S. Hengproprohm and P. Chongstitvatana. Selective crossover in genetic programming. In *ISCIT International Symposium on Communications and Information Technologies*, ChiangMai Orchid, ChiangMai Thailand, 14-16 November 2001.
4. Takuya Ito, Hitoshi Iba, and Satoshi Sato. Non-destructive depth-dependent crossover for genetic programming. In Wolfgang Banzhaf, Riccardo Poli, Marc Schoenauer, and Terence C. Fogarty, editors, *Proceedings of the First European Workshop on Genetic Programming*, volume 1391 of *LNCS*, pages 71–82, Paris, 14-15 April 1998. Springer-Verlag.
5. John R. Koza. *Genetic Programming II: Automatic Discovery of Reusable Programs*. MIT Press, Cambridge Massachusetts, May 1994.
6. Hammad Majeed. A new approach to evaluate GP schema in context. In Franz Rothlauf, Misty Blowers, Jürgen Branke, Stefano Cagnoni, Ivan I. Garibay, Ozlem Garibay, Jörn Grahl, Gregory Hornby, Edwin D. de Jong, Tim Kovacs, Sanjeev Kumar, Claudio F. Lima, Xavier Llorà, Fernando Lobo, Laurence D. Merkle, Julian Miller, Jason H. Moore, Michael O'Neill, Martin Pelikan, Terry P. Riopka, Marylyn D. Ritchie, Kumara Sastry, Stephen L. Smith, Hal Stringer, Keiki Takadama, Marc Toussaint, Stephen C. Upton, and Alden H. Wright, editors, *Genetic and Evolutionary Computation Conference (GECCO2005) workshop program*, pages 378–381, Washington, D.C., USA, 25-29 June 2005. ACM Press.
7. David J. Montana. Strongly typed genetic programming. BBN Technical Report #7866, Bolt Beranek and Newman, Inc., 10 Moulton Street, Cambridge, MA 02138, USA, 7 May 1993.

8. Riccardo Poli and William B. Langdon. On the search properties of different crossover operators in genetic programming. In John R. Koza, Wolfgang Banzhaf, Kumar Chellapilla, Kalyanmoy Deb, Marco Dorigo, David B. Fogel, Max H. Garzon, David E. Goldberg, Hitoshi Iba, and Rick Riolo, editors, *Genetic Programming 1998: Proceedings of the Third Annual Conference*, pages 293–301, University of Wisconsin, Madison, Wisconsin, USA, 22-25 July 1998. Morgan Kaufmann.

9. Walter Alden Tackett. *Recombination, Selection, and the Genetic Construction of Computer Programs*. PhD thesis, University of Southern California, Department of Electrical Engineering Systems, USA, 1994.

10. K. P. Vekaria. *Selective Crossover as an Adaptive Strategy for Genetic Algorithms*. PhD thesis, University of London, Department of Selective Recombination (Dominance Crossover) Computer Science, University College London, UK, 1999.

11. Chi Chung Yuen. Selective crossover using gene dominance as an adaptive strategy for genetic programming. Msc intelligent systems, University College, London, UK, September 2004.

AQUAGP: Approximate QUery Answers Using Genetic Programming

Jason B. Peltzer, Ankur M. Teredesai, and Garrett Reinard

Department of Computer Science, Rochester Institute of Technology (RIT),
20 Lomb Memorial Drive, Rochester, NY 14623
{jbp1500, amt, glr7495}@cs.rit.edu

Abstract. Speed, cost, and accuracy are crucial performance parameters while evaluating the quality of information and query retrieval within any Database Management System. For some queries it may be possible to derive a similar result set using an approximate query answering algorithm or tool when the *perfect/exact* results are not required. Query approximation becomes useful when the following conditions are true: (a) a high percentage of the relevant data is retrieved correctly, (b) irrelevant or extra data is minimized, and (c) an approximate answer (if available) results in significant (notable) savings in terms of the overall query cost and retrieval time. In this paper we discuss a novel approach for approximate query answering using Genetic Programming (GP) paradigms. We have developed an evolutionary computing based query space exploration framework which, given an input query and the database schema, uses tree-based GP to generate and evaluate approximate query candidates, automatically. We highlight and discuss various avenues of exploration and evaluate the success of our experiments based on the speed, cost, and accuracy of the results retrieved by the re-formulated (GP generated) queries and present the results on a variety of query types for TPC-benchmark and PKDD-benchmark datasets.

1 Introduction

Query processors in most modern database management systems include some form of query approximation or query optimization component(s). There are several scenarios where an exact answer may not be required and the end-user may prefer a fast approximate answer. For example, say the exact answer to the query: *Find the number of employees with salary greater than ε 50,000* is 48 employees and it takes 6 hours to run the query. On the other hand, an approximate query answering system may return the answer, "50 employees" in 6 seconds. If the original query was intended to gain a general idea about the underlying data, the approximate query has saved a significant amount of time and effort. Further demonstrating its usefulness, the approximate query answering system can also provide appropriate confidence bounds to advise the user of the validity of the approximate answer as compared to the exact answer. i.e. 50 (+/- 5 employees) as in the previous example.

P. Collet et al. (Eds.): EuroGP 2006, LNCS 3905, pp. 49–60, 2006.

Query processors typically perform several optimizations and approximations on-the-fly as queries are presented in a pervasive manner without specific direction from the end-user. Two such systems currently exist: AutoAdmin from Microsoft, and the Aqua project from Bell Laboratories. AutoAdmin is a self-tuning and self-administering system for the MS SQL Server DBMS. Using an index tuning wizard, a database administrator can optimize a database relatively easily and inexpensively [http://research.microsoft.com/dmx/autoadmin/default.asp]. Aqua is a visualization tool designed for approximate query answering and can be used with SQL-Compliant DBMS. Aqua pre-computes statistical summaries of data, generally in the form of histograms. One of its key features is that it provides error/confidence bounds on the answer returned [1]. Conversely, most query optimization is interactive in nature where the data analyst has effective domain knowledge of the underlying relations, indices and constraints to speed up or approximate the query by hand.

All of this, typically, is based on the query plan for the original query. The database system, in itself, proposes efficient ways of restructuring the query plan based on statistical analysis of the underlying database using histograms and other data summarization techniques [6]. Roughly twenty years ago, logic based approaches and semantic transformations were proposed to solve this problem [5]. As the level of statistical analysis techniques improve, efficient user interaction provides even greater insight and value to the overall optimization process. One case in point example is the Microsoft SQL-Server 2005's query optimizer, which takes a query and creates a parse tree for it. From the parse tree of the query, statistical information, such as, (a) **estimated IO Time**, (b) **estimated CPU Time**, (c) **estimated rows resulting from a Join**, (d) **estimated total subtree cost**, etc. is computed and translated into various types of query costs. The main idea is to make use of the statistics that the DBMS provides, and to use them to approximate/optimize queries, no matter the implementation.

Such statistics then indicate an aggregate query cost estimate. The entire process of generating a parse tree, computing statistics, and estimating query costs accompanies the generation of a query plan for the original input query. The query processor will then (typically) try and come up with several different permutations of the parse tree, and assess the different individual costs associated with each parse tree. For example, using relational algebra, different operator trees can implement the same algebraic expressions [2]. Equation 1 shows how two join orders result in equivalent tuple sets but might have different query costs associated with them based on the size and order of the intermediate joins:

$$((A \bowtie B) \bowtie C) \cong ((B \bowtie C) \bowtie A) \tag{1}$$

The focus of the work presented in this paper is the development of a query processor that presents the DBMS with a *re-formulated* query using GP such that its result set is similar to that of the original input query, yet is superior to the original query in terms of speed and cost. The resulting query may differ in the overall structure from the input query and the output is a new query plan that returns the same, or approximately the same, result set as the original query.

This implementation differs from other prior frameworks. Prior attempts at using evolutionary computation techniques for approximate query answering have focused on a single relation or on specific join operations. The GP implementation used in [8] attempts to optimize the different $\bowtie$ algorithms. The operator tree is made up of specific $\bowtie$ operations and the relations being joined, using standard TREE crossover operations to recombine parents to develop children queries. Ours is a multi-relational implementation designed to search the schema space of a database for referential ties to the input query's select attributes. In other words, since the input query's select attributes tend to be distributed throughout the database as primary and foreign keys, the same values can occur in other tables under the same, or different, attribute names. In some cases optimization can be accomplished by building a new query that uses the attributes of some other table in the schema as long as those new attributes can be formally mapped back to the original input query's attributes through key references. Using these references, a tool can look deeper into the data and take advantage of certain aspects of the relationships between database entities. Further, using the primary and foreign key relationships of the schema to find and join data allows an approximator to take advantage of the built in efficiency of using the indices placed on those keys by the DBMS.

1.1   Problem Formulation

The approximate query answering problem we are trying to solve using this GP based implementation can be defined as follows:

Definition 1. *Approximate Query:* Find a query Q_x such that:

$$C_{Q_i} >= C_{Q^o_i} >= C_{Q_x} \tag{2}$$

and

$$\tau_{Q_i} = \tau_{Q^o_i} \approx \tau_{Q_x} \tag{3}$$

where C_{Q_i} represents the cost of executing query Q_i and τ_{Q_i} represents the accuracy of Q_i.

Hence, the idea is to search the query space using a heuristic search procedure. This search procedure is a multi-objective optimization problem where the goal is to minimize the query processing costs and maximize the accuracy of the query results. The objective is to build a GP framework which searches different subsets of the schema iteratively, one candidate query at a time, calculating different values such as cost, time, and accuracy. All of these calculations are valuable to the query processor while performing approximations and/or optimizations. These metrics apply both to this GP based algorithm and to other standard DBMS algorithms. The job of this GP is to exploit all of these inter-relationships such that they produce proper optimizations which eventually yield a very accurate (as high as 100%) approximation of the correct result set in significantly less time and with a substantially smaller cost.

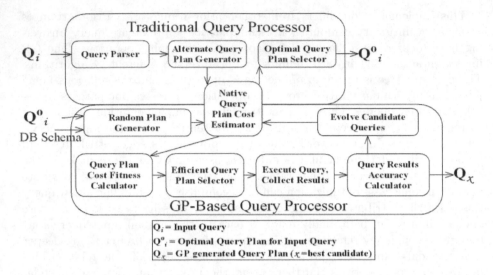

Fig. 1. Overall architecture of the proposed GP based Approximate Query Answering System. The upper portion of the diagram describes the traditional query processor, while the lower portion describes components of the proposed GP based system.

Figure 1 shows that the traditional query processor typically accepts an input query Q_i and passes it to the parser to generate alternative query plans. The query plan cost estimator provides the cost of each plan to the optimal plan selector. The optimal plan selector then decides the optimal query plan for execution as specified by Q^o_i. The lower portion of the figure describes our implementation. Beginning with the optimal query plan Q^o_i for query Q_i and the database schema, this algorithm randomly generates a population of alternate query plans and uses the query plan cost estimator provided by the native database engine to estimate the cost of these plans. The most efficient plans are selected from this initial population and the queries are executed to collect query statistics. The accuracies of the candidate queries are collated to evaluate the quality of approximation. The best candidates are selected for further evolution according to the specified GP algorithm. This process continues for a predetermined number of iterations or until a specific termination criterion is met. Typical termination criteria may be a predefined accuracy threshold, or any other such fitness measure.

1.2   Background and Related Work

There is a substantial body of work available for review in the fields of query optimization and query approximation. We note the most important and related efforts in this section. The major effort for optimization deals with cost analysis of queries based on different attributes. Query optimizers have to iterate, efficiently, through different parse trees for each query to decide on an optimal query plan. Traditional query optimizers tend not to enumerate all possibilities for query plans due to computational constraints. The query optimizer prunes the plan space while enumerating plans in order to meet these constraints. Such pruning significantly reduces the amount of space and time an optimizer requires for queries that contain a lot of Joins. Generally this pruning is done using dynamic programming (DP) algorithms. Hellerstein proposed one such popular DP based approach [4]. Earlier efforts include the work by Graefe et al where many techniques are surveyed for executing complex queries over large data sets [3]. Steinbrunn et. al. [7] outline other algorithms such as deterministic algorithms, dynamic programming solutions, minimum selectivity, Krishnamurty-Boral-Zanialo (KBZ) algorithm, the AB algorithm, randomized algorithms, iterative improvement, simulated annealing, two phase optimization, toured simulated annealing, and random sampling as relevant heuristic optimizations for the join ordering problem. They also explain the use of genetic algorithms (GA) as a query optimization technique.

2   The AQUAGP Framework

The overall architecture of the proposed framework was described in Figure 1. The user defined query Q_i and the database schema are used as input to the system. In traditional databases the input query follows a certain path to execution. The job of the query optimizer is to produce an alternate query, Q^o_i, based on the inherent properties (types) of the query, the meta-data available to the optimizer and the database schema. Our goal was to demonstrate that it is possible to extend the query optimizer further by including a GP based query optimization routine that lowers the query cost significantly without resulting in inaccurate results.

The simplest approach to develop a GP based system would be to take the original query Q_i as the input query, evolve several combinations of the query based on this input and the underlying schema and evaluate each candidate query for its query cost to find the most optimal query plan. There are several problems with this approach. The first and the foremost problem is 'semantic mapping.' Since the query space is very large for such a problem every possible query posed to the underlying database can be a candidate query. In fact one can see why it will be impossible to establish the internal logical consistency of what an optimal query might mean in this context since we will have to adopt principles of reasoning so complex that their internal consistency will be as open to interpretation as the optimal query itself (somewhat like Gödel's incompleteness proof). On the other hand developing a heuristic system that is constrained by semantic considerations and follows a logical query plan when searching for the optimal query within the constrained set of parameters might actually result in an alternative query plan that has an effective cost less than the original query plan. For this reason the framework uses the original input query and the query Q^o_i- the optimal version of some input query, as calculated by a native DBMS system (MS SQL Server 2005 in our case) , as seed queries. The population of candidate queries of is a parameter of the system denoted by n and the candidate queries are denoted by $Q_1, Q_2, ..., Q_{n-1}, Q_n$.

Framework Components. The first component of our GP framework is an automatic query generator. Automatic query generation is a complicated task requiring significant constraint processing efforts. To generate queries, efficiently, a database needs to be represented in terms of its meta data, such that the schema can be examined and the complex relationships between entities can be understood. Due to space constraints we do not describe how a database's schema can be used to generate random candidate queries using the attributes of the input query in this paper.

3   GP Based Candidate Query Generation: Parameters and Issues

3.1   Fitness Evaluation

Fitness evaluation of any query Q_x is based on a few different pieces of information about the query. The following statistics, about a given query Q, must be derived:

1. The execution time of the query (in seconds).
2. The estimated cost of the query, which is based on:
   (a) The estimated CPU time.
   (b) The estimated IO time.
   (c) The estimated number of rows a $\bowtie$ (join) will cause.
   (d) The estimated total subtree cost.
3. The resulting set of information that the query returns when executed.

From the meta-data, query cost estimates, and other such information provided by the DBMS, we developed a function to evaluate the GP fitness such that the value returned is a normalized value on the interval $(0, 1]$ where a fitness of 1 indicates the best possible individual in a given population and 0 is the worst. During query evolution, two quantitative criteria can be minimized as discussed earlier. These entities, time and cost, are denoted as T_{Q_x} and C_{Q_x} respectively. A third qualitative measure is a query's accuracy in comparison to the optimal query, denoted as τ_{Q_x}.

Calculating the accuracy of all generated candidate queries is computationally infeasible. In fact, even for a reduced set of queries, a large portion of the randomly generated queries take an extremely long time to execute. Thus, the initial set of queries, whose accuracy the GP will examine, must be pruned. To facilitate pruning, a "costFitness" value is introduced. costFitness can be used to weed out the poorly formed queries that would take too long to execute. The costFitness formula is comprised of four components as follows:

$$ioFit(Q_x) = (Q^o{}_i.io/(Q_x.io + Q^o{}_i.io)) \tag{4}$$

$$cpuFit(Q_x) = (Q^o{}_i.cpu/(Q_x.cpu + Q^o{}_i.cpu)) \tag{5}$$

$$rowFit(Q_x) = (Q^o{}_i.row/(Q_x.row + Q^o{}_i.row)) \tag{6}$$

$$streeFit(Q_x) = (Q^o{}_i.stree/(Q_x.stree + Q^o{}_i.stree)) \qquad (7)$$

$$costFitness(Q_x) = \qquad\qquad\qquad\qquad\qquad\qquad (8)$$
$$((ioFit(Q_x) * W_1) + (cpuFit(Q_x) * W_2) \qquad\qquad (9)$$
$$+ (rowFit(Q_x) * W_3) + (streeFit(Q_x) * W_4))/100 \qquad (10)$$

where W_i = the weight of that particular fitness in the costFitness calculation, and $W_1 + \ldots + W_4 = 100$.

The costFitness value of any query lies in the interval $(0, 1]$. It is an estimate of how fast the query would take to complete, if it were actually executed. The framework has a hard coded costFitness threshold, ρ ($\rho = 0.7$ in our implementation) which is used to prune queries whose $costFitness < \rho$.

Given a pruned population of test queries, accuracy is calculated by examining the results returned ($q_x.r$) from both the current and optimal queries in the following manner:

$$inaccuracy(Q_x) = |Q^o{}_i.r \bigcup Q_x.r| - |Q^o{}_i.r \bigcap Q_x.r| \qquad (11)$$

$$accuracyQ_x = \frac{|Q^o{}_i.r|}{|Q^o{}_i.r| + inaccuracy(Q_x)} \qquad (12)$$

The initial query result set, $Q^o{}_i.r$, is the standard by which accuracy is measured. Inaccuracy of the test query, Q_x, can be defined, concretely, as the set of tuples which are returned by either query but do not appear in the intersection. Clearly, the lower the value of $inaccuracy(Q_x)$, the more similar the result sets. The results of measuring inaccuracy are normalized on the interval, $(0, 1]$, in the $accuracy(Q_x)$ function.

A similar procedure is defined for determining the actual execution time of the query. Each query's execution time is measured and tabulated, and an efficiency function is used to derive a normalized value over the interval, $(0, 1]$:

$$efficiency(Q_x) = \frac{Q^o{}_i.t}{Q^o{}_i.t + Q_x.t} \qquad (13)$$

The accuracy and efficiency of a particular query is formalized in the following equation:

$$Fitness(Q_x) = accuracy(Q_x) * efficiency(Q_x) \qquad (14)$$

Any query whose fitness exceeds 0.5 is considered "better than" the initial query, $Q^o{}_i$, as $Fitness(Q^o{}_i) = 0.5$. The strength of this fitness equation is that it favors neither criterion at the expense of the other. Queries which show perfect performance in one area, and abysmal performance in the other will not be ranked higher than the initial query.

3.2 Query Tree Crossover

Next, we describe the GP crossover operation as implemented for generating approximate query plans. Assuming all queries within this system have the following structure:

```
SELECT      <s_list>
FROM        <f_list>
WHERE       <w_list>
```

where any $< *\_list >$ is a list of valid strings that can be placed in that part of the query to generate valid SQL syntax and semantics. During SELECT list crossover, one of the biggest obstacles we had to overcome was making sure that attributes of a certain data type were compared only with other attributes of the same data type that corresponded to the same data in the schema. Although everything cannot be restricted, it is necessary to impose restrictions on how pieces are compared and how much comparing actually gets done. From two parent queries, the crossover operation does its work in three main steps:

1. Iterate for the number of SELECT attributes (each parent will have the same number of SELECT attributes) and at each iteration randomly take the corresponding attribute from one of the two parents. Create a new $< f\_list >$ and fill it with all of the required tables corresponding to the new set of SELECT attributes in the new $< s\_list >$.
2. Combine the $< w\_list >$'s from both parent queries and randomly select a subset of that list to create a new $< w\_list >$ for the offspring. If not already added, append any necessary parent tables to the $< f\_list >$ to accommodate the WHERE clause.
3. Construct the new child query from the newly generated $< s\_list >$, $< f\_list >$, and $< w\_list >$.

This crossover process results in evolving semantically equivalent (albeit in a limited context of this implementation) candidate queries.

3.3 Query Tree Mutation

We developed the GP mutations to focus exclusively on the WHERE clause portion of the queries. The rationale behind this decision is that the WHERE clause is more than likely the key determining factor in how accurate a randomly generated query will be. Each mutation operation consists of the following steps:

1. Separate the where clauses into the individual clause types (i.e. LIKE, BE-TWEEN, predicate). Ignore wiring (join defining) and nested clauses.
2. Randomly generate new values for the LIKE, BETWEEN, and predicate clauses of the query. This must be done with consideration of the data type and range of the attributes being mutated. Both measures are available via meta data from the schema.
3. Randomly insert or remove NOT operators to negate the current functionality of each clause.
4. Randomly select AND and OR operators to be placed between the clauses. We favored AND's in this step to decrease the chances of creating overly complex, and therefore inefficient, queries.

4   Experiments and Results

We used the MS Visual Studio 2005 IDE, C#, and Microsoft SQLServer 2005 Beta 2 June CTP consisting of native query parsing and cost estimators, as the development platform. Experiments were conducted on an IBM PC with an Intel Pentium 4 processor with 1GB RAM. The two datasets used include: (a) The PKDD Cup Multi-relational transaction dataset, and (b) the TPC-H benchmark dataset containing business transaction data. Recall, that the idea is to evolve new queries, efficiently, evaluate their fitnesses, and determine if they meet the accuracy criterion as approximate queries for the original queries. For simplicity of explanation, we divide the discussion in two subsections; one containing results from the generational GP implementation, and the second containing results from the steady-state GP implementation. For both of the GP strategies we evolve queries of the following types: (i) 2-table join without projection, (ii)2-table join with projection, (iii) 3-table join without projection, and (iv) 3-table join with projection. The complexity of various queries broadly depends on the join condition and depending on the constraints if projections can/need be achieved prior or post join. Queries over both the datasets mentioned above were computed for all 4 of the above categories and results were evaluated. Figure 2 describes the comparison between the optimal query as proposed by query plan analyzer built into the MS SQL Server 2005 and the cost of executing the GP generated best fit candidate query. The accuracy threshold was set to 80% for this plot.

Generational GP Implementation. Table 1 contains the GP parameters set as defaults in all test runs. Mid (0.5) to high (0.99) mutation rate leads

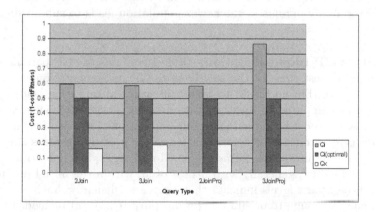

Fig. 2. Graph of Cost Reduction Comparison for Differing Query Types. This graph shows a comparison between the cost of executing the original input query, Q_i, the cost of executing the optimal form of that query, Q^o_i, and the cost of executing our GP's best candidate query, Q_x. The costs compared were all calculated for queries Q_x which return results with an accuracy of 80% or greater. Results are shown for queries of the following types: 2-table join without projection, 2-table join with projection, 3-table join without projection and 3-table join with projection.

Table 1. Default parameter values for Generational and Steady-State GP implementations

Parameter	Value: Generational	Value: Steady-State
Population Size	100	100
Generations	20	n/a
Loops	n/a	2000
Selection Size	10	5
Percentage of Copies	20%	n/a
Percentage of Crossovers	80%	n/a
Desired Accuracy	.85	.85
Mutation Rate	50%	50%
W_1, W_2, W_3, W_4	25	25

to faster convergence compared to lower rates. As shown in Figure 3(a) the increase in fitness over a number of evaluations indicates progress towards convergence. Average fitness levels such as 0.5 were quickly achieved irrespective of the mutation rates. Since fitness is a measure proportional to accuracy of the tuples returned, our understanding is that the generational GP based approximate query answering system finds an average fit query within the initial population most of the time and it takes some effort later on to fine tune the candidate queries towards the most optimal query. This fact is apparent in Figure 3(b), where fitness varies as a parameter of the population size. Large population sizes tend to converge slowly, but this could be a dataset specific phenomenon and could not be conclusively proved. Figure 3(c) demonstrates the result of modifying the selection size on fitness and suggests that keeping too few or too many parents in the newer population leads to sub-optimal local minima.

Steady-State GP Implementation. Table 1 contains the GP parameters set as defaults in all test runs for the steady-state GP implementation. As per the generational algorithm mid (0.5) to high (.99) rates of mutation lead to faster convergence as compared to lower mutation rates. These rates show a steady progression of the most fit individual in our population. The need for higher mutation rates is apparent in the determination of the proper constants and logical operators that produce a well-formed query. In all cases, in Figure 4(a), we see an average individual, generally with fitness of .5, within the initial population. However, these fitness levels indicate that they are efficient enough to execute, but not accurate enough to be suitable for our purpose. Mutation leads to better individuals in later iterations of the steady-state GP. Figure 4(b) shows that convergence varies with population size. Finally, Figure 4(c) demonstrates the use of different selection sizes on the populations. When the selection/tournament size is too low (2) convergence may not occur in the specified number of iterations. But given too high a selection size (>18) leads to drastic over fitting of a non optimal minimum. Figure 4(c) suggests that selection size (6-10) leads to fast convergence with a higher accuracy.

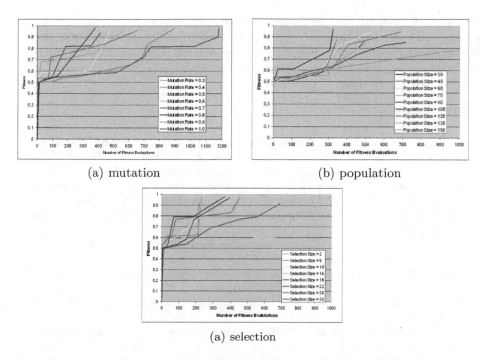

(a) mutation   (b) population

(a) selection

Fig. 3. The effects of different parameters on the generational algorithm

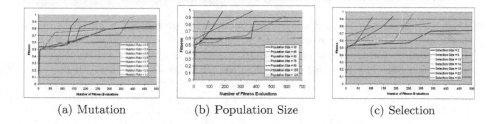

(a) Mutation   (b) Population Size   (c) Selection

Fig. 4. The effects of different parameters on the steady-state algorithm

5   Summary and Discussion

In this paper we described a novel approach for approximate query answering using Genetic Programming. We evaluated different GP techniques for generating approximate queries and then developed a cost model to determine how fit a given candidate query is compared to the original query in terms of the results returned. The framework described in this paper handles a variety of queries involving relational joins, multi-joins, projections, and select project joins. The current framework can be extended to include an enhanced tree-generation module and a semantic constraint verification module that will allow greater flexibility with respect to the queries that the framework can handle. Other models of GP such as linear GP might be suitable comparative techniques for query generation compared to tree-based GP for searching through the query space. Based on the speed, cost, and accuracy we derived methods to show that an evolved query can result in an accurate approximation of an input query.

References

1. Swarup Acharya, Phillip B. Gibbons, Viswanath Poosala, and Sridhar Ramaswamy. The aqua approximate query answering system. *Proceedings of the 1999 ACM SIG-MOD international conference on Management of data*, pages 574–576, 1999.
2. Surajit Chaudhuri. An overview of query optimization in relational systems. *Symposium on Principles of Database Systems Proceedings of the seventeenth ACM SIGACT-SIGMOD-SIGART symposium on Principles of database systems*, pages 34–43, 1998.
3. Goetz Graefe. Query evaluation techniques for large databases. *ACM Comput. Surv.*, 25(2):73–169, 1993.
4. Joseph M. Hellerstein. Optimization techniques for queries with expensive methods. *ACM Trans. Database Syst.*, 23(2):113–157, 1998.
5. Matthias Jarke and Jurgen Koch. Query optimization in database systems. *ACM Comput. Surv.*, 16(2):111–152, 1984.
6. Hang T. A. Pham and Kenneth C. Sevcik. Structure choices for two-dimensional histogram construction. *Proceedings of the 2004 conference of the Centre for Advanced Studies on Collaborative research*, pages 13–27, 2004.
7. Michael Steinbrunn, Guido Moerkotte, and Alfons Kemper. Heuristic and randomized optimization for the join ordering problem. *The VLDB Journal*, 6(3):191–208, 1997.
8. Michael Stillger and Myra Spiliopoulou. Genetic programming in database query optimization. In John R. Koza, David E. Goldberg, David B. Fogel, and Rick L. Riolo, editors, *Genetic Programming 1996: Proceedings of the First Annual Conference*, pages 388–393, Stanford University, CA, USA, 28–31 1996. MIT Press.

Blindbuilder: A New Encoding to Evolve Lego-Like Structures

Alexandre Devert, Nicolas Bredeche, and Marc Schoenauer

TAO team - INRIA Futurs - LRI, Bat 490 - Université Paris-Sud - France

Abstract. This paper introduces a new representation for assemblies of small Lego®-like elements: structures are indirectly encoded as construction plans. This representation shows some interesting properties such as hierarchy, modularity and easy constructibility checking by definition. Together with this representation, efficient GP operators are introduced that allow efficient and fast evolution, as witnessed by the results on two construction problems that demonstrate that the proposed approach is able to achieve both compactness and reusability of evolved components.

1 Introduction

In recent years, there have been many important achievements in the domain of Evolutionary Design using Evolutionary Computation in general [2], and Genetic Programming in particular [9]. These works range from evolving robots [10] to the design of satellite antennas [11]. Among these works, there is a strong interest for evolving constructions or robots using simple elements such as Lego bricks [13, 8].

The work described in this paper aims at evolving complete structures from small atomic elements (such as Lego® bricks or Kapla® elements) in order to obtain walls, bridges and so on. Many representations have been proposed for such constructions (see section 3), but many of them easily lead to either non-physical structures (overlapping elements), or structures that are impossible to actually construct (even though no element overlap).

One way to overcome this difficulty is to indirectly represent a structure through a construction plan. Indeed, construction plans provide a rather expressive representation formalism, and Evolutionary Computation provides an efficient way to evolve a plan (a genotype) such that the structure resulting from the application of this plan (a phenotype) is optimal for given objectives. One of the critical issues is then to provide evolution with efficient variation operators (crossover, and mutation) that explore some relevant part of the search space.

This paper proposes *BlindBuilder*, a representation for indirect encoding of structures that uses a direct representation for construction plans, described as Directed Acyclic Graphs (DAG). The variation operators borrow from the Embryogenic approaches of GP [6]. The paper is organized this following way:

Section 2 describes the framework of this work. Section 3 briefly reviews some important contributions in the field of Evolutionary Design of assemblies of small

P. Collet et al. (Eds.): EuroGP 2006, LNCS 3905, pp. 61–72, 2006.

elements, in both structural design (walls, bridges, tables and chairs, ...) and robotics (evolving both the morphology and the controller of robots). Sections 4 and 5 present the contributions of this work regarding *BlindBuilder*, respectively describing the language used to represent plans as DAGs, and the associated variation operators that have been defined to bias the exploration of such a search space. Section 6 shows the results on several classical problems of structural design. As usual, the final section discusses the results and sketches some directions for future work.

2   Problem Setting

The framework of this paper is the automatic building of constructions made of small elements such as (but not limited to) Lego-like bricks. Such set of elements gives to the user a huge expressivity (endless possible constructions) with very few biases (such elements are not targeted toward building any specific constructions). The basic objective of this work is to provide an efficient encoding language as well as the corresponding relevant variation operators to evolve constructions that are optimal with respect to given objective functions (e.g. filling space, building high-and-wide bridges, ...). An other longer-term goal is to evolve element-based morphologies for mobile robots.

In the context of Evolutionary Design, the following three issues must be addressed: (1) **Representation**: what is the search space to explore? should direct or indirect encoding be used? Can a given coding achieve generality, modularity, robustness ; (2) **Variation operators**: How to design relevant crossover and mutation operators to enable efficient evolution? (3) **Evaluation and Simulation**: how to evaluate structures regarding some given objective function(s)? Should the resulting structures be built and tested in the real world, though this usually is far too time consuming? And if going for a simulated evaluation, how to tackle the trade-off between precise but costly physical simulations and faster but inaccurate heuristic computations?

The next section will survey how these issues have been addressed in the literature for similar Evolutionary Design problems, focusing on the representations used to encode the structures.

3   Related Work

Representations for structures made of small elements can broadly be broken in two categories: *direct encoding* representations encode the position of elements in the environment; *indirect encoding* representations rely on a language that specifies *how to assemble the elements*.

Indirect encoding is largely favored in the literature, be it in the field of robotics or Structural Design, because it provides an easy and efficient way to bias evolution towards relevant structures. A remarkable exception is that of the GOLEM project [10] where real world implementation of evolved robots is achieved through a direct encoding that specifies anchor points that are linked by rigid sticks. But most other works rely on some indirect encoding: Karl Sims [15] evolves the building process of simulated robots through graph-based flow machines; more recently, the TinkerBots project [8] relies on L-systems to indirectly encode the construction process to build virtual and real world creatures. In both cases, the use of grammar- or L-system-based encoding makes it possible to obtain highly modular representations. In the field of Structural Design, [4] describe the evolution of a construction process that successfully builds 2D cantilever bridges, and [13] introduces a DAG-based representation to represent *construction plans* that are used to build small constructions such as pillars, walls and staircases.

Some previous works [1, 7] have shown that such indirect encoding representations are indeed much more efficient than direct encoding representations. The efficiency of an indirect encoding seems to have two main causes : *compactness* and *bias*. Indirect encoding is more expressive than direct encoding thanks to the possibility of reusing portions of the code; thus, appropriate factorisation in the representation may occur, that makes it possible to have more expressive code with shorter length, and, as a direct consequence, to speed up evolution. Indirect encoding also makes it possible to potentially represent only part of all possible structures, i.e. only a specific class of physical structures can be expressed; with the appropriate choice of implementation this enables the introduction of relevant domain knowledge.

Thus, several important properties should be considered[1] : *modularity* (the ability to reuse a part of the construction plan. Modularity may or may not be recursive) *hierarchy* (the ability to consider as one single element what has already been built as opposed to having to target specific sub-elements for any new operations) *generality* (the property according to which the representation can be easily extended to accept new kind of elements), and *3D representation* (some representations only consider 2-D structures, or don't scale-up well to 3-D structures).

The main drawbacks of indirect encoding is that they usually achieve some trade-off between language expressivity and constructibility. As a result, there is a clear separation between works that rely on direct encoding approach and that are actually implemented in the real world and works that exploit the power of the indirect encoding approach but are usually limited to simulation. A noteworthy exception is [8], where an indirect encoding approach is used to build real-world robots; but the approach is limited to a rather small number of elements.

Yet, it is possible to avoid, or at least limit, the problem of non constructibility by relying on an indirect encoding approach that works in the space of *construction plans* as proposed in [13]. A *construction plan* is evaluated to build a physical structure through a sequence of construction operations. In [13], construction plans are represented as Directed Acyclic Graphs where nodes are physical Lego

---

[1] Note that in [7], some of these terms are used in the context of programs rather than graphs, with different meaning.

elements and arcs are connection operators. With such a representation, it is possible to iteratively check at each construction step if the physical structure is buildable rather than evaluating the whole structure only at the end of the construction procedure.

4   BlindBuilder: A New Indirect Encoding Language

This section introduces *BlindBuilder*, an indirect encoding language for the description of construction plans. Basically, a *BlindBuilder* individual is a Directed Acyclic Graph (DAG) where nodes can be either atomic elements (e.g. Lego-elements, Kapla-Elements, Joints, Sticks, Tubes) offering *connectors* to other elements, or construction operators of a given arity (e.g. SNAP, CONNECTWITH-HINGEJOINT, CONNECTWITHBALLJOINT) parameterized by the connections they achieve between their arguments. More precisely :

- **Atomic element** are terminals of the DAG (i.e. they don't have any argument since their arity is zero). However, they are not considered as *physical* elements but rather as element templates that may be instantiated when needed. Each element template is defined with a given geometry and a set of connectors. Examples of atomic elements are Lego-elements, Kapla-elements (that have 0 connectors), tubes, wheels, artificial muscles, servomotors.
- **Construction operators** are functional nodes with a fixed number (*arity*) of arguments, i.e. targeted sub-nodes in the DAG, that specify what the defined function should be applied on (either other construction nodes or atomic elements). Moreover, each construction operator has internal parameter that specify how to connect its arguments together and that are subject to evolution. An example of a simple operator used in the following is the SNAP operator, that takes as arguments two elements to connect (e.g. *elements 1 and 2*) as well as parameters that define the anchor points and orientation. SNAP is formally written as : SNAP *[element1 target connector, element1 orientation connector, element2 target connector, element2 orientation connector] (element1 , element2)* . The *connector* arguments are used to pick up one actual connector from each argument-element (modulo the number of connectors of the actual argument), and the orientation of the connection is determined according to the *orientation* parameters (the number of parameters is thus independent of the size of bricks).

A well-formed *BlindBuilder* individual is hence a DAG such that the atomic elements are terminal nodes while the construction operators have as many sub-nodes as their arity. Moreover, there is a unique special node called the *top-level operator* (i.e. the entry point), so as to generate a single construction. The program run when using such a DAG to build a structure starts from the top-level operator and iteratively builds the structure by evaluating every operators until all terminal elements have been reached.

Figure 1 gives a very simple example of a construction plan with such properties together with the resulting structure. As a matter of fact, this example also illustrates some useful properties of this representation: **hierarchy**, when the snap operator at the top (right) reuses the results of its subgraph (at his left); and **modularity**, as four physical elements are built from the same element template. Moreover, as already mentioned, the ability to work in the construction space makes it possible to check for

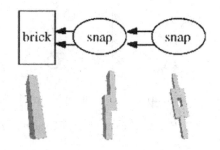

Fig. 1. A simple construction plan example and the resulting structure. The parameters of the Snap operators are not shown.

constructibility at each steps of the DAG evaluation, thus reducing the chances to obtain a non-constructible structure.

BlindBuilder is somewhat related to the graph-based approach described in [13]. Both languages are represented by a DAG and rely on similar construction operators (e.g. the *snap* operator). However, *BlindBuilder* considers both elements **and** construction operators as possible nodes of the graph. Moreover, element nodes are considered as templates and instantiated into physical elements, which makes it possible to endow hierarchy as well as modularity [2].

To summarize, *BlindBuilder* implements a language that is hierarchical, modular, and general while focusing on buildable plans in 3 dimensions, thus departing from previous work in the literature. Moreover, no a priori assumption is given for the definition of operators. It is hence possible to define a wide range of operators, as will be described in next section. As a consequence, it should be highlighted that all works described in section 3 can easily be expressed within *BlindBuilder* framework – from Karl Sims' creatures to Pollack's GOLEM robots and Lego-like constructions – as soon as the appropriate elements are properly designed.

5   Variation Operators

In order to evolve *BlindBuilder* individuals, it is necessary to design variation operators. Some examples of GP-based evolution of graphs exist in the literature [16]. However, the DAGs resulting from the variation operators for *BlindBuilder* must comply with the definition of a well-formed *BlindBuilder* individuals, as stated in the previous section.

Classical operators in graph-based GP such as *crossover* (creating a construction plan from two existing plans) and *mutation* (altering a construction plan) may be used to evolve a *BlindBuilder* DAG. However, two main problems arise. First, performing even a syntactically correct crossover upon two DAGs may result in very different structures in the end because of the very structure of a DAG

---

[2] While recursivity is possible, it is not yet implemented in the present work.

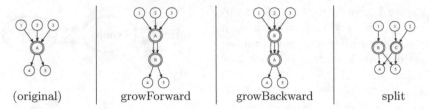

(original) | growForward | growBackward | split

Fig. 2. Effects of *growForward, growBackward* and *split* operators

(i.e. semantic) is ignored in the blind process of standard crossover. Because the topology of *BlindBuilder* DAGs is of utter importance, no useful crossover operator could be designed, and the evolutionary process described hereafter only relies on mutation. Second, simple random mutation operator (i.e. replacing a (group of) node(s) by randomly generated nodes) is confronted to the difficulty of matching arities between deleted and inserted (group of) node(s).

However, though the proposed approach is definitely not an embryogenic approach, the operators used as nodes in the seminal work in embryogeny-inspired GP [6] were used as inspiration for the present work and led to introducing the following five mutation operators:

1. *GrowForward* (fig. 2-b): a new non-terminal node B is added downstream from the target non-terminal node A. All arcs outgoing from A are connected with B. B is randomly chosen among all operators with the same arity than A, and its parameters are uniformly initialized;
2. *GrowBackward*: a new non-terminal node B is added upstream from the target non-terminal node A. The ingoing arcs to A become ingoing arcs to B. B is randomly chosen among all non-terminal node and its parameters are uniformly initialized;
3. *Split*: target node A is split into B and C, two nodes at the same level. Ingoing arcs to A are randomly assigned to B or C, while outgoing arcs are duplicated. These new nodes are randomly chosen among the set of arity-compatible nodes. This operator cannot be applied to the upper level node;
4. *Permute*: outgoing arcs of the target non-terminal node are randomly permuted *and* parameters are uniformly reset;
5. *Replace* : the target node is replaced by a randomly chosen node with the same arity *and* its parameters are uniformly reset.

The only restriction in those operators is that the *split* operator cannot be applied to the top level node, to avoid conflicting entry points for the evaluation process. This feature ensures that all plans can be generated (in theory) from DAG made of a single terminal: this is what will be used in the initial population.

6   Experimental Results

This section presents the experimental setup (software and evolution parameters) along with two experiments. Each experiment relies on the use of one specific

species of construction elements: Lego-like and Kapla-like[3]. Due to the type
of elements involved, *BlindBuilder* construction operator list is limited to the
SNAP operator described in section 4. For Lego-like elements, the SNAP operator
results in establishing a real physical connection while for Kapla-like elements,
it is only used to position the various elements (i.e. the resulting construction
may be destroyed because of gravity).

6.1   Experimental Setup

As said above, all individuals in the initial population are single-node DAGs,
for which the unique terminal is uniformly chosen among the set of element
templates.

The selection is a tournament selection (typically of size 7) based on a hierarchical multi-criterion comparison operator that incorporates both the target
objective(s) and some parsimony pressure in a lexicographic way similar to that
proposed by [12]. Note that this is **not** a Pareto-based optimization (e.g., two
individuals are always comparable).

- Define the relative distance between two values a and b as $\frac{|a-b|}{max(a,b)}$;
- Order the list of objectives from most to less important;
- Two individuals are said to be equivalent for a given objective if the relative
  distance between their values for this objective is less than a given threshold
  (typically 0.1);
- The comparison of two individuals is then lexicographic, i.e. individual x is
  better than individual y if, for some objective rank i, x and y are equivalent
  for objectives $1, \ldots, i-1$, they are not equivalent for objective i, and the
  value of x for objective i is larger than that of y.

In the following experiments, tournament size is set to 7 and population size
to 1000. The threshold for the comparison of objective values is set to 0.1. All
experiments were run 13 to 20 times. Each experiment took about 16 hours on
a PC with Intel Pentium 4 running at 3.6 GHz under Linux.

A few preliminary experiments (not shown here) showed that a Pareto approach (relying on NSGA-2 algorithm [3]) was slower the hierarchical approach
described above. Moreover, a standard generational GA evolution (i.e. 1000 offspring are generated at each generation and replace all parents) using tournament selection was observed to be more efficient than both $(\mu, lambda)$-ES and
$(\mu + lambda)$-ES, with $\mu = 15$ or $\mu = 30$ and $\lambda = 7\mu$, the latter giving better
result than the former. Finally, a maximal size of 50 for a construction plan was
set to avoid uncontrolled code growth – but the limit was hardly ever reached.

The preliminary experiments also showed the relative importance of the variation operator *replace*: Indeed, this operator is much more conservative than the
others, and is mandatory to fine tune existing structures, while all other operators result in important changes in the resulting structure. As a consequence,

---

[3] http://www.kapla.com

the rate for the *replace* operator is set to 0.7 while all other operators have a rate of 0.075 in the following experiments.

The *BlindBuilder* approach was implemented within *Open-BEAGLE*, a framework for artificial evolution written in $C++$ [5]. *Newton Game Dynamics*[4], was used in order to simulate and evaluate the resulting structure in a physical environment. All the experiments are in three dimensions.

6.2   The Pillar Experiment

The goal is to build the biggest possible structure using Lego-like elements (1x2, 2x2, 2x3, 2x4 and 2x6 bricks). Lego-like elements are characterized by physical connections that hold them together. The objective functions to maximise are, ordered by priority:

1. The *volume*: $V = \sum V_i$, where V_i is the volume of ith atomic element i.
2. The *compacity*: $C = \frac{V}{V_{full}}$ where V_{full} is the volume of the convex hull of the whole structure.
3. The *parsimony*: $P = 50 - S$ where S is the number of nodes of the construction plan (max. 50 elements).

Figures 3 and 4 shows evolution results and an example of obtained structure when using only a 2x2 element. Results show that for this simple constrained problem, maximum compacity is achieved very quickly. Moreover, optimal individuals are found with the smallest possible construction plan. Figures 5 and 6 shows the same experiment but with all 5-elements templates possible. The bigger and thus most appropriate element (2x6) is always used, even though the optimal plan is not yet reached at the end of evolution (it may be reached if evolution is carried on further). The two examples shown on Figure 6 are very different construction plans, the latter being larger, but leading to a more compact construction. In all experiments, reusability has been heavily exploited, as can be observed in the sample plans of Figure 6.

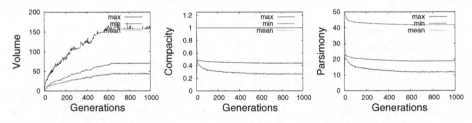

Fig. 3. Averge results for Pillar experiment using only the 2x2 Lego-element template

6.3   The Bridge Experiment

Kapla-like elements can be defined as Lego-like elements with no connections. Thus, Kapla construction are much more unstable. Moreover, by changing the set

---
[4] Freeware but not open-source, see http://www.newtondynamics.com/

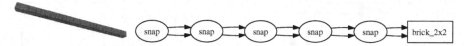

Fig. 4. Example of best solution for the Pillar experiment using only the 2x2 Lego-element template. Snap parameters not shown.

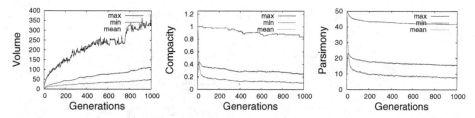

Fig. 5. Average results for Pillar experiment using five possible Lego-element templates

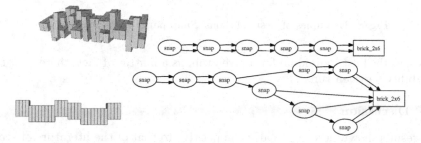

Fig. 6. Examples of best solutions found for the Pillar experiment using five possible Lego-element templates. Snap parameters not shown.

of possible values of the *orientation* parameter in the Snap construction operator, the user can decide to go from "flat" structure (allowing a single value 0) to square structures (allowing 0, 90, 180 and 270 degree orientations) to complex 3D structure (allowing any floating-point value). The goal of this experiment is to build the longest horizontal structure with as few elements on the floor using Kapla-like elements. The objective functions to maximise are:

1. The *length*, the horizontal length of the structure.
2. The *grounding*, $n - f$ where n is the number of atomic elements of the construction, and f the number of atomic elements that are in direct contact with the floor.
3. The *parsimony* defined as in the Pillar experiment above.

Figure 7 show results of obtained individuals. Every runs succeeded in generating quite successful individuals, either by deeply optimizing one of the objective function or making a compromise between the three objective functions. The most striking results is that evolution has been able to build *cantilever* bridges with *arches*, for which various examples are shown in figure 8. Each example

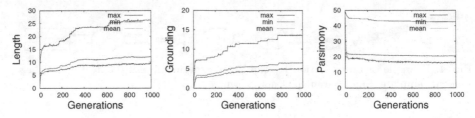

Fig. 7. Results for the Bridge experiment

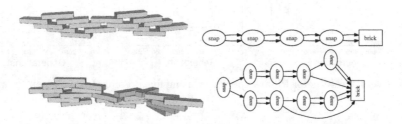

Fig. 8. Examples of best solutions. Snap parameters not shown.

represent the best individual for a given run, as a matter of fact, there is a great variability between runs.

6.4 Discussion

The results shown here are clearly competitive to that of the literature of evolutionary design using Lego-like elements. The approach of [13] and *BlindBuilder* both use a DAG-based representation of construction plans. However, the former lacks properties of modularity due to the intrinsic nature of the graph (node are physical elements only, arcs are functions that connect these elements and the language is limited to Lego elements). As a consequence, experiments are limited to simple constructions (walls, pillars) and evolution is slower than what has been shown here - for instance, construction size can only grow by adding one element after another while a *BlindBuilder* construction can double in size thanks to the addition of a single SNAP operator at the top of a graph.

The experiments presented in [4] also demonstrated that bridges made of Lego elements can be evolved according to the cantilever principle. However, evolution took place in a two-dimensional environment (even though "flat" 3D models were shown). Moreover, the language used in [4] lacks reusability. On the opposite, the *BlindBuilder* approach leads to comparable results in a true 3D environment, with a more compact representation, thanks again to modularity (here : ability to reuse arches and cantilever principle as soon as their definitions are evolved in a construction plan).

One current limitation of our work is that for every run, the evolution process failed to maintain diversity. As a results, best individuals are very different from one run to another, but very similar within one given run. A current track under investigation is that of introducing island models so as to maintain candidate solutions with similar performance but different structures within one single run.

7   Conclusion and Perspectives

This paper has introduced a new indirect encoding language for structures made of small elements called *BlindBuilder*. It is designed to represent construction plans, i.e. plans to iteratively build structures such as bridges or robots from atomic elements. *BlindBuilder* shows interesting features such as compactness and reusability thanks to hierarchy and modularity. Moreover, construction plans make it possible to check for constructibility at each time steps of the evaluation instead of having to evaluate the whole structure. To our knowledge, this language is the first to endow all these properties in a single framework.

Alongside, a set of mutation operators have been defined to perform efficient evolution. These kind of mutation operators explore the space of construction plans and alter existing construction plans in such a way that resulting individuals are well-formed *BlindBuilder* graphs.

The experiments showed that *BlindBuilder* features are exploited by the evolution process and do achieve compact representation with reusable components. Interesting results were achieved when building bridges with Kapla-like elements, such as the rediscovery of arches and cantilever principle so as to minimise contact points while maximising bridge length.

Future works on *BlindBuilder* include adding recursivity, though there is no way to easily specify a terminating condition within a graph. We also intend to refine the variation operators, especially the *permute* and *replace* operators, with respect to the modification of the parameters; parameters are at the moment modified uniformly, while more real-value-oriented mutations, such as Gaussian mutation for the orientation in the case of Kapla elements, should be more appropriate and should allow both more variety in the results and better finetuning of the final solution. As for constructibility issues, recent works [14] have shown that a promising way is to evaluate candidates as they are built, and not just the resulting structure, which can be easily implemented using *BlindBuilder* – but this will have some computational cost.

References

1. Peter Bentley and Sanjeev Kumar. Three ways to grow designs: A comparison of embryogenics for an evolutionary design problem. In *Proceedings of the Genetic and Evolutionary Computation Conference*, volume 1, pages 35–43, Orlando, Florida, USA, 13-17 1999. Morgan Kaufmann.
2. Peter J. Bentley. *Evolutionary Design by Computers*. Morgan Kaufmann Publishers Inc., San Francisco, CA, USA, 1999.
3. K. Deb, S. Agrawal, A. Pratab, and T. Meyarivan. A Fast Elitist Non-Dominated Sorting Genetic Algorithm for Multi-Objective Optimization: NSGA-II. In M. Schoenauer et al., editor, *Proceedings of the 6th Conference on Parallel Problems Solving from Nature*, pages 849–858. Springer-Verlag, LNCS 1917, 2000.

4. Pablo J. Funes and Jordan B. Pollack. Computer evolution of buildable objects, Chapter 17 in [2], 1999.
5. Christian Gagné and Marc Parizeau. Open BEAGLE: A new C++ evolutionary computation framework. In *GECCO 2002: Proceedings of the Genetic and Evolutionary Computation Conference*, page 888, New York, 9-13 July 2002. Morgan Kaufmann Publishers.
6. F. Gruau. *Neural Network Synthesis using Cellular Encoding and the Genetic Algorithm*. PhD thesis, Ecole Normale Supérieure de Lyon, France, 1994.
7. Gregory S. Hornby. Measuring, enabling and comparing modularity, regularity and hierarchy in evolutionary design. In *GECCO 2005: Proceedings of the 2005 conference on Genetic and evolutionary computation*, volume 2, pages 1729–1736, Washington DC, USA, 25-29 June 2005. ACM Press.
8. Gregory S. Hornby, Hod Lipson, and Jordan B. Pollack. Generative representations for the automated design of modular physical robots. *IEEE transactions on Robotics and Automation*, 19(4):709–713, August 2003.
9. John R. Koza, David Andre, Forrest H Bennett III, and Martin Keane. *Genetic Programming 3: Darwinian Invention and Problem Solving*. Morgan Kaufman, April 1999.
10. Hod Lipson and Jordan B. Pollack. Automatic design and manufacture of robotic lifeforms. *Nature*, 406:974–978, 2000.
11. Jason Lohn, Gregory Hornby, and Derek Linden. Evolutionary antenna design for a NASA spacecraft. In *Genetic Programming Theory and Practice II*, chapter 18, pages 301–315. Springer, Ann Arbor, 13-15 May 2004.
12. Sean Luke and Liviu Panait. Lexicographic parsimony pressure. In *GECCO-2002: Proceedings of the Genetic and Evolutionary Computation Conference*, pages 829–836. Morgan Kaufmann, 2002.
13. Maxim Peysakhov, Vlada Galinskaya, and William C. Regli. Representation and evolution of lego-based assemblies. In *Proceedings of the Seventeenth National Conference on Artificial Intelligence and Twelfth Conference on Innovative Applications of Artificial Intelligence*, page 1089. AAAI Press / The MIT Press, 2000.
14. John Rieffel and Jordan Pollack. Automated assembly as situated development: using artificial ontogenies to evolve buildable 3-d objects. In *GECCO '05: Proceedings of the 2005 conference on Genetic and evolutionary computation*, pages 99–106, New York, NY, USA, 2005. ACM Press.
15. Karl Sims. Evolving 3d morphology and behavior by competition. *Artificial Life*, 1(4):353–372, 1994.
16. Astro Teller and Manuela Veloso. PADO: A new learning architecture for object recognition. In *Symbolic Visual Learning*, pages 81–116. Oxford University Press, 1996.

Dynamic Scheduling with Genetic Programming

Domagoj Jakobović and Leo Budin

Faculty of Electrical Engineering and Computing, University of Zagreb, Croatia
{domagoj.jakobovic, leo.budin}@fer.hr

Abstract. This paper investigates the use of genetic programming in automatized synthesis of scheduling heuristics. The applied scheduling technique is priority scheduling, where the next state of the system is determined based on priority values of certain system elements. The evolved solutions are compared with existing scheduling heuristics for single machine dynamic problem and job shop scheduling with bottleneck estimation.

1 Introduction

Scheduling is concerned with the allocation of scarce resources to activities with the objective of optimizing one or more performance measures, which can assume minimization of makespan, job tardiness, number of late jobs etc. Due to inherent problem complexity and variability, a large number of scheduling systems employ heuristic scheduling methods. Among many available heuristic algorithms, the question arises of which heuristic to use in a particular environment, given different performance criteria and user requirements. The problem of selecting the appropriate scheduling policy is an active area of research [1][2], and a considerable effort is needed to choose or develop the algorithm best suited to the problem at hand. A solution to this problem may be provided using machine learning, genetic programming in particular, to create problem specific scheduling algorithms.

The combinatorial nature of most scheduling problems allows the use of search based and enumerative techniques [1], such as genetic algorithms, branch and bound etc. These methods usually offer good quality solutions, but at the cost of a large amount of computational time needed to produce such a solution. Furthermore, search based techniques are not applicable in dynamic or uncertain conditions where there is need for frequent schedule modification or reaction to changing system requirements. Scheduling with heuristic algorithms that define only the next state of the system is therefore highly effective in most instances.

Genetic programming has rarely been employed in scheduling, mainly because it is unpractical to use it to search the space of potential solutions (i.e. schedules). It is, however, very suitable for the search of the space of algorithms that provide solution to the problem. Previous work in this area of research includes evolving scheduling policies for single machine unweighted tardiness problem [3][4][5], single machine scheduling subject to breakdowns [6], classic job shop tardiness scheduling [7][8] and airplane scheduling in air traffic control [9][10].

P. Collet et al. (Eds.): EuroGP 2006, LNCS 3905, pp. 73–84, 2006.

In most cases the authors observe performance comparable to the human-made algorithms. The scheduling procedure is however defined only implicitly for a given scheduling environment. In this paper we structure the scheduling algorithm in two components: a meta-algorithm which uses priority values to perform scheduling and a priority function which defines values for different elements of the system. This approach allows easier creation of various heuristics in an arbitrary scheduling environment. To illustrate this methodology we address the problem of scheduling with dynamic job arrivals, for which there is a possibility of inserted idleness in resource usage. We also tackle the problem of bottleneck identification in multiple machine environments and define an appropriate algorithm structure for job shop scheduling. The obtained results can be used in a more realistic weighted variant of the presented problems.

2 Priority Scheduling with Genetic Programming

A natural representation for the solution of a scheduling problem is a sequence of activities to be performed on each of the machines. While this representation is most suitable for use in combinatorial optimization, it presents only a solution to the specific scheduling instance, which means that a new solution must be found for different initial conditions. With genetic programming, we have the ability to represent a solution for all the problem instances in a scheduling environment with an algorithm that can be used to generate a schedule.

The scheduling method applied in this work is priority scheduling, in which certain elements of the scheduling system are assigned priority values. The choice of the next activity being run on a certain machine is based on their respective priority values. This kind of scheduling algorithm is also called, variously, 'dispatching rule', 'scheduling rule' or just 'heuristic'. The term scheduling rule, in a narrow sense, often represents only the *priority function* which assigns values to elements of the system (jobs in most cases). For instance, a scheduling process may be described with the statement 'scheduling is performed using SPT rule'. While in most cases the method of assignment of jobs on machines based on priority values is trivial, in some environments it is not. This is particularly true in dynamic conditions where jobs arrive over time or may not be run before some other job finishes. That is why a *meta-algorithm* must be defined for each scheduling environment, dictating the way activities are scheduled based on their priorities and possible system constraints. This meta-algorithm encapsulates the priority function, but the same meta-algorithm may be used with different priority functions and vice versa. The time complexity of priority scheduling algorithms depends on the meta-algorithm, but it is in most cases negligible compared to search-based techniques, which allows the use of this method in on-line scheduling [11] and dynamic conditions (all heuristics presented here provide a solution for several hundred instances in less than a second).

The described structure of the scheduling algorithm allows modular development and the possibility of iterative refinement, which is particularly suitable for machine learning methods. In this work the meta-algorithm part is defined manually for a specific scheduling environment, such as dynamic one machine or job shop. The priority function is evolved with genetic programming using appropriate functional and data structures. This way, using the same meta-algorithm, different scheduling algorithms best suited for the current criteria can be devised. The task of genetic programming is to find such a priority function which would yield the best results considering given meta-algorithm and user requirements.

3   Single Machine Dynamic Scheduling

Problem Statement. In a single machine environment, a number n of jobs J_j are processed on a single resource. In a static problem each job is available at time zero, whereas in a dynamic problem each job has a release date r_j. The processing time of the job is p_j and its due date is d_j. The relative importance of a job is denoted with its weight w_j. In this environment the non-trivial optimization criteria include weighted tardiness and weighted number of late jobs, which are defined as follows: if C_j denotes the finishing time of job j, the job tardiness T_j is defined as

$$T_j = \max\{C_j - d_j, 0\} \ . \tag{1}$$

Lateness of a job U_j is taken to be 1 if a job is late, i.e. if its tardiness is greater than zero, and 0 otherwise. Weighted tardiness for a set of jobs is defined as

$$T_w = \sum_j w_j T_j \tag{2}$$

and weighted number of late jobs as

$$U_w = \sum_j w_j U_j \ . \tag{3}$$

In the evaluation of scheduling heuristics we use a large number of test cases with different number of jobs, job durations and weights. In order for all the test cases to have a similar influence to the overall quality estimate of an algorithm, we define normalized criteria for each test case. Normalized weighted tardiness is defined as

$$\overline{T_w} = \frac{\sum\limits_{j=1}^{n} w_j T_j}{n \cdot \bar{w} \cdot \bar{p}} \ , \tag{4}$$

and normalized number of late jobs as

$$\overline{U_w} = \frac{\sum\limits_{j=1}^{n} w_j U_j}{n \cdot \bar{w}} \ , \tag{5}$$

where n represents the number of jobs in a test case, $\bar{w}$ the average weight and $\bar{p}$ the average duration of all jobs. The average duration is not included in weighted number of late jobs because that criteria does not include any quantity of time dependent on job's processing time. The total quality estimate of an algorithm is expressed as the sum of normalized criteria over all the test cases.

Scheduling Heuristics. In a dynamic environment the scheduler can use algorithms designed for a static environment, but two things need to be defined for those heuristics: the first is the subset of the jobs to be taken into consideration for scheduling, since some jobs may arrive in some future moment in time. The second issue is the method of evaluation of jobs which have not yet arrived, i.e. the question should the priority function for those jobs be different and in what way. This can be resolved in the following ways:

1. no inserted idleness - we only consider jobs which are immediately available;
2. inserted idleness - waiting for a job is allowed and waiting time is added to job's processing time in priority calculation;
3. inserted idleness with arbitrary priority - waiting is allowed but the priority function must be defined so it takes waiting time into account.

When using existing heuristics for comparison, we apply the second approach where necessary, i.e. if priority function does not take job's release date into account. The genetic programming, on the other hand, is coupled with the third approach, as it has the ability to learn and make use of waiting time information on itself. Scheduling heuristics that presume all the jobs are available are modified so that the processing time of a job includes job's time till arrival (waiting time), denoted with

$$wt_j = \max\{r_j - time, 0\} \ . \tag{6}$$

Thus, if an algorithm uses the processing time of a job, that time is increased by wt_j of the job. This modification is not necessary for algorithms that are specifically designed for dynamic conditions, i.e. which already include release date information in priority calculation. It can be shown that, for any regular scheduling criteria [12], a job should not be scheduled if the waiting time for that job is longer than the processing time of the shortest of all currently available unscheduled jobs. In other words, we may only consider jobs j for which

$$wt_j \leq \min_i \{p_i\}, \forall i : r_i \leq time \ . \tag{7}$$

This approach may be illustrated with the following meta-algorithm using an arbitrary priority function:

> **while** there are unscheduled jobs **do**
>   wait until machine is ready;
> p_{MIN} = the duration of the shortest available job;
>   calculate priorities of all jobs with $wt_j < p_{MIN}$;
>   schedule job with best priority;
> **end while**

In the above algorithm, 'best' priority may be defined as the one with the greatest or the lowest value, which is purely a matter of definition. For purposes of efficiency comparison we used the following heuristics: weighted shortest processing time (WSPT), earliest due date (EDD), weighted Montagne heuristic [12] (MON), Rachamadugu & Morton heuristic [13] (RM) and X-dispatch bottleneck dynamics heuristic [12] (XD). Each heuristic is defined with its priority function which is used as described in the above meta-algorithm. All except the XD heuristic, which is the only one designed for dynamic job arrivals, are modified to include job waiting time; WSPT heuristic, for instance, has the priority function

$$\pi_j = w_j/(p_j + wt_j) \ . \tag{8}$$

Test Cases. Each scheduling instance is defined with the following parameters: the number of jobs, their processing times, due dates, release dates and weights. Job durations may take integer values between 1 and 100 and their weights values between 0.01 and 1 in steps of 0.01. The values of processing times are generated using uniform, normal and quasi-bimodal probability distributions among the different test cases. Release times are chosen randomly in the interval

$$r_j \in \left[0, \ \frac{1}{2}\sum_{i=1}^{n} p_i\right] \ . \tag{9}$$

Job due dates are generated using two parameters: T as due date tightness and R as due date range, which both assume values in interval $[0,1]$. For each test case due dates are generated with uniform distribution in the interval

$$d_j \in \left[r_j + \left(\sum_{i=1}^{n} p_i - r_j\right) \cdot (1 - T - R/2), \ r_j + \left(\sum_{i=1}^{n} p_i - r_j\right) \cdot (1 - T + R/2)\right] \ . \tag{10}$$

Due date tightness parameter represents the expected percentage of late jobs and due date range defines the dispersion of due date values. The numbers of jobs in test cases are 12, 25, 50 and 100 whereas parameters T and R assume values of 0.2, 0.4, 0.6, 0.8 and 1 in various combinations. We define 100 scheduling instances that are used as fitness cases in learning process and additional 600 instances that are used for evaluation purposes only.

Scheduling with Genetic Programming. The task of genetic program is to find a priority function which is best suited for use with given criteria and meta-algorithm. After the learning process, the best found priority function is tested on evaluation test cases. The solution of genetic programming is represented with a single tree that embodies the priority function. The choice of functions and terminals is a crucial step in the overall optimization process since they must allow the program to use all the relevant information and form an efficient solution. The complete set of primitives used as tree elements is presented in Table 1.

Weighted Tardiness Problem. The described genetic programming process can be used for optimization of an arbitrary scheduling criteria, but the most common one for single machine environment is weighted tardiness. Fitness value of a genetic program solution is defined as sum of normalized criteria values, defined as (4), over all 100 learning test cases (smaller values are better). The genetic programming parameters are given in Table 2 (we did not perform any

Table 1. The function and terminal set for dynamic one machine problem

Function name	Definition
ADD, SUB, MUL	binary addition, subtraction and multiplication operators
DIV	protected division: DIV $(a, b) = \begin{cases} 1, \text{if } |b| < 0.000001 \\ a/b, \text{otherwise} \end{cases}$
POS	POS $(a) = \max \{a, 0\}$
Terminal name	**Definition**
pt	processing time of a job (p_j)
dd	due date (d_j)
w	weight (w_j)
N	total number of jobs
Nr	number of remaining (unscheduled) jobs
SP	sum of processing times of all jobs
SPr	sum of processing times of remaining jobs
SD	sum of due dates of all jobs
SL	positive slack, $\max \{d_j - p_j - time, 0\}$
AR	job arrival time (waiting time), $\max \{r_j - time, 0\}$

Table 2. The genetic programming parameters

Parameter / operator	Value / description
population size	10000
selection	steady-state, tournament of size 3
stopping criteria	maximum number of generations (300) or maximum number of consecutive generations without best solution improvement (50)
crossover	85% probability, standard crossover
mutation	standard, swap and shrink mutation, 3% probability for each
reproduction	5% probability
initialization	ramped half-and-half, max. depth of 5

additional parameter tuning to show that even with 'common' parameter values good results could be obtained).

We conducted 20 runs using the defined meta-algorithm and achieved mean best result of 331.0 with standard deviation $\sigma = 1.92$. The overall solution was chosen among best solutions of each run as the one with the best performance on the unseen set of 600 evaluation test cases. The results in the form of total normalized criteria values are presented in the lefthand side of Table 3 ('Twt' denotes weighted tardiness and 'Uwt' weighted number of tardy jobs). Apart from total criteria values, the performance measure for each heuristic may also be described as the percentage of test cases in which the heuristic achieved the best known result (or the result that is not worse than any other heuristic). This value can be denoted as the dominance percentage, and comparative results for all the heuristics are shown in the righthand side of Table 3.

Table 3. Normalized criteria and dominance percentages for one machine problem

	Normalized criteria		Dominance percentage	
	Twt	Uwt	Twt	Uwt
GP	330.6	188.8	80 %	49 %
XD	389.7	194.1	21 %	30 %
RM	451.7	210.6	9 %	17 %
MON	623.1	216.7	3 %	8 %
WSPT	845.0	201.6	0 %	21 %
EDD	1280.9	440.0	14 %	13 %

It can be perceived that the evolved scheduling heuristic achieved the best overall performance for both scheduling criteria. In addition, we performed experiments with weighted number of tardy jobs as the fitness function and, as expected, the evolved algorithm's efficiency for that criteria was improved. At the same time, the performance in regard of weighted tardiness decreased significantly, so we may conclude that optimization with weighted tardiness as performance criteria pays off better considering overall algorithm quality.

4   Job Shop Scheduling

Problem Statement. Job shop scheduling includes running n jobs on m machines where each job has m operations and each operation is to be processed on a specific machine (more general model involves arbitrary number of operations for any job). Duration of one operation of job j on machine i is denoted with p_{ij}. Every machine and job is considered to be available for processing from the beginning. The operations of each job have to be completed in a specific sequence which differs from job to job. In addition to weighted tardiness and number of tardy jobs, another non-trivial and widely used criteria are weighted flowtime and makespan. Normalized weighted flowtime of a set of jobs is defined as

$$\overline{F_w} = \frac{\sum\limits_{j=1}^{n} w_j F_j}{n \cdot \bar{w} \cdot \bar{p}} \ , \tag{11}$$

where F_j equals to the completion time of the last operation of a job, C_j. Normalized makespan is similarly defined as

$$\overline{C_{max}} = \frac{\max\{C_j\}}{n \cdot \bar{p}} \ . \tag{12}$$

Although the jobs are considered to be available from the time zero, scheduling on a given machine is inherently dynamic because an operation may only be ready at some time in the future (after the completion of the job's previous operation). We therefore modify the processing time of an operation as in the single machine dynamic problem (inserted idleness approach).

Scheduling Heuristics. Job shop priority scheduling involves determining the next operation to be processed on a given machine. The scheduling on a machine may only occur if the machine is available and if either of the following is true: there are operations ready to be processed on that machine or there are operations which will be ready for processing at a known time in future. The latter situation occurs if the previous operation of a job has already started and we know the time it will finish. This procedure can be described with the following meta-algorithm:

> **while** there are unprocessed operations **do**
> > wait for a machine with pending operations;
> > calculate priorities of all pending operations;
> > schedule best priority operation;
> > update machine and next job's operation ready time;
> **end while**

The choice of operations considered for scheduling is still restricted to those operations whose waiting time (6) is smaller than the duration of the shortest available operation. In efficiency comparison we used the following job shop heuristics: WSPT, processing time to the total work remaining (WSPT/TWKR), weighted total work remaining (WTWKR), dynamic slack per remaining process time (SLACK/TWKR), COVERT (cost over time) and Rachamadugu & Morton job shop heuristic (RM). Each heuristic is described with its priority function; detailed descriptions of the listed heuristics can be found in [14] and [12].

Test Cases. The operations processing times and job weights are generated randomly as for the one machine environment. Job numbers are 12, 25, 50 and 100 whereas the number of machines takes values of 5, 10, 15 or 20 in a test case. The expected total duration of all the jobs is defined as

$$\hat{p} = \frac{1}{m} \sum_{j=1}^{n} \sum_{i=1}^{m} p_{ij} \; , \tag{13}$$

and job due dates are generated randomly with parameters T and R in the following interval:

$$d_j \in [\hat{p}(1 - T - R/2), \hat{p}(1 - T + R/2)] \; . \tag{14}$$

We define 160 test cases for learning and 320 evaluation test cases, in addition to 80 instances taken from [15], used for evaluation only.

Scheduling with Genetic Programming. As in the single machine case, the solution of genetic programming is a single tree which represents the priority function to be used with defined meta-algorithm. The choice of functions is similar to the previous implementation, but the terminals are radically different, because they must include different information of the system state. The set of functions and terminals is presented in Table 4.

Table 4. The function and terminal set for job shop problem

Function name	Definition
ADD, SUB, MUL, DIV, POS	as in Table 1
SQR	protected unary square root: $SQR(a) = \begin{cases} 1, & \text{if } a < 0 \\ \sqrt{a}, & \text{otherwise} \end{cases}$
IFGT	comparison operator: $IFGT(a,b,c,d) = \begin{cases} c, & \text{if } a > b \\ d, & \text{otherwise} \end{cases}$
Terminal name	Definition
pt	operation processing time (p_{ij})
dd	job due date (d_j)
w	job weight (w_j)
CLK	current time
AR	operation waiting time: $\max\{r_{ij} - time, 0\}$, where r_{ij} denotes finishing time of the previous operation (before machine i)
NOPr	number of remaining job operations
TWK	total processing time of all operations of a job
TWKr	processing time of remaining operations of a job
PTav	average duration of all the operations on a given machine
HTR	head time ratio: the ratio of the total time the job has been in the system and total duration of job's completed operations

Table 5. Normalized criteria and dominance percentages for job shop problem

	Normalized criteria				Dominance percentage			
	Twt	Uwt	Fwt	Cmax	Twt	Uwt	Fwt	Cmax
GP	146.1	70.9	105.8	133.5	88 %	12 %	73 %	0 %
RM	158.0	68.5	110.0	121.6	5 %	14 %	1 %	5 %
COVERT	179.8	73.4	119.0	118.7	0 %	11 %	0 %	31 %
WSPT	161.6	69.3	107.9	121.7	2 %	13 %	16 %	5 %
SPT/TWKR	195.5	74.6	123.2	118.9	0 %	11 %	0 %	35 %
WTWKR	166.1	68.4	109.0	127.8	4 %	17 %	10 %	4 %
SL/TWKR	225.5	77.0	134.3	123.7	0 %	11 %	0 %	14 %
EDD	206.1	76.5	123.7	128.0	1 %	11 %	0 %	6 %

We conducted 20 experiments optimizing weighted tardiness criteria with mean best value over the runs 147.5 and $\sigma = 1.07$. The best solution was compared with the existing scheduling heuristics on the evaluation set of 400 (320 + 80) test cases. The results in normalized criteria values and dominance percentages are shown in Table 5.

Scheduling with Adaptive Heuristic. It has already been shown [8] that the identification of the bottleneck resource, i.e. the resource with substantially higher load, may improve the scheduling process. As it is generally not known in advance which machine could become a bottleneck, we may try and develop a heuristic to determine such resource on line. We propose a genetic programming

Table 6. The terminal set for decision tree

Terminal name	Definition
MTWK	total processing time of all operations on a machine
MTWKr	processing time of all remaining operations on a machine
MTWKav	average duration of all operations on all machines
MNOPr	number of remaining operations on a machine
MNOPw	number of waiting operations on a machine
MUTL	utilization: the ratio of duration of all processed operations on a machine and total elapsed time

approach where there are two distinctive agents, or scheduling heuristics, and GP is responsible for evolving the rule to decide which heuristic is to be applied on a given machine. The solution of genetic programming consists of three parts (represented as trees): the first part, or the decision tree, determines which heuristic should be used at a given moment. The other two parts (scheduling trees) are applied depending on the result of the decision tree. Scheduling trees use the same primitives as in Table 4, but the decision tree should be able to recognize increased load on a machine with appropriate set of terminals. The terminals which can be used in the decision tree are presented in Table 6 (the functions are the same in all trees).

As the result of the decision tree is a numeric value, we have to interpret it in some way and define the scheduling process. This procedure can be described with the following meta-algorithm:

for each machine i **do**
    calculate decision tree value (P_i);
end for
while there are unprocessed operations **do**
    wait for a machine with pending operations;
    P_i = decision tree value for current machine;
    if $P_i > P_m$, $\forall m$ **then**
        calculate priorities using the second tree;
    else
        calculate priorities using the first tree;
    end if
    schedule best priority operation;
    update machine and next job's operation ready time;
end while

Using the above adaptive structure, we conducted 20 runs with the same evolution parameters and achieved mean best result of 146.05 and $\sigma = 1.25$. The overall best solution (denoted GP-3) is compared with existing scheduling algorithms and with single tree heuristic (denoted GP). The first row of Table 7 shows the results in comparison with existing heuristics and the bottom two rows compare the described methods (we include only GP values for brevity since the other heuristics are unchanged). The t-test on the results of the methods rejects

Table 7. Performance of single tree (GP) and multiple tree solution (GP-3)

	Normalized criteria				Dominance percentage			
	Twt	Uwt	Fwt	Cmax	Twt	Uwt	Fwt	Cmax
GP-3	143.8	67.2	104.5	132.9	94 %	17 %	86 %	0 %
GP	146.1	70.9	105.8	133.5	31 %	11 %	24 %	1 %
GP-3	143.8	67.2	104.5	132.9	64 %	17 %	64 %	0 %

the null hypothesis with $t = 1.89$ and $p < 0.067$ for normalized criteria and with $t = 4.08$ and $p < 3.34 \times 10^{-3}$ for dominance percentages (when compared to existing heuristics). The difference between the two algorithms in terms of absolute criteria values is not great, which can in part be attributed to the relative proximity to the optimal solution. On the other hand, the relative dominance of the multiple tree algorithm is much greater, as it is able to find non-dominated solution in a majority of problem instances.

5   Conclusion

This paper shows genetic programming can be used to build scheduling algorithms whose performance is measurable with human-made heuristics for a specific scheduling environment. We addressed the issue of dynamic single machine scheduling for which a suitable meta-algorithm and appropriate data structures are defined. Additionally, a multiple tree adaptive heuristic is proposed for job shop scheduling problem, where decision tree is used to distinguish between resources based on their load characteristics. The results are promising, as for given problems the evolved heuristics exhibit better performance than existing scheduling methods. The presented methodology can be particularly useful in scheduling environments where there are no adequate algorithms and could alleviate the design of an appropriate scheduling procedure.

References

1. Jones, A., Rabelo, L.C.: Survey of job shop scheduling techniques. Technical report, NISTIR, National Institute of Standards and Technology, Gaithersburg (1998)
2. Walker, S.S., Brennan, R.W., Norrie, D.H.: Holonic job shop scheduling using a multiagent system. IEEE Intelligent Systems (2) (2005) 50
3. Dimopoulos, C., Zalzala, A.: A genetic programming heuristic for the one-machine total tardiness problem. In: Proceedings of the Congress on Evolutionary Computation. Volume 3. (1999)
4. Dimopoulos, C., Zalzala, A.M.S.: Investigating the use of genetic programming for a classic one-machine scheduling problem. Advances in Engineering Software **32**(6) (2001) 489
5. Adams, T.P.: Creation of simple, deadline, and priority scheduling algorithms using genetic programming. In: Genetic Algorithms and Genetic Programming at Stanford 2002. (2002)

6. Yin, W.J., Liu, M., Wu, C.: Learning single-machine scheduling heuristics subject to machine breakdowns with genetic programming. In: Proceedings of the 2003 Congress on Evolutionary Computation CEC2003, IEEE Press (2003) 1050

7. Atlan, B.L., Polack, J.: Learning distributed reactive strategies by genetic programming for the general job shop problem. In: Proceedings 7th annual Florida Artificial Intelligence Research Symposium, IEEE, IEEE Press (1994)

8. Miyashita, K.: Job-shop scheduling with gp. In: Proceedings of the Genetic and Evolutionary Computation Conference (GECCO-2000), Morgan Kaufmann (2000) 505

9. Cheng, V., Crawford, L., Menon, P.: Air traffic control using genetic search techniques. In: IEEE International Conference on Control Applications, Hawai'i, IEEE (1999)

10. Hansen, J.V.: Genetic search methods in air traffic control. Computers and Operations Research **31**(3) (2004) 445

11. Pinedo, M.: Offline deterministic scheduling, stochastic scheduling, and online deterministic scheduling: A comparative overview. In Leung, J.Y.T., ed.: Handbook of Scheduling. Chapman & Hall/CRC (2004)

12. Morton, T.E., Pentico, D.W.: Heuristic Scheduling Systems. John Wiley & Sons, Inc. (1993)

13. Mohan, R., Rachamadugu, V., Morton, T.E.: Myopic heuristics for the weighted tardiness problem on identical parallel machines. Technical report, The Robotics Institute, Carnegie-Mellon University (1983)

14. Chang, Y.L., Sueyoshi, T., Sullivan, R.: Ranking dispatching rules by data envelopment analysis in a job shop environment. IIE Transactions **28**(8) (1996) 631

15. Taillard, E.: Scheduling instances. "http://ina.eivd.ch/Collaborateurs/etd/problemes.dir/ordonnancement.dir/ordonnancement.html" (2003)

Emergent Generality of Adapted Locomotion Gaits of Simulated Snake-Like Robot

Ivan Tanev[1,2]

[1] Department of Information Systems Design, Doshisha University,
1-3 Miyakodani, Tatara, Kyotanabe, Kyoto 610-0321, Japan
[2] ATR Network Informatics Laboratories,
2-2-2 Hikaridai, "Keihanna Science City", Kyoto 619-0288, Japan
itanev@mail.doshisha.ac.jp

Abstract. In this work we consider the generality of locomotion gaits of simulated snake-like robot (Snakebot), adapted (via genetic programming, GP) to both (i) a challenging terrain and (ii) a partial mechanical damage. Discussing the emergence of common traits in these gaits, we elaborate on the strong correlation between their respective genotypes. We experimentally verify the generality of the adapted gaits in different "unexpected" environmental conditions and for various mechanical failures of the Snakebots. From an engineering standpoint, we suppose that in response to an eventual degradation of velocity, the Snakebot might activate a general locomotion gait, without the need to diagnose and treat the concrete underlying reason for such degradation. We view this work as a step towards building real Snakebots, which are able to perform robustly in difficult environment.

Keywords: Genetic programming, generality, snake-like robot, locomotion.

1 Introduction

Wheelless, limbless snake-like robots (Snakebots) feature potential robustness characteristics beyond the capabilities of most wheeled and legged vehicles – ability to traverse terrain that would pose problems for traditional wheeled or legged robots, and insignificant performance degradation when partial damage is inflicted. The useful features of Snakebots (smaller size of the cross-sectional areas, stability, traction, redundancy, and complete sealing of the internal mechanisms [2, 3]) open up several critical applications in exploration, reconnaissance, medicine and inspection. However, compared to the wheeled and legged vehicles, Snakebots feature (i) more difficult control of locomotion gaits and (ii) inferior speed characteristics. Focusing on these drawbacks, we intend to address the following challenge: how to develop control sequences of Snakebot's actuators, which allow for achieving the fastest possible speed of locomotion.

For many tasks and robot morphologies, it might be seen as a natural approach to handcraft the locomotion control code by applying various theoretical approaches [12, 18]. However, handcrafting might not be feasible for developing the control code of real Snakebot due to its morphological complexity and the need of prompt adaptation under degraded mechanical abilities or unanticipated environmental conditions [4, 6, 10, 13, 14, 17]. The proposed approach of employing genetic programming (GP)

P. Collet et al. (Eds.): EuroGP 2006, LNCS 3905, pp. 85–96, 2006.

implies that the code, which controls the locomotion of Snakebot is automatically designed by a computer system via simulated evolution through a selection and survival of the fittest in a way similar to the natural evolution of species [7].

However, it is recognized that the lack of generalization (or robustness) of the evolved solutions is among the most serious disadvantages of the evolutionary approaches, including GP [5, 8]. The methods that address the challenge of dealing with the performance of the evolved solutions in changeable fitness landscapes in evolutionary robotics usually consider an online adaptation to the changes through either evolution or learning [4, 10, 14]. Although these techniques do really provide a feasible way to address the problem of the brittleness of the evolved solutions, they usually require a series of trials in which the incrementally adapting artifact interacts with the surrounding environment. These trials, conducted online, might be costly, time- and energy consuming, and even dangerous for the artifact itself.

In our previous work [14] we discussed the feasibility of applying GP to design fast locomotion of the Snakebot and investigated the beneficial effects of learning mutation strategies on the efficiency of its evolution and adaptation [16]. In this work our objective is to explore the generality (analogy) of the gaits, emerged as a result of adaptation of the Snakebot to two distinct changes in the fitness landscape which, in the real-world, are most likely to cause a performance degradation of the Snakebot: (i) a challenging terrain and (ii) a partial damage. Our work is motivated by the anticipated engineering implications of the eventual analogy of the gaits adapted to these two situations: we assume that in response to an eventual degradation of velocity, the Snakebot might activate some general locomotion gaits without the need to diagnose and treat the concrete underlying reason for such degradation (e.g., a challenging terrain or degraded Snakebots' abilities).

The remainder of this document is organized as follows. Section 2 emphasizes the main features of the GP proposed for evolution of locomotion gaits of the simulated Snakebot. Section 3 presents empirical results of emergent properties and the generality of the evolved and adapted locomotion gaits. Section 4 draws a conclusion.

2   GP for Automatic Design of Locomotion Gaits of Snakebot

2.1   Representation of Snakebot

Snakebot is simulated as a set of identical spherical morphological segments ("vertebrae"), linked together via universal joints. All joints feature identical (finite) angle limits and each joint has two attached actuators ("muscles"). In the initial, standstill position of Snakebot the rotation axes of the actuators are oriented vertically (vertical actuator) and horizontally (horizontal actuator) and perform rotation of the joint in the horizontal and vertical planes respectively. Considering the representation of Snakebot, the task of designing the fastest locomotion can be rephrased as developing temporal patterns of desired turning angles of horizontal and vertical actuators of each segment, that result in fastest overall locomotion of Snakebot. The proposed representation of Snakebot as a homogeneous system significantly reduces the search space size of GP, and consequently, allows for achieving a favorable scalability of GP.

2.2 Algorithmic Paradigm

GP. GP [7] is a domain-independent problem-solving approach in which a population of computer programs (individuals' genotypes) is evolved to solve problems. The simulated evolution in GP is based on the Darwinian principle of reproduction and survival of the fittest. The fitness of each individual is based on the quality with which the phenotype of the simulated individual is performing in a given environment.

Function Set and Terminal Set. In applying GP to evolution of Snakebot, the genotype is associated with two algebraic expressions, which represent the temporal patterns of desired turning angles of both the horizontal and vertical actuators of each morphological segment. Because locomotion gaits, by definition, are periodical, we include the trigonometric functions sin and cos in the GP function set in addition to the basic algebraic functions. From another perspective, these functions allow to mimic (to some extend) the functionality of central pattern generator (CPG) in the central nervous system, which is believed to be necessary and sufficient for the generation of rhythmic patterns of activities of animals [9]. The approach of employing CPG for developing the locomotion gaits of the Snakebot would be based on an iterative tuning of the parameters of CPG (e.g., the common frequency across the coupled oscillators, the phase-relationship between the oscillators, and the amplitude of each of oscillations). The proposed approach of applying GP for evolution of Snakebot shares some of the features of CPG such as the open-loop control scheme and the incorporation of coupled oscillators. Conversely to the CPG however, the proposed method incorporates too little domain-specific knowledge about the task. As argued in [14], the flexibility of GP, resulting from not considering all the domain-specific constrains, can potentially yield an optimal solution with the following (typically uncommon for CPG) properties: (i) the oscillations of segments might result from arbitrary superposition of several oscillations with different frequencies, (ii) the relationship between the oscillators in the segments of Snakebot is not necessarily a simple phase relationship, and (iii) the phase relationship between the oscillators in the morphological segments might vary along the body of Snakebot, rather than being fixed. These features can be achieved by incorporating the terminal symbol segment_ID (a unique index of the segments of Snakebot), which allows GP to discover how to specialize (by phase, amplitude, frequency etc.) the temporal motion patterns of actuators of each of the segments of the Snakebot. In addition, the terminal symbols of GP include the variable time and two constants: Pi, and a random constant within the range [0, 2]. The introduction of variable time reflects our objective to develop temporal patterns of turning angles of actuators. The main parameters of the GP are summarized in Table 1.

Fitness Evaluation. The fitness function is based on the velocity of Snakebot, estimated from the distance, which the center of the mass of Snakebot travels during the trial. Fitness of 100 (the one of termination criteria shown in Table 1) is equivalent to a velocity, which displaced Snakebot a distance equal to twice its length.

Representation of Genotype. Inspired by its flexibility, and the recently emerged widespread adoption of document object model (DOM) and extensible markup language (XML), we represent evolved genotypes of simulated Snakebot as DOM-parse

Table 1. Main parameters of GP

Category	Value
Function set	{sin, cos, nop, +, -, *, /}
Terminal set	{time, segment_ID, Pi, random constant}
Population size	200 individuals
Selection	Binary tournament, selection ratio 0.1, reproduction ratio 0.9
Elitism	Best 4 individuals
Mutation	Random subtree mutation, ratio 0.01
Fitness	Velocity of simulated Snakebot during the trial
Trial interval	180 time steps, each time step account for 50ms of "real" time
Termination criterion	(Fitness >100) *or* (Generations>30) *or* (no improvement of fitness for 16 generations)

trees featuring equivalent flat XML-text in a way as originally implemented in [15]. Both (i) the calculation of the desired turning angles during fitness evaluation and (ii) the genetic operations are performed on DOM-parse trees using API of off-the shelf DOM-parser.

Genetic Operations. Binary tournament selection is employed – a robust, commonly used selection mechanism, which has proved to be efficient and simple to code. Crossover operation is defined in a strongly typed way in that only the DOM-nodes (and corresponding DOM-subtrees) of the same data type (i.e. labeled with the same tag) from parents can be swapped. The sub-tree mutation is allowed in strongly typed way in that a random node in genetic program is replaced by syntactically correct

Table 2. ODE-related parameters of simulated Snakebot

Parameter	Value
Number of phenotypic segments in snake	15
Model and size of the segment	Sphere with radius 3cm
Density of the segment, g/cm^3	0.9
Mass of the segment, g	100
Type of joint between segments	Universal
Number of actuators per joint	2 (horizontal – along X-axis and vertical – along Z-axis of the world)
Operational mode of actuators	dAMotorEuler
Actuators stops (angular limits), degrees	±50
Max torque of actuators, gcm	12000
Max angular velocity of actuators, degrees/s	100
Coefficient of friction between segments and surface (μ)	0.5
Friction model	Pyramid approximation of Coloumb friction model
Sampling frequency of simulation, Hz	20 Hz

sub-tree. The mutation routine refers to the data type of currently altered node and applies randomly chosen rule from the set of applicable rewriting rules as defined in the grammar of GP.

ODE. We have chosen Open Dynamics Engine (ODE) [11] to provide a realistic simulation of physics in applying forces to phenotypic segments of Snakebot. ODE is a free, industrial quality software library for simulating articulated rigid body dynamics. It is fast, flexible and robust, and it has built-in collision detection. The ODE-related parameters of simulated Snakebot are summarized in Table 2.

3 Empirical Results

In this section we present the experimental results verifying the feasibility of applying GP for evolution of the fast locomotion gaits of Snakebot. In addition, we investigate the emergent properties of (i) the fastest locomotion gaits, evolved in unconstrained environmental conditions and (ii) the robust locomotion gaits evolved in challenging environments. The section also discusses (iii) the gradual adaptation of the locomotion gaits to degraded mechanical abilities of Snakebot. The abilities of Snakebot to address these challenges are relevant for the success of the anticipated real-world exploration, reconnaissance, medicine- and inspection missions.

In all of the considered cases, the fitness of Snakebot reflects the basic objective (i.e. *what* is required to be achieved) of Snakebot in these missions, namely, to be able to move fast regardless of environmental challenges or mechanical failures. The results of experiments shown in this section illustrate the ability of evolving Snakebot to learn *how* (e.g. by discovering beneficial locomotion traits) to accomplish the required objective without being explicitly taught about the means to do so. Such *know-how* acquired by Snakebot automatically and autonomously can be viewed as a demonstration of an emergent intelligence in that the task-specific knowledge of *how* to accomplish the task emerges in the Snakebot from the interaction between the problem solver and the fitness function [1].

3.1 Emergent Properties of Evolved Fastest Locomotion Gaits in Unconstrained Environment

Figure 1 shows the fitness convergence characteristic of 10 independent runs of GP (Figure 1a) and sample snapshots of evolved best-of-run locomotion gaits (Figures 1b and 1c) when fitness is measured in any direction in a smooth and unconstrained environment. Despite that fitness is measured as a velocity in any direction, sidewinding locomotion (i.e., locomotion predominantly perpendicular to the long axis of Snakebot) emerged in all 10 independent runs of GP, suggesting that it provides superior speed characteristics for the given morphology of the Snakebot. The evolved locomotion gait is quite similar to the locomotion of the natural snake *Crotalus cerastes*, or "Sidewinder". In the proposed representation of Snakebot, similarly to the natural snake, no anisotropic (directional) friction between the morphological segments and the surface is considered. It is easy to eventually simulate (and design) segments featuring anisotropic friction with the surface, e.g. by attaching simple passive wheels [3]. However, this would feature the following serious drawbacks: (i) wheels, attached to the morphological segments of Snakebot are mainly effective in two-dimensional locomotion gaits, when neither the fastest gaits in a smooth environments nor the adaptive gaits in challenging environments (e.g., with obstacles) or partial damage are necessarily two-dimensional, (ii) wheels may compromise the intended generality (robustness) of Snakebot because they can be trapped, locked or rendered useless easily in challenging environments (rugged terrain, obstacles, shifting surfaces, etc.), and (iii) wheels potentially reduce the application areas of the Snakebot because their engineering design implies a lack of complete sealing of all mechanisms of Snakebot.

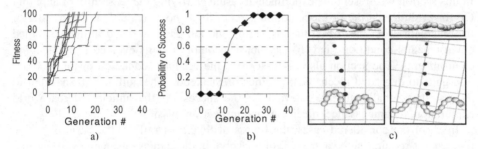

a)   b)   c)

Fig. 1. Evolution of locomotion gaits for cases where fitness is measured as a velocity in any direction – the fitness convergence characteristics of 10 independent runs (a), the probability of success (b), and snapshots of frontal view (c, top) and view from above (c, bottom) of sample evolved best-of-run sidewinding locomotion gaits. The dark trailing circles in the view from above depict the trajectory of the center of the mass of Snakebot.

The genotype of sample best-of-run genetic program is shown in Figure 2. The dynamics of evolved turning angles of actuators in sidewinding result in characteristic circular motion pattern of segments around the center of the mass as shown in Figure 3a. The circular motion pattern of the segments and the characteristic track on the ground as a series of diagonal lines (as illustrated in Figure 3b) suggest that during sidewinding the shape of Snakebot takes the form of a rolling helix (Figure 3c). Figure 3 demonstrates that the simulated evolution of locomotion via GP is able to invent the improvised "cylinder" of the sidewinding Snakebot to achieve fast locomotion.

```
GenH = (sin(((sin(-8))*(segment id - time)) + (3*time)))/(sin(-8));
GenV = sin(ADF), where ADF = GenH
```

Fig. 2. Normalized algebraic expressions of the genotype of sample best-of-run genetic program: dynamics of turning angle of horizontal (GenH) and vertical (GenV) actuators

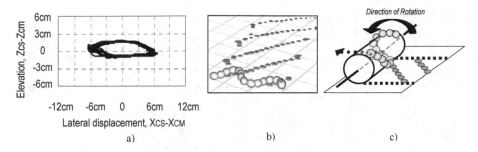

Fig. 3. Trajectory of the central segment (cs) around the center of mass (cm) of Snakebot for a sample evolved best-of-run sidewinding locomotion (a), traces of ground contacts (b), and Snakebot, wrapped around an imagined cylinder taking the form of a rolling helix

3.2 Adaptation to Challenging Environment

Adaptation in Nature is viewed as an ability of species to discover the best phenotypic (i.e. pertaining to biochemistry, morphology, physiology, and behavior) traits for survival in continuously changing fitness landscape. In our approach we employ GP for adaptation of Snakebot to changes in the fitness landscape caused by (i) challenging environment and (ii) partial damage to 1, 2, 4 and 8 (out of 15) morphological segments. The former case is discussed in this subsection, while the latter case is elaborated in the following subsection 3.3. In both cases of adaptation, GP is initialized with a population comprising 20 best-of-run genetic programs, obtained from 10 independent runs of evolution of Snakebot in unconstrained environment, plus additional 180 randomly created Snakebots.

The challenging environment is modeled by the introduction of immobile obstacles comprising 40 small, randomly scattered boxes, a wall with height equal to the 0.5 diameters of the cross-section of Snakebot, and a flight of 3 stairs, each with height equal to the 0.33 diameters of the cross-section of Snakebot. The results of adaptation of Snakebots, obtained over 10 independent runs reveal the poor initial performance of the Snakebots, obtained via evolution in unconstrained environment. Indeed, the fitness of these Snakebots immediately drops from the initial value of 100 in unconstrained environment to only 65 when Snakebots are first tested (at generation #0) on the challenging terrain. However, adapting to the new environment, the evolving Snakebots are able to discover robust locomotion gaits, which ultimately allow them to overcome the obstacles. The computational effort (required to reach fitness values of 100 with probability of success 0.9) of adaptation is about 20 generations. Snapshots illustrating the performance of sample best-of-run Snakebot initially evolved in unconstrained environment, before and after the adaptation to the challenging environment are shown in Figure 4.

The robust sidewinding gaits (Figure 5) feature an additional elevation of the body - the emergent know-how in the adapting Snakebot, relevant for negotiating the obstacles faster. As shown in Figure 5d, the trajectory of the central segment around the center of the mass of sample adapted Snakebot is almost twice higher than before the adaptation, as depicted, both qualitatively and quantitatively in Figures 1c and 3a. Moreover, as Figure 5b and Figure 5c reveal, the robust locomotion gaits feature

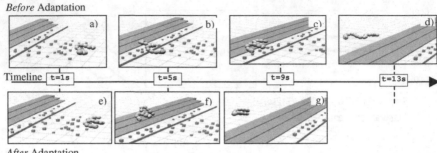

Before Adaptation

After Adaptation

Fig. 4. Snapshots illustrating the sidewinding Snakebot, initially evolved in unconstrained environment, before the adaptation – initial (a), intermediate (b and c) and final stages of the trial (d), and after the adaptation to challenging environment via GP - initial (e), intermediate (f) and final stages of the trial (g)

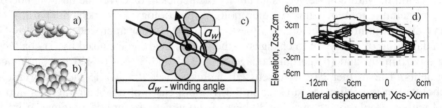

Fig. 5. Snapshots of a frontal view (a) and a view from the above (b and c) of sample sidewinding Snakebots after the adaptation to challenging terrain

higher winding angle of locomotion (more than 120°) yielding a longitudinally more compact sidewinding Snakebots. Again, as with the emergence of sidewinding, the result of the artificial evolution is analogous to the solution discovered by Nature – it is recognized that natural snakes also change the winding angle of the locomotion in order to adapt themselves to the various environmental conditions.

3.3 Adaptation to Partial Damage

The experiments on adaptation of sidewinding Snakebot to partial damage is conducted over 10 independent runs for each case of partial damage to 1, 2, 4 and 8 (out of 15) segments. The damaged segments are evenly distributed along the body of Snakebot. Damage inflicted to a particular segment implies a complete loss of functionality of both horizontal and vertical actuators of the corresponding joint. Experimental results indicate that Snakebot quickly and completely recovers from damage to single segment attaining its previous velocity only in 7 generations. Snakebots also recovers to average of 100% of its previous velocity also in 12 generations in the case of 2 damaged segments. With 4 and 8 damaged segments the degree of recovery is 92% (in 14 generations) and 72% (in 26 generations) respectively. The emergent properties of adapted sidewinding locomotion gaits are shown in Figure 6.

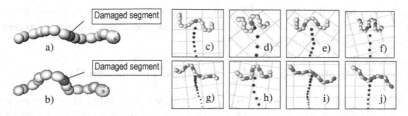

Fig. 6. The emergent properties of adapted sidewinding locomotion gaits: frontal view of the Snakebot before (a) and after the adaptation (b) to the damage of single segment demonstrates the additional elevation of the adapted Snakebot. The view of the Snakebot from the above reveals the emergent tendency of increasing the winding angle of locomotion in the way much similar to the adaptation to challenging environment (as shown in Figure 5b and 5c): Snakebot with 1 (c, d), 2 (e, f), 4 (g, h) and 8 (i, j) damaged segments before and after the adaptation, respectively.

3.4 Genetic Similarity of Adapted Snakebots

In order to investigate whether the analogy in the emergent properties of locomotion gaits result from similar genotypes, we analyzed the correlation between the frequencies of occurrence of tree nodes in a particular context (i.e. the parent- and the descendant tree nodes) in the genetic representations of the three categories of Snakebots – (i) evolved in smooth unconstrained environment, (ii) adapted to challenging environment, and (ii) adapted to the degraded mechanical abilities – as elaborated earlier in Sections 3.1, 3.2 and 3.3 respectively. For each of these three categories of Snakebots we aggregated the frequencies of occurrence of tree nodes obtained from the genotypes of the 20 best-of-run Snakebots (from 10 independent runs of GP). The results are as follows:

(i)   The correlation between genotypes of the Snakebots evolved in smooth environment and the Snakebots adapted to challenging environment is $C_{S-C}=0.34$,

(ii) The correlation between genotypes of the Snakebots evolved in smooth environment and the Snakebots adapted to degraded mechanical abilities due to partial damage is $C_{S-D}=0.32$, and

(iii) The correlation between genotypes of the Snakebots adapted to challenging environment and the Snakebots adapted to degraded mechanical abilities due to partial damage is $C_{C-D}=0.91$.

These results suggest that there is a little similarity between the genotypes of Snakebots adapted to both changes in the fitness landscape (i.e., due to challenging environment and partial damage) and the Snakebot evolved in smooth environment. We assume that this limited similarity ($C_{S-C}=0.34$, and $C_{S-D}=0.32$) is due to the shared genotypic fragments, which are relevant for the very ability of Snakebot to move, regardless of the environmental conditions and/or the mechanical failures. These results also show that in both cases the genotype of Snakebots adapts to changes in the fitness landscape by drifting away from the genotype of the common ancestor – the Snakebot evolved in smooth environment, used to initially feed the adapting populations of Snakebots. Moreover, the strong correlation between the genotypes of adapted Snakebots ($C_{C-D}=0.91$) suggests that the adaptation in both cases is achieved through a drift towards adjacent niches in the genotypic space of the Snakebot. This, in turn, yields the discovered phenotypic analogy between the adapted Snakebots, as discussed above in Sections 3.2 and 3.3.

3.5 Cross-Verification of Generality of Adapted Locomotion Gaits

The anticipated practical implications of the analogy between the emergent properties of the sidewinding gaits, adapted to different fitness landscapes, are related to the possibility to develop a general locomotion gait which could be autonomously activated in case of any degradation of velocity of Snakebot. This activation could be done without the necessity for the Snakebot to diagnose the underlying reason for such degradation (e.g., either a challenging environment or degraded mechanical abilities). To verify the feasibility of such an approach, we examined the performance of the same three categories of best-performing Snakebots – (i) evolved in a smooth environment, (ii) adapted to challenging environment, and (ii) adapted to degraded mechanical abilities due to damage of 8 segments (as elaborated earlier in Sections 3.1, 3.2 and 3.3 respectively). The performance, aggregated over 20 best-performing Snakebots, obtained from 10 independent runs of an evolution with the condition Fitness>100 removed from the termination criterion of GP (refer to Table 1), is shown in Figure 7.

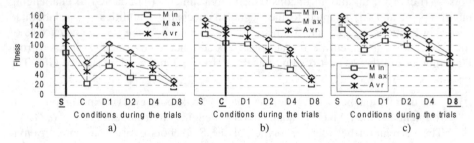

Fig. 7. Performance of the best-performing Snakebots evolved in a smooth environment (a), evolved in challenging environment (b), and adapted to the degraded mechanical abilities due to damage of eight morphological segments (c) in various "unexpected" fitness landscapes corresponding to a smooth environment (S), challenging terrain (C), and degraded mechanical abilities due to a damage to one- (D1), two- (D2), four- (D4) and eight (D8) – out of 15 – morphological segments

As Figure 7a illustrates, the average fitness of the Snakebots, evolved in smooth environment drops more than twice in challenging terrain to 70%, 55%, 45% and 10% of the initial value for Snakebots with one, two, four and eight damaged segments, respectively, indicating relatively poor generality of these locomotion gaits. Conversely, the average fitness of the Snakebots, evolved in challenging terrain (Figure 7b) increases to 116% of its initial value in smooth terrain, and drops only to 97%, 75%, and 60% of the initial value for Snakebots with one-, two- and four- damaged segments, respectively. However, the average fitness of the Snakebots with eight damaged segments is only 25% of the initial value, suggesting that the degradation of the performance, inflicted by such damage is so heavy that it requires an especially adapted locomotion gait. The performance of Snakebots, adapted to degraded mechanical abilities due to damage of eight segments, shown in Figure 8c, support this conclusion. Indeed, the average fitness of the heavily damaged (with eight broken segments), especially adapted Snakebots is more than twice higher than of the equally damaged Snakebots, obtained from an evolution in challenging environment (Figure 7c). For Snakebots with one-, two- and four damaged segments these locomotion gaits are slightly superior to the gaits obtained from evolution in challenging terrain, and, naturally, somehow inferior to them in challenging environment.

4 Conclusion

We considered the adaptation of evolved locomotion gaits of simulated snake-like robot (Snakebot) to two distinct changes in the fitness landscape which, in the real-world, are most likely to cause a degradation of the performance of Snakebot – (i) a challenging terrain and (ii) a Snakebot's partial mechanical damage. We focused on the generality of the locomotion gaits, adapted to these changes in the fitness landscape, and observed the emergence of an additional elevation of the body and increased winding angle as common traits in these gaits. Discovering the strong correlation between the genotypes of the adapted gaits, we concluded that the adaptation is achieved through a drift towards adjacent niches in the genotypic space of the evolving Snakebots. Finally, we verified experimentally the generality of the adapted gaits in various fitness landscapes corresponding to a smooth environment, challenging terrain, and mechanical failures of one-, two-, four- and eight (out of 15) morphological segments. We argue that due to the explored generality of the adapted gaits, in response to an eventual degradation of its velocity, the Snakebot might only activate a general locomotion gait, without the need to diagnose and treat the concrete underlying reason for such degradation. We consider this work as a step towards building real Snakebots, which are able to perform robustly in difficult environment.

Acknowledgments

The author thanks A.Buller, V.Gerasimov, M.Prokopenko, T.Ray and K.Shimohara for their support of this work. The research was supported in part by the National Institute of Information and Communications Technology of Japan.

References

1. Angeline, P. J.: Genetic Programming and Emergent Intelligence. In Kinnear, K.E. Jr., editor, Advances in Genetic Programming, MIT Press (1994) 75-98
2. Dowling, K.: Limbless Locomotion: Learning to Crawl with a Snake Robot, doctoral dissertation, tech. report CMU-RI-TR-97-48, Robotics Institute, Carnegie Mellon University (1997)
3. Hirose, S.: Biologically Inspired Robots: Snake-like Locomotors and Manipulators, Oxford University Press (1993)

4. Ijspeert, A., Crespi, A., and Cabelguen, J. (2005). Simulation nd robotics studies of sala-mander locomotion. Applying neurobiological principles to the control of locomotion in robots. *Neuroinformatics*, 3(3):171–196
5. Kinnear Jr., K.E., Generality and difficulty in genetic programming: Evolving a sort. In Proceedings of the 5th International Conference on Genetic Algorithms, ICGA-93 (1993) 287–294
6. Kimura, H., Yamashita, T., and Kobayashi, S., Reinforcement Learning of Walking Be-havior for a Four-Legged Robot, 40th IEEE Conference on Decision and Control (2001) 411-416
7. Koza, J. R., Genetic Programming: On the Programming of Computers by Means of Natu-ral Selection, Cambridge, MA, MIT Press (1992)
8. Kushchu, I., Genetic Programming and Evolutionary Generalization, IEEE Transactions On Evolutionary Computation, Vol. 6, No. 5 (2002) 431-442
9. Levitan, I. B. and Kaczmarek, L. K., The Neuron: Cell and Molecular Biology, Oxford University Press, New York (2002)
10. Mahdavi, S., Bentley, P.J.: Evolving Motion of Robots with Muscles. In Proc. of Evo-ROB2003, the 2nd European Workshop on Evolutionary Robotics, EuroGP 2003 (2003) 655-664
11. Smith, R.: Open Dynamics Engine (2001-2003) http://q12.org/ode/
12. Stoy, K., Shen W.-M., Will, P.M., A simple approach to the control of locomotion in self-reconfigurable robots, Robotics and Autonomous Systems, Vol.44 , No.3 (2003) 191-200
13. Takamura, S., Hornby, G. S., Yamamoto, T., Yokono, J. and Fujita, M., Evolution of Dy-namic Gaits for a Robot, IEEE International Conference on Consumer Electronics (2000) 192-193
14. Tanev, I., Ray, T., and Buller, A., Automated evolutionary design, robustness, and adapta-tion of sidewinding locomotion of a simulated snake-like robot. IEEE Transactions On Robotics, 21 (2005) 632–645
15. Tanev, I., DOM/XML-Based Portable Genetic Representation of Morphology, Behavior and Communication Abilities of Evolvable Agents, Artificial Life and Robotics, Vol.8, Number 1 (2004) 52-56
16. Tanev, I, Incorporating Learning Probabilistic Context-sensitive Grammar in Genetic Pro-gramming for Efficient Evolution and Adaptation of Snakebot, in M. Keijzer et al. (Eds.): Proceedings of the 8th European Conference on Genetic Programming (EuroGP-2005), LNCS 3447, pp.155 – 166 (2005) 30 March - 1 April 2005, Lausanne, Switzerland
17. Teo, J. and Abbass, H.A., Multi-objectivity and Complexity in Embodied Cognition. IEEE Transactions on Evolutionary Computation, 9(4) (2005) 337-360
18. Zhang, Y., Yim, M. H., Eldershaw, C., Duff, D. G., and Roufas, K. D., Phase automata: a programming model of locomotion gaits for scalable chain-type modular robots, IEEE/RSJ International Conference on Intelligent Robots and Systems (IROS 2003), October 27 - 31; Las Vegas, NV (2003) 2442- 2447

Evolving Crossover Operators for Function Optimization

Laura Dioşan and Mihai Oltean

Department of Computer Science,
Faculty of Mathematics and Computer Science,
Babeş-Bolyai University, Cluj-Napoca, Romania
{lauras, moltean}@cs.ubbcluj.ro

Abstract. A new model for evolving crossover operators for evolutionary function optimization is proposed in this paper. The model is a hybrid technique that combines a Genetic Programming (GP) algorithm and a Genetic Algorithm (GA). Each GP chromosome is a tree encoding a crossover operator used for function optimization. The evolved crossover is embedded into a standard Genetic Algorithm which is used for solving a particular problem. Several crossover operators for function optimization are evolved using the considered model. The evolved crossover operators are compared to the human-designed convex crossover. Numerical experiments show that the evolved crossover operators perform similarly or sometimes even better than standard approaches for several well-known benchmarking problems.

1 Introduction

Evolutionary algorithms are relatively robust over many different types of search spaces. This is why they are often chosen for use where there is little domain knowledge.

However, for particular problem domains, their performance can often be improved by tuning their parameters (such as type of operators, probabilities of applying the genetic operators, population size etc). One possible way to obtain good parameters is to let them to be adjusted along with the population of solutions. Another possibility is to evolve a population of parameters (or operators) which are applied for solving a particular problem. This is usually referred in the literature as Meta EA (or Meta GP) and it has been successfully applied for evolving complex structures (such as computer programs) [4], [8], [10], [12], [13].

Usually the genetic operators are fixed by the programmer and are not modified during the search process. Moreover, the same particular operators are used for a wide range of problems. This could lead to non-optimal behavior of the considered algorithms for some particular problems.

Our purpose is to find (by using evolutionary techniques) genetic operators which are suitable for solving particular problems. Roughly speaking, we will let the problem find by itself the genetic operators that correspond to its structure.

P. Collet et al. (Eds.): EuroGP 2006, LNCS 3905, pp. 97–108, 2006.

A new model for evolving crossover operators is proposed in this paper[1]. The model is a hybrid technique that combines Genetic Programming (GP) [6] and Genetic Algorithms (GAs) [5] within a two-level model. Each GP chromosome encodes a crossover operator which contains standard symbols (mathematical operators, constants and some variables). The evolved crossover is embedded into a standard Genetic Algorithm which is used for solving a particular problem (function optimization in our case).

The evolved crossover operators are compared to the human-designed convex crossover. For numerical experiments we have used ten artificially constructed functions and one real-world problem. Results show that the evolved crossover operators perform similarly or sometimes even better than standard approaches for several well-known benchmarking problems.

This research was motivated by the need of answering several important questions concerning genetic operators. The most important question is: *Can genetic operators be automatically synthesized by using only the information about the problem being solved?* And, if yes, which are the symbols that have to be used within a genetic operator (for a given problem)? We better let the evolution find the answer for us.

The paper is structured as follows: section 2 discusses work related to the evolution of evolutionary structures (such as genetic operators or evolutionary algorithms). The proposed model is described in section 3. Several numerical experiments are performed in section 4. Conclusions and further work directions are discussed in section 5.

2   Related Work

Several attempts for evolving variation operators for different techniques were made in the past.

Teller [13] describes a procedure for automatic design and the use of new genetic operators for GP. These SMART operators are co-evolved with the main population of programs and they learn to recombine the new population better than random genetic recombination. The SMART operators are programs that learn to do a graph crossover better than standard GP crossover.

Meta-Genetic Programming (MGP) [4] encodes the genetic operators as trees. These operators "act" on other tree structures to produce the next generation of individuals. In his paper on Meta-Genetic Programming [4], Edmonds used two populations: a standard GP population and a co-evolved population of operators that act on the main population. This technique introduces extra computational cost, which must be weighed against any advantage gained. Also the technique turns out to be very sensitive to biases in the syntax, from which the operators are generated, therefore it is less robust.

Peter Angeline [1] investigated the possibility of a "self-adaptive" crossover operator. In this work, the basic operator action is fixed (as a crossover) but

---

[1] The source code for evolving crossover operators and all the evolved operators will be available on www.eea.cs.ubbcluj.ro

probabilistic guidance is used to help the operator to choose the crossover nodes so that the operation is more productive.

Note that all these approaches are focused on evolving a crossover operator for GP technique. Their purpose was to obtain a better GP crossover. Our approach is quite different: we use a standard GP technique (with standard GP crossover) for evolving a crossover operator for evolutionary function optimization. We have trained our GP algorithm to find the expression of a crossover operator using one test function, and then we test this operator for other 10 functions.

3 Proposed Model

3.1 Representation

Consider the standard convex crossover operator [2], [5], [9]:

$$\text{Offspring} = x * \alpha + (1 - \alpha) * y.$$

The right-hand expression may be easily represented as a GP individual depicted in Figure 1.

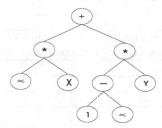

Fig. 1. Convex crossover. Two parents x and y are recombined in order to obtain an offspring. α is a real value randomly generated between 0 and 1. If the function to be optimized has multiple dimensions, the convex crossover operator will be applied for each of them.

Our purpose is to evolve a crossover operator (for function optimization) based on the information taken from a function to be optimized. The evolved crossover will be represented as a GP tree. The set of GP function symbols will consist in mathematical operators that can appear into a crossover operator:

$$F = \{+, -, *, sin, cos, exp\}$$

Our aim is to design a crossover operator which is able to optimize functions defined over any real domain. Not all genetic operators can do that. For instance, a genetic operator defined as $sin(x) + sin(y)$ will considerably reduce the search space to the interval [-2, 2]. If the optimal solution is not in that interval, our algorithm, which uses only that variation operator, will not be able to find it.

An idea is to have a crossover operator whose inputs (the parents and any other values placed in the leaves of the tree) are real values between 0 and 1. The output of that chromosome should also be a real number between 0 and 1. When we apply this operator for a particular problem, first we need to scale the parents to the [0, 1] interval and then we need to scale the output of the crossover to the definition domain of the function to be optimized. For instance, if the domain of the function to be optimized is [-5, 5], we need to scale down the parents to the interval [0, 1] and then we apply crossover and then we need to scale up the [0, 1] result to the interval [-5, 5].

Because we are dealing with real-valued definition domains (e.g. [0,1]) we have to find a way of protecting against overflowing these limits. For instance if we employ a standard addition of two numbers greater than 0.5 we would get a result greater than 1 (domain upper bound). Thus, each operator has been redefined in order to output result in the standard interval [0,1]. The redefinitions are given in Table 1.

Table 1. The redefinitions of the operators so that the output should always be between 0 and 1 if the inputs are between 0 and 1

Operator	Definition
$\widehat{+}$	$(x + y)/2$
$\widehat{-}$	$|x - y|$
$\widehat{*}$	**None** (If you multiply two numbers between 0 and 1 you will always get a number between 0 and 1.)
$\widehat{sin}$	$\sin(x)/\sin(1)$
$\widehat{cos}$	$\cos(x)/\cos(1)$
$\widehat{exp}$	$\exp(x)/\exp(1)$

The terminal set is composed by several, uniformly distributed, constants between 0 and 1. Our purpose is to design a genetic operator that recombines two parents. Thus, the terminal set should also contain two symbols reserved for parents (x and y).

$$T = \{0.1, 0.2, 0.3, 0.4, 0.5, 0.6, 0.7, 0.8, 0.9, 1.0, x, y, R\},$$

where R is actually a function with no arguments that always outputs a random value between 0 and 1. This terminal symbol was added in order to simulate the α parameter from the convex crossover. Note that if the function has multiple dimensions the evolved crossover operator will be applied for each of them.

3.2   The Model

The proposed approach is a hybrid technique divided in two levels: a macro level and a micro level. The macro level is a GP algorithm that evolves crossover operators for function optimization. The micro level is a GA used for computing the quality of a GP individual.

When we compute the quality of a GP chromosome we actually have to compute the quality of the crossover operator encoded in that GP tree. For assessing the performance of a crossover operator we have to embed that operator within an evolutionary algorithm and we have to run the obtained algorithm for a particular problem. Since our problem is a function optimization we embed the evolved crossover within as standard Genetic Algorithm as described in [2], [9].

The fitness of a GP individual is equal to the fitness of the best solution generated by the Genetic Algorithm which uses the GP tree as the crossover operator. But, since the GA uses pseudo-random numbers, it is very likely that successive runs of the same algorithm will generate completely different solutions. This problem can be fixed in a standard manner: the GA embedding the GP individual is run more times (200 runs in fact) and the fitness of the GP chromosome is averaged over all runs.

3.3   The Algorithms

The algorithms used for evolving a crossover operator are described in this section. As we said before we are dealing with a hybrid technique which has a macro level and a micro level.

The Macro-level Algorithm. The macro level algorithm is standard GP algorithm [6] used for evolving crossover operators for function optimization.

We use steady-state evolutionary model as underlying mechanism for our GP implementation. The GP algorithm starts by creating a random population of individuals (trees). The following steps are repeated until a given number of generations is reached: Two parents are selected using a standard selection procedure. The parents are recombined in order to obtain two offspring. The offspring are considered for mutation. The best offspring O replaces the worst individual W in the current population if O is better than W.

The Micro-level Algorithm. The micro level algorithm is a Genetic Algorithm [5] used for computing the fitness of each GP individual from the macro level. The GA starts by creating a random population of individuals. Each individual is a real-valued array whose number of dimensions is equal to the number of dimensions of the function to be optimized. The entire process is run along a fixed number of generations. The best individual in the current population is automatically copied to the next generation. The following steps are repeated until the new population is filled: two parents are selected randomly and are recombined in order to obtain one offspring which will be added to the new population.

We have removed the mutation operator and we have performed random selections. In this way, the performance of the algorithm will mainly be guided by the crossover operator only.

The recombination operator is evolved by the macro level algorithm. During the training stage, the micro-level algorithm is run multiple times and the results are averaged (see section 3.2).

4   Numerical Experiments

In this section, several numerical experiments for evolving crossover operators for function optimization are performed. After evolving it, the crossover operator is embedded into a Genetic Algorithm and used to solve eleven difficult benchmarking problems. Ten functions are artificially constructed and one test problem (the Portfolio Selection Problem) is an important real-world problem (Table 2). Several numerical experiments, with a standard Genetic Algorithm [5] that use a convex crossover for function optimization, are also performed. Finally the results are compared.

The Portfolio Selection Problem. Modern computational finance has its historical roots in the pioneering portfolio theory of Markowitz [7]. This theory is based on the assumption that investors have an intrinsic desire to maximize return and minimize risk on investment. Mean or expected return is employed as a measure of return, and variance or standard deviation of return is employed as a measure of risk. This framework captures the risk-return tradeoff between a single linear return measure and a single convex nonlinear risk measure.

The solution typically proceeds as a two-objective optimization problem where the return is maximized while the risk is constrained to be below a certain threshold. The well-known risk-return efficient frontier is obtained by varying the risk target and maximizing on the return measure.

The Markowitz mean-variance model [7] gives a multi-objective optimization problem, with two output dimensions. A portfolio p consisting of N assets with specific volumes for each asset given by weights w_i is to be found, which minimizes the variance of the portfolio:

$$\sigma_p = \sum_{i=1}^{N} \sum_{j=1}^{N} w_i w_j \sigma_{ij} \tag{1}$$

maximizes the return of the portfolio:

$$\mu_p = \sum_{i=1}^{N} w_i \mu_i \tag{2}$$

subject to: $\sum_{i=1}^{N} w_i = 1, 0 \leq w_i \leq 1$, where $i = 1...N$ is the index of the asset, N represents the number of assets available, μ_i the estimated return of asset i and σ_{ij} the estimated covariance between two assets. Usually, μ_i and σ_{ij} are to be estimated from historic data. While the optimization problem given in (1) and (2) is a quadratic optimization problem for which computationally effective algorithms exist, this is not the case if real world constraints are added. In this paper we treat only the cardinality constraints problem [11].

Cardinality constraints restrict the maximal number of assets used in the portfolio

$$\sum_{i=1}^{N} z_i = K, \tag{3}$$

where $z_i = sign(w_i)$. Let K be the desired number of assets in the portfolio, ϵ_i be the minimum proportion that must be held of asset i, $(i = 1, ..., N)$ if any of asset i is held, δ_i be the maximum proportion that can be held of asset i, $(i = 1, ..., N)$ if any of asset i is held, where we must have $0 \leq \epsilon_i \leq \delta_i \leq 1 (i = 1, ..., N)$. In practice, ϵ_i represents a "min-buy" of "minimum transaction level" for asset i and δ_i limits the exposure of the portfolio to asset i.

$$\epsilon_i z_i \leq w_i \leq \delta_i z_i, i = 1...N \tag{4}$$

$$w_i \in [0, 1], i = 1...N. \tag{5}$$

Eq. (3) ensures that exactly K assets are held. Eq. (4) ensures that if any of asset i is held ($z_i = 1$) its proportion w_i must lie between ϵ_i and δ_i, whilst if none of asset is held ($z_i = 0$) its proportion w_i is zero. Eq. (5) is the integrality constraint. The objective function (Eq. (1)), involving as it does the covariance matrix, is positive semi-definite and hence we are minimizing a convex function. The chromosome - within the GA heuristic - supposes (conform to [3]) a set Q of K distinct assets and K real numbers s_i, $(0 \leq s_i \leq 1)$, $i \in Q$.

Now, given a set Q of K assets, a fraction $\sum_{j \in Q} \epsilon_j$ of the total portfolio is already accounted for and so we interpret s_i as relating to the share of the *free* portfolio proportion $(1 - \sum_{j \in Q} \epsilon_j)$ associated with asset $i \in Q$.

Thus, our GA chromosome will encode real numbers s_i and the proportion of asset i from Q in portfolio will be:

$$w_i = \epsilon_i + \frac{s_i}{\sum_{j \in Q} s_j}(1 - \sum_{j \in Q} \epsilon_j) \tag{6}$$

For this experiment we have used the daily rate of exchange for a set of assets quoted to Euronext Stock [16] during June to December, 2002.

4.1 Experimental Results

We evolve a crossover operator (used by Genetic Algorithm for function optimization) and then we assess its performance by comparing it with the standard convex crossover.

Experiment 1. A crossover operator is evolved in this experiment. For evolving this kind of genetic operator we use a modified version of function f_1 as the training problem. We need this modification to function f_1 because its optimal solution is $x^* = (0, 0, \quad , 0)$. This means that a crossover (obtained by evolution) which always outputs value 0 will be able to solve this problem in one generation (in fact after the first crossover operation). An example of this kind of crossover is $x - x$ or $0.3 - 0.3$ or other similar structures. The same issue could appear for all training problems whose optimal solution is an array containing the same constant (e.g. $x^* = (1.56, 1.56... 1.56)$). In all these cases the macro level algorithm could evolve a tree (crossover operator) whose output is always a constant value.

Table 2. Test functions used in our experimental study. The parameter n is the space dimension ($n = 5$ in our numerical experiments) and f_{min} is the minimum value of the function. All functions should be minimized.

Test function	Domain	f_{min}
$f_1(x) = \sum_{i=1}^{n} (i \cdot x_i^2)$.	$[-10, 10]^n$	0
$f_2(x) = \sum_{i=1}^{n} x_i^2$.	$[-100, 100]^n$	0
$f_3(x) = \sum_{i=1}^{n} |x_i| + \prod_{i=1}^{n} |x_i|$.	$[-10, 10]^n$	0
$f_4(x) = \sum_{i=1}^{n} \left(\sum_{j=1}^{i} x_j \right)^2$.	$[-100, 100]^n$	0
$f_5(x) = \max_i \{x_i, 1 \leq i \leq n\}$.	$[-100, 100]^n$	0
$f_6(x) = \sum_{i=1}^{n-1} 100 \cdot (x_{i+1} - x_i^2)^2 + (1 - x_i)^2$.	$[-30, 30]^n$	0
$f_7(x) = 10 \cdot n + \sum_{i=1}^{n} (x_i^2 - 10 \cdot \cos(2 \cdot \pi \cdot x_i))$	$[-5, 5]^n$	0
$f_8(x) = -a \cdot e^{-b\sqrt{\frac{\sum_{i=1}^{n} x_i^2}{n}}} - e^{\frac{\sum \cos(c \cdot x_i)}{n}} + a + e$.	$[-32, 32]^n$ $a = 20,\ b = 0.2,\ c = 2\pi$.	0
$f_9(x) = \frac{1}{4000} \cdot \sum_{i=1}^{n} x_i^2 - \prod_{i=1}^{n} \cos(\frac{x_i}{\sqrt{i}}) + 1$.	$[-500, 500]^n$	0
$f_{10}(x) = \sum_{i=1}^{n} (-x_i \cdot \sin(\sqrt{|x_i|}))$	$[-500, 500]^n$	$-n* 418.98$
$f_{11} =$ The Portfolio Selection Problem	$[0, 1]^n$	0

In order to avoid this problem we have to modify the training function. We do this by adding some randomly generated constants to each variable x_i. We obtain the function: $f_1(x) = \sum_{i=1}^{n} (i \cdot (x_i - r_i)^2)$, where r_i are some randomly generated constants between -10 and 10. In this case the optimal solution is $x^* = (r_1, r_2 ... r_n)$.

We have two possibilities for generating the constants: we could keep them fixed during training or we could generate new constants each time the function is called. The second strategy seems to be more general. However, we have tested both strategies, but, for our simple case, both provided similar results.

Note that the modified function is used in the training stage only. During testing stage we use the unmodified (see Table 2) version of the function.

The parameters of the GP algorithm (macro level) are given in Table 3. For GA we use a population with 200 individuals, each of them with 5 dimensions. During 50 generations we apply random selection and recombination (using the evolved crossover) with probability 0.8.

We performed 30 independent runs for evolving operators. In all runs we obtained a very good crossover operator able to compete with the standard

Table 3. The parameters of the GP algorithm (the macro level algorithm) used for evolving genetic operators

Parameter	Value
Population size	50
Number of generations	100
Maximum size (depth) for a tree	10
Initialization	Ramped half and half
Crossover probability	0.8
Mutation probability	0.1
Function set	$F = \{\widehat{+}, \widehat{-}, \widehat{*}, \widehat{sin}, \widehat{cos}, \widehat{exp}\}$
Terminal set	$T = \{0.1, 0.2, 0.3, 0.4, 0.5, 0.6,$ $0.7, 0.8, 0.9, 1.0, x, y, R\}$

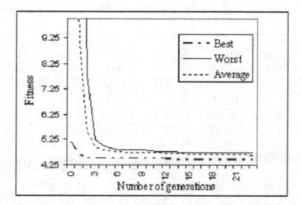

Fig. 2. The evolution of the fitness of the best/worst GP individual, and the average fitness (of all GP individuals in the population) in a particular run. We have depicted a window of 25 generations for a better visualization of the results.

convex crossover. The results obtained in one of the runs (randomly selected from the set of 30 runs) are presented in Figure 2.

Crossover operators of different complexities have been evolved. The simplest operators contain 5 nodes, whereas the most complex evolved operator has 17 nodes. One of the simplest evolved operators is depicted (as GP tree) in Figure 3. We can see that the complexity of the evolved operator is similar to the complexity of the standard convex crossover.

The crossover operator (given in Figure 3) will be used in the numerical experiments performed in the next section.

Experiment 2. This experiment serves our purpose to compare the evolved crossover operator with a convex crossover operator [5]. A Genetic Algorithm [5] is used for testing the quality of the crossover operators. This algorithm has the same structure as the one used in the previous experiment (the micro level algorithm), the only difference being the employed recombination operators. First

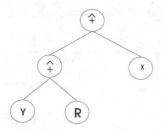

Fig. 3. One of the evolved crossover operators represented as a GP tree. The function symbols have been defined in Table 1.

Table 4. The results obtained by applying the evolved operator and the standard convex crossover to the considered test functions. *Best/Worst* stands for the fitness of the best individual in the best/worst run. The results are averaged over 500 runs.

Func-tions	Evolved crossover				Convex crossover			
	Best	Worst	Mean	StdDev	Best	Worst	Mean	StdDev
f_1	0.036	1.157	0.513	0.215	0.093	16.320	2.945	2.490
f_2	3.630	194.718	78.036	32.348	12.796	2884.690	438.121	343.631
f_3	0.415	2.590	1.561	0.342	0.644	9.586	3.589	1.514
f_4	5.263	202.777	76.756	34.022	14.588	4512.660	496.383	524.641
f_5	1.325	9.496	6.030	1.355	1.720	37.528	13.243	5.286
f_6	58.786	4936.8	1198.430	833.183	102	1.65E+06	57400	1.33E+05
f_7	1.387	16.745	8.881	2.600	2.007	34.621	16.877	5.973
f_8	2.681	8.272	5.986	0.895	3.497	17.300	9.719	72.452
f_9	0.557	2.223	1.426	0.250	0.619	19.568	3.576	2.188
f_{10}	-1436.21	-417.259	-849.782	189.805	-1470.00	-454.968	-884.159	198.569
f_{11}	1.49E-04	1.98E-04	1.64E-04	8.75E-06	1.47E-04	3.32E-04	1.87E-04	3.12E-05

Table 5. The results of F-test and t-test

Functions	F-test	t-test	Functions	F-test	t-test
f_1	7.48E-03	2.32E-15	f_7	1.89E-01	5.16E-42
f_2	8.86E-03	4.91E-13	f_8	1.33E-01	1.77E-43
f_3	5.10E-02	5.41E-33	f_9	1.31E-02	1.46E-12
f_4	4.21E-03	2.99E-08	f_{10}	9.14E-01	1.45E-01
f_5	6.57E-02	1.42E-31	f_{11}	3.71E-51	1.96E-143
f_6	3.95E-05	1.77E-03			

we run the GA employing the evolved crossover and later we run the same GA, with the same parameters, using the convex crossover this time. The results of this experiment are presented in Table 4.

Taking into account the average values presented in Table 4 we can conclude that the evolved operator performs significantly better than the classical recombination in 10 out of 11 cases. Taking into account the best values we can see that the evolved crossover performs better than the convex crossover in 10 cases (out of 11).

In order to determine whether the differences between the evolved crossover and the convex crossover are statistically significant, we use a t-test with a 0.05 level of significance. Before applying the t-test, an F-test is used for determining whether the compared data have the same variance. The P-values of a two-tailed t-test with 499 degrees of freedom are given in Table 5. Table 5 shows that the differences between the results obtained by standard convex crossover and by the evolved crossover are statistically significant ($P < 0.05$) in 9 cases.

5 Conclusions and Further Work

A new hybrid technique for evolving crossover operators has been proposed in this paper. The model has been used for evolving crossover operators for function optimization. Numerical experiments have shown that the evolved crossover performs better than the standard convex crossover for most of the test problems. However, taking into account the No Free Lunch theorems for Search and Optimization [15] we cannot make any assumption about the generalization ability of the evolved crossover operators. Further numerical experiments are required in order to assess the power of the evolved operators. Further work will be focused on: evolving better crossover operators for real encoding, evolving more complex genetic operators which can act as both crossover and mutation, evolving genetic operators for other problems.

References

1. P. J. Angeline, "Two self-adaptive crossover operators for genetic programming", *Advances in Genetic Programming II*, pp. 89-110, MIT Press, 1996.
2. H. J. Bremermann, "Optimization through evolution and recombination", M.C. Yovits, G.T. Jacobi, and G.D. Goldstein, editors, *Self-Organizing Systems 1962*, Proceedings of the Conference on Self-Organizing Systems, Chicago, Illinois, 22.- 24.5.1962, pp. 93-106, 1962.
3. T. -J. Chang, N. Meade, J. E. Beasley, and Y. M. Sharaiha, "Heuristics for cardinality constrained portfolio optimisation" Comp. & Opns. Res. 27, pp. 1271-1302, 2000.
4. B. Edmonds, "Meta-genetic programming: coevolving the operators of variation", *Electrik on AI*, Vol. 9, pp. 13-29, 2001.
5. D. Goldberg, *Genetic algorithms in search, optimization and machine learning*, Addison-Wesley, 1989.
6. J. R. Koza, *Genetic programming, On the programming of computers by means of natural selection*, MIT Press, Cambridge, MA, 1992.
7. H. Markowitz, "Portfolio Selection", *Journal of Finance*, 7, pp. 77-91, 1952.
8. M. Oltean and C. Grosan, "Evolving EAs using Multi Expression Programming", *European Conference on Artificial Life*, pp. 651-658, Springer-Verlag, 2003.
9. H.-P. Schwefel, *Numerical optimization of computer models*, John Wiley & Sons, New York, 1981.

10. L. Spector and A. Robinson, A., "Genetic Programming and Autoconstructive Evolution with the Push Programming Language", *Genetic Programming and Evolvable Machines*, Issue 1, pp. 7-40, Kluwer, 2002.
11. F. Streichert, H. Ulmer, and A. Zell, "Comparing Discrete and Continuous Genotypes on the Constrained Portfolio Selection Problem", *Genetic and Evolutionary Computation Conference - GECCO 2004, Proceedings*, Part II., pp. 1239-1250, Springer-Verlag, 2004.
12. J. Tavares, P. Machado,A. Cardoso, F.-B. Pereira and E. Costa, "On the evolution of evolutionary algorithms", in Keijzer, M. (et al.) editors, *European Conference on Genetic Programming*, pp. 389-398, Springer-Verlag, Berlin, 2004.
13. A. Teller, "Evolving programmers: the co-evolution of intelligent recombination operators", *Advances in Genetic Programming II*, pp. 45-68, MIT Press, USA, 1996.
14. X. Yao, Y. Liu and G. Lin, "Evolutionary programming made faster", *IEEE Transaction on Evolutionary Computation*, pp. 82-102, IEEE Press, 1999.
15. D. H. Wolpert and W. G. McReady, "No Free Lunch Theorems for Search", *Technical Report SFI-TR-05-010*, Santa Fe Institute, USA, 1995.
16. http://www.euronext.com

Genetic Programming, Validation Sets, and Parsimony Pressure

Christian Gagné[1,2,3], Marc Schoenauer[1],
Marc Parizeau[2], and Marco Tomassini[3]

[1] Équipe TAO – INRIA Futurs,
LRI Bat. 490, Université Paris Sud, 91405 Orsay CEDEX, France
{christian.gagne, marc.schoenauer}@lri.fr
[2] Laboratoire de Vision et Systèmes Numériques (LVSN),
Département de Génie Électrique et de Génie Informatique,
Université Laval, Québec (QC), G1K 7P4, Canada
parizeau@gel.ulaval.ca
[3] Information Systems Institute,
Université de Lausanne, CH-1015 Dorigny, Switzerland
marco.tomassini@unil.ch

Abstract. Fitness functions based on test cases are very common in Genetic Programming (GP). This process can be assimilated to a learning task, with the inference of models from a limited number of samples. This paper is an investigation on two methods to improve generalization in GP-based learning: 1) the selection of the best-of-run individuals using a three data sets methodology, and 2) the application of parsimony pressure in order to reduce the complexity of the solutions. Results using GP in a binary classification setup show that while the accuracy on the test sets is preserved, with less variances compared to baseline results, the mean tree size obtained with the tested methods is significantly reduced.

This paper is an experimental study of methodologies for Evolutionary Computations (EC) inspired by common practices in the Machine Learning (ML) and Pattern Recognition (PR) communities. More specifically, using Genetic Programming (GP) for supervised learning, we aim at evaluating both the effect of using a *three data sets methodology* (training, validation, and test sets) and the effect of minimizing the classifiers complexity. Our experiments show that these approaches preserve the performances of GP, while significantly reducing the size of the best-of-run solutions, which is in accordance with Occam's Razor principle.

The structure of the paper goes as follow. Section 1 starts with a high-level description of the tested approaches and their justifications. A presentation of relevant work follows in Section 2. Thereafter, the methodology used in the experiments is detailed in Section 3. Finally, Section 4 presents the experimental results obtained on six binary classification data sets, and Section 5 concludes the paper.

P. Collet et al. (Eds.): EuroGP 2006, LNCS 3905, pp. 109 120, 2006.
© Springer-Verlag Berlin Heidelberg 2006

1   Introduction

GP is particularly suited for problems that can be assimilated to learning tasks, with the minimization of the error between the obtained and desired outputs for a limited number of test cases – the training data, using a ML terminology. Indeed, the classical GP examples of symbolic regression, boolean multiplexer and artificial ant [1] are only simple instances of well-known learning problems (i.e. respectively regression, binary classification and reinforcement learning). In the early years of GP, these problems were tackled using a single data set, reporting results on the same data set that was used to evaluate the fitnesses during the evolution. This was justifiable by the fact that these are toy problems used only to illustrate the potential of GP. In the ML community, it is recognized that such methodology is flawed, given that the learning algorithm can overfit the data used during the training and perform poorly on unseen data of the same application domain [2, 3]. Hence, it is important to report results on a set of data that was not used during the learning stage. This is what we call in this paper a *two data sets methodology*, with a training set used by the learning algorithm and a test set used to report the performance of the algorithm on unseen data, which is a good indicator of the algorithm's generalization (or robustness) capability. Even though this methodology has been widely accepted and applied in the ML and PR communities for a long time, the EC community still lags behind by publishing papers that are reporting results on data sets that were used during the evolution (training) phase. This methodological problem has already been spotted (see [4]) and should be less and less common in the future.

The two data sets methodology prevents reporting flawed results of learning algorithms that overfit the training set. But this does not prevent by itself overfitting the training set. A common approach is to add a third data set – the validation set – which helps the learning algorithm to measure its generalization capability. This validation set is useful to interrupt the learning algorithm when overfitting occurs and/or select a configuration of the learning machine that maximizes the generalization performances. This third data set is commonly used to train classifiers such as back-propagation neural networks and can be easily applied to EC-based learning. But this approach has an important drawback: it removes a significant amount of data from the training set, which can be harmful to the learning process. Indeed, the richer the training set, the more representative it can be of the real data distribution, and the more the learning algorithm can be expected to converge toward robust solutions. In the light of these considerations, an objective of this paper is to investigate the effect of a validation set to select the best-of-run individuals for a GP-based learning application.

Another concern of the ML and PR communities is to develop learning algorithms that generate simple solutions. An argument behind this is the Occam's Razor principle, which states that between solutions of comparable quality, the simplest solutions must be preferred. Another argument is the minimum description length principle [5], which states that the "best" model is the one that minimizes the amount of information needed to encode the model and the data given the model. Preference for simpler solutions and overfitting avoidance are closely related: it is more likely that a complex solution incorporates specific information from the training set, thus overfitting the training set, compared to a simpler solution. But, as mentioned in [6], this argumentation should be taken with care as too much emphasis on minimizing complexity can prevent the discovery of more complex yet more accurate solutions.

There is a strong link between the minimization of complexity in GP-based learning and the control of code bloat [1, 7], that is an exaggerated growth of program size in the course of GP runs. Even though complexity and code bloat are not exactly the same phenomenon, as some kind of bloat is generated by neutral pieces of code that have no effect on the actual complexity of the solutions, most of the mechanisms proposed to control it [8, 9, 10, 11] can also be used to minimize the complexity of solutions obtained by GP-based learning.

This paper is a study of GP viewed as a learning algorithm. More specifically, we investigate two techniques to increase the generalization performance and decrease the complexity of the models: 1) use of a validation set to select best-of-run individuals that generalize well, and 2) use of lexicographic parsimony pressure [10] to reduce the complexity of the generated models. These techniques are tested using a GP encoding for binary classification problems, with vectors taken from the learning sets as terminals, and mathematical operations to manipulate these vectors as branches. This approach is tested on six different data sets from the UCI ML repository [12]. Even if the proposed techniques are tested in a specific context, we argue that they can be extended to the frequent situations where GP is used as a learning algorithm.

2 Related Work

Some GP learning applications [13, 14, 15] have made use of a three data sets methodology, but without making a thorough analysis of its effects. Panait and Luke [16] conducted some experiments on different approaches to increase the robustness of the solutions generated by GP, using a three data sets methodology to evaluate the efficiency of each approach. Rowland [17] and Kushchu [18] conducted studies on generalization in EC and GP. Both of their argumentations converge toward the testing of solutions in previously unseen situations for improving robustness.

Because of the bloat phenomenon, typical in GP, parsimony pressure has been more widely studied [9, 19, 20, 21]. In particular, several papers [22, 23, 24] have produced interesting results around the idea of using a parsimony pressure to increase the generalization capability of GP-evolved solutions. However, a counter-argumentation is given in [25], where solutions biased toward low complexity have, in some circumstances, increased generalization error. This is in accordance with the argumentation given in [6], which states that less complex solutions are not always more robust.

3 Methodology

The experiments conducted in this work are based on a GP-setup specialized for binary classification problems. The data processed by the primitives are vectors of two possible sizes, either of size one (a scalar value), or of size n, the feature set size. Table 1 presents the set of primitives used to build the programs.

Three main families of primitives were used: the *mathematical function primitives* (ADD, SUB, MUL, DIV, MXF, MNF, ABS, and SLN), the *vector-to-scalar primitives* (SUM, MEA, MXV, MIV, and L2), and the *vectorial terminals* (E and X). The mathematical function primitives with two arguments (ADD, SUB, MUL, DIV, MXF, and MIF) are defined to deal with arguments of different sizes by applying the function to each component of the n-sized arguments, when necessary repeatedly using the value of the scalar arguments. More formally, if $f(x_1, x_2)$ denotes the function associated to the primitive presented in Table 1, the output of these primitives is:

- A scalar $[f(x_1(1), x_2(1))]$, if both arguments are scalars;
- A size n vector $[f(x_1(1), x_2(1))\ \ f(x_1(1), x_2(2))\ \ \ldots\ \ f(x_1(1), x_2(n))]^T$, if the first argument is a scalar and the second a vector;
- A size n vector $[f(x_1(1), x_2(1))\ \ f(x_1(2), x_2(1))\ \ \ldots\ \ f(x_1(n), x_2(1))]^T$, if the first argument is a vector and the second a scalar;
- A size n vector $[f(x_1(1), x_2(1))\ \ f(x_1(2), x_2(2))\ \ \ldots\ \ f(x_1(n), x_2(n))]^T$, if both arguments are vectors.

Table 1. GP primitives used to build the classifiers

Name	# args.	Description
ADD	2	Addition, $f_{\mathrm{ADD}}(x_1, x_2) = x_1 + x_2$.
SUB	2	Subtraction, $f_{\mathrm{SUB}}(x_1, x_2) = x_1 - x_2$.
MUL	2	Multiplication, $f_{\mathrm{MUL}}(x_1, x_2) = x_1 x_2$.
DIV	2	Protected division, $f_{\mathrm{DIV}}(x_1, x_2) = \begin{cases} 1 & |x_2| < 0.001 \\ x_1/x_2 & \text{otherwise} \end{cases}$.
MXF	2	Maximum value, $f_{\mathrm{MXF}}(x_1, x_2) = \max(x_1, x_2)$.
MNF	2	Minimum value, $f_{\mathrm{MNF}}(x_1, x_2) = \min(x_1, x_2)$.
ABS	1	Absolute value, $f_{\mathrm{ABS}}(x) = |x|$.
SLN	1	Saturated symmetric linear function, $f_{\mathrm{SLN}}(x) = \begin{cases} 1 & x > 1 \\ -1 & x < -1 \\ x & \text{otherwise} \end{cases}$.
SUM	1	Sum of vector's components, $f_{\mathrm{SUM}}(\mathbf{x}) = \sum_i x_i$.
MEA	1	Mean of vector's components, $f_{\mathrm{MEA}}(\mathbf{x}) = \frac{\sum_i x_i}{\mathrm{card}(\mathbf{x})}$.
MXV	1	Maximum of vector's components, $f_{\mathrm{MXV}}(\mathbf{x}) = \max_i x_i$.
MIV	1	Minimum of vector's components, $f_{\mathrm{MIV}}(\mathbf{x}) = \min_i x_i$.
L2	1	L_2 norm of the vector, $f_{\mathrm{L2}}(\mathbf{x}) = \sqrt{\sum_i x_i^2}$.
E	0	Ephemeral random vector, generated by copying the value of a randomly selected training set data.
X	0	Vector with the value of the data to classify.

On the other hand, the vector-to-scalar primitives are defined to convert a vector argument of size n into a scalar output. When the argument is a scalar, it is returned as output value as is, without modification, except for the L2 primitive which returns the absolute value of the input scalar. Finally, the vectorial terminals are always vectors of size n, with either randomly selected data of the training set (terminal E), used as constants, or the value of the data to classify (terminal X), used as the variable of the problem.

The data evaluated is classified according to the output of the GP tree, that is assigned to the first class for an output value positive or zero, otherwise assigned to the second class. If necessary, the output of the GP program is converted into a scalar beforehand, by a summation of each vector's components, as does the primitive SUM.

In order to test the effect of using a validation set and applying some parsimony pressure, GP will be tested on common binary classification data sets taken from the *Machine Learning Repository* at UCI [12]. The selected data set are presented in Table 2. The selection of these data sets was guided by the following main criteria: 1) select appropriate sets for binary classification, 2) select appropriate sets for 10-folds cross-validation (see below), that is data sets without predefined separated training and testing sets, and 3) select sets of relatively large size or high dimensionality. The first two criteria were chosen in order to fit into our general methodology, to avoid special data manipulations, while the last criterion was postulated in an attempt to select not too easy data sets, that should help to generate discriminant results.

Table 2. Description of UCI data sets used for the experimentations

Data set	Size	# of features	Application domain
bcw	699	9	Wisconcin's breast cancer, 65.5 % benign and 34.5 % malignant.
cmc	1473	9	Contraceptive method choice, 42.7 % not using contraception and 57.3 % using contraception.
ger	1000	24	German credit approval, 70 % approved and 30 % not approved.
ion	351	34	Ionosphere radar signal, 35.9 % without structure detected and 64.9 % with a structure detected.
pid	768	8	Pima Indians diabetes, 65.1 % tested negative and 34.9 % tested positive for diabetes.
spa	4601	57	Spam e-mail, 60.6 % non-junk e-mail and 39.4 % junk e-mail.

Before the experiments, each data set was randomly divided into 10 folds of equal size, taking care to balance the number of data of each class between the folds. A 10-folds cross-validation [2] has been conducted using the data in 9 folds as the training set for an evolution, reporting the test set error rate on the remaining fold. For each tested configuration, the process is repeated 10 times for each fold, for a total of 100 evolutions per configuration. The reported results consist in the means for these 100 evolutions.

Our experimentations are conducted on four different configurations:

1. **Baseline:** The fitness measure consists in minimizing the error rate on the complete training set. The best-of-run individual is simply the individual of the evolution with the lowest error rate on the training set, with the smallest individual selected in cases of ties.

2. **With validation:** For each evolution, the training set is randomly divided into two data sets: the fitness evaluation data set, with 67% of the training data, and the validation set, with the remaining 33%. The class distribution of the data is well-balanced between the sets. The fitness measure consists in minimizing the error rate on the fitness evaluation set. At each generation, a two-objective sort is conducted in order to extract a set of non-dominated individuals (the Pareto front), with regards to the lowest fitness evaluation set error rate and the smallest individuals. These non-dominated individuals are then evaluated on the validation set, with the best-of-run individual selected as the one of these with the smallest error rate on the validation set, ties being solved by choosing the smallest individual.

3. **With parsimony pressure:** A lexicographic parsimony pressure [10] is applied to the evolution by minimizing the error rate on the complete training set, using the individual size as second point of comparison in cases of identical error rates. As with the baseline configuration, the best-of-run individual is the individual of the evolution with the lowest error rate on the training set, with the smallest individual selected in cases of ties (strict equality).

4. **With validation and parsimony pressure:** A mix of the two previous configurations, by separating the training set into two sets, the fitness evaluation set (67% of the data) and the validation set (33% of the data), and making use of the lexicographic parsimony pressure. The fitness evaluation set is used to compute the error rate that guides the evolution while the validation set is used only to select the best-of-run individual. The selection of this best-of-run individual is identical to the *with validation* configuration, by extracting a Pareto front of the non-dominated individuals of the current generation (fitness evaluation set error rates vs individual sizes). At each generation, all these non-dominated individuals are tested on the validation set. The best-of-run individual is selected as the solution that minimizes the validation error rate, breaking ties by preferring the smallest individuals.

Thus, for the second and fourth settings, the Pareto front is extracted at each generation for testing against the validation set. This is motivated by two main reasons: 1) it is important to reduce the number of solutions tested against the validation set, in order not to select best-of-run solutions that are just "by chance" performing well on the validation set, and 2) it is desirable to test on the validation set a range of solutions with different accuracy/size trade-offs. It should be stressed that tournament selection is used in all evolutions, with lexicographic ranking for the third and fourth configurations. Strictly speaking, this is not a Pareto domination-based multi-objective selection algorithm.

Table 3. Tableau of the GP evolutions

Parameter	Description and parameter values
Terminals and branches	See Table 1.
Population size	One panmictic population of 1000 individuals.
Stop criterion	Evolution ends after 100 generations.
Replacement strategy	Genetic operations applied following generational scheme.
Selection	Tournaments selection with 2 participants (relative ranking).
Fitness measure	**Without parsimony pressure:** minimize the error rate. **With parsimony pressure:** minimize the error rate and, in case of ties, select the smallest individuals (lexicographic ranking).
Crossover	Classical subtree crossover [1] (probability 0.7).
Standard mutation	Replace a subtree with a new randomly generated one (probability 0.05).
Swap mutation	Exchange a primitive with another of the same arity (probability 0.05).
Shrink mutation	Replace a branch with one of its children and remove the branch mutated and the other children's subtrees (if any) (probability 0.05).
Ephemerals mutation	Randomly select a new ephemeral random vector (probability 0.05).
Reproduction	Copy without modification an existing individual (probability 0.1).
Data normalization	The data of the different sets are scaled in $[-1, 1]$ along the different dimensions.

Table 3 presents the GP parameters used during the experiments. No special tweaking of these parameter values was done, which correspond in most cases to the default values of the software tool used. The experimentations have been implemented using the GP facilities of the Open BEAGLE framework [26].

4   Results

Table 4 presents the detailed results obtained by testing the four configurations presented in the previous section, using the six data sets of Table 2. The error rates and tree sizes that are reported consist in the mean and standard deviation values of the best-of-run individuals for the 100 runs (10 different runs for each folds). The *effort*[1] consists in a measure of the computations done during the evolutions. It is calculated by summing the number of GP primitives evaluated during the runs. More precisely, for configurations without validation, the effort is computed by counting in the number of primitives in each individual times the training set size, for all evaluated individuals during the run. For configurations with validation, the size of the individuals on Pareto front times the

---

[1] Note that the notion of "effort" presented here is different from the one defined by Koza in [1].

Table 4. Error rates, tree sizes and effort for the evolution of GP-based classifiers using the UCI data sets. Results in *italic* are not statistically different from those of the baseline configuration, according to a 95% confidence two-tailed Student's *t*-test. Results in **bold** are more than 50% smaller than the corresponding baseline results.

Approach	Train set rate Mean error	Std. dev.	Valid. set rate Mean error	Std. dev.	Test set rate Mean error	Std. dev.	Tree size Mean size	Std. dev.	Effort Mean (×10⁹)	Stdev. (×10⁹)
					bcw					
Baseline	1.7 %	0.5 %	–	–	3.4 %	2.3 %	83.4	55.2	4.92	1.5
Validation	2.3 %	0.7 %	2.3 %	0.8 %	*3.3 %*	2.3 %	**34.2**	38.8	4.08	1.2
Parsimony	2.1 %	0.5 %	–	–	*3.5 %*	2.3 %	**22.0**	18.9	1.10	0.83
Both	2.8 %	0.7 %	2.7 %	1.0 %	*3.3 %*	2.1 %	**6.5**	11.2	0.72	0.55
					cmc					
Baseline	26.3 %	2.2 %	–	–	31.2 %	4.8 %	174.8	68.2	11.2	3.5
Validation	28.6 %	3.2 %	30.8 %	3.0 %	*32.5 %*	4.5 %	106.4	68.3	8.43	2.7
Parsimony	27.0 %	2.8 %	–	–	*31.7 %*	4.9 %	151.6	62.4	10.1	3.9
Both	29.3 %	3.0 %	29.6 %	3.0 %	*32.1 %*	5.0 %	**63.7**	39.8	6.17	2.2
					ger					
Baseline	22.7 %	1.6 %	–	–	29.3 %	3.8 %	175.3	77.9	7.43	2.7
Validation	25.3 %	2.6 %	27.3 %	1.5 %	*29.5 %*	3.5 %	**78.2**	68.8	5.13	1.6
Parsimony	*22.6 %*	1.7 %	–	–	*29.1 %*	3.8 %	141.8	69.2	5.73	2.6
Both	25.7 %	2.7 %	26.7 %	1.6 %	*29.6 %*	3.2 %	**54.8**	47.1	3.79	2.0
					ion					
Baseline	4.1 %	1.2 %	–	–	10.5 %	5.4 %	149.4	53.0	2.80	0.76
Validation	5.9 %	3.1 %	7.5 %	3.5 %	*11.3 %*	6.8 %	94.2	56.3	2.08	0.55
Parsimony	*4.2 %*	1.3 %	–	–	*10.1 %*	6.0 %	84.4	38.8	1.88	0.59
Both	7.7 %	2.9 %	7.5 %	2.8 %	*11.0 %*	6.3 %	**41.6**	28.3	**1.10**	0.35
					pid					
Baseline	19.9 %	1.2 %	–	–	25.2 %	4.5 %	149.5	56.8	5.47	1.6
Validation	22.0 %	2.1 %	22.9 %	2.2 %	*25.2 %*	4.5 %	**60.4**	55.5	4.25	1.3
Parsimony	20.1 %	1.2 %	–	–	*24.7 %*	4.4 %	99.6	59.0	3.85	1.2
Both	23.5 %	2.0 %	22.4 %	2.0 %	*25.1 %*	4.4 %	**28.0**	25.4	**2.45**	0.89
					spa					
Baseline	12.8 %	2.2 %	–	–	13.6 %	2.7 %	166.6	62.4	34.4	9.4
Validation	*12.9 %*	2.3 %	13.7 %	2.7 %	*13.9 %*	2.6 %	148.7	61.7	21.7	6.6
Parsimony	*13.3 %*	2.6 %	–	–	*14.2 %*	3.2 %	141.3	56.4	28.6	10.1
Both	*13.1 %*	2.2 %	13.5 %	2.2 %	*13.9 %*	2.5 %	109.3	47.0	18.7	6.4

validation set size is also taken into account. Italic results in Table 4 are not statistically different from the corresponding baseline result; hence all other results are statistically distinct from the baseline.

Figure 1 presents the box plots that stem from a one-way analysis of variance (ANOVA) conducted on the test set error rates. Looking at the results, it seems that no approach is clearly superior to the others in term of test set accuracy. But, taking a closer look we can see that the approach using both the validation set and parsimony pressure reduces the variance of the test set error rates (first to third quartile range) for the bcw, ger, pid and spa data sets, having a comparable

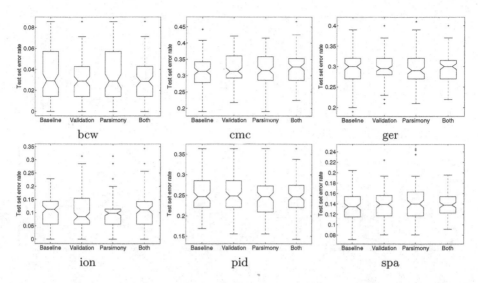

Fig. 1. One-way analysis of variance (ANOVA) box plots of the best-of-run solutions test set error rates. The center box is bounded by the first and third quartiles of the data distribution, with the median as the central line in the box. The notches surrounding the median show the 95% confidence interval of this median. The whiskers above and below the boxes represent the spread of the data value within 1.5 times the interquartile range, with the + symbol showing outliers.

or slightly worse variance for the two other sets. This is an important result as getting reproducible and stable solutions is often more interesting than finding only infrequently a marginally better individual.

Taking a closer look at the error rates on the different sets in Table 4, important differences can be noted between the train and validation set rates, on one hand, and the test set rates on the other hand. The differences between the train and test rates can be explained by an overfitting of the training data. But, it is surprising to see the importance of the differences between the validation and test rates. This may indicate that, because too many solutions are still tested against the validation set at each generation, the risk of selecting solutions that fit the validation set "by chance" is not negligible.

Figure 2 presents the one-way ANOVA box plots for the best-of-run tree sizes. This time, it seems clear that the tested methods significantly reduce the best-of-run individual tree sizes for all tested data sets. It is interesting to note that the configurations with a validation set have generated significantly smaller best-of-run individual tree sizes compared with the parsimony pressure only approach. This is expected given that the validation set is directly used in the best-of-run individual selection process, while the parsimony pressure is used only to limit the tree sizes during the runs. Also, the important size reduction of the best-of-run solutions, especially noticeable with the combination of validation and parsimony pressure, is valuable when simplicity or comprehensibility is necessary for the application at hand. Finally, taking a look at the mean effort

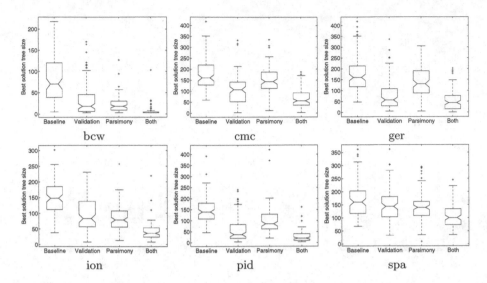

Fig. 2. One-way analysis of variance (ANOVA) box plots of the best-of-run solutions tree sizes

in Table 4, the reduction goes up to 50 % with the validation and parsimony pressure approach, compared to the baseline effort.

5   Conclusion

In this paper, methodologies were investigated to improve GP as a learning algorithm. More specifically, using the GP-based setup for binary classification, the use of a validation set for selecting best-of-run individuals was tested, in order to pick solutions that generalize well. The effect of a lexicographic parsimony pressure was also tested, in order to avoid unnecessary complexity in the evolved solutions. Experimental results indicate that the use of a validation set improves a little the stability of the best-of-run solutions on the test sets, by maintaining accuracy while slightly reducing variance in most cases. This is important given the stochastic nature of GP, which can introduce important variations of the results, from one run to another. Moreover, it was shown that mild parsimony pressure applied during evolutions can sustain performance in general, while effectively reducing both solution size and effort. The combination of these two approaches apparently gives the best of both worlds, by reducing the variance of test set errors, simplifying drastically the complexity best-of-run solutions, and cutting down effort by half.

As future work, still using a GP-based learning setup, it is planned to develop new stopping criteria based on the difference between training and validation set error rates. It is also planned to study the effect of changing the test cases during the course of the evolution for GP-based learning, using methods such as competitive co-evolution and boosting.

Acknowledgments

This work was supported by postdoctoral fellowships from the ERCIM (Europe) and the FQRNT (Québec) to C. Gagné.

References

1. Koza, J.R.: Genetic Programming: On the Programming of Computers by Means of Natural Selection. MIT Press, Cambridge (MA), USA (1992)
2. Duda, R.O., Hart, P.E., Stork, D.G.: Pattern Classification. Second edn. John Wiley & Sons, Inc., New York (NY), USA (2001)
3. Mitchell, T.M.: Machine Learning. McGraw-Hill (1997)
4. Eiben, A.E., Jelasity, M.: A critical note on experimental research methodology in EC. In: Proceedings of the 2002 Congress on Evolutionary Computation (CEC 2002), Honolulu (HI), USA, IEEE Press (2002) 582–587
5. Rissanen, J.: Modeling by shortest data description. Automatica **14** (1978) 465–471
6. Domingos, P.: The role of occam's razor in knowledge discovery. Data Mining and Knowledge Discovery **3**(4) (1999) 409–425
7. Banzhaf, W., Langdon, W.B.: Some considerations on the reason for bloat. Genetic Programming and Evolvable Machines **3**(1) (2002) 81–91
8. Langdon, W.B.: Size fair and homologous tree genetic programming crossovers. Genetic Programming and Evolvable Machines **1**(1/2) (2000) 95–119
9. Ekárt, A., Németh, S.Z.: Selection based on the pareto nondomination criterion for controlling code growth in genetic programming. Genetic Programming and Evolvable Machines **2**(1) (2001) 61–73
10. Luke, S., Panait, L.: Lexicographic parsimony pressure. In: Proceedings of the 2002 Genetic and Evolutionary Computation Conference (GECCO 2002), New York (NY), USA, Morgan Kaufmann Publishers (2002) 829–836
11. Silva, S., Almeida, J.: Dynamic maximum tree depth. In: Proceedings of the 2003 Genetic and Evolutionary Computation Conference (GECCO 2003), Chicago (IL), USA, Springer-Verlag (2003) 1776–1787
12. Newman, D., Hettich, S., Blake, C., Merz, C.: UCI repository of machine learning databases. http://www.ics.uci.edu/~mlearn/MLRepository.html (1998)
13. Sherrah, J., Bogner, R.E., Bouzerdoum, A.: The evolutionary pre-processor: Automatic feature extraction for supervised classification using genetic programming. In: Genetic Programming 1997: Proceedings of the Second Annual Conference, Stanford University (CA), USA, Morgan Kaufmann (1997) 304–312
14. Brameier, M., Banzhaf, W.: Evolving teams of predictors with linear genetic programming. Genetic Programming and Evolvable Machines **2**(4) (2001) 381–407
15. Yu, T., Chen, S.H., Kuo, T.W.: Discovering financial technical trading rules using genetic programming with lambda abstraction. In: Genetic Programming Theory and Practice II, Ann Arbor (MI), USA (2004) 11–30
16. Panait, L., Luke, S.: Methods for evolving robust programs. In: Proceedings of the 2003 Genetic and Evolutionary Computation Conference (GECCO 2003). Volume 2724 of LNCS., Chicago (IL), USA, Springer-Verlag (2003) 1740–1751
17. Rowland, J.J.: Generalisation and model selection in supervised learning with evolutionary computation. In: EvoWorkshops 2003. Volume 2611 of LNCS., University of Essex, UK, Springer-Verlag (2003) 119–130

18. Kushchu, I.: Genetic programming and evolutionary generalization. IEEE transactions on Evolutionary Computation **6**(5) (2002) 431–442
19. Nordin, P., Banzhaf, W.: Complexity compression and evolution. In: Proceedings of the Sixth International Conference Genetic Algorithms, Pittsburgh (PA), USA, Morgan Kaufmann (1995) 310–317
20. Soule, T., Foster, J.A.: Effects of code growth and parsimony pressure on populations in genetic programming. Evolutionary Computation **6**(4) (1998) 293–309
21. Gustafson, S., Ekart, A., Burke, E., Kendall, G.: Problem difficulty and code growth in genetic programming. Genetic Programming and Evolvable Machines **5**(3) (2004) 271–290
22. Iba, H., de Garis, H., Sato, T.: Genetic programming using a minimum description length principle. In: Advances in Genetic Programming. Complex Adaptive Systems, Cambridge (MA), USA, MIT Press (1994) 265–284
23. Zhang, B.T., Mühlenbein, H.: Balancing accuracy and parsimony in genetic programming. Evolutionary Computation **3**(1) (1995) 17–38
24. Rosca, J.: Generality versus size in genetic programming. In: Genetic Programming 1996: Proceedings of the First Annual Conference, Stanford University (CA), USA (1996) 381–387
25. Cavaretta, M.J., Chellapilla, K.: Data mining using genetic programming: The implications of parsimony on generalization error. In: Proceedings of the 1999 Congress on Evolutionary Computation (CEC 1999), Washington (DC), USA (1999) 1330–1337
26. Gagné, C., Parizeau, M.: Open BEAGLE: A new versatile C++ framework for evolutionary computation. In: Late-Breaking Papers of the 2002 Genetic and Evolutionary Computation Conference (GECCO 2002), New York (NY), USA (2002)

Geometric Crossover for Biological Sequences

Alberto Moraglio[1], Riccardo Poli[1], and Rolv Seehuus[2]

[1] Department of Computer Science,
University of Essex,
Wivenhoe Park, Colchester, CO4 3SQ, UK
{amoragn, rpoli}@essex.ac.uk
[2] Department of Computer Science,
Norwegian University of Science and Technology,
Sem selands v 7-9, 7000 Trondheim, Norway
rolv.seehuus@idi.ntnu.no

Abstract. This paper extends a geometric framework for interpreting crossover and mutation [4] to the case of sequences. This representation is important because it is the link between artificial evolution and biological evolution. We define and theoretically study geometric crossover for sequences under edit distance and show its intimate connection with the biological notion of sequence homology.

1 Introduction

Evolutionary algorithms (EAs) mimic, in a simplified manner, natural evolution. However, very few theoretical results are available which apply equally well to both forms of evolutionary search.

One important cause of the lack of connection between evolutionary computation theory and evolutionary biology is that they focus on different kinds of genotypes (different solution representations), namely DNA strands (variable-length strings or sequences) and binary strings. Most importantly, even if DNA strands and binary strings appear to be very similar at a first sight, the crossover operator for binary strings is just a caricature of the biological recombination acting on DNA strands. The main difference is that DNA strands align on the basis of their contents (at meiosis) before exchanging genetic material and do not align only positionally as it is the case for binary strings. Such an alignment is flexible in that two DNA strands can stretch and fold to better align with each other. Moreover, DNA strands do not need to be aligned on the extremities. After alignment, the two DNA strands cut in one or more regions in which they match well and exchange DNA segments. This last phase is present in crossovers for EAs, in which, however, typically no alignment process based on content takes place.

Geometric crossover and geometric mutation [4] are representation-independent search operators that generalise by abstraction many pre-existing search operators for the major representations used in EAs, such as binary strings, real vectors, permutations and syntactic trees. They are defined in geometric terms using the notions of line segment and ball. These notions and the

P. Collet et al. (Eds.): EuroGP 2006, LNCS 3905, pp. 121–132, 2006.

corresponding genetic operators are well-defined once a notion of distance in the search space is well-defined. This way of defining search operators as function of the search space is opposite to the standard way [5] in which the search space is seen as a function of the search operators employed. This viewpoint greatly simplifies the relationship between search operators and fitness landscape and allows different search operators to share the same search space thereby clarifying their roles.

Is biological recombination geometric? In this paper we are able to answer this question in the affirmative by extending the geometric framework mentioned above to sequences under edit distance. This has the remarkable consequence that the theory of geometric crossover applies to biological crossover as well, bridging the gap between biological evolution and artificial evolution. Our results reveal a deep connection between crossover for binary strings and biological recombination, showing that standard EA crossover is less of a caricature than it appears at first.

The paper is organised as follows. In section 2, we introduce the geometric framework. In section 3, we show that in the case of sequences endowed with edit distances geometric crossover is a form of homologous crossover which performs the alignment on sequence contents before mixing genetic material. We prove various properties of this crossover and, in section 4, extend it to weighted alignments and alignment with gaps. In section 5 we argue that biological recombination is geometric and discuss the consequences of this.

2   Geometric Framework

2.1   Geometric Preliminaries

In the following we give necessary preliminary geometric definitions and extend those introduced in [4] and [2]. The following definitions are taken from [6].

The terms *distance* and *metric* denote any real valued function that conforms to the axioms of identity, symmetry and triangular inequality. A simple connected graph is naturally associated to a metric space via its *path metric*: the distance between two nodes in the graph is the length of a shortest path between the nodes. Similarly, an edge-weighted graph with strictly positive weights is naturally associated to a metric space via a *weighted path metric*.

In a metric space (S, d) a *closed ball* is the set of the form $B(x; r) = \{y \in S | d(x, y) \leq r\}$ where $x \in S$ and r is a positive real number called the radius of the ball. A *line segment* (or closed interval) is the set of the form $[x; y] = \{z \in S | d(x, z) + d(z, y) = d(x, y)\}$ where $x, y \in S$ are called extremes of the segment. Metric ball and metric segment generalise the familiar notions of ball and segment in the Euclidean space to any metric space through distance redefinition. These generalised objects look quite different under different metrics. Notice that a metric segment does not coincide to a shortest path connecting its extremes (*geodesic*) as in an Euclidean space. In general, there may be more than one geodesic connecting two extremes; the metric segment is the union of all geodesics.

We assign a structure to the solution set by endowing it with a notion of distance d. $M = (S, d)$ is therefore a solution *space* and $L = (M, g)$ is the corresponding fitness landscape. Notice that d is arbitrary and need not have any particular connection or affinity with the search problem at hand.

2.2   Geometric Crossover Definition

The following definitions are *representation-independent* therefore crossover is well-defined for any representation. It is only *function of the metric d* associated with the search space being based on the notion of metric segment.

Definition 1. *(Image set) The* image set $Im[OP]$ *of a genetic operator OP is the set of all possible offspring produced by OP with non-zero probability.*

Definition 2. *(Geometric crossover) A binary operator is a geometric crossover under the metric d if all offspring are in the segment between its parents.*

Definition 3. *(Uniform geometric crossover) Uniform geometric crossover UX is a geometric crossover where all z laying between parents x and y have the same probability of being the offspring:*

$$f_{UX}(z|x,y) = \frac{\delta(z \in [x;y])}{|[x;y]|}$$

$$Im[UX(x,y)] = \{z \in S | f_{UX}(z|x,y) > 0\} = [x;y].$$

A number of general properties for geometric crossover and mutation have been derived in [4].

2.3   Geometric Crossover Landscape

Geometric operators are defined as functions of the distance associated to the search space. However, the search space does not come with the problem itself. The problem consists only of a fitness function to optimise, that defines what a solution is and how to evaluate it, but it does not give any structure on the solution set. The act of putting a structure over the solution set is part of the search algorithm design and it is a designer's choice. A fitness landscape is the fitness function plus a structure over the solution space. So, for each problem, there is one fitness function but as many fitness landscapes as the number of possible different structures over the solution set. In principle, the designer could choose the structure to assign to the solution set completely independently from the problem at hand. However, because the search operators are defined over such a structure, doing so would make them decoupled from the problem at hand, hence turning the search into something very close to random search.

In order to avoid this one can exploit problem knowledge in the search. This can be achieved by carefully designing the connectivity structure of the fitness landscape. For example, one can study the objective function of the problem and select a neighbourhood structure that couples then distance between solutions and their fitness values. Once this is done problem knowledge can be exploited by search operators to perform better than random search, even if the search operators are problem-independent (as in the case of geometric crossover and mutation).

Under which conditions is a landscape well-searchable by geometric operators? As a rule of thumb, geometric mutation and geometric crossover work well on landscapes where the closer pairs of solutions, the more correlated their fitness values. Of course this is no surprise: the importance of landscape smoothness has been advocated in many different context and has been confirmed in uncountable empirical studies with many neighbourhood search meta-heuristics [7].

3   Geometric Crossover for Sequences

In this section, we extend the geometric framework to the case of sequences. In particular we will focus on edit distances that associate with sequence homology.

3.1   Preliminaries: Sequences, Edit Distance and Alignments

A sequence is a variable length string of characters. In particular, DNA strands are sequences of characters from the alphabet $\Sigma_{dna} = \{a, c, t, g\}$. The *edit distance* between two sequences is defined as the minimum number of edit operations – insertions, deletions, and substitutions – needed to transform the first string into the second. The edit distance is a metric in that it respects all the metric axioms. Hence, the space of sequences endowed with edit distance is a metric space. There are a number of extensions to the simple edit distance such as weighted edit distance, block-edit distance, reversals and transpositions distances (see Sections 4 and 5 for a discussion on their use). The edit distance between two sequences is a measure of their syntactic dissimilarity. This syntactic dissimilarity is intimately connected with the notion of sequence alignment.

An *alignment* of two sequences is obtained by first appropriately inserting spaces (which we represent with dashes), either into or at the ends of the two sequences, and then placing the two resulting sequences one above the other so that every character or space in one sequence is aligned with a character or space in the other sequence. The *score of an alignment* is the number of aligned characters that are different in the two sequences. There may be more that one optimum alignment between two sequences. The score of an optimum alignment of two sequences equals their edit distance. Changing the scoring system, one can obtain optimal alignments associated to weighted edit distances and block-edit distances. Edit distances and optimal alignments can be computed efficiently using dynamic programming.

The (edit) *transcript* T associated to an alignment q is a vector that specifies what edit move to apply to parent 1 to reach parent 2 for each position. For each alignment q there is only one transcript T and vice versa. For example, $T = (\texttt{RIMDMDMMI})$ and $q = \begin{pmatrix} \texttt{v-intner-} \\ \texttt{wri-t-ers} \end{pmatrix}$, where R, I and D stand for replace, insert, delete and match, respectively, while M is a just place holder.

3.2   Homologous Crossover and Geometric Crossover

Homologous crossover for sequences has been introduced by [8] in the context of linear GP. We formalise and generalise it, we prove that it is geometric crossover and then list some of its properties.

Definition 4. *(Alignment-based homologous crossover operators)*

1. Let Q be the set of all optimal alignments of two sequences S_1 and S_2 under simple edit distance. Homologous crossover picks a random optimal alignment $q \in Q$ with a given probability distribution over Q. Let $\overline{S}_1$ and $\overline{S}_2$ be the two sequences aligned with gaps according to q.
2. Let l be the length of q and m be a mask drawn from $\{0,1\}$ with a given probability distribution. m specifies for each position of q from which parent to copy the corresponding character to produce an aligned offspring $\overline{S}_3$
3. The actual offspring S_3 is obtained by remove the dashes from $\overline{S}_3$.

Example 1. If $S_1 = $ agcacaca and $S_2 = $ acacacta and the chosen optimal alignment is $q = \begin{pmatrix} \text{agcacac-a} \\ \text{a-cacacta} \end{pmatrix}$ then $l = 9$, $\overline{S}_1 = $ agcacac-a and $\overline{S}_2 = $ a-cacacta. If $m = 111100000$ we obtain the offspring $\overline{S}_3 = $ a-cacac-a. After gap removal we obtain $S_3 = $ acacaca.

Theorem 1. *All alignment-based homologous crossover operators are geometric crossovers under edit distance.*

Proof. An optimal edit transcript T contains a smallest set E of edit moves to transform u in v. $|E| = d(u,v)$. The edit moves in E are independent because they can be applied in any order and transform u into v. Any intermediate sequence z obtained by applying a subset $E' \subseteq E$ of edit moves to u is on a shortest path between u and v because z is $d(u,z) = |E'|$ moves away from u and $d(z,v) = |E \setminus E'|$ moves to v hence $d(u,z) + d(z,v) = d(u,v)$. A mask m selects a subset of edit moves $E_m \subseteq E$ from the transcript T to apply to u and produce the offspring z. Hence z is on the shortest path.

Theorem 2. *Every sequence O in the segment between two sequences P1 and P2 under edit distance is reachable by homologous alignment-based crossover applied to the parent sequences P1 and P2.*

Proof. We need to prove that for each $O \in [P_1, P_2]_{ed}$ there exists an optimal alignment q of P1 and P2 and a mask m that applied to q gives O. We prove it by constructing q and m given any O.

If $O \in [P_1, P_2]_{e}d$ then there exists a shortest path sp between P1 and P2 in the search space of sequences endowed with the edit distance such that $O \in sp$. Then there exists a transcript T such as all the edit moves in T are the same of the set of edit moves that generate sp. The transcript T may comprise also one or more M characters that do not correspond to any edit move. The transcript T is optimal by construction because the number of edit moves in T (non-M characters) is exactly $ed(P1, P2)$.

Given T, $P1$ and $P2$, it is possible to build the unique alignment q of $P1$ and $P2$ associated with T. The alignment q is optimal because T is optimal. Consider now the crossover mask m of the same length of the transcript T obtained by setting at 1 the loci corresponding to those edit moves in the transcript T that in the path sp transform $P1$ into O. The crossover mask m applied to the optimal alignment q produces O.

Theorems 1 and 2 establish that a crossover is an alignment-based homologous crossover if and only if it is a geometric crossover under simple edit distance.

3.3 Optimal Alignments and Segment Subsets

The family of crossovers introduced in the previous section can be seen as an extension to sequences of the family of alignment-based crossovers for fixed-length binary strings. [4] proved that for binary strings, uniform crossover, where crossover masks are obtained by flipping n times a unbiased coin, picks offspring with uniform probability distribution on the line segment between parents under Hamming distance. In this section we introduce a generalisation of uniform crossover based on masks for sequences and show that, unlike the binary string case, this crossover, surprisingly, does not pick offspring uniformly in the segment between parents under edit distances.

Definition 5. *(Uniform alignment-based homologous crossover) Uniform homologous crossover is an alignment-based crossover operator that chooses optimal alignments and crossover masks with uniform probability.*

In Table 1, we enumerate all possible offspring under homologous crossover of the sequences "vint" and "writ". For these sequences there are three possible optimal alignments. The edit distance between the sequences is 3. This can be seen also from the edit transcript associated to each optimal alignment in which there are 3 non-M characters. These characters describe the edit operations and the location of their application on the alignment to transform the first sequence into the second one. In the first column, all the possible crossover masks are shown. For space limitations we report only the bits corresponding to the three non-M symbols, thereby obtaining 8 effective crossover masks. The entry at the intersection of a row (effective crossover mask) and a column (optimal alignment) contains the offspring obtained by the application of the mask on the alignment. Alignment-based uniform crossover returns any of the offspring in the table at random with uniform probability ($\frac{1}{24}$). However, some offspring can be generated by more than one alignment, and so they have higher chances to be picked. "vint" and "writ", for example, are produced with a probability $\frac{3}{24}$, while "vit", "wrint", "vrit" and "wint" are returned with probability $\frac{2}{24}$.

The image set of an optimal alignment q is the set of offspring that can be generated by homologous crossover using any mask m over q.

Theorem 3. *Consider the image sets $Im(q_1) \ldots Im(q_n)$ of homologous crossover applied to all optimal alignment $q_1 \ldots q_n$ of the sequences $P1$ and $P2$.*

Table 1. Possible offspring under uniform alignment-based homologous crossover

	Alignment 1	Alignment 2	Alignment 3
mask	mm*m*	mm*m*	mmm*
transcript	IRMDM	RIMDM	RRRM
parent 1	-vint	v-int	vint
parent 2	wri-t	wri-t	writ
000	-vint	v-int	vint
001	-vi-t	v-i-t	viit
010	-rint	vrint	vrnt
011	-ri-t	vri-t	vrit
100	wvint	w-int	wint
101	wvi-t	w-i-t	wiit
110	wrint	wrint	wrnt
111	wri-t	wri-t	writ

The union of $Im(q_1) \ldots Im(q_n)$ is $[P1, P2]$ but they do not form a partition of $[P1, P2]$.

Proof. For theorem 1, the image set of any optimal alignment is subset of the segment. For theorem 2, any sequence z in the segment $[P1, P2]$ can be generated by homologous crossover. Hence, there must exist at least an alignment such as its image set includes z. This means that every point in the segment is at least in $Im(q_i)$, hence the union of all $Im(q_i)$ is the segment $[P1, P2]$. Proof by counterexample: example 2 shows that all $Im(q_i)$ do not form a partition of the segment $[P1, P2]$ because their intersections are non-empty.

Theorem 4. *Uniform alignment-based homologous crossover is not the uniform geometric crossover under edit distance.*

Proof. Proof by counterexample: example 2 shows that the frequency of some offspring sequences under uniform homologous crossover is higher than others. So the probability is not uniformly distributed over the segment.

The non-uniformity of this crossover is the result of the same offspring sequence being generated by multiple different optimal alignments. Parent sequences, for example, are in this category because they can be generated by all optimal alignments using masks 0...0 and 1...1. Other offspring sequences can be generated more than once when two optimal transcripts share non-M characters at the same positions. For example, if two transcripts have a D at position 1, then the mask 0X...X where X...X is either 0...0 or 1...1 will produce the same offspring with both alignments. The mask 1X...X will have the same effect.

3.4 Bounds on Offspring Size

In this section we explore how offspring and parent sizes are related in homologous crossover.

Theorem 5. *Given two parent sequences P1 and P2 of length l_1 and l_2 with $l_1 \leq l_2$ and edit distance ed, the length l_3 of any offspring sequence O obtained by homologous recombination is bounded as follows:*

1. *Edit distance ed known: $(l_1 + l_2 - ed)/2 \leq l_3 \leq (l_1 + l_2 + ed)/2$*
2. *Edit distance ed not known: $l_1/2 \leq l_3 \leq l_1/2 + l_2$*
3. *Parents of same length $l_1 = l_2 = l$: $l/2 \leq l_3 \leq 3l/2$*
4. *Non-empty parents imply non-empty offspring*

Proof. Trivial edit distance bounds: (i) $d(a,b) \geq |l(a) - l(b)|$ and (ii) $d(a,b) \leq max(l(a), l(b))$. From bound (i) applied to P1 and P3: $d(P1, P3) \geq |l1 - l3|$ that breaks into two cases: (1) $l_1 - l_3 \leq 0 \rightarrow l_1 \leq l_3 \leq d(P1, P3) + l_1$ (worst case upper bound) (2) $l_1 - l_3 \geq 0 \rightarrow l_1 - d(P1, P3) \leq l_3 \leq l_1$ (worst case lower bound). Analogously, applying bound (i) to P2 and P3 we obtain other two alternative cases: (3) $l_2 - l_3 \leq 0 \rightarrow l_2 \leq l_3 \leq d(P2, P3) + l_2$ (worst case upper bound) (4) $l_2 - l_3 \geq 0 \rightarrow l_2 - d(P2, P3) \leq l_3 \leq l_2$ (worst case lower bound).

Let us consider the upper bound for l_3. Both the conditions (1) and (3) must hold true, so $2l_3 \leq d(P1, P3) + d(P2, P3) + l_1 + l_2$. For all P3: $d(P1, P3) + d(P2, P3) = d(P1, P2) = ed$. Hence for all P3: $l_3 \leq (l_1 + l_2 + ed)/2$. If the distance ed between parents P1 and P2 is unknown we can use bound (ii) to bound it: $ed \leq max(l_1, l_2) \rightarrow ed \leq l_2$. Hence for all P3 in the worst case we have: $l_3 \leq l_1/2 + l_2$. In case $l_1 = l_2 = l$ we have for all P3: $l_3 \leq 3l/2$.

Let us consider the lower bound for l_3. Both the conditions (2) and (4) must hold true, so $l_1 + l_2 - (d(P1, P3) + d(P2, P3)) \leq 2l_3$. For all P3: $d(P1, P3) + d(P2, P3) = d(P1, P2) = ed$. Hence for all P3: $(l_1 + l_2 - ed)/2 \leq l_3$. If the distance ed between parents P1 and P2 is unknown we can use bound (ii) to bound it: $ed \leq max(l_1, l_2) \rightarrow ed \leq l_2$. Hence for all P3 in the worst case we have: $l_1/2 \leq l_3$. In case $l_1 = l_2 = l$ we have for all P3: $l/2 \leq l_3$.

Homologous crossover cannot produce empty offspring from non-empty parents. This can be shown by using the second inequality: $l_1/2 \leq l_3 \leq l_1/2 + l_2$. Independently from the distance between parents the minimum lower bound of the length of any offspring is half of the length of the shortest parent. When such parent is not empty ($l_1 \geq 1$) then $l_3 \geq 1/2$. Since the length is an integer we have $l_3 \geq 1$. So even for parents of length 1 the offspring are non-empty.

Under geometric crossover, the more different the parents are, the more "unrelated", or "innovative", the offspring become. From the previous theorem, the size of the offspring is bounded by: $(l_1 + l_2 - ed)/2 \leq l_3 \leq (l_1 + l_2 + ed)/2$. Hence, the bigger the difference between the parents the bigger the range of the size of possible offspring. Note, however, that when using weighted edit distances it is possible to create situations were an empty offspring can be returned.

4   Extensions of Homologous Crossover

4.1   Weighted Edit Distances and Geometric Crossover

Extending homologous crossover to the case of weighted edit distances is crucial to capture more realistic details of real biological sequences. Weighted edit distances allow to specify relative preferences in the alignment before recombination such as character mismatches vs. sequence interruptions (spaces), positional preferences (for example, matches at the extremities vs. matches at the centre of the sequences) or preferences on the mismatching pairs (for example, preferring a mismatch (a, t) to a mismatch (a, c)).

The following theorem is a very general and useful result that connects weighted edit moves for any solution representation and metric spaces.[1]

Theorem 6. *Any weighted edit distance with strictly positive weights on edit moves is a metric.*

Proof. A space of configurations endowed with an edit distance with strictly positive weights can be represented by a weighted graph in which nodes are syntactic configurations and weighted edges represent (reversible) weighted edit moves transforming one configuration into neighbour configuration. Any graph with strictly positive weights on edges is a metric space [6] hence an edit distance with strictly positive weights on edit moves, that is isomorphic to such a graph, is a metric.

The cost of a weighted alignment is the sum of the weights associated to each character alignment. The weight of each couple of characters is symmetric and matching characters have weight 0. An optimal alignment is an alignment with minimal cost. The cost of the optimal weighted alignment between two sequences equals their weighted edit distance where the edit moves allowed correspond to the set of couple of characters corresponding with their alignment weights.

The following theorem extend the geometricity result of homologous crossover to weighted edit distances and weighted alignments.

Theorem 7. *Alignment-based homologous crossover on the optimal alignments under weighted edit distance d_w is geometric crossover under d_w.*

Proof. An optimal edit transcript T contains a set E of edit moves to transform u in v whose cost $w(E) = \sum_{e \in E} w_e$ is minimal. The weighted edit distance is $d_w(u, v) = w(E)$. The edit moves in E are independent because they can be applied in any order and transform u into v. Any intermediate sequence z obtained by applying a subset $E' \subseteq E$ of edit moves to u is on a shortest weighted path between u and v because $d_w(u, z) = w(E')$ and $d(z, v) = w(E \setminus E') = w(E) - w(E')$ hence $d(u, z) + d(z, v) = d(u, v)$. A mask m selects a subset of edit moves $E_m \subseteq E$ from the transcript T to apply to u and produce the offspring z. Hence z is on the shortest path.

4.2 Gaps and Geometric Crossover

In this section we extend homologous crossover to the case of edit distances based on replacement move and a block ins/del move. This edit distance allows

---

[1] This is a fairly simple result. However, it appears that this is not been proved in published literature, leading to significant confusion, particularly in the bio-informatics literature, in which edit distances and scoring matrices are extensively used.

to specify preference to few big gaps against many small gaps in the alignment before recombination and allows to model loops in the alignments.

Theorem 8. *Alignment-based homologous crossover with one locus for each entire gap on the optimal alignments under weighted edit distance with block moves d_{bw} is geometric crossover under d_{bw} with convex weight gap model.*

Proof. Let us consider a weighted block ins/del edit move such as its weights depends only on the length of the block in a way that shorter blocks have smaller cost per length unit: $l_1 < l_2 \rightarrow w(l_1)/l_1 > w(l_2)/l_2$. An optimal edit transcript must necessarily comprise the largest block ins/del edit move. The crossover mask has to treat each edit move as a unity: for block edit moves there must be only one locus in the crossover mask. The rest follows from theorem 7.

5   Bridging Natural and Artificial Evolution

In this section we discuss the feasibility of homologous crossover as a model of biological recombination and its implications.

Is biological recombination geometric? Most of pre-existing recombination operators for the most-used representations are geometric. So this geometric property unifies by abstraction across representations the notion of "crossoverness" emerged experimentally over the years. All geometric crossovers do the same type of search (convex search). This question if answered affirmatively would show a deep unity in the way EAs and biological evolution search and would allow to apply the geometric framework to study both natural and artificial evolution jointly casting a computational and geometric perspective on natural evolution.

Many details of real biological recombination are unknown and it is focus of active research to elicit them. There are various models for studying different aspects of biological evolution at different levels of granularity.

At the genetic level, the model of homologous recombination based on fixed-size strings used in population genetics, is a simple extension of the traditional crossover for binary strings to the multi-valued case and it is geometric under Hamming distance. Unequal crossover at a genetic level happens when the homologous alignment of the strands is not perfect. This can be the result of an error in the alignment due to environmental noise (this can be considered as a mutation) or being one of the possible best inexact alignments under edit distance at the level of genes. In this case unequal crossover would be geometric.

The reason why strands tend to align according to the edit distance can be understood at a molecular level. Our working hypothesis is that an edit distance, weighted and based on edit moves such as insertion/deletion (to model frame-shift), replacement (to model base mismatch), block-insertion/deletion (to model folds/loops), block-reversal (to model subsequence inversion) and block-transposition (to model subsequence transposition), is expressive enough to model the resulting configuration obtained at the equilibrium of all the forces that lead to the inexact homologous alignment of two chromosomes at a molecular level (before crossing over). The notion of minimum distance connects naturally with the notion of optimal alignment (best trade-off among all forces involved, or chemical equilibrium) of two macromolecules (chromosomes) that, as any other chemical reaction, tends to evolve toward the state of "minimum free energy". In summary:

1. the geometric crossovers associated with edit distances naturally capture the notion of homology, or inexact alignment based on the sequences contents.
2. there is a natural parallel between weighted edit distances and DNA pairing up at the molecular level because the weights on edit moves can be interpreted in chemical terms as attraction and repulsion forces.
3. there are a variety of edit distances that allow to show that pre-existing model of biological crossovers and many variants are still geometric. This suggests that assuming that biological recombination is geometric is reasonable even in the lack of full-knowledge about all its details.

Is the natural landscape smooth? The natural adaptive landscape of a population is not static but changes over time in response to environmental changes and in response to the change in the population composition adapting to the new environment due to evolutionary forces. Evolution (adaptation) happens when the adaptive landscape is non-flat.

Despite the inherent dynamical character of the natural adaptive landscape, it has a smooth trend: most of the mutations are neutral [9], do not affect the phenotype or quasi-neutral in that they affect the phenotype marginally and so its fitness. Very rarely a single mutation is lethal, creating "cracks" in the landscape. The landscape may be rugged and may present various neutral paths but the overall trend is smooth and when evolution (adaptation) is in progress, non-flat. Hence, we can safely state that the closer genotypes under edit distance (mutation) the more correlated their fitness values. Indeed, this is the same principle on which bio-informatics is firmly based upon: similarity of genotypes allows us to infer similarity in the phenotype (hence, in fitness) without doing any experimental work except searching databases of known genotypes by homology [1].

Geometric biological operator + smooth natural landscape = quick adaptation. What is the fitness function to optimise in case of natural evolution? Natural evolution, seen as a search algorithm, is trying to optimise the fitness function that is obtained from the adaptive landscape by removing the space structure (see section 2). While doing this optimisation, the fitness function is constantly changing, because the adaptive landscape is constantly changing under the effect of population change due to evolution (optimisation) itself. The evolution (optimisation) ends when the fitness landscape becomes flat and the fitness function becomes constant. This means that the population is completely adapted to the environment. Hence, the performance of biological evolution, seen as a search algorithm, is in terms of speed of adaptation.

If one accepts that (i) biological recombination is geometric under edit distance and that (ii) the natural landscape has a smooth trend then, since smoothness of the landscape is the condition we need to enforce to the landscape to be well-searched by geometric crossover and geometric mutation, the logical conclusion is that biological recombination and mutation are well-matched with the natural fitness landscape. So their performance in terms of adaptation is expected to be much better than pure random search. This is to say that biological evolution is very efficient at doing adaptation.[2]

6   Conclusions

In this paper we have extended the geometric framework to the important case of sequences. We have given a number of theoretical results and started investigating the hypothesis that biological recombination is geometric and discussed its consequences.

References

1. D. Gusfield. Algorithms on Strings, Trees and Sequences. *Cambridge University Press, 1997.*
2. A. Moraglio, R. Poli. Geometric landscape of homologous crossover for syntactic trees. In *Proceedings of CEC 2005*, pages 427–434.
3. A. Moraglio, R. Poli. Topological crossover for the permutation representation. In *Workshop on theory of representations at GECCO 2005.*
4. A. Moraglio, R. Poli. Topological interpretation of crossover. In *Proceedings of GECCO 2004*, pages 1377–1388.
5. T. Jones. Evolutionary Algorithms, Fitness Landscapes and Search. *PhD dissertation, University of New Mexico, 1995.*
6. M. Deza, M. Laurent. Geometry of cuts and metrics. *Springer, 1991.*
7. P.M. Pardalos, M.G.C. Resende. Handbook of Applied Optimization. *Oxford University Press, 2002.*
8. M.D. Platel, M. Clergue, P. Collard. Maximum homologous crossover for linear genetic programming. In *Proceedings of EuroGP 2003*, pages 194–203.
9. M. Kimura. Neutral theory of molecular evolution. *Cambridge University Press, 1983.*

---

[2] This offers an answer to the anti-evolutionist William Dembski that has used the no free lunch theorems to criticise the theory of evolution, stating that the No Free Lunch theorems demonstrate that evolution is no better than random chance at selecting optimal outcomes.

Incentive Method to Handle Constraints in Evolutionary Algorithms with a Case Study

Edward Tsang and Nanlin Jin

Department of Computer Science, University of Essex,
Colchester CO4 3SQ, United Kingdom
{edward, njin}@essex.ac.uk

Abstract. This paper introduces Incentive Method to handle both hard and soft constraints in an evolutionary algorithm for solving some multi-constraint optimization problems. The Incentive Method uses hard and soft constraints to help allocating heuristic search effort more effectively. The main idea is to modify the objective fitness function by awarding differential incentives according to the defined qualitative preferences, to solution sets which are divided by their satisfaction to constraints. It does not exclude the right to access search spaces that violate some or even all constraints. We test this technique through its application on generating solutions for a classic infinite-horizon extensive-form game. It is solved by an Evolutionary Algorithm incorporated by Incentive method. Experimental results are compared with results from a penalty method and from a non-constraint setting. Statistic analysis suggests that Incentive Method is more effective than the other two techniques for this specific problem.

1 Introduction

Many optimization problems involve constraints. Hard constraints describe feasibility of solutions. Soft constraints describe preferences, which often encode our partial knowledge about good solutions. The best known constraints handling techniques used in evolutionary algorithms include: penalty methods; repair algorithms; multi-objective functions; and co-evolutionary models. The penalty method, penalizes infeasible (or unfavorable) individuals. In general, it transforms a constrained optimization problem $max\ f(x)$ subject to $w(x) \leq C$ to an unconstrained problem $max\ Y(x) = f(x) - Penalty(x)$ by defining the Penalty function. A death penalty method would reject infeasible individuals. Repair methods use domain specific operators to modify infeasible individuals to feasible ones. They have been used for solving many combinatorial optimization problems.

In some problems, candidate solutions can be classified into three qualitatively different sets: feasible, infeasible and preferred. No matter how many soft constraints a candidate solution satisfies, its satisfaction to hard constraints still has the first priority. Those candidate solutions that satisfy hard constraints, are preferable differently by soft constraints. For such problems, it is sometimes difficult to define penalties for penalty methods or to repair solutions to satisfy hard constraints, while taking soft constraints into consideration. It is also hard

P. Collet et al. (Eds.): EuroGP 2006, LNCS 3905, pp. 133–144, 2006.

to decide which of the many soft constraints can be sacrificed to ensure the hard constraint to be satisfied.

This paper presents Incentive Method as a complementary method to penalty and repair methods, hybrid methods possible, for handling multi constraints in evolutionary algorithms. By introducing Incentive Method, we attempt to deal with each type of constraints individually, by differentially rewarding individuals depending on the level of constraints they satisfy. Moreover, Incentive Method is designed to enable us to integrate extra problem-specific knowledge into fitness functions. Constraints are used to guide the search, as opposed to being seen as obstacles to the search, a view deeply rooted in constraint satisfaction research [7].

We examine the performance of Incentive Method on an infinite extensive-form game: Basic Alternating-Offers Bargaining Problem. Firstly, experimental outcomes for this application by using Evolutionary Algorithms integrated by Incentive Method will be measured against game-theoretic solutions; Secondly, such experimental outcomes will further be compared with outcomes by a Penalty Method and by an evolutionary algorithm without constraint handling technique.

2   The Incentive Method

An optimization problem Φ, has hard constraint(s) that defines feasibility of solutions, and soft constraint(s) that defines preference properties in solutions. Let S be the search space and $E \subseteq S$ be the set of feasible solutions. Further, let $P \subseteq E$ be the set of feasible solutions that violate no soft constraints at all. The objective is to find $x \in S$ to optimize $f(x)$ where x can be in the form of a number, a vector or a computer program.

Definition 1: Incentive Method

$$R(x) = \begin{cases} f(x) + C & \text{if } x \in P \\ g(x) & \text{if } x \in E \cap x \notin P \\ h(x) & \text{if } x \notin E \end{cases} \tag{1}$$

To formulate the above problem Φ under Incentive Method, one must define functions g and h for evaluating the fitness of an individual. Functions g and h must satisfy the condition $h(x) < g(x) < f(x) + C$ where C is a constant. Note that C is not strictly necessary; it is included so that g and h do not have to return negative values to meet the above condition. Problem-dependent knowledge is required to define $g(x)$ and $h(x)$ in Incentive Method. Effective definitions of $g(x)$ and $h(x)$ will help the search to allocate its effort more effectively. Therefore, the definition of $g(x)$ and $h(x)$ can be seen as a burden on users, but it can also be seen as an opportunity for channeling domain knowledge into the search method.

The conditions in Equation (1) make sure that solutions sets are strictly ordered, so that no matter how many soft constraints a feasible solution violates, it is still better than an infeasible one. A solution x that violates no constraints at all is preferred to a solution x' that violates one or some soft constraints, no matter how poor x is, or how good x' is, according to f. The incentive Method does not prevent a search from considering infeasible regions of the search space. This is because infeasible solutions may contain valuable genetic material that is needed for finding global optimal solutions. However, the fitness measure will discourage candidate solutions in infeasible regions to produce offspring.

3   A Bargaining Problem

An optimization problem with both hard and soft constraints is chosen as a test-bed to examine the quality and performance of Incentive Method. It is a classic game, the Alternating-Offers bargaining problem which can be formulated as an optimization problem and it has both hard and soft constraints.

The Basic Alternating-Offers Bargaining Problem modeled and solved by Rubinstein [5] describes a bargaining scenario wherein participant A starts by making a proposal to his counterpart B on dividing a cake $\pi = 1$ at time of 0. B has options to accept this offer immediately or to make a counter offer at time 1. Similarly, participant A can choose to accept the offer immediately, or to make a counter offer at time 2. The bargaining process ends once a proposal is accepted by the counterpart. For convenience, we denote an offer x_i proposed by player i for himself and $x_j = 1 - x_i$ for the other.

An offer simply takes the form of a percentage of the cake, which is a number between 0 and 1. For the game to be interesting, utility deteriorates over time for both players, which motivates the players to make agreements as soon as possible. For the same share, it is worth more in round t than in round $t + 1$, round $t + 2$, etc. Player i's discount factor $\delta_i \in (0,1)$ is his bargaining cost per time interval, $\delta_i = e^{-r_i}$ where r_i is the player i's discount rate. If an agreement is reached at time t, the payoff p_i gained by player i who has a share x_i from this agreement is determined by the payoff function: $p_i = x_i \delta_i^t$. This problem's game-theoretic solution is that the first player obtains:

$$x_A^* = \frac{1 - \delta_B}{1 - \delta_A \delta_B} \tag{2}$$

The second player obtains the rest of cake, $(1 - x_A^*)$. This solution is called the *Perfect Equilibrium Partition* (P.E.P). Game-theoretic analysis and proof can be found in [5] and [4].

4   Experiments Design

4.1   Overview of Experimental Design

We solve this bargaining problem by evolutionary computation, specially co-evolution algorithm. The goal is to evolve competitive strategies. Co-evolution has been demonstrated to be effective for solving finite extensive-form games by

Koza [1] and a repeated normal-form game by Miller [2]. Tsang and Li [6] used a constrained objective function in a co-evolutionary system EDDIE/FGP, which aids investors to seek dealing rules in financial market.

In the evolutionary system for this problem, players are assumed to learn bargaining strategies through trial-and-error playing. It is a two-population co-evolving system, each population representing a player. They are called Population A for the player A and Population B for the player B. This enables different strategies to be evolved as the first player may have a first-move advantage [4]. It also allows extensibility for potential differences between the two players (for example, one player may have more information than the other) in future work. Each population consists of a set of individuals, each of which is the evolving part of a bargaining strategy.

During the co-evolution process, every individual of the population A bargains with every individual in the population B, if the individual meets the basic criteria (hard constraint) that it makes offers and counteroffers between 0 and 1. The game fitness of an individual is the average payoff of its corresponding strategy's bargaining outcomes. On the occasion when an individual does not fit the basic criteria, a value based on its structure is calculated as (part of) its fitness (see Subsection 4.3).

Individuals of a population independently undergo natural selection based on their performance (fitness). Better performed individuals have higher probability to be taken as "raw materials" which will be genetically modified in order to breed new individuals for the forthcoming generation. Newly created individuals will bargain with the updated counterpart population that has gone through a similar evolutionary process. Note that the same genetic operators (selection method, crossover rate and mutation rate) are employed for both populations. Co-evolution pushes individuals of both populations to continue improving over time.

4.2   Genetic Programming Representation

Since strategies are represented by functions in theoretic solutions, we use Genetic Programming (GP) [1] which is an easy way to cope with function-based representation. Although Rubinstein's solution [5] does not involve time at all, time can be an important element in real life bargaining. To limit our search space, we assume that player i bids b_i at time t:

$$b_i = g_i \times (1 - r_i)^t \tag{3}$$

where g_i is a function generated by genetic programming, an individual in a population. The part of $(1 - r_i)^t$ guarantees that players bid decreasing shares of the cake while time elapses, which is considered to be practical. A g_i is constructed with the function set $\{+, -, \times$ and $\div$ (protected) $\}$ and the terminal set $\{1, -1, \delta_i, \delta_j \}$. By changing the function and terminal sets, we could model different strategies. For example, if adding time t into the terminal set, we would allow the system to generate time-dependent strategies beyond what is restricted by Equation (3).

A strategy determines what action (acceptance or making a new proposal) it takes at time t. The following rule determines whether a strategy s_i accepts or rejects a proposal $(1 - x_j, x_j)$ at time t:

$$s_i = \begin{cases} accept : x_i = 1 - x_j \\ \quad if\ (1 - x_j)\delta_i^t \geq b_i(t+1)\delta_i^{t+1} \\ counteroffer\ at\ (t+1) : x_i = b_i(t+1) \\ \quad if\ (1 - x_j)\delta_i^t < b_i(t+1)\delta_i^{t+1} \end{cases} \tag{4}$$

This means that when a player with strategy s_i receives an offer $(1 - x_j)$ from his opponent who asks x_j for herself, he will compare the payoff $(1 - x_j)\delta_i^t$ of this offer with the payoff that he will get should his counter offer $b_i(t+1)$ be accepted in the next round. If the later is not higher than the former, then the offer will be accepted.

4.3   Design of Fitness Function Using Incentive Method

Success of evolutionary algorithms relies on appropriate fitness measures that evaluate performance of individuals. In order to define $g(x)$ and $h(x)$ in Equation (1), favorable features of solutions in the above problem are studied. Incentives are defined based on these features. The alternating-offer bargaining problem has a hard constraint regarding feasibility: any proposal of division of the cake must be within the size of cake. Any offer that does not obey this constraint is infeasible. Besides, the common sense tells that a player has a relatively higher discount factor (lower cost) is in a stronger position to bargain. This is because each round of delay would cost him less than his opponent. We list the hard constraint *C1* and two soft constraints *C2* and *C3*:

C 1. Any proposal on the partition of a cake should be a value within the range $x_i \in (0, 1]$;

C 2. Everything else being equal, the higher discount factor a player i has, the larger share x_i he can obtain.

C 3. Everything else being equal, the higher discount factor the opponent j has, the lower share x_i a player i can get.

Sensibility Measure and Evaluation of Attribution. Obviously not all genetic programs meet the above constraints, especially when the genetic programs are created randomly at the initial generation. *Sensibility Measure SM* is invented to measure whether a genetic program characterizes *C2* and/or *C3*. Let $g_i(p, q)$ be the instantiation of the program g_i with δ_i being substituted by p and δ_j being substituted by q. With an arbitrary real numbers $\alpha \in (0, 1)$.

Definition 2: Sensibility Measure of a genetic program g_i

$$SM_i(\delta_i, \delta_j, \alpha) = \begin{cases} -\frac{g_i(\delta_i, \delta_j) - g_i(\delta_i \times (1+\alpha), \delta_j)}{g_i(\delta_i, \delta_j)} \\ \quad if\ \delta_i \times (1+\alpha) < 1; \\ \frac{g_i(\delta_i, \delta_j) - g_i(\delta_i \times (1-\alpha), \delta_j)}{g_i(\delta_i, \delta_j)} \\ \quad if\ \delta_i \times (1+\alpha) \geq 1; \end{cases} \tag{5}$$

$$SM_j(\delta_i, \delta_j, \alpha) = \begin{cases} \dfrac{g_i(\delta_i,\delta_j)-g_i(\delta_i,\delta_j \times (1+\alpha))}{g_i(\delta_i,\delta_j)} \\ \qquad \text{if } \delta_j \times (1+\alpha) < 1; \\ -\dfrac{g_i(\delta_i,\delta_j)-g_i(\delta_i,\delta_j \times (1-\alpha))}{g_i(\delta_i,\delta_j)} \\ \qquad \text{if } \delta_j \times (1+\alpha) \geq 1; \end{cases} \tag{6}$$

SM describes $C2$ and $C3$ in a mathematic manner: when player i's discount factor increases from δ_i to $(\delta_i \times (1+\alpha)) \in (0,1)$, the genetic program g_i that positively correlates to δ_i should be rewarded. The amount of reward depends on the degree of the increment from $g_i(\delta_i, \delta_j)$ to $g_i(\delta_i \times (1+\alpha), \delta_j)$. In the case of α is too large to make $\delta_i \times (1+\alpha)$ satisfy the definition $\delta \in (0,1)$, we decrease the discount factor δ_i to $\delta_i \times (1-\alpha)$. The value of g_i should decrease accordingly. So $g_i(\delta_i, \delta_j)$ should be larger than $g_i(\delta_i \times (1-\alpha), \delta_j)$. When taken account into the opponent j's discount factor, the genetic program g_i that negatively correlates to δ_j should be rewarded. $SM_j(\delta_i, \delta_j, \alpha)$ returns such rewards. In short, positive values returned from both $SM_i(\delta_i, \delta_j, \alpha)$ and $SM_j(\delta_i, \delta_j, \alpha)$ mean that the genetic program g_i satisfies the constraints $C2$ and $C3$, respectively.

Definition 3: Evaluation of Attribution (ATT) defines the incentive value to a genetic program g_i whose Sensibility Measures are SM_i and SM_j. The incentive is calculated by g_i's satisfaction to constraints.

$$ATT(i) = \begin{cases} 1 & \text{if } SM_i(\delta_i, \delta_j, \alpha) \geq 0 \\ -e^{\frac{1}{SM_i(\delta_i,\delta_j,\alpha)}} & \\ & \text{if } SM_i(\delta_i, \delta_j, \alpha) < 0 \end{cases} \tag{7}$$

$$ATT(j) = \begin{cases} 1 & \text{if } SM_j(\delta_i, \delta_j, \alpha) \geq 0 \\ -e^{\frac{1}{SM_j(\delta_i,\delta_j,\alpha)}} & \\ & \text{if } SM_j(\delta_i, \delta_j, \alpha) < 0 \end{cases} \tag{8}$$

When SM_i or SM_j returns positive values, meaning that they satisfy soft constraints, $ATT(i)$ or $ATT(j)$ is the highest incentive 1. When SM_i or SM_j return negative values, ATT gives an incentive less than 0. The exact incentive value depends on how close SM_i or SM_j is to 0. The closer SM_i or SM_j to 0, the more reward is given by the $ATT(i)$ or $ATT(j)$. Here we adopt the function $-e^{\frac{1}{SM}}$ to control this incentive rewarding algorithm. For an negative value of SM, ATT is always negative in the range between $(-1,0)$. For $SM \rightarrow 0^-$, ATT goes quickly to near 0. For $SM < -1$ and $SM \rightarrow -\infty$, ATT goes quickly to -1. The function $-e^{\frac{1}{SM}}$ is problem-dependent and is not the only way to implement the idea of incentive rewarding. It is chosen here as its simple structure.

Fitness Function. A genetic program g_i that satisfies the constraints $C1$ is converted to a bargaining strategy s_i by the function (3) and (4). Strategies pair-wisely play the alternating-offers bargaining game.

Definition 4: Game Fitness $GF(s_i)$ of s_i is the average payoff of a strategy s_i gained from bargaining against every bargaining strategy in its opponent j's population which has a set (S_y) consisting of the number of n bargaining strategies where the integer n is an experimental parameter.

$$GF(s_i) = \frac{\sum_{j \in S_y} p_{s_i \to s_j}}{n} \qquad (9)$$

where $p_{s_i \to s_j}$ is the payoff obtained by the strategy s_i from an agreement with the strategy s_j. $GF(s_i)$ estimates the bargaining competence of the strategy s_i in its generation.

Definition 5: Fitness Function $F(i)$ incorporated with Incentive Method determines the fitness of an individual g_i whose corresponding strategy is s_i, whose Sensibility Measures are SM_i and SM_j and whose Evaluation of Attribution are $ATT(i)$ and $ATT(j)$.

$$F(i) = \begin{cases} GF(s_i) + 3 \\ \quad \text{if } g_i \in (0,1] \cap SM_i > 0 \cap SM_j > 0 \\ GF(s_i) + ATT(i) + ATT(j) \\ \quad \text{if } g_i \in (0,1] \cap (SM_i < 0 \cup SM_j < 0) \\ ATT(i) + ATT(j) - e^{\frac{-1}{|g_i|}} \\ \quad \text{if } g_i \notin (0,1] \end{cases} \qquad (10)$$

This is the top-level evaluation using Incentive Method, applied to all individuals in both populations. A little reflection should convince the readers that, in $F(i)$, $GF(s_i) + 3 > GF(s_i) + ATT(i) + ATT(j) > ATT(i) + ATT(j) - e^{\frac{-1}{|g_i|}}$. Genetic programs that satisfy all three constraints are rewarded a bonus of 3 plus the game fitness $GF(s_i)$. This will ensure that they dominate the rest who fail to meet all constraints and then to encourage desired genetic programs to propagate. Individuals that satisfy the constraint $C1$, but do not meet $C2$ and/or $C3$, are still eligible for playing bargaining games. Their fitness are the game fitness adding a value $(ATT(i) + ATT(j))$ that reflects how close they meet any of the two soft constraints. Such individuals that violate the constraint $C1$ are not eligible for entering bargaining games. Instead they are allocated a fitness solely based on the structures of their genetic programs by SM and ATT measurements. Their fitness is definitely lower than any individual that satisfies at least, the constraint $C1$.

4.4   Parameters of Co-evolving System

In general, a co-evolutionary system is more sensitive to the values of genetic operators than an evolutionary system. Even a slight modification on either population will duplicate its effects due to dynamic properties of the landscapes. So crossover and mutation rates in co-evolutionary systems should be smaller than normally taken values by evolution. This concept is also supported by our experimental results. A rang of crossover and mutation rates are tested to reduce their bias on experiential results. Our system performs relatively stable while the crossover rate is within 0 to 0.1 and the mutation rate ranges from 0.01 to 0.3. Jin et al [3] explains how to choose crossover and mutation rates for a co-evolutionary system through a case study.

In a typical run, the fitness of two populations tends to be stabilized before 200th generation. To ensure the stabilization and limited by computational resources, we terminate runs at the 300th generation. Each population has 100 individuals.

5   Experimental Results and Observations

5.1   Using Incentive Method

We select total 25 game settings (game parameters) for testing, $\delta_A, \delta_B \in \{0.1, 0.3, 0.5, 0.7, 0.9\}$. The combinations of selected δ_A and δ_B evenly distributed over the space $\delta_A \times \delta_B$. 100 runs are conducted for every pair of (δ_A, δ_B). It is considered to be statistically sufficient to collect samples.

In one run, x_A is player A's share from an observed agreement made by the pair of the best-of-generation (highest fitness) strategies, one from the population A and another from population B, at the end of evolution (300th generation in our experiments). $\bar{x_A}$ is the average of 100 x_As from 100 runs with the same (δ_A, δ_B) but with different random sequences. The results of $\bar{x_B}$ is not reported here because it is merely the complement of $\bar{x_A}$.

Two methods are taken into investigation of experimental results. (1) For all test results, a T-test over the hypothesis $(x_A^* - \bar{x_A} = 0)$ is done. The result of the t-test shows that there is no statistically significant difference between the experimentally observed $\bar{x_A}$ and P.E.P, with 95% level of confidence. (t Critical Value two-tail = 2.06 and t Statistic Value = −0.85) (2)Two types of variations are defined to measure the difference between x_A^* and experimentally observed $\bar{x_A}$ of a given game setting.

Definition 6: Absolute Variation (av) is an unsigned difference between the P.E.P x_A^* and experimentally observed $\bar{x_A}$ for a given (δ_A, δ_B).

$$av = |x_A^* - \bar{x_A}| \qquad (11)$$

Definition 7: Relative Variation (rv) is an unsigned relative increment of $\bar{x_A}$ over x_A^*.

$$rv = \frac{|x_A^* - \bar{x_A}|}{x_A^*} = \frac{av}{x_A^*} \qquad (12)$$

Results of the absolute variation by Incentive Method are given in Table 1. They are very small variations from P.E.P, especially for game settings reported in Table 3. That of relative variation by Incentive Method can be calculated

Table 1. Absolute Variation by Incentive Method (x_A^* is the P.E.P. $\bar{x}_A$ is the experimental mean of Player A's shares from agreements by the best-of-generation individuals at the 300th generations of 100 trials)

δ_B value	Incentive Method ($|x_A^* - \bar{x}_A|$)				
	$\delta_A = 0.1$	$\delta_A = 0.3$	$\delta_A = 0.5$	$\delta_A = 0.7$	$\delta_A = 0.9$
0.1	0.0135	0.0715	0.0520	0.0308	0.0098
0.3	0.2775	0.2308	0.1741	0.1075	0.0371
0.5	0.1606	0.0963	0.0087	0.0841	0.1643
0.7	0.0002	0.0258	0.1016	0.2287	0.1266
0.9	0.0821	0.0280	0.0780	0.0001	0.0122

according to the definition of relative variation from Table 1 [1]. The results of rv are omitted here due to the page limitation. The results from both the T-test and two variation measures demonstrate that the evolutionary system combining Incentive Method has produced results that approximate to Perfect Equilibrium solutions in majority cases.

   Having obtained a general view on the results, we further look into the effectiveness of Incentive method. The questions to be answered are: whether Incentive method outperforms some other constraint-handling techniques, for instance, widely applied Penalty method? Does Incentive Method produce better results than an evolutionary algorithm having no constraint handling technique?

5.2   Using a Penalty Method

To evaluate the performance of Incentive Method, a control experiment using a penalty method is conducted. Another fitness function $F(i)'$ is defined to deal with the hard constraint: $x_i \in (0, 1]$. To be fairly comparable to the fitness function $F(i)$ in which Incentive Method is used, $F(i)'$ implements the penalty function for infeasible individuals is $ATT(i) + ATT(j) - e^{\frac{-1}{|g_i|}}$.

Definition 8: Fitness Function $F(i)'$ incorporated with Penalty Method

$$F(i)' = \begin{cases} GF(s_i) + ATT(i) + ATT(j) \\ \quad \text{if } g_i \in (0, 1] \\ ATT(i) + ATT(j) - e^{\frac{-1}{|g_i|}} \\ \quad \text{if } g_i \notin (0, 1] \end{cases} \tag{13}$$

---

[1] The reasons that we adopt two variation measures are that (i) for Absolute variation, $|x_A^* - \bar{x}_A| = |x_B^* - \bar{x}_B|$ is true. But for relative variation, $\frac{av}{x_A^*} = \frac{av}{x_B^*}$ is always not hold. Relative variation may produce two different results for one run with the same set of all parameters;(ii) absolute variation alone is not enough to express the variation on the base of the target point P.E.P. For example, two sets of results $(x_A^* = 0.05, \bar{x}_A = 0.06)$ and $(x_A^* = 0.95, \bar{x}_A = 0.96)$, both have the same absolute variation $av = 0.01$, but the former set has a 0.17 increment based on x_A^* and the latter set has only a 0.01 increment based on x_A^*. In this sense, the relative variation is more informative and indicative.

The same sequence of random seeds, the same genetic operators and the same sets of discount factor pairs as before are used in this experiment. Fitness function is $F(i)'$. As before, each game setting runs 100 times. The experimental results on absolute variation are shown in Table 2.

We can see from Table 1 and Table 2 that there are 17 out of the total 25 game-parameter combinations for which the incentive method outperforms the penalty one; one has the same absolute variation for both methods; for the rest 7, the penalty one does better. Moreover, for certain combinations of game parameters (δ_A, δ_B), the evolutionary algorithm is unable to approach the P.E.P equilibriums. Notice that this is not due to the method used, neither Incentive Method nor Penalty Method, but only depends on the combinations of game parameters. For example, the exactly corresponding cells in both absolute variation by Incentive Method (Table 1) and absolute variation by Penalty Method (Table 2) meet $av > 0.15$ condition. In the form of (δ_A, δ_B), these cells are $(0.1, 0.3)(0.1, 0.5)(0.3, 0.3)(0.5, 0.3)(0.7, 0.7)$ and $(0.9, 0.5)$. So the factor(s) of approximation failures is independent of the constraint handling technique chosen. We therefore exclude these failed cases from the performance comparison of two methods, which are only compared on successful-tested game-parameter combinations. Table 3 and Table 4 list the average absolute and relative variations of the incentive method and the penalty method, grouped by three conditions, namely $av(rv) < 0.15$, $av(rv) < 0.10$ and $av(rv) < 0.05$. A clear pattern displays: for all these three

Table 2. Absolute Variation by Penalty Method (x_A^* is the P.E.P. $\bar{x}_A$ is the experimental mean of Player A's shares from agreements by the best-of-generation individuals at the 300th generations of 100 trials)

δ_B value	Penalty Method ($\|x_A^* - \bar{x}_A\|$)				
	$\delta_A = 0.1$	$\delta_A = 0.3$	$\delta_A = 0.5$	$\delta_A = 0.7$	$\delta_A = 0.9$
0.1	0.0909	0.0722	0.0526	0.0323	0.0110
0.3	0.2784	0.2308	0.1765	0.1139	0.0411
0.5	0.1625	0.0986	0.0058	0.0813	0.1555
0.7	0.0066	0.0238	0.1025	0.2356	0.0855
0.9	0.0765	0.0184	0.0458	0.0021	0.0252

Table 3. Comparisons of the average absolute variation of selected settings. "m" is the number of $\bar{x}_A$s which meet the specified condition, amongst the 25 game settings.

Method	Average Absolute variation $\frac{\sum av}{m}$ when $av < 0.15$	Average Absolute variation $\frac{\sum av}{m}$ when $av < 0.10$	Average Absolute variation $\frac{\sum av}{m}$ when $av < 0.05$
Incentive Method	0.0509	0.0394	0.0166
Penalty Method	0.0519	0.0453	0.0212

Table 4. Comparisons of the average absolute variation of selected settings. "n" is the number of $\bar{x}_A$s which meet the specified condition, amongst the 25 game settings.

Method	Average relative variation $\frac{\sum rv}{n}$ when $rv < 0.15$	Average relative variation $\frac{\sum rv}{n}$ when $rv < 0.10$	Average relative variation $\frac{\sum rv}{n}$ when $rv < 0.05$
Incentive Method	0.0433	0.0302	0.0166
Penalty Method	0.0628	0.0426	0.0246

groups, both on absolute variation and relative variations measures, the incentive method yields less variation than the penalty method does. $\bar{x}_A$ found by the incentive method deviates from the P.E.P less than those found by the penalty method. Therefore, Incentive method is more effective than Penalty method in this case study.

5.3   Imposing No Constraints

To examine the usefulness of the constraints, we further do experiments whose fitness functions contain none of three mentioned constraints. All individuals play the bargaining game. In this non-constrained setting, although the majority of the 100 runs result with strategies that propose x_A within the cake size, i.e. satisfying the hard constraint, their value $\bar{x}_A$s have very large variations $|x_A^* - x_A|$, far away from the P.E.P prediction. Besides, a few runs end up with some x_As being exceptionally large or exceptionally small (including negative) values, which shows that the search probably had no chance to enter the area of $(0, 1]$. The average of 100 runs $\bar{x}_A$ is then surely far from meeting the fundamental requirement $x_i \in (0, 1]$. Therefore, imposing no constraints into the fitness function is impractical in this case.

6   Concluding Summary

In this work, we have introduced Incentive Method, which is a constraint handling technique, in evolutionary algorithms. It is especially suitable for problems where solutions can be categorized into different groups by the nature of the constraints. The main idea of Incentive Method is to define the relevance of each type of constraint to the quality of a solution. Thus all candidate solutions can be categorized into partially ordered sets. For example, the set of solutions violate hard constraints are definitely less favorable to the set of solutions that violate some soft constraints, which are in turn less favorable to solutions that violate no constraints. Note that some soft constraints may not be strictly ordered. The partial order of the constraints is translated into the objective fitness function. Thus evolution rewards favorable candidate solutions according to this partial ordering mechanism. This helps to guide the evolutionary search to allocate more effort to search areas that are more promising, without totally denying access to other areas.

We equipped a genetic programming with Incentive Method and used it to search strategies for the classic bargaining problem. A candidate solution is represented by tree structure. This method has successfully produced experimental outcomes, in terms of statistics, consistent with the game theoretically perfect equilibrium. In addition, we compared the incentive-based evolutionary algorithm with a penalty method and with a non-constraint setting on how close their solutions approximate game-theoretic perfect equilibrium partition P.E.P. Experimental results show that Incentive Method has found more precise approximation to the game-theoretic partition. This result encourages us to apply Incentive Method to other bargaining problems and some other optimization problems with similar constraints features in future.

Acknowledgement

Authors would like to thank Alberto Moraglio who has given important feedbacks on the initial submission.

References

1. Koza, J.: Genetic Programming: On the Programming of Computers by Means of Natural Selection. The MIT Press, USA (1992)
2. Miller, J.: The Co-evolution of Automata in the Repeated Prisoner's Dilemma. Journal of Economic Behavior and Organization, (1996) 29(1), 87-112,
3. Jin, N. and Tsang, E. (2005) Co-evolutionary Strategies for an Alternating-Offer Bargaining Problem, IEEE Symposium on Computational Intelligence and Games (IEEE CIG), Colchester, UK 4-6 April 2005
4. Muthoo, A.: Bargaining Theory with Applications, Cambridge University Press (1999)
5. Rubinstein, A.: Perfect Equilibrium in a Bargaining Model, Econometrica, (1982) 50: 97-110
6. Tsang, E., Li, J.: EDDIE for financial forecasting, in S-H. Chen (ed.), Genetic Algorithms and Programming in Computational Finance, Kluwer Series in Computational Finance, 2002, Chapter 7, 161-174
7. Tsang, E.P.K., Foundations of Constraint Satisfaction, Academic Press, London and San Diego, 1993

Iterative Filter Generation
Using Genetic Programming

Marc Segond, Denis Robilliard, and Cyril Fonlupt

Laboratoire d'Informatique du Littoral,
Maison de la Recherche Blaise Pascal,
50 rue Ferdinand Buisson - BP 719,
62228 CALAIS Cedex, France
segond@lil.univ-littoral.fr
http://lil.univ-littoral.fr/~segond/

Abstract. Oceanographers from the IFREMER institute have an hypothesis that the presence of so-called "retentive" meso-scale vortices in ocean and coastal waters could have an influence on watery fauna's demography. Up to now, identification of retentive hydro-dynamical structures on stream maps has been performed by experts using background knowledge about the area. We tackle this task with filters induced by Genetic Programming, a technique that has already been successfully used in pattern matching problems. To overcome specific difficulties associated with this problem, we introduce a refined scheme that iterates the filters classification phase while giving them access to a memory of their previous decisions. These iterative filters achieve superior results and are compared to a set of other methods.

1 Introduction

Watery fauna concentration in coastal waters seems to be correlated with the presence of physical structures that may retain eggs and larvae in favorable environmental conditions. In the case of the anchovy in the Gulf of Biscay, biologists from the IFREMER institute are studying the correlation between retentive meso scale vortices, whose size ranges from 10km to 200 km, and the demography of these fishes. The detection of these structures is made by experts on stream vector maps using background expertise about plausible structures.

Maps are actually generated by hydro-dynamical simulations such as the Mars3D or the Mercator models[1]. A typical stream map is a 3 dimensional matrix containing the x and y components of the stream vector at 10 meters depth on a discrete grid with 10km by 10km cells, collected at regular time steps, usually every 24 hours. The maps are stored in the NetCDF[2] format.

To verify the hypothesis at hand, the frequency and location of interesting vortices has to be recorded and summed up over many years, yielding a very large

---

[1] http://www.mercator-ocean.fr
[2] http://my.unidata.ucar.edu/content/software/netcdf/index.html

P. Collet et al. (Eds.): EuroGP 2006, LNCS 3905, pp. 145–153, 2006.

amount of maps to be processed. Thus an automatic and efficient detection tool is needed to conduct the study.

When the specialist highlights retentive structures by hand on the stream maps, he uses expertise based on his knowledge of the area, of the characteristics of the simulation model and his understanding of the phenomenon he studies. During this process some structures that could be retained by a naive observer are rejected, e.g. because the stream aspect is chaotic in the neighborhood, suggesting these are only transient patterns or artifacts due to the model digitization. Thus the physics-based vortices detection problem is topped by a hidden criteria learning task. An efficient detection scheme for this problem must therefore build over these two aspects: using hydrodynamics and being able to learn part of the expert's knowledge.

An ant algorithm was proposed in [1] to solve this problem. In this scheme, ants used physical information from the stream vector field and a further parameter tuning phase brought the algorithm closer towards matching the hidden criteria. This approach was satisfactory and superseded standard vorticity threshold methods (see [3, 4] for a presentation of such techniques).

Nonetheless the question was still open whether a supervised machine learning scheme could achieve superior results. In this paper we introduce genetic programming filters that are able to take into account the physical characteristics of the problem and to learn from example maps.

2   Genetic Programming Filters

The basic scheme is inspired by the work of Daida [2] on detecting pressure ridges in the arctic ice cover. We evolve filters (i.e. classifier programs) in a supervised learning framework. These are selected on their ability to correctly classify cells of a stream map whether they belong or not to a structure of interest. Each filter classify one map cell at a time, and it is successively applied to every cell of the map. Evaluation is done on a set of reference maps tagged by the expert (see Figure 1).

Filters are implemented with the ECJ[3] Java evolutionary library, using the standard Lisp-like tree representation. Inputs available to a filter are floating point physical data such as stream strength and vorticity. We keep the closure property and use only GP nodes that return a floating point value.

The conversion between this floating point matrix and the boolean values expected for classification is done with a threshold value. Continuously increasing the threshold from 0 to 1, we obtain a monotonous increase of the true positive and false positive rates, from 0% to 100%: we can draw a Reicever Operating Characteristics (ROC) curve. This is a standard technique (see e.g. [6]) that will be used later when evaluating and comparing heuristics. The end-user will have the choice of the threshold level that corresponds to his preferred trade-off between sensibility and specificity.

---

[3] http://cs.gmu.edu/eclab/projects/ecj/

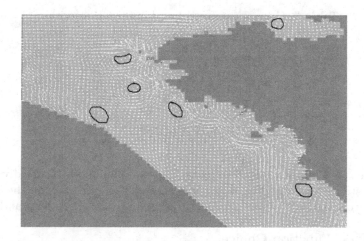

Fig. 1. An example of detection performed by an expert: interesting vortices are circled in black

2.1   Basic GP Filters Presentation

The set of function and terminal nodes is shown in table 1, and it has been chosen to allow computations on the physical characteristics of the stream.

For example, it seems relevant to use information from the 8 neighbors of the cell we are working on: the "strength3x3" terminal returns the mean value of the stream strength in the neighboring cells, and the "angle3x3" terminal gives the mean value of the angle of the vector stream in those same cells. The "min" and "max" function nodes have been introduced to allow comparisons. The "curl" and "divergence" are standard operators used in vortices detection. Notice that

Table 1. Summary of non-terminal and terminal nodes used in the basic GP filters

Name	Meaning	Input	Output
add	addition	2 reals	1 real
sub	subtraction	2 reals	1 real
mul	multiplication	2 reals	1 real
div	protected division	2 reals	1 real
min	minimum of 2 arguments	2 reals	1 real
max	maximum of 2 arguments	2 reals	1 real
cos	cosine	1 real	1 real
sin	sine	1 real	1 real
strength	stream strength	null	1 real $\in [0, 1]$
strength3x3	stream strength averaged over a 3x3 cells matrix	null	1 real $\in [0, 1]$
angles3x3	stream vector angle averaged over a 3x3 cells matrix	null	1 real
curl	cell vorticity	null	1 real
divergence	cell divergence	null	1 real
erc	ephemeral random constant	null	1 real

Table 2. General parameters used in the GP algorithm

Name	Value
Number of generations	80
Size of the population	600
Max depth for a tree	15
Mutation rate	5%
Crossover rate	85%
Reproduction rate (with elitism)	5%

in order to speed up the evaluation phase, most terminal nodes (curl, divergence, strength, strength3x3, angle3x3) are pre-computed for the maps in the learning set. The evolution parameters are shown in table 2, and are quite standard.

2.2 Fitness Function Choice

One of the difficulty in Genetic Programming is to find the adequate fitness function to optimize. Basically, the fitness of individuals is evaluated by measuring their performance on a learning set of 10 maps tagged by an expert. However the actual performance of a filter depends on the choice of the threshold level. A possible choice is maximizing the area under the ROC curve, denoted as AUC — Area Under Curve — (see Sebag et al. [5] for a discussion about efficient computation of this area). Optimizing the AUC delivers pretty good results, but the ant algorithm still dominate when the threshold trade-off is aimed at very low false positive rates.

We therefore propose to focus on having a steeper slope in the left part of the ROC curve (low false positive rates). This is achieved by choosing a set of 10 values on the ROC x-axis, 5 in the range $[0.25, 0.35]$, the others equally spaced on the range $[0, 1] \setminus [0.25, 0.35]$, and minimizing the following fitness function:

$$f = \frac{\sum_{i=1}^{n} \frac{y_i}{x_i}}{n}$$

were x_i is a value chosen on the x-axis and y_i the corresponding value on the y-axis according to the ROC curve.

2.3 First Results and Discussion

Unfortunately the GP approach we just described fails to give conclusive results, although it relies on state-of-the-art evolutionary techniques previously successful on classification and pattern detection cases. On our problem, the filters ROC curves are dominated by the results obtained from the ant algorithm. GP produces rough and noisy classification specially near the coast, that reminds of results obtained by vorticity analysis.

We conjecture that these filters have a too reduced "sight range" to recognize global vortices shapes that can be spread over 20 grid cells or more. We saw in the introduction that whether or not a structure is considered retentive certainly depends on each cell of that structure, but also on distant surrounding cells that are not member of the vortices. In this regard, the "strength3x3" and "angle3x3" nodes probably give a too local information, and we need to add more problem specific knowledge to allow GP to cross the gap.

Experiments have been conducted to let the evolution process determine the size of these matrix-shaped terminals, but these were not successful, leading us to propose a solution based on the propagation of classification results across the grid, as explained in the next section.

3   Iterative Genetic Programming Filters

To remedy the failure of the previous scheme, we need to provide some means of communicating information over the grid, while keeping a manageable search space: a large increase in the number of terminals to access a variety of distant cells would prevent successful learning by GP.

Our proposition is iterative filters, i.e. filters that are applied in several successive classifications steps on a map, retaining the final last decision, and that have a memory of their previous decisions at each classification step (see Figure 2). If the filter operating at a given cell accesses such memory from neighbors, information will slowly spread along the grid at every iteration.

3.1   Iterative GP Filters Presentation

From a technical point of view, two nodes are added to the terminal set: `lastValue` and `meanLastValue`.

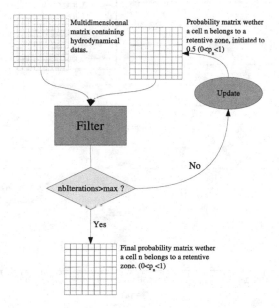

Fig. 2. Description of the way an iterative filter works

- `lastValue`: returns a value that aggregates the filter results at previous iterations. This value is 0.5 during the first classification step (no previous result), and it is updated using the following equation:

$$\mathtt{lastValue}_{i+1} = \frac{2 * \mathtt{lastValue}_i + F}{3}$$

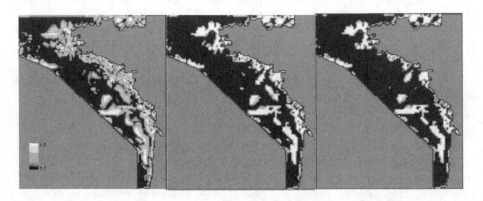

Fig. 3. Evolution of the classification after 1, 15 and 30 iterations, without `distCoast` terminal

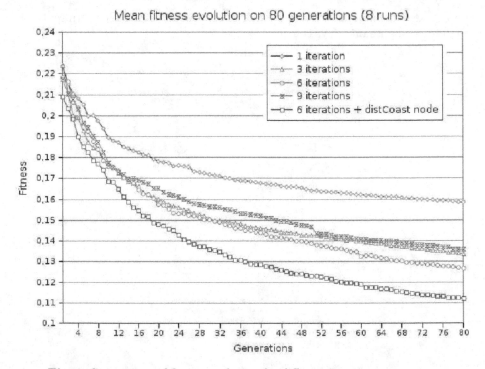

Fig. 4. Comparison of fitness evolution for different iteration parameters

were `lastValue`$_i$ is the value returned by this terminal at iteration i, and F is the classification value computed by the filter.

– `meanLastValue`: returns the mean of `lastValue` for the 8 neighboring cells.

Thanks to `meanLastValue`, a filter is now able to take into account classification results from its immediate neighbors, and, within successive iterations, it can grasp classification information about cells distant from two, three or more grid cells, depending on how many iterations we allow. The F value produced by the individual during the last iteration will be the its final classification and will serve to compute its fitness.

Experiments also show that it is very difficult for a filter to avoid false positives near the coast line, almost setting a higher bound to performances. To tackle this problem, a `distCoast` node is introduced that returns 1 if the cell is farther than 2 grid steps from the coast, else 0.

3.2   Iterative Filters Results

On Figure 3 we plot the evolution of the classification result for three iteration limits. We observe that the classification is refined in the first iterations before becoming stable.

Figure 4 is a standard fitness versus generations plot. We can see that iterative filters have an increased efficiency, with a maximum at 6 iterations. The `distCoast` node also boosts the performance.

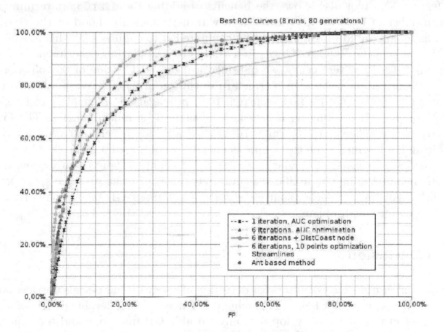

Fig. 5. ROC curve based comparison between GP filters and other methods

Fig. 6. A map filtered using the "distCoast" node

A comparison with the ant algorithm and streamlines schemes introduced in [1] is given in Figure 5 using ROC curves. Depending on the trade-off desired, either the "steeper slope" fitness function or the AUC maximization may be preferred. This plot also shows the benefits of adding the `distCoast` terminal. The number of false positive is reduced within the neighborhood of the coast line, as is illustrated on Figure 6 to be compared with Figure 3 for this matter.

Maximizing the ROC AUC within a 5-fold cross validation experiment (1600 training cells, 7200 test cells), we obtained a mean AUC value of 0.8955 (normalized, maximum is 1) with a standard deviation of 0.0093. We performed a similar experiment with a non-recurrent back-propagation artificial neural network (see e.g. [7]), taking 54 inputs i.e. the same 6 terminal inputs as GP for 9 cells evenly spaced in a 70km x 70km area around the classification focus. Limiting the learning time to 15 min as for GP, we obtained a mean AUC value of 0.7515 with a standard deviation of 0.0178. We cannot claim to have spent as much time in tuning the artificial neural network (ANN) as we have spent for the GP algorithm, nonetheless it gives some hints about GP being competitive with ANN for this problem.

4   Conclusion

We presented iterative GP filters for detection of retentive meso-scale vortices on simulated stream vector fields. This scheme has needed considerable insights into the problem in order to develop not only suitable GP functions and terminals, but also an original iterated scheme for GP classification and an alternative to the AUC maximization fitness function.

With our GP based filtering method, we are able to learn some part of the expert knowledge, while also performing meaningful computations in term of vector field analysis, as can be judged by the results. We think that this iterating scheme for GP classification may well be of interest in the image analysis domain and possibly for general classification tasks.

Although preliminary work with ADFs have shown no increase in performances, we also plan to investigate further this way.

References

1. M. Segond, C. Fonlupt, D. Robilliard, Ant Algorithms for Detection in Coastal Waters, *EA'03*, Vol. 1, pp. 1-100, 2003.
2. J. M. Daïda, C. T. F. Bersano-Begey, S. J. Ross, J. F. Vesecky, Computer Assisted Design of Image Classification Algorithms: Dynamic and Static Fitness Evaluations in a Scaffolded Genetic Programming Environment, *GP'96*, 1996.
3. T. Corpetti, E. Mémin, P. Pérez, Dense estimation of fluid flows, *IEEE transaction on pattern analysis and machine intelligence*, 24(3), pp. 365-380, 2002.
4. T. Corpetti, E. Mémin, P. Pérez, Extraction of singular points from dense motion fields: an analytic approach, *Journal of mathematical imaging and vision*, 2003.
5. M. Sebag, J. Azé, N. Lucas, ROC-Based Evolutionary Learning: Application to Medical Data Mining, *Artificial Evolution 2003*, pp.384-396, 2003.
6. W.B. Langdon, B.F. Buxton, Evolving Receiver Operating Characteristics for Data Fusion, *Proceedings of EuroGP'2001*, pp.87–96, LNCS 2038, Springer-Verlag, 2001.
7. T. M. Mitchell, Machine Learning, Mc Graw-Hill, 1997.

Iterative Prototype Optimisation with Evolved Improvement Steps

Jiri Kubalik and Jan Faigl

Department of Cybernetics, CTU Prague,
Technicka 2, 166 27 Prague 6, Czech Republic
{kubalik, xfaigl}@labe.felk.cvut.cz

Abstract. Evolutionary algorithms have already been more or less successfully applied to a wide range of optimisation problems. Typically, they are used to evolve a population of complete candidate solutions to a given problem, which can be further refined by some problem-specific heuristic algorithm. In this paper, we introduce a new framework called *Iterative Prototype Optimisation with Evolved Improvement Steps*. This is a general optimisation framework, where an initial prototype solution is being improved iteration by iteration. In each iteration, a sequence of actions/operations, which improves the current prototype the most, is found by an evolutionary algorithm. The proposed algorithm has been tested on problems from two different optimisation problem domains - binary string optimisation and the traveling salesman problem. Results show that the concept can be used to solve hard problems of big size reliably achieving comparably good or better results than classical evolutionary algorithms and other selected methods.

1 Introduction

In the evolutionary optimisation framework, the evolutionary algorithms (EAs) are typically used to evolve a population of candidate solutions to a given problem. Each of the candidate solutions encodes a complete solution - a complete set of problem control parameters, a complete schedule in the case of scheduling problems, a complete tour for the traveling salesman problem, etc. This implies, that especially for large instances of the solved problem the EA searches enormous space of potential solutions. In this paper, a new approach is presented, where the EA does not handle the solved problem as a whole. Instead, the EA is employed within the iterative optimisation framework to evolve the best modification of the current solution prototype in each iteration. Thus, the load of searching for the best complete solution at once is cut into pieces, each of them representing a process of seeking the best transformation of the current solution prototype to the new possibly better one.

The structure of the paper is as follows. In section 2, the general outline of the algorithm of Iterative **P**rototype **O**ptimisation with **E**volved IM**p**rovement **S**teps (POEMS) is described. Section 3 describes the problems and the experimental set-up used for the proof-of-concept validation of POEMS. In section 4, POEMS is compared with other evolutionary approaches and other selected

P. Collet et al. (Eds.): EuroGP 2006, LNCS 3905, pp. 154–165, 2006.

methods. The paper ends with conclusions on effectiveness of POEMS, its advantages and disadvantages, and its further extensions.

2   POEMS

The main idea behind POEMS (Figure 1) is that some initial prototype solution is further improved in an iterative process, where the most suitable modification of the current prototype is sought for using an evolutionary algorithm (EA) in each iteration. The modifications are represented as a sequence of primitive actions/operations, defined specifically for the solved problem. Such a sequence can be considered a program and the employed EA a special case of a linear genetic programming. The evaluation of action sequences is based on how good/bad they modify the current prototype, which is an input parameter of EA. Sequences that do not change the prototype at all are penalized in order to avoid generating trivial solutions. After the EA finishes, it is checked whether the best evolved sequence improves the current prototype or not. If an improvement is found, then the sequence is applied to current prototype and the result becomes a new prototype. Otherwise the current prototype remains unchanged for the next iteration.

Representation. The EA evolves linear chromosomes of length *MaxGenes*, where each gene represents an instance of certain action chosen from a set of elementary actions defined for given problem. Each action is represented by a record, with an attribute *action_type* followed by parameters of the action. Besides actions that truly modify the prototype there is also a special type of action called *nop* (no operation). Any action with *action_type = nop* is interpreted as a void action with no effect on the prototype, regardless of the values of its parameters. A chromosome can contain one or more instances of the *nop* operation. This way a variable effective length of chromosomes is implemented.

Operators. The crossover operator generates a child chromosome so that each gene of the new chromosome is a copy of randomly chosen gene either from the first or the second parent. Both parents have the same probability of contributing its genes to the generated child, and each gene can be used only once. This can be considered a generalized uniform crossover, where any combination of parental genes can form a valid offspring. After the new chromosome has been

```
1      generate(Prototype)
2      repeat
3            BestSequence ← run_EA(Prototype)
4            if(apply_to(BestSequence, Prototype) is better than Prototype)
5                  then Prototype ← apply_to(BestSequence, Prototype)
6      until(POEMS termination condition)
7      return Prototype
```

Fig. 1. An outline of POEMS algorithm

```
1    initialize(OldPop)
2    BestSequence ← best_of(OldPop)
3    repeat
4        NewPop ← BestSequence
5        repeat
6            Parents ← select(OldPop)
7            Children ← cross_over(Parents)
8            mutate(Children)
9            evaluate(Children)
10           NewPop ← Children
11       until(NewPop is completed)
12       BestSequence = best_of(NewPop)
13       switch(OldPop, NewPop)
14   until(EA termination condition)
15   return BestSequence
```

Fig. 2. An outline of a simple generational evolutionary algorithm

finished, it is checked for gene duplicates and left with just one copy of each non *nop* action. Each duplicate of some non *nop* action is converted into *nop* action, simply by setting $action\_type = nop$. This means that the population genotype can contain many "inactive" action specifications. These can be activated again by changing their $action\_type$ from *nop* to some effective action. Action can be activated/inactivated by mutation operator, which can also change the parameters of the action.

Evolutionary model. The design and configuration of the EA can differ for each particular optimisation problem. Figure 2 shows a simple generational evolutionary algorithm (gEA) with tournament selection, and elitism preserving the best individual in the population. Figure 3 shows a mutation-based iterational EA (iEA) that iteratively modifies a population of individuals. In each iteration a chromosome is selected by tournament selection. Then the chromosome is mutated so that one action out of its active actions (i.e. genes with $action\_type$ other than *nop*) is selected and inactivated ($action\_type$ set to *nop*). If the fitness of the chromosome did not worsen after this change the modified chromosome is accepted and replaces other bad performing chromosome in the population.

In general, the EA is expected to be executed many times during the whole run of the POEMS. Thus, it must be configured to converge fast in order to get the output in short time. As the EA is evolving sequences of actions to improve the solution prototype, not the complete solution, the maximal length of chromosomes *MaxGenes* can be short compared with the size of the problem. For example *MaxGenes* would be much smaller than the size of the chromosome in case of binary string optimisation or much smaller than the number of cities in case of the TSP problem. The relaxed requirement on the expected EA output and the small size of evolved chromosomes enables to setup the EA so that it converges within a few generations. It is important to note, that POEMS does not perform prototype optimisation via improvement steps that are purely

```
 1  initialize(Population)
 2  repeat
 3       Parents ← select(Population)
 4       Children ← cross_over(Parents)
 5       mutate(Children)
 6       evaluate(Children)
 7       Replacement = find_replacement(Population)
 8       Population[Replacement] ← Child1
 9       Replacement = find_replacement(Population)
10       Population[Replacement] ← Child2
11  until(EA termination condition)
12  BestSequence ← best_of(Population)
13  return BestSequence
```

Fig. 3. An outline of a mutation-based iterational evolutionary algorithm

local with respect to the current prototype. In fact, long phenotypical as well as genotypical distances between the prototype and its modification can be observed if the system possesses a sufficient explorative ability. The space of possible modifications of the current prototype is determined by the set of elementary actions and the maximum allowed length of evolved action sequences *MaxGenes* (as demonstrated in section 6). The less explorative actions are and the shorter sequences are allowed the more the system searches in a prototype neighborhood only and the more it is prone to get stuck in a local optimum, and vice versa.

3   Test Problems

The first set of test problems belongs to a binary string optimisation problem domain. It includes simple onemax, royal road, deceptive, hierarchical, multimodal and non-linear function optimisation problems.

OneMax. This is a simple problem, where the chromosome is assigned a value equal to the number of ones it contains. Thus the optimal sought string is of fitness equal to the size of the chromosome (that is 100, here). Note that this function is considered to be easy for GAs.

DF3. This is a representative of deceptive problems, i.e. problems that are intentionally designed to make a GA converge towards local deceptive optimum. The problem is composed of 25 copies of a 4-bit fully deceptive function DF3 taken from [8]. DF3 has a global optimum in the string 1111 with fitness 30 and a deceptive attractor 0000 with low fitness 10, which is surrounded, in the search space, by four strings of just one 1 with fitness values 28, 27, 26, and 25. The whole 100-bit long chromosome has the global optimum of value 750.

Rosenbrock. This problem uses as the basic building block the well-known Rosenbrock function of two parameters x and y, each of them coded on 12 bits. The function has high degree of dependency between variables, which makes it hard to optimize using standard genetic algorithms. The sought minimum value of the function is 0.0 at the point [1.0, 1.0]. The problem consists of 4 copies of the function whose contributions are summed up in the final fitness value. Any solution of fitness less than or equal to 0.001 is considered to be an optimum.

F103. This test problem is based on function $F103(x, y)$ taken from [9]. It is a non-linear non-separable and highly multimodal function of two variables, where the parameters x and y are each coded on 10 bits. The global minimum is of value 0.0. Our problem consists of 5 copies of the function, where the fitness of the whole chromosome is given as the sum of the five function contributions. Again, any solution of fitness less than or equal to 0.001 is considered an optimum.

RR. This is a 16-bit version of the RR1 single-level royal road problem described in [2]. The problem is defined by enumerating the schemata, where each schema s_i has assigned its contribution coefficient c_i. The evaluation of an arbitrary chromosome is given as a sum of all contributions of those schemata that are covered by the chromosome. Only the combination of all ones on the bits pertinent to a given schema contributes to the fitness with the nonzero value, any other combination has value 0. Here, the problem is defined as a concatenation of six 16-bit long schemata, so the optimum solution is the string of all ones of the fitness 96.

H-IFF. A hierarchical-if-and-only-if function proposed in [6] is the representative of hierarchically decomposable problems. The hierarchical block structure of the function is a balanced binary tree. Leaf nodes, corresponding to single genes, contribute to the fitness by 1. Each inner node is interpreted as 1 if and only if its children are both 1's, and as 0 iff they are both 0's - in such cases the inner node contributes to the fitness by a positive value $2^{height(x)}$, where $height(x)$ is the distance from the node x to its antecedent leaves. Otherwise the node is interpreted as null and its contribution is 0. The function has two global optima - one consists of all 1's and the other one has all 0's. We have used the 128-bit version with global optima of value 1024.

TSP. The second set of test problems are instances of the well-known Traveling Salesman Problem. We have used datasets for 100, 200, 500, 1000, and 2000 cities, where the cities were generated randomly in the area of size 100 by 100.

4   Optimisation Techniques Used for Comparisons

On the binary string optimisation problems, we have compared the proposed POEMS algorithm with the following approaches :

- *Simple Genetic Algorithm* (SGA). This is a generational genetic algorithm, with tournament selection, 2-point crossover, a simple bit-swapping mutation operator, and an elitism, which preserves the best individual in the population. Population size 500 was used. The probability of crossover was 0.9. The mutation rate was set so that one bit of each chromosome is inverted.
- *Genetic Algorithm with Gene Based Adaptive Mutation Strategy* (GBAM). Uyar et al. [5] proposed this adaptive approach for adjusting mutation rates

for the gene locations based on the feedback obtained by observing the relative success or failure of the individuals in the population. There are two mutation rates for each locus - one for allele 1 and the other for allele 0. For each generation the mutation rates are updated for each locus so that the mutation rate for the better-performing allele decreases, and vice versa. This certainly speeds up the convergence so the strategy is implemented with a convergence control mechanism for escaping local optima.

- *A Genetic Algorithm with Limited Convergence* (GALCO). Kubalik et al. [4] proposed this approach for preserving population diversity. It is based on an idea that the population is explicitly prevented from becoming homogenous by simply imposing limits on its convergence. This is done by specifying the maximum difference between frequency of ones and zeros at any position of the chromosome calculated over the whole population. A steady-state evolutionary model and a special replacement operator are used to keep the desired distribution of ones and zeros during the whole run.

Note that all of these techniques are more or less modifications of the standard genetic algorithm. As such they rely on the proper spacial structure of the chromosome. In other words, they work well if the groups of dependent genes are spatially clustered within the chromosome. This is called a tight linkage. In the opposite case, when the linkage is loose (i.e. the dependent genes are far from each other), the genetic algorithm can not combine building blocks of two parental chromosomes properly, see [3]. In order to show the effect of the linkage on the performance of the algorithms, two series of experiments were carried out - one for the *tight linkage*, and the other for the *loose linkage* (this was implemented so that the sequence of genes within the chromosome was chosen by random for each experiment). Obviously, the evolutionary algorithm used in POEMS is linkage independent, so it was tested on the loose linkage only.

The following approaches have been compared with POEMS on the TSP:

- *Genetic Algorithm with E-R crossover* (ER). This is a steady-state genetic algorithm, with the edge-recombination crossover proposed by Whitley et al. [7]. Mutation operator exchanges positions of two randomly selected cities within a given path. First, two parental chromosomes are selected by tournament selection, and crossed over to generate its offspring. The new chromosome undergoes the mutation and is evaluated. Finally, the newly generated chromosome replaces a chosen poorly performing chromosome in the population if the new chromosome outperforms the replacement one.
- *Self Organising Maps* (SOM). The salesman's city tour is represented by a ring of neurons, where the neighboring neurons are connected. The general schema of SOM algorithm consists of two procedures: (1) a selection of winner neuron, where the closest neuron for each city is selected and (2) an adaptation of the winner neuron, where the neuron along with its several neighbors are moved towards the closest city. These two procedures are repeated until a stopping condition is satisfied. The algorithm implemented in this work is based on [1].

- *2-opt heuristic* (2-opt). This algorithm is based on simple local search heuristic called 2-opt, that was proposed by Flood and Croes in fifties. The algorithm starts with some feasible (random) solution. Than it searches for two edges $e_1 = (v_1, v_3), e_2 = (v_2, v_4)$ such that a recombination of the edges to $e_1 = (v_1, v_2), e_2 = (v_3, v_4)$ improves the current solution. The algorithm stops if no two edges for improvement recombination are found.

5   Experimental Setup

For the binary string optimisation problems the action sequences evolved in POEMS were composed of just one type of action called *invert(gene)*. The action simply inverts specified *gene* within the prototype.

For the TSP problem a direct path representation of the tour was used. The prototype tour in POEMS was modified by action sequences composed of actions of the following types

- *move(city$_1$, city$_2$)* moves *city$_1$* right after *city$_2$* in the tour,
- *invert(city$_1$, city$_2$)* inverts a subtour between *city$_1$* and *city$_2$*,
- *swap(city$_1$, city$_2$)* swaps *city$_1$* and *city$_2$*.

Both versions, POEMS with gEA and POEMS with iEA were tested on the binary string optimisation problems. Both of them used the same parameter setup as follows: chromosome length 10 (the maximal number of active actions in the action sequence, see Section 2), population size 200, number of fitness function evaluations 3000, tournament selection with $N = 3$, crossover and mutation operators as described in Section 2 with $P_c = 0.8$ and $P_m = 0.1$, respectively.

The other algorithms were used with the following common setting: population size 500, 2-point crossover with $P_c = 0.8$, tournament selection with $N = 3$. SGA used a mutation operator with the probability $P_m = 0.01$, GALCO does not use any explicit mutation operator, and GBAM was used with the mutation rate interval $(0.0001 - 0.2)$, the initial mutation rate 0.025, and the mutation adaptation step 0.001. All algorithms were running for 10^6 fitness evaluations.

The following configurations of POEMs and ER algorithms were used in experiments on TSP problem. The population size was set to the number of cities (*Cities*) and 2·*Cities* for POEMS and ER, respectively. EA used in POEMS (line 3 in Figure 1) worked with chromosomes of length 10 and lasted for $1000 \cdot PopSize$ fitness evaluations.

Two strategies for generating of the starting prototype were used - the random initialisation and the heuristic one. When generating a tour, a decision of what city should be visited from the current city is made by random in the random strategy whilst the heuristic strategy prefers the next city to be from the neighborhood of the current city. Similarly, the concept of the neighborhood was used with the ER crossover so that the operator prefers links to cities from the current city's neighborhood.

Both POEMs and ER were running for *Cities* · 1000 fitness function evaluations. The tournament selection parameter and the neighborhood size were set

Table 1. Configurations of POEMs and ER used for TSP problem

PopSize	Tournament	Cities	Neighborhood
100	3	100	20
200	4	200	15
500	5	500	10
1000	6	1000	7
2000	7	2000	5
4000	8		

depending on the population size and the number of cities as shown in Table 1. The crossover operator was applied on the parents with the probability 0.9. If the parents did not undergo crossover they were mutated so that positions of two randomly chosen cities were swapped. The following statistics were calculated based on 50 runs of each experiment

- *Mean.* Mean *best-of-run* value calculated over the 50 independent runs.
- *StDev.* Standard deviation of the *best-of-run* values.
- *#Succ.* A number of runs, in which the optimum solution was found.
- *When.* The average number of fitness evaluations needed to get the optimum.
- *BestPath.* The shortest path out of 50 runs for each TSP experiment.

6   Results

Table 2 shows results obtained with POEMS-gEA and POEMS-iEA on binary string optimisation problems. It shows that POEMS-iEA is better than POEMS-gEA on OneMax, DF3, Rosenbrock, and F103 problem. POEMS-iEA achieves either better mean quality of the best-of-run solutions or finds the optimal solutions more often or is faster in converging to the optimal solution on those problems. This may be attributed to the fact that the iEA is designed to converge very fast so it might be able to come up with better action sequence than gEA in each iteration. On the other hand, the performance of both variants of POEMS is very poor for the RR and H-IFF problems. For the royal road problem this might be surprising as those problems are considered easy for genetic algorithms. The explanation of why POEMS does not work for these problems

Table 2. Performance of POEMS on binary string optimisation problems

problem	POEMS-gEA				POEMS-iEA			
	Mean	*StDev*	*#Succ*	*When*	*Mean*	*StDev*	*#Succ*	*When*
OneMax	100.0	0.0	50	20732	100.0	0.0	50	12168
DF3	749.1	3.7	47	617034	750	0.0	50	307820
Rosenbrock	0.36	0.52	7	656342	0.029	0.14	17	516988
F103	0.0127	0.0093	0	-	0.0063	0.0061	1	769400
RR	5.1	7.5	0	-	6.7	9.7	0	-
H-IFF	568.8	58.8	0	-	580.8	15.2	0	-

is that *it lacks the ability to combine several solution into a new one* as the standard genetic algorithms do. POEMS seeks the optimal solution via a process of iteratively modifying (mutating) the prototype solution. Thus, the algorithm can get stuck with such a prototype, for which it is very hard (or even impossible) to evolve any improving action sequence. In case of RR problem, for POEMS is very hard to find a sequence of single bit inversions such that it would discover a new 16-bit long building block of all ones without simultaneously damaging any of already existing blocks in the prototype. Similarly this applies for H-IFF problem, where POEMS optimizes the prototype up to some level, where any further improvement would require to invert a large block of genes.

When comparing POEMS with the other algorithms (see Table 3) on the binary string optimisation problems we can observe that if the chromosome

Table 3. Performance of SGA, GBAM and GALCO on binary string optimisation problems

	problem	tight linkage				loose linkage			
		Mean	*StDev*	*#Succ*	*When*	*Mean*	*StDev*	*#Succ*	*When*
SGA	OneMax	100.0	0.0	50	13448	100.0	0.0	50	13564
	DF3	750	0.0	50	595359	707.1	6.8	0	-
	Rosenbrock	0.063	0.084	4	724888	0.502	0.591	0	-
	F103	0.005	0.0035	2	680329	0.0197	0.0156	0	-
	RR	91.5	7.3	36	654756	88.8	9.7	35	706064
	H-IFF	710.4	87.8	1	295261	617.6	34.7	0	-
GBAM	OneMax	100.0	0.0	50	10935	100.0	0.0	50	10847
	DF3	750.0	0.0	50	558097	728.3	6.9	0	-
	Rosenbrock	1.22	0.46	0	-	2.11	0.8	0	-
	F103	0.32	0.11	0	-	0.47	0.17	0	-
	RR	96.0	0.0	50	43984	96.0	0.0	50	68378
	H-IFF	790.8	57.4	0	-	625.6	38.1	0	-
GALCO	OneMax	100.0	0.0	50	141190	100.0	0.0	50	142170
	DF3	750.0	0.0	50	108685	714.6	5.2	0	-
	Rosenbrock	0.0103	0.0137	1	936201	0.36	0.26	0	-
	F103	0.0008	0.0004	38	642325	0.025	0.013	0	-
	RR	94.7	4.4	23	453373	43.5	8.6	0	-
	H-IFF	1024.0	0.0	50	22620	574.4	46.9	0	-

Table 4. Performance of POEMS-gEA on TSP problem

cities	random			heuristic		
	Mean	*StDev*	*BestPath*	*Mean*	*StDev*	*BestPath*
100	831.9	15.7	803.8	818.6	14.5	786.1
200	1190.1	25.6	1156.3	1132.9	16.2	1098.1
500	2025.9	40.3	1975.6	1746.3	13.5	1718.0
1000	9970.0	290.0	9475.9	2523.0	15.0	2491.6
2000	34829.0	503.9	34281.5	3692.2	20.4	3655.1

representation with tight linkage is used the GALCO algorithm slightly outperforms POEMS on DF3 and F103 problems. However, the situation changes when solving problems with loose linkage. Then the POEMS performs considerably better than the other algorithms on DF3, Rosenbrock and F103 problems.

Tables 4 and 5 provide a comparison of the POEMS with ER, ER-heuristic, SOM, and 2-opt. We can observe that POEMS with random initialisation of the prototype works poorly on large TSP datasets. This is because starting from a very bad tour it would require many more iterations to find a good solution than allowed here. On the other hand, when the heuristic is used for generation of the initial prototype the POEMS outperform all the other approaches even on the large datasets of 2000 cities.

Table 5. Performance of ER, ER-heuristic, SOM, and 2-opt on TSP problem

cities	ER			ER-heuristic		
	Mean	*StDev*	*BestPath*	*Mean*	*StDev*	*BestPath*
100	1192.9	54.7	1115.6	935.1	27.1	884.1
200	2096.3	74.6	1973.6	1406.1	54.6	1289.1
500	4562.4	155.5	4424.0	2753.3	66.4	2666.6
1000	8256.5	223.9	7964.1	3799.6	91.4	3678.8
2000	16956.1	480.7	16402.4	5983.5	95.1	5875.8
cities	SOM			2-opt		
	Mean	*StDev*	*BestPath*	*Mean*	*StDev*	*BestPath*
100	830.4	13.0	811.7	853.5	18.2	797.3
200	1155.4	12.4	1124.7	1196.1	24.1	1149.2
500	1776.0	14.0	1751.2	1866.8	123.1	1772.9
1000	2533.0	12.0	2508.4	2650.1	160.0	2572.1
2000	3725.3	14.9	3695.6	3908.1	122.8	3789.2

Table 6. Performance of POEMS-gEA using just one type of the elementary function

action type	*Mean*	*StDev*	*BestPath*
invert	2554.7	13.3	2526.2
move	2689.1	20.1	2653.6
swap	2824.8	31.5	2775.1

Results in Table 6 demonstrate how the selection of elementary functions affects the performance of the POEMS approach. The results were obtained for TSP problem with 1000 cities. It shows that if just one function out of the three functions *invert*, *move*, and *swap* is enabled the POEMS performs worse than if all the functions are allowed to be combined in the action sequences. A fragment of an execution of POEMS on TSP with 100 cities is shown in Figure 4.

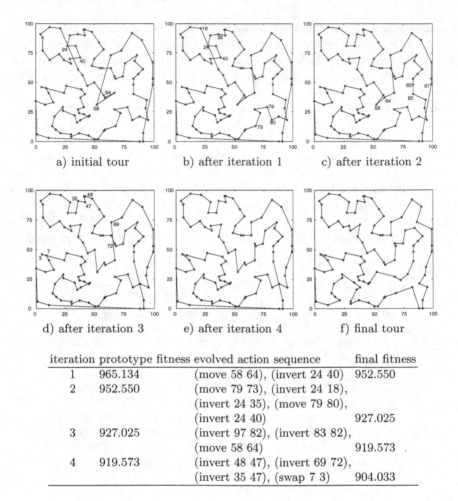

a) initial tour   b) after iteration 1   c) after iteration 2

d) after iteration 3   e) after iteration 4   f) final tour

iteration	prototype fitness	evolved action sequence	final fitness
1	965.134	(move 58 64), (invert 24 40)	952.550
2	952.550	(move 79 73), (invert 24 18),	
		(invert 24 35), (move 79 80),	
		(invert 24 40)	927.025
3	927.025	(invert 97 82), (invert 83 82),	
		(move 58 64)	919.573
4	919.573	(invert 48 47), (invert 69 72),	
		(invert 35 47), (swap 7 3)	904.033

Fig. 4. A fragment of an execution of POEMS on TSP with 100 cities. a) an initial tour prototype of length 965.134. b) the tour obtained after applying the action sequence evolved in iteration 1 on the current prototype. c) the tour obtained after iteration 2. d) the tour obtained after iteration 3. e) the tour obtained after iteration 4. f) the final tour of length 824.874.

7   Conclusions

In this paper, an algorithm called *Iterative Prototype Optimisation with Evolved Improvement Steps* (POEMS) is proposed. POEMS iteratively improves the prototype solution via evolving the best sequence of actions to be applied to the current prototype in each iteration.

The POEMS concept has been tested on the binary string optimisation problems and the traveling salesman problem and compared with other optimisation algorithms. The presented experiments show that the proposed approach achieves competitive or better results than the compared algorithms. However, as a mutation-based optimisation approach it possesses a limited ability to identify and process building blocks of higher order.

On the other hand, this approach might be well suited for solving problems where the representation does not allow to design crossover operators that would effectively mix important building blocks of the parental solutions. In other words, these are the problems where the crossover performs just as a hyper-mutation.

Future research will focus on the analysis of the proposed algorithm behavior as well as on the identification of problems the algorithm is well suited for.

Acknowledgments. The research has been supported by the research program No. MSM6840770012 "Transdisciplinary Research in the Area of Biomedical Engineering II" of the CTU in Prague, sponsored by the Ministry of Education, Youth and Sports of the Czech Republic. Authors would like to thank Petr Pošík (CTU Prague) for many valuable comments improving the paper.

References

1. Faigl, J., Kulich, M., Přeučil, L.: Multiple traveling salesmen problem with hierarchy of cities in inspection task with limited visibility. In proceedings of the 5th Workshop on Self-Organizing Maps. Universit Paris-Sud, (2005) 91–98
2. Forrest, S. and Mitchell, M.: Relative building-block fitness and the Building Block Hypothesis. In Whitley, L. D. (Ed.), *Foundations of Genetic Algorithms 2*. San Mateo, CA: Morgan Kaufmann, (1993) 109–126
3. Goldberg, D.E.: *The Design of Innovation: Lessons from and for Competent Genetic Algorithms*. Genetic Algorithms and Evolutionary Computation, Volume 7. Kluwer Academic Pub; ISBN: 1402070985, (2002)
4. Kubalík, J., Rothkrantz, L.J.M., Lažanský, J.: Genetic Algorithms with Limited Convergence. In Grana, M.; Duro, R.J.; Anjou, A.d.; Wang, P.P. (Eds.), *Information Processing with Evolutionary Algorithms: From Industrial Applications to Academic Speculations*, ISBN: 1-85233-866-0, (2005) 233–254
5. Uyar, A.S., Sariel, S., Eryigit, G.: "A Gene Based Adaptive Mutation Strategy for Genetic Algorithms", GECCO 2004: Genetic and Evolutionary Computation Conference, (2004) 271–281
6. Watson, R.A., Hornby, G.S. and Pollack, J.B.: Modeling Building-Block Interdependency. In *Fifth International Conference PPSN V*. Springer, (1998) 97–106
7. Whitley, D., Starkweather, T., D'Ann Fuquay: Scheduling Problems and Traveling Salesmen: The Genetic Edge Recombination Operator. ICGA 1989. (1989) 133–140
8. Whitley, D.: Fundamental Principles of Deception in Genetic Search. In: *Foundations of Genetic Algorithms*. G. Rawlins (ed.), Morgan Kaufmann, (1991) 221–241
9. Whitley, D., Mathias, K., Rana, S., Dzubera, J.: Evaluating Evolutionary Algorithms. *Artificial Intelligence*, Volume 85, (1996) 245–2761

Learning Recursive Functions with Object Oriented Genetic Programming

Alexandros Agapitos and Simon M. Lucas

Department of Computer Science,
University of Essex, Colchester CO4 3SQ, UK
{aagapi, sml}@essex.ac.uk

Abstract. This paper describes the evolution of recursive functions within an Object-Oriented Genetic Programming (OOGP) system. We evolved general solutions to factorial, Fibonacci, exponentiation, even-n-Parity, and nth-3. We report the computational effort required to evolve these methods and provide a comparison between crossover and mutation variation operators, and also undirected random search. We found that the evolutionary algorithms performed much better than undirected random search, and thats mutation outperformed crossover on most problems.

1 Introduction

One of the most challenging areas of research in GP is to investigate ways of scaling its ability to evolve computer programs to larger and more complex problem domains. Modularity is arguably the main mechanism that conventional programming uses to address complex problems, and enables solutions to such problems to be specified as relatively simple compositions of sub-components. Past research has attempted to integrate modularity into the GP paradigm. Several approaches have been followed, including, Automatically Defined Functions (ADFs) [1], Module Acquisition [2], Adaptive Representation through Learning [3] and Automatically Defined Macros [4]. Much of modern software development, however, is based on object-oriented (OO) programming. Object-oriented software design couples the design of data structures [5] (Object classes or types) with methods that operate on those structures, thereby providing better modularity and reuse than non-OO techniques. We believe that object-oriented programs should also be amenable to evolutionary search, and may enable GP to scale up to tackle complex problems that would otherwise be infeasible. This is a very significant challenge, however, and in this paper we focus our attention on the evolution of simple recursive methods within OOGP. The reason for doing this is to demonstrate that OOGP is able to provide competitive performance on this class of problem.

Recursion is a powerful concept, and when appropriate can be used to specify very elegant programs. Where applicable, recursive programs tend to be more compact than non-recursive (or non-iterative) expression trees. From a machine learning perspective, one of the main goals of GP is to create a program given a

P. Collet et al. (Eds.): EuroGP 2006, LNCS 3905, pp. 166–177, 2006.

set of training data such that the program will have a low error rate on unseen test data. Previous research [6] has shown that more parsimonious evolved solutions are less prone to over-fitting. Finally, it has been argued [7] that programs of shorter effective length have better chances of surviving the destructive effects of crossover than programs with larger effective length.

The main problem GP faces when evaluating recursive programs is the handling of infinite loops which result from recursive function calls that never satisfy a termination criterion. Here we use a function call limit within our interpreter. Programs that exceed their limit are terminated and assigned minimum fitness (maximum error). An interesting alternative is the competing coroutines method of Maxwell [8], where a population of programs is run concurrently, with best fitness being assigned to the first programs to provide correct output. For now, however, we use the function call limit, as it is more straightforward to implement and to configure.

Previous research [9, 10, 11, 12, 13, 14, 15, 16, 17, 18, 19, 20] has addressed the issue of evolving recursive programs, using either implicit or explicit recursion mechanisms. It is clearly not possible in a paper of this length to review all previous attempts on the subject and provide specific comparisons to other approaches. It is worth mentioning that past research has been devoted to evolving recursion using tree, linear (binary machine code) and stack-based hypothesis representations. However, to our knowledge, no solutions to factorial nor exponentiation, using a tree-type representation, have been attempted at the time of writing. Furthermore, Fibonacci sequence, with a tree-type genome, was induced in [11] using Automatically Defined Recursion and Architecture Altering Operations but the evolved program did not generalize beyond the first twelve elements of the sequence used as fitness cases during training. Even-N-Parity with explicit recursion and tree-type representation was studied in [14]. Their work used trees derived from logic grammars, an approach quite different from the one taken in this paper.

This paper focuses on evolving Object Oriented (OO) recursive programs. Of direct relevance to this paper is the work of Bruce [21] and Langdon [5] on evolving abstract data types. The most similar prior work on evolution of OO methods is Abbott's [22] and Lucas's [23] initial explorations of reflection-based OOGP systems as well as Suarez's et al [24] investigation of evolving OO agent programs. Abbott used reflection to make method invocations, and mentioned the ability to use existing class libraries as an advantage of the approach, though the parity problem he used as an example did not demonstrate that, and instead used specially defined classes and methods to help solve the problem. Lucas investigated the use of Java Reflection to enable evolutionary algorithms to directly exploit existing class libraries and demonstrated the feasibility of his approach with the aid of an evolutionary art example.

The most extensive set of evolved recursive programs presented so far was due to Spector et al [9] with their PushGP system. They evolved many ingenious recursive solutions to a number of problems. Here, we show that we can obtain similar results in terms of evolved functionality within our OOGP system, with all the potential benefits that could ensue from using an OO model, together with the ability to use the power of the Java class libraries in to potentially evolve solutions to interesting real-world problems, with very little human input.

2   OOGP: Evolutionary Computation Research System

OOGP is a Java-based *Object Oriented Genetic Programming* system capable of evolving OO method implementations that match a specified interface. This section describes the main features of the OOGP experimentation framework.

OOGP uses a panmictic, generation-based breeding policy to evolve object-oriented programs. For this paper, we are fixing the set of available classes, objects, variables and method signatures, and evolving only the method implementations, which are specified as program-trees. Each run begins with a population of randomly initialized program-trees.

The generational model is combined with elitism, in that a fixed percentage of the best individuals are preserved from generation to generation. The genetic algorithm for OOGP is the same as that for standard GP. The system provides implementations of three tree generation methods most widely used in literature namely, Full, Grow, Ramped Half-and-Half [20]. We used tournament selection and standard variation operators of crossover (XO), macro-mutation (MM — substituting a node in the tree with an entire randomly generated subtree with the same return type) and point-mutation[1] (PM — substituting a non-terminal node with another non-terminal node with the same return and parameter types or substituting a terminal node with another terminal node of the same return type). We used a standard crossover operator (not homologous).

Recursion in conventional programming can be achieved by making the name of a procedural abstraction appear in its own body, and thus enabling it to call itself. Similarly, recursion in GP can be most naturally expressed by assigning a name to the evolved method and allow this name to be called from within the evolved method's body [12, 14, 19]. An important issue is regarding what we consider to be a non-terminal element. Using the above approach we make no distinction between built-in methods and the evolved method, thus making the evolved method available to the method set serving as the alphabet for constructing hypotheses. Importantly, this representation of recursion is generic and in-line with conventional programming's implementation of recursive calls. It does not require high-level recursive operators to be supplied in the method set. Thus, the ability to synthesize arbitrary recursive behaviour from non-recursive primitives makes recursion an emergent property of the GP run.

Given a method signature (its return type and list of parameter types), the system evolves the code that implements the method. We consider an evolved method's representation to be a tree-type structure of objects of interface type Expr. This interface is presented in Figure 1. Note that each expression has a set of children, and an evaluation environment. The evaluation environment

---

[1] Analogue of bit-flip mutation in standard Genetic Algorithm.

```
public interface Expr {
  public Object eval(Expr[] env);
  public Expr[] getChildren();
  public Class getType();
}
```

Fig. 1. The interface for an `Expr`, the building block of the tree-type representation

provides bindings for any formal method parameters, and this model directly enables recursive calls [25].

Wrapper classes have been used to define the building blocks of the tree representation. These classes include `Function`[2], `IFThenElse`, `Cond`[3], `Constant`, and `Parameter`[4], all implementing the `Expr` interface in order to achieve polymorphism during recursive tree evaluation and tree manipulation operations. Following the discussion above, a `Function` object must be able to represent both an evolved method and a primitive non-terminal element. The solution we preferred is to declare a `Function` class instance variable of interface type `Callable`[5] and define two classes, namely, `Funcall` and `MethodCall` implementing this interface. The former holds a reference to the root node of an evolved tree-structure and triggers its evaluation, while the latter represents a primitive OO method invocation.

The system exploits reflection to automatically discover features about the environment (the existing classes and objects) it is to operate on. Therefore, it is possible to discover the set of all methods that can be called on an object of a particular class and hence invoke these during tree interpretation. Towards this direction, we use a set of active `Class` types in order to populate our primitive OO non-terminal (i.e methods) set. If desirable, manual intervention is still possible by specifying the set of existing methods to be used. The complete OOGP method set is large and cannot be fully documented here, but the set of the OO primitive methods used in the experiments is presented in Table 1.

In addition, every evolved method should be able to use its own objects to invoke methods on. The solution we preferred is to define an `ObjectHolder` wrapper class, which has two fields: `Class objectClass`, and `Object objectValue`. This structure provides local fine-grain control of the object classes and values. The `ObjectManager` class dynamically instantiates objects of active `Class` types[6] and makes them available for use to an evolved method during its creation. The interface of Figure 1 shows that each tree-node, represented as a class that implements this interface, is a self-evaluated entity (i.e. `eval(Expr[] env)`). Our reflection-based interpreter starts the evolved method evaluation from the root

---

[2] To avoid confusion with existing `java.lang.reflect.Method` we call our tree-node, representing an OO method, a `Function`.

[3] Analogous to Lisp's `Cond` function.

[4] `Constant` and `Parameter` classes represent primitive terminal elements.

[5] It's only method is: `public Object call(Object[] args)`.

[6] Via reflection-based constructor invocation.

Table 1. Sample OOGP method set

Description	Methods	Argument(s) type	Return type
Arithmetic	add, sub, mul, div, pow	Double, Double	Double
	exp, log, sqrt	Double	Double
Boolean Logic	and, or, nand, nor	Boolean, Boolean	Boolean
List Processing	cdr	List	List
	car	List	Double
	isEmpty	List	Boolean
	length	List	Integer
Predicate	=, >, >=, <, <=	Double, Double	Boolean

node of its tree-type structure and recursively calls the `eval` method on each node. Conditional nodes (i.e instances of `IfThenElse` and `Cond` classes) are evaluated using the delayed evaluation model (otherwise recursive programs would never halt). All other nodes are strictly evaluated.

The heavy reliance on reflection does have an unfortunate performance cost, and for real-world applications a better option might be to compile the code. This can be done by using Java toolkits that allow run-time manipulations of classes, or by generating Java source code and then compiling it. For the simple problems under investigation here, however, the compilation or class construction cost could outweigh the evaluation cost.

The tree-based structures that undergo adaptation are strongly typed. This is similar to Montana's *Strongly Typed Genetic Programming* [26] in that each `Parameter` and `Constant` has an assigned type (i.e. an instance of `Class`) and each `Function` has a specified type for each argument and for the value it returns. To assist in enforcing type constraints, while creating and manipulating parse-trees, we implemented a class called `TypeManager`. This maintains three look-up tables called *typedMethods*, *typedTerminals* and *elementPossibility*, all of type `HashMap` from *Java's Collection API*. The purpose of *typedMethods* and *typedTerminals* is to provide direct access to the set of non-terminal and terminal primitive elements, of a specific type, respectively. The *elementPossibility* data structure is reminiscent of Montana's [26] *"type possibilities table"*. It constrains the choice of non-terminal primitives, as tree nodes, in order to ensure that the tree can grow to its maximum depth.

An important issue of Object Orientation is polymorphism (i.e methods can be defined that allow parameters of type `Object`, the root of *Java's Object Hierarchy*). This mechanism of passing polymorphic parameters is clearly desirable in a framework that evolves OO software. Argument objects, represented by elements of the primitive terminal set, should be allowed many entries in the *typedTerminals* map, one for each parameter type they can be passed as. System enhancement of this kind is currently under development.

We implemented an `ExpressionSimplifier` class in order to syntactically simplify the programs evolved by OOGP. The expression simplification algorithm used the universal domain-independent editing rule defined in [20] along with a simple hill-climber that iteratively performs a random simplification and retains

the simpler program only if it is equally good. Random simplifications include:
(a) the substitution of a subtree with a terminal node from a predefined terminal
set, and (b) the removal of a subtree from a bigger subtree and reconnection of
the two loose ends. This approach has been remarkably successful, reducing full-
depth trees to the simplified ones shown in Figure 2.

```
(If-Then-Else              (Cond                        (If-Then-Else
  (Method:gt                 (Method:et                   (Method:gt
    Parameter[0]               Parameter[0]                 Parameter[1]
    Constant:0.0               Constant:0.0)                Constant:0.0
  )                          Constant:1.0                 )
  (Method:mul                (Method:et                   (Method:mul
    Parameter[0]               Parameter[0]                 (Evolved_Method
    (Evolved_Method            Constant:1.0)                 Parameter[0]
      (Method:sub            Constant:1.0                   (Method:sub
        Parameter[0]         (Method:add                      Parameter[1]
        Constant:1.0           (Evolved_Method                Constant:1.0
      )                          (Method:sub                )
    )                            Parameter[0]             )
  )                              Constant:1.0))           Parameter[0]
  Constant:1.0               (Evolved_Method             )
)                              (Method:sub               Constant:1.0
                                 Parameter[0]            )
                                 Constant:2.0)))
                           )

        (a)                        (b)                        (c)
```

Fig. 2. Sample simplified evolved methods for (a) Factorial; (b) Fibonacci; (c)
Exponentiation

3   Experiments

Five different problems have been tackled in order to assess the feasibility and
generality of our approach in evolving recursive methods. These include the
computations of factorial, Fibonacci sequence, exponentiation, even-n-parity and
nth-3. The experiments used a variety of control parameters. Population sizes
ranged from 7,000 to 12,000 individuals and the number of generations was set to
50. It seemed unnecessary to extend the number of generations as the runs tended
to stagnate after approximately 30 generations. In order to enforce diversity in
the initial random generation, ramped half-and-half was used as a tree generation
method with maximum initial depth set to 4 and maximum depth produced by
the genetic operators set to 10 or 12. Tournament selection (tournament sizes
of 7 or 10) along with elitism (1%) was used as the selection mechanism. The
distribution of selection of crossover points was set to 90% probability of selecting
interior nodes (uniformly) and 10% probability of selecting a leaf node. In order

to avoid the problem caused by non-terminating recursive structures we limited the recursive calls to between 20 and 288. The upper bound of 288 was chosen to be slightly larger than the largest number of recursive calls required by our hand-coded implementation of the most recursively expensive problem, Fibonacci. By limiting the recursive calls in this way, we may have been providing a very weak form of guidance to the evolutionary algorithm, but this was done simply to place a reasonable limit on the run time. When limited in this way, each single run of the EA still took several hours.

When a program reaches the execution limit, evaluation is abandoned and the individual is assigned the maximum error (making it unlikely that a violating program will produce offspring, unless it participates in a tournament of equally unfit individuals). The evolution terminated if the maximum number of generations was reached or an individual reproduced successfully the training set outputs. Test sets measured the ability of an evolved solution to generalize to unseen data and recognized the success of a run. No individual that has passed all of the training cases has ever been shown to fail on any test case subsequently presented to it. At no stage were the test sets used during training. In each problem, unless otherwise stated, we used the normalized absolute mean error on the training set as the fitness function. The normalization gives equal weight to the errors resulting from each training case by placing each error within the range of $\{0.0, \ldots, 1.0\}$. Thus, it restricts big errors from dominating the mean error, which is important for problems such as factorial. The fitness function is specified in Equation 1 (the lower the numerical value the better the individual's performance),

$$Error = \frac{\sum_{i=1}^{n} \frac{|actual_i - estimate_i|}{|actual_i| + |estimate_i|}}{n} \tag{1}$$

where $actual_i$ is the correct value for the training/test case i, $estimate_i$ is the value returned by the evolved method for the training/test case i, and n is the size of the training/test set.

We used three different search regimes to search the space of recursive programs. The first regime used 99% XO combined with 1% PM. The second regime used 99% MM combined with 1% PM. Note here that the exploitative nature of PM can be used to complement the global search power of XO and MM. However, the small probability of its application dictates a behaviour that guards against premature loss of primitives. The third regime used random search (RS) (i.e. no selection pressure), but arranged in generations of purely random individuals in order to plot the fitness on the same graphs as for the other methods.

We performed 100 independent runs on each experiment in order to get statistically meaningful results. The computational effort $I(M,i,z)$ was computed in the standard way, as described by Koza [20]. A summary of the computational effort, sufficient to yield a solution to the considered problems with 99% confidence, is illustrated in Table 2. The standard error estimates derive from treating a successful outcome as the result of flipping a biased coin, and can be used to judge the statistical significance of the differences (there is a greater than

Table 2. Summary of results for each method on each problem (bold face indicates best performance on a given problem, standard errors in parentheses for prob. success)

		Prob. of Success (%)	Minimum I(M,i,z)	Fitness Evaluations
Factorial	XO	40 (4.8)	1,520,000	15,200,000
	MM	**74 (4.4)**	**600,000**	**6,000,000**
	RS	6 (2.4)	20,340,000	203,400,000
Fibonacci	XO	19 (3.9)	4,557,000	45,570,000
	MM	**25 (4.3)**	**2,002,000**	**20,020,000**
	RS	0 (-)	-	-
Exponentiation	XO	**6**	**14,238,000**	**142,380,000**
	MM	2 (1.4)	38,304,000	383,040,000
	RS	2 (1.4)	52,440,000	524,400,000
Even-N-Parity	XO	69 (4.6)	600,000	7,200,000
	MM	**78 (4.1)**	**680,000**	**8,160,000**
	RS	1 (1.0)	9,180,000	110,160,000
Nth-3	XO	55 (5.0)	1,224,000	24,480,000
	MM	**82 (3.8)**	**512,000**	**10,240,000**
	RS	2 (1.4)	44,064,000	881,280,000

99% chance that the true probability of success lies within 3 standard errors of the estimate). Note that when showing the sample evolved methods, we show only the simplified versions; the evolved versions prior to simplification tend to be bloated to maximum tree depth. This may have been avoidable had we used some form of parsimony pressure.

Factorial: We seek to evolve a recursive implementation of the factorial function. Figure 3 shows the best-of-generation individuals of 100 independent runs using (a) XO; (b) MM; and (c) RS. Figure 3(d) presents the cumulative probability of success resulting from the three different search regimes. We used integers $\{1, \ldots, 10\}$ as training set arguments, and $\{11, \ldots, 30\}$ for the test set. A simplified sample evolved solution is illustrated in Figure 2(a). It was possible to coerce the system to produce different solutions by varying the primitive non-terminal set of a given run. We experimented with evolving a factorial sequence approximation using the arithmetic methods presented in Table 1, but excluded the evolved method name from the function set, hence preventing the evolution of recursion. In this experiment we used the first 100 integers for training. The system was able to come up with many novel solutions to the approximation of factorial. The best evolved individual gave an error of $3,140702 \times 10^{-8}$ over the complete training set. We plotted the evolved solution against the recursive version and Stirling's approximation and observed that the evolved approximation came closer to the recursive solution for the integer values in the range of $\{1, \ldots, 120\}$. We have omitted the evolved tree for space reasons.

Fibonacci sequence: We used the first 12 elements of the sequence as the training cases. The test set was set to elements of $\{13, \ldots, 17\}$. An evolved *general solution* simplified to the program of Figure 2(b).

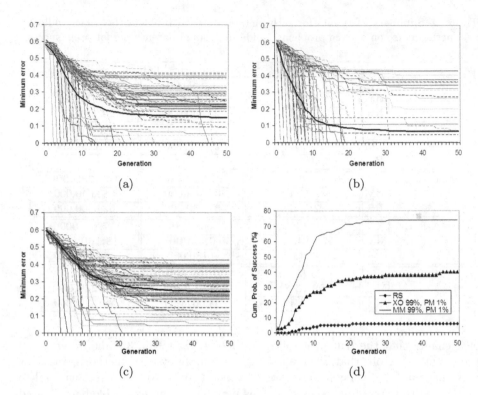

Fig. 3. Evolving Factorial. (a) Best-of-generation individuals using XO; (b) Best-of-generation individuals using MM; (c) Best-of-generation individuals using RS; (d) Comparison of cumulative probabilities of success between the search operators.

Exponentiation: We seek solutions to the general recursive definition of computing the integer exponential a^b. The training set was set to instances of 2^n, n in the range of $\{1, \ldots, 9\}$. Ten unique test cases were randomly generated. Both the base and the exponent were taken from the range of $\{1, \ldots, 10\}$. Figure 2(c) presents a general evolved solution.

Even-N-Parity: Takes a list of N boolean inputs, returning True if an even number of inputs are True and False otherwise. Again, we seek solutions to the general even-n-parity problem. The even-2- and even-3-parity problems were used as the training data. These 12 cases constitute a well-defined set for learning the recursive definition of this problem. The even-7-parity problem (128 fitness cases) was used as the test set. The fitness function in this problem is the total number of misclassifications on the 12 training cases.

Nth-3: This problem takes two arguments, an integer N and a list L and returns the Nth element of L. If $N < 1$, it returns the first element of L. If $N > length(L)$, it returns the last element of L. We took training list L to be a list of length 10 and test list L' to be a list of length 20 with all of their entries unique. The training set contained 20 cases of N in the range of $\{-4, \ldots, 15\}$. The test set contained 30 cases of N in the range of $\{-4, \ldots, 25\}$. The fitness function is given in Equation 2; the lower the error the better the performance.

$$Error = \frac{\sum_{i=1}^{n} 1 - \frac{1}{2^{d_i}}}{n} \tag{2}$$

where d is the distance between the correct position and the return value position for the training/test case i and n is the size of the training/test set.

4   Discussion

Macro-mutation outperformed crossover on most problems. A possible reason could be the sometimes deceptive fitness assignment inherent in fitness evaluation of recursive code. Recall from Section 3 that an individual is being assigned the maximum error in case where its evaluation reaches the execution limit. For example, a recursive program that contains a correct transition rule but an incorrect base case may be discarded from the population if its evaluation results in the maximum error due to unending recursion. A program that does not halt may still contain useful parts that need to be propagated and combined in further generations. Programs containing erroneous recursive structures are most likely non-terminating ones unless these recursive structures lie in tree parts not being evaluated due to delayed evaluation. It may therefore be the case that recursive nodes are being prematurely lost from the population and the low probability of mutation application cannot guard against convergence to local optima. Crossover cannot play the role of a building-block proliferation engine, and is instead degenerated into a mutation operator whose randomly generated material is restricted by population content. Run stagnation may have been avoidable had we put more effort to optimize the algorithm's control parameters.

Exponentiation evolution has a relatively low success rate. This is probably due to the function having two formal parameters of the same type, thus hindering the discovery of their semantic dependencies when these parameters are used within the function body.

5   Conclusions

It is possible to routinely evolve a range of recursive functions within an object-oriented genetic programming system. The functions can be reliably evolved from small samples of data and generalize perfectly. Evolution significantly outperformed random search. The recursion mechanism used is general; recursive behaviour emerges from non-recursive primitives. The tree-type representation produces elegant, easy-to-understand solutions, and can naturally integrate with the *Java API*. This initial exploration gives impetus to concentrate on evolving more interesting recursive algorithms, such as $n\log n$ sorting algorithms, and to provide a comparative assessment with other approaches. Beyond that, we believe that OOGP is an area with immense possibilities, including the evolution of complete classes, and cooperating sets of classes.

Acknowledgements

The authors thank the Natural and Evolutionary Computation research group (especially Bill Langdon) at the University of Essex, UK, and the anonymous reviewers, for their feedback on this work.

References

1. J.R. Koza, *Genetic Programming II: automatic discovery of reusable programs*, MIT Press, (1994).
2. Peter J. Angeline and Jordan Pollack, "Evolutionary module acquisition", in *Proceedings of the Second Annual Conference on Evolutionary Programming*, 25-26 February 1993, pp. 154–163.
3. Justinian P. Rosca and Dana H. Ballard, "Discovery of subroutines in genetic programming", in *Advances in Genetic Programming 2*, Peter J. Angeline and K. E. Kinnear, Jr., Eds., chapter 9, pp. 177–202. MIT Press, 1996.
4. Lee Spector, "Simultaneous evolution of programs and their control structures", in *Advances in Genetic Programming 2*, Peter J. Angeline and K. E. Kinnear, Jr., Eds., chapter 7, pp. 137–154. MIT Press, 1996.
5. William B. Langdon, "Evolving data structures with genetic programming", in *Proc. of the Sixth Int. Conf. on Genetic Algorithms*, Larry J. Eshelman, Ed. 1995, pp. 295–302, Morgan Kaufmann.
6. Justinian Rosca, "Generality versus size in genetic programming", in *Genetic Programming 1996: Proceedings of the First Annual Conference*. 28–31 July 1996, pp. 381–387, MIT Press.
7. Wolfgang Banzhaf, Peter Nordin, Robert E. Keller, and Frank D. Francone, *Genetic Programming – An Introduction; On the Automatic Evolution of Computer Programs and its Applications*, Morgan Kaufmann, January 1998.
8. Sidney R. Maxwell, "Experiments with a coroutine execution model for genetic programming", in *IEEE Conference on Evolutionary Computation*. 1994, pp. 413 – 417, IEEE.
9. Lee Spector, Jon Klein, and Maarten Keijzer, "The push3 execution stack and the evolution of control", in *GECCO '05: Proceedings of the 2005 conference on Genetic and evolutionary computation*, 2005, pp. 1689–1696.
10. Lorenz Huelsbergen, "Learning recursive sequences via evolution of machine-language programs", in *Genetic Programming 1997: Proceedings of the Second Annual Conference*, 13-16 July 1997, pp. 186–194.
11. John R. Koza, David Andre, Forrest H Bennett III, and Martin Keane, *Genetic Programming 3: Darwinian Invention and Problem Solving*, Morgan Kaufman, (1999).
12. Chris Clack and Tina Yu, "Performance enhanced genetic programming.", in *Proceedings of the Sixth Conference on Evolutionary Programming*, 1997, vol. 1213 of *Lecture Notes in Computer Science*.
13. P. A. Whigham and R. I. McKay, "Genetic approaches to learning recursive relations", in *Progress in Evolutionary Computation*, X. Yao, Ed., vol. 956 of *Lecture Notes in Artificial Intelligence*, pp. 17–27. Springer-Verlag, 1995.
14. Man Leung Wong and Kwong Sak Leung, "Evolving recursive functions for the even-parity problem using genetic programming", in *Advances in Genetic Programming 2*, Peter J. Angeline and K. E. Kinnear, Jr., Eds., chapter 11, pp. 221–240. MIT Press, Cambridge, MA, USA, 1996.

15. Tina Yu and Chris Clack, "Recursion, lambda abstractions and genetic programming", in *Genetic Programming 1998: Proceedings of the Third Annual Conference*, 22-25 July 1998, pp. 422–431.
16. Mykel J. Kochenderfer, "Evolving hierarchical and recursive teleo-reactive programs through genetic programming", in *Genetic Programming, Proceedings of EuroGP'2003*, 14-16 April 2003, vol. 2610 of *LNCS*, pp. 83–92.
17. Peter Nordin and Wolfgang Banzhaf, "Evolving turing-complete programs for a register machine with self-modifying code", in *Genetic Algorithms: Proceedings of the Sixth International Conference (ICGA95)*, L. Eshelman, Ed. 15-19 July 1995, pp. 318–325, Morgan Kaufmann.
18. Masato Nishiguchi and Yoshiji Fujimoto, "Evolutions of recursive programs with multi-niche genetic programming (mnGP)", in *Proceedings of the 1998 IEEE World Congress on Computational Intelligence*. 5-9 May 1998, pp. 247–252, IEEE Press.
19. Scott Brave, "Evolving recursive programs for tree search", in *Advances in Genetic Programming 2*, Peter J. Angeline and K. E. Kinnear, Jr., Eds., chapter 10, pp. 203–220. MIT Press, 1996.
20. J.R. Koza, *Genetic Programming: on the programming of computers by means of natural selection*, MIT Press, (1992).
21. Wilker Shane Bruce, "Automatic generation of object-oriented programs using genetic programming", in *Genetic Programming 1996: Proceedings of the First Annual Conference*, Stanford University, CA, USA, 28–31 July 1996, pp. 267–272.
22. Russell J. Abbott, "Object-oriented genetic programming, an initial implementation", in *Procceedings of the Sixth International Conference on Computational Intelligence and Natural Computing*, September 26-30 2003.
23. Simon M. Lucas, "Exploiting reflection in object oriented genetic programming", in *Genetic Programming 7th European Conference, EuroGP 2004, Proceedings*, 5-7 April 2004, vol. 3003 of *LNCS*, pp. 369–378.
24. David Enrique Suarez Pinzon, Julian Yezid Olarte Ramos, and Sergio Andres Rojas Galeano, "Evolving object oriented agent programs in robocup domain", in *Genetic and Evolutionary Computation Conference (GECCO2005) workshop program*, Washington, D.C., USA, 25-29 June 2005, pp. 407–410, ACM Press.
25. Harold Abelson and Gerald Jay Sussman, *Structure and Interpretation of Computer Programs*, MIT Press, 1984.
26. David J. Montana, "Strongly typed genetic programming", BBN Technical Report #7866, Bolt Beranek and Newman, Inc., Cambridge, MA, 1994.

Negative Slope Coefficient: A Measure to Characterize Genetic Programming Fitness Landscapes

Leonardo Vanneschi[1], Marco Tomassini[2], Philippe Collard[3], and Sébastien Vérel[3]

[1] Dipartimento di Informatica, Sistemistica e Comunicazione (D.I.S.Co.),
University of Milan-Bicocca, Milan, Italy
[2] Computer Systems Department, University of Lausanne, Lausanne, Switzerland
[3] I3S Laboratory, University of Nice, Sophia Antipolis, France

Abstract. Negative slope coefficient has been recently introduced and empirically proven a suitable hardness indicator for some well known genetic programming benchmarks, such as the even parity problem, the binomial-3 and the artificial ant on the Santa Fe trail. Nevertheless, the original definition of this measure contains several limitations. This paper points out some of those limitations, presents a new and more relevant definition of the negative slope coefficient and empirically shows the suitability of this new definition as a hardness measure for some genetic programming benchmarks, including the multiplexer, the intertwined spirals problem and the royal trees.

1 Introduction

What makes a problem easy or hard for Evolutionary Algorithms? A first effort to answer this challenging question has been done by Goldberg and coworkers (e.g., see [3, 5]) in the field of Genetic Algorithms (GAs). Their approach consisted in constructing functions that should *a priori* be easy or hard for GAs to solve. These ideas have been followed by many others (e.g. [12, 4]) and have been the source of many hypotheses as to what makes a problem easy or difficult for GAs. One concept that underlies many of these approaches is the notion of *fitness landscape* [15]. A fitness landscape is a plot where the points in the horizontal subspace represent the different individual genotypes in a search space and the points in the vertical direction represent their fitness [9]. Individual genotypes are usually placed on the horizontal subspace according to a certain neighborhood structure. If genotypes can be visualized in two dimensions, the plot can be seen as a three-dimensional surface, which may contain peaks and valleys. The task of finding the best solution to the problem is equivalent to finding the highest peak (for maximization problems). The problem solver is seen as a short-sighted explorer searching for it. The fitness landscape plot can be helpful to understand the difficulty of a problem, i.e. the ability of a searcher to find the optimal solution for that problem (see for instance [17] for a deep analysis). Nevertheless, fitness landscapes are impossible to be plotted in practice, given the generally huge size of the space of solutions and the multi-dimentionality and complexity of the possible neighborhood structures. For this reason, in the last few years researchers have been looking for an algebraic measure able to capture some of the interesting properties of fitness landscapes. Early attemps

P. Collet et al. (Eds.): EuroGP 2006, LNCS 3905, pp. 178–189, 2006.

are represented by [22, 11, 7]. A signicant contribution to this field has been given by Jones [6] with the introduction of an hardness measure for GAs called *fitness distance correlation (fdc)*. This measure has been extended to tree-based Genetic Programming (GP) and proven a suitable hardness indicator in [17, 16, 19, 20, 2]. Nevertheless, these contributions have also shown that *fdc* has some flaws, the most important one being the fact that *fdc* is not predictive, i.e. the optimal solution (or solutions) must be known beforehand, which is almost unrealistic in applied search and optimization problems. Thus, it is important to investigate other approaches based on quantities that can be measured without any explicit knowledge of the genotype of optimal solutions. Preliminary results of this enquiry can be found in [18], where a new measure called *negative slope coefficient (nsc)* has been introduced.

This paper aims at extending and generalizing the study of *nsc* for tree-based GP. It is structured as follows: section 2 introduces the concept of *fitness cloud* on which *nsc* is based. Section 3 takes up the original definition of the *nsc* as it has been presented in [18] and section 4 points out its main limitations. Section 5 proposes a new method for calculating the *nsc* and shows some experimental results pointing out that this method enables to overcome some drawbacks of the original definition of the *nsc*. Finally, section 6 offers our conclusions and hints for future research.

2   Fitness Clouds

Evolvability is a feature that is intuitively related, although not exactly identical, to problem difficulty. It has been defined as the capability of genetic operators to improve fitness quality [1]. The most natural way to study evolvability is, probably, to plot the fitness values of individuals against the fitness values of their neighbors, where a neighbor is obtained by applying one step of a genetic operator to the individual. Such a plot has been first introduced for binary landscapes by Vérel and coworkers [21] and called by them *fitness cloud*. In this paper, the genetic operator used to generate fitness clouds is standard subtree mutation [8], i.e. mutation obtained by replacing a subtree of the selected individual with a randomly generated tree.

2.1   Definition

Let $\Gamma = \{\gamma_1, \gamma_2, \ldots, \gamma_n\}$ be the whole search space of a GP problem and let $V(\gamma_j) = \{v_1^j, v_2^j, \ldots, v_{m_j}^j\}$ be the set of all the neighbors of individual $\gamma_j, \forall j \in [1,n]$. Now let f be the fitness function of the problem at hand. The following set of points can be defined: $S = \{(f(\gamma_j), f(v_k^j)), \forall j \in [1,n], \forall k \in [1,m_j]\}$. The graphical representation of S on a bidimentional plane, or fitness cloud, is the scatterplot of the fitness of all the individuals belonging to the search space against the fitness of all their neighbors. The main idea is that the shape of this scatterplot can give an indication of the evolvability of the genetic operators used and thus some hints about the difficulty of the problem at hand. The fitness cloud also implicitly gives some insight on the genotype to phenotype map: the set of genotypes that all have equal fitness is a *neutral set*. Such a set corresponds to one abscissa in the fitness/fitness plane; according to this abscissa, a vertical slice from the cloud represents the set of fitnesses that could be reached from this set of neutrality.

For a given offspring fitness value $\tilde{f}$, an horizontal slice represents all the fitnesses from which one can reach $\tilde{f}$.

2.2 Sampling Methodology

In general, the sizes of the search space and of the neighborhoods do not allow one to consider all the possible individuals. Thus, samples are needed. Since selection used by GP is likely to eliminate bad individuals from the population, importance sampling techniques must to be used. As in [17, 18], also in this work the well-known *Metropolis-Hastings* technique [10] is used to sample the search space and the k-tournament selection algorithm [8] (with $k = 10$) is used to sample neighborhoods (see [17] for a detailed motivation of these choices). Using random samples would assume that the space is relatively uniform, e.g. that the measurement in one region of space (the sampled space) applies to all regions of space (or at least a large enough percentage of the space). The choice of important samplings has also been done to limitate this drawback. The terminology of section 2.1 is thus updated: from now on, Γ represents a sample of individuals obtained with the Metropolis-Hastings technique and, for each γ_j belonging to Γ, $V(\gamma_j)$ is a subset of its neighbors, obtained by the applying tournament selection.

3 Negative Slope Coefficient

The fitness cloud can be of help in determining some characteristics of the fitness landscape related to evolvability and problem difficulty. But the mere observation of the scatterplot is not sufficient to quantify these features. In [17, 18] an algebraic measure called *negative slope coefficient* (*nsc*) has been introduced. It can be calculated as follows: the abscissas of a scatterplot can be partitioned into k segments $\{I_1, I_2, \ldots, I_k\}$ of the same length. From those segments, one can deduce the set $\{J_1, J_2, \ldots, J_k\}$, where each J_i contains all the ordinates corresponding to the abscissas contained in I_i. Let $M_1, M_2, \ldots, M_k$ be the averages of the abscissa values contained inside the segments $I_1, I_2, \ldots, I_k$ and let $N_1, N_2, \ldots, N_k$ be the averages of the ordinate values in $J_1, J_2, \ldots, J_k$. Then, the set of segments $\{S_1, S_2, \ldots, S_{k-1}\}$ can be defined, where each S_i connects the point (M_i, N_i) to the point (M_{i+1}, N_{i+1}). For each one of these segments S_i, the *slope* P_i is defined as $P_i = (N_{i+1} - N_i)/(M_{i+1} - M_i)$. Finally, the negative slope coefficient is defined as $nsc = \sum_{i=1}^{k-1} min\,(0, P_i)$. The hypothesis proposed in [18] is that *ncs* should classify problems in the following way: if $nsc = 0$, the problem is easy; if $nsc < 0$ the problem is difficult and the value of *nsc* quantifies this difficulty: the smaller its value, the more difficult the problem. The idea behind this hypothesis is that the presence of a segment with negative slope indicates a bad evolvability for individuals having fitness values contained in that segment (see [17] for a detailed discussion on this issue). Results shown in [18], using the previous definition, are encouraging, nevertheless the technique used to partition the fitness cloud into segments was totally arbitrary: fitness clouds were partitioned into a certain number of bins of the same size; the number of segments and their size was chosen in an arbitrary way (10 segments of the same size in [18]). This may have some undesirable consequences: for instance, segments containing too few points may be generated (and thus the averages calculated on their abscissas and ordinates may lack statistical significance). In the next section, we present some experiments showing that *nsc* calculated by partitioning the fitness cloud into a fixed number of segments can give wrong indications about the difficulty of some GP problems.

4   Limitations of the Original Definition

The *nsc* has been tested as a measure of problem hardness on a set of well-known GP benchmarks, namely the multiplexer problem [8], the intertwined spirals problem [8] and the royal trees [14]. These benchmarks have been chosen because *nsc* has never been tested on them before and because they are problems of different nature and often showing different behaviors. Below, we briefly describe these three benchmarks (see [8] and [14] for a more detailed description) and the parameters used in the experiments.

*k***-Multiplexer.** The problem is to design a Boolean function with k inputs and one output. The first x of the k inputs can be considered as address lines. They describe the binary representation of an integer number. This integer chooses one of the 2^x remaining inputs. The correct output for the multiplexer is the input on the line specified by the address lines. The terminals are the k inputs to the function. The non-terminals are the boolean operators *AND, OR, NOT, IF*. The raw fitness is calculated by counting the number of correct outputs returned by the boolean function over all the possible 2^k inputs (fitness cases). Subtracting 2^k to raw fitness makes this problem a maximization one and dividing the result by 2^k allows to normalize all fitness values into range $[0, 1]$. Empirical results show that the difficulty of the multiplexer problem increases as the number of inputs k increases.

Intertwined Spirals. The goal of this problem is to find a program to classify a given point in the $x - y$ plane as belonging to one of two well defined spirals. These two spirals are defined by a set of 194 given points. The functions and terminals set used to build this function are: $\mathcal{F} = \{+, -, *, //, IFLTE, SIN, COS\}$ and $\mathcal{T} = \{X, Y, \mathcal{R}\}$, where $\mathcal{R}$ is an ephemeral random floating point constant ranging between -1 and 1 and $//$ is a protected division returning 1 instead of an error if the denominator is 0. In order to calculate fitness, individuals are evaluated and mapped into 1 if they return a positive value and into -1 otherwise. The fitness is calculated by subtracting 194 to the number of correctly classified points, among the 194 points which define the spirals. In this way, the problem is transformed into a maximization one and values are normalized into the range $[0, 1]$ by dividing them by 194. Empirical results show that it is difficult for GP to find a perfect solution to this problem.

Royal Trees. The language used to code individuals is composed by a set of functions A, B, C, etc. with increasing arity (i.e. $arity(A) = 1, arity(B) = 2$, and so on) and a single terminal X (i.e. $arity(X) = 0$). Royal trees are based on the concept of "perfect tree", which is a tree in which all the links are "perfect links". A link is perfect if it joins a node of arity n (at level l in the tree) with a node of arity $n - 1$ (at level $l - 1$). The fitness of each tree is calculated by assigning a *bonus* to each perfect link and a *penalty* to each non-perfect link. The global optimum is the perfect tree having the node with the maximum arity as root. In [14], Punch and coworkers have empirically shown that the difficulty of royal trees increases as the maximum arity allowed for the tree nodes increases.

Performance Measure and GP Parameters. Once a measure of hardness and the way to compute it have been chosen, the problem remains of finding a means to validate the prediction of the measure with respect to the problem instance and the algorithm. The easiest way is to use a *performance* measure [13]. For the purposes of the present work, performance is defined as being the proportion of the runs for which the global optimum has been found in less than 500 generations over 100 runs. Even if this definition is informal and prone to criticism, good or bad performance values correspond to our intuition of what "easy" or "hard" means in practice. All GP runs executed to calculate performance values have used the same set of GP parameters used in [17, 18]: generational GP, population size of 200 individuals, standard GP mutation used as the sole genetic operator with a rate of 95%, tournament selection of size 10, ramped half-and-half initialization, maximum depth of individuals equal to 10, elitism (i.e. survival of the best individual into the newly generated population).

4.1 Experimental Results

Empirical results for the royal trees are not shown here for lack of space. Nevertheless, they can be found in [17] and they confirm the consistency of the *nsc* as an hardness indicator. Results for the multiplexer problem are summarized by figures 1(a) and 1(b) and by table 1. Figure 1(a) as well as the first row in table 1 concern the 6 multiplexer problem. For this instance of the problem, performance (*p*) of GP using only standard mutation as a genetic operator is equal to 0.58 (which means that a global optimum has been found in 58 runs over 100 before generation 500). Given that *p* is larger than 0.5, this problem can be considered as an "easy" one for GP (even though, being the value of *p* so close to 0.5, the term "uncertain" would probably be more appropriate). On the

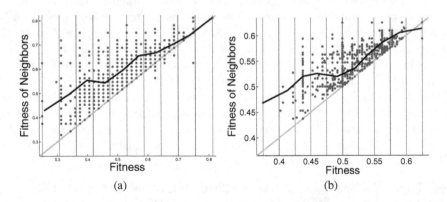

Fig. 1. Multiplexer problem, fitness cloud and segments. (a): 6 multiplexer. (b): 11 multiplexer.

Table 1. Multiplexer. Indicators related to scatterplots of figure 1.

scatterplot	problem	p	nsc
Fig. 1(a)	6 multiplexer	0.58	-0.16
Fig. 1(b)	11 multiplexer	0	-0.24

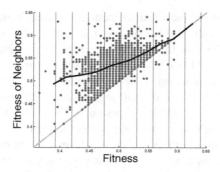

Fig. 2. Intertwined Spirals Problem. Fitness cloud with segments.

Table 2. Intertwined Spirals Problem. Indicators related to the scatterplot of figure 2.

scatterplot	problem	p	nsc
Fig. 2	intertwined spirals	0	0

other hand, the value of the *nsc* is equal to -0.16, which means that, according to the *nsc* measure, the 6 multiplexer problem should be difficult to solve. Thus, the *nsc* does *not* give the correct indication about the hardness of this problem.

Figure 1(b) and the second row of table 1 concern the 11 multiplexer problem. For this instance of the problem, no global optimum has been found by GP using mutation over the 100 runs performed. Thus the problem is clearly difficult and, consistently, *nsc* has a negative value.

The intertwined spirals problem is difficult to solve by GP. In fact, no optimum has been found over 100 runs. On the other hand, as shown by figure 2 and table 2, the *nsc* value is equal to zero, which means that, according to the *nsc* measure, the problem should be easy. While the lack of reliability of the *nsc* reported in the case of the 6 multiplexer problem could eventually be considered as "marginal", since GP performance in that case is very close to 0.5 (and thus hardness is very difficult to measure), the wrong indication on the intertwined spirals problem leaves no room for doubts: the *nsc*, as it has been used in [18] and until now in this paper, cannot be used as a general hardness indicator for GP. Thus, the next sections are dedicated to the definition of a new technique for partitioning fitness clouds into segments, in order to assure a higher statistical significance to the set of points belonging to each segment. Successively, some new empirical results are shown, confirming that the new partitioning technique allows to overcome the *nsc* drawbacks presented here.

5   Size Driven Bisection

One of the most natural ways to automatically partition a fitness cloud into a set of segments consists in applying the well-known *bisection* algorithm: as a first step, the fitness cloud may be partitioned into two segments, each one containing the same number of points; then the algorithm may be recursively applied to each one of these two segments until at least one of the segments contains a smaller number of points than a prefixed threshold. This technique has been tested and it has a major drawback: let the *size* of a segment be defined as the difference between the rightmost and the leftmost abscissas of that segment. After a few number of steps, very small bins (i.e. bins with a very small size) may be generated (see [17], at page 162, for a practical case where this problem arises). In such cases, if small segments have negative slopes, the *nsc* may take very large values (around 10^6 in the example shown in [17], page 162). This is clearly unacceptable, even in consideration of the fact that all the points included inside that segments give more or less the same information. In other words, a segment of such a small size is clearly not a significant one. Such a pathologic situation manifests very often if the bisection strategy is applied [17]. Thus, a different strategy is needed.

In an informal way, one may say that the arbitrary criteria used in [18] and in section 4 took into account the size of the segments, but not the number of points they contain, while the bisection algorithm does exactly the opposite. In this section, a technique which takes into account *both* the size of the segments and the number of points they contain, called *size driven bisection* for brevity, is proposed. The starting point of this algorithm is the same as for bisection: the fitness cloud is partitioned into two segments, each of which contains the same number of points. After that, instead of recursively applying bisection to both these segments, only the segment with larger size is further partitioned. Partition is done, once again, by bisection, i.e. the segment is partitioned into two bins, each one containing the same number of points. The algorithm is iterated until one of the two following conditions is satisfied: either a segment contains a smaller number of points than a prefixed threshold, or a segment has become smaller than a prefixed minimum size. In this paper, as a first approximation, 50 has been chosen as a threshold for the number of points belonging to a bin, and the 5% of the distance between the leftmost and the rightmost points in the fitness cloud has been chosen as the minimum size of a segment.

5.1 Experimental Results

Empirical results for the multiplexer problem using size driven bisection are summarized by figures 3 and table 3. Figure 3(a) and figure 3(b) as well as the first row in table 3 concern the 6 multiplexer problem. This time, the value of the *nsc* is equal to 0 and this value is consistent with the fact that GP performance is > 0.5. Nevertheless, figure 3(b) (containing standard deviations of the same points as in figure 3(a)) shows that the slope of some segments is not statistically significant. Our interpretation of it is that, since the GP performance value is near 0.5, it is difficult to state if the problem is "easy" or "hard". We could informally say that it is "moderatedly easy" or maybe "uncertain" and the standard deviations of some segments seem to confirm this "uncertainty".

Figures 3(c) and 3(d) and the second row of table 3 concern the 11 multiplexer problem. The *nsc* calculated with the size driven bisection has a negative value and, this time, standard deviations leave few chances to segment slopes to change. In conclusion, *nsc* using size driven bisection seems a reasonable hardness indicator for the multiplexer problem.

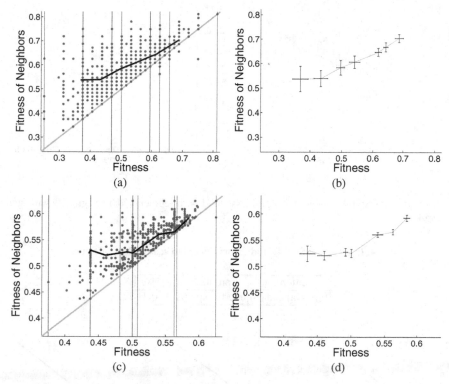

Fig. 3. Multiplexer problem. (a): 6 multiplexer, fitness cloud and segments. (b): 6 multiplexer, segments with standard deviations. (c): 11 multiplexer, fitness cloud and segments. (d): 11 multiplexer, segments with standard deviations.

Table 3. Multiplexer. Indicators related to scatterplots of figure 3.

scatterplot	problem	p	*nsc*
Fig. 3(a) and (b)	6 multiplexer	0.58	0
Fig. 3(c) and (d)	11 multiplexer	0	-0.21

Figure 4 shows the scatterplot and segments with their standard deviations for the intertwined spirals problem. Table 4 shows that the value of the *nsc* calculated using size driven bisection is negative. Standard deviations confirm that all the segment slopes are statistically significant. We conclude that *nsc* gives reasonable indications on the hardness of this problem too.

Finally, figures 5(a), 5(b) and 5(c) show the scatterplot and segments for the royal tree problem in the case where $\mathcal{F} = \{A, B\}$, $\mathcal{F} = \{A, B, C\}$ $\mathcal{F} = \{A, B, C, D\}$. In these cases, performance values (p) confirm that the problem is easy for GP. The first three rows of table 5 show that *nsc* is equal to zero in all these cases. Furthermore (see figures 6(a), 6(b) and 6(c)) standard deviations confirm that all the segment slopes are statistically significant. On the other hand, if E, F and G nodes are added to the set

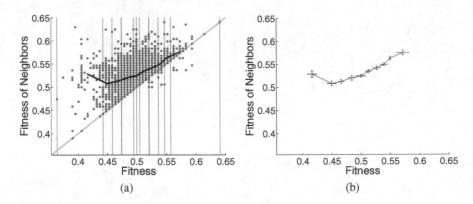

Fig. 4. Intertwined Spirals Problem. (a) : Fitness cloud with segments. (b) : Segments with standard deviations.

Table 4. Intertwined Spirals. Indicators related to scatterplots of figure 4.

scatterplot	problem	p	nsc
Fig. 4(a) and (b)	intertw. spirals	0	-0.41

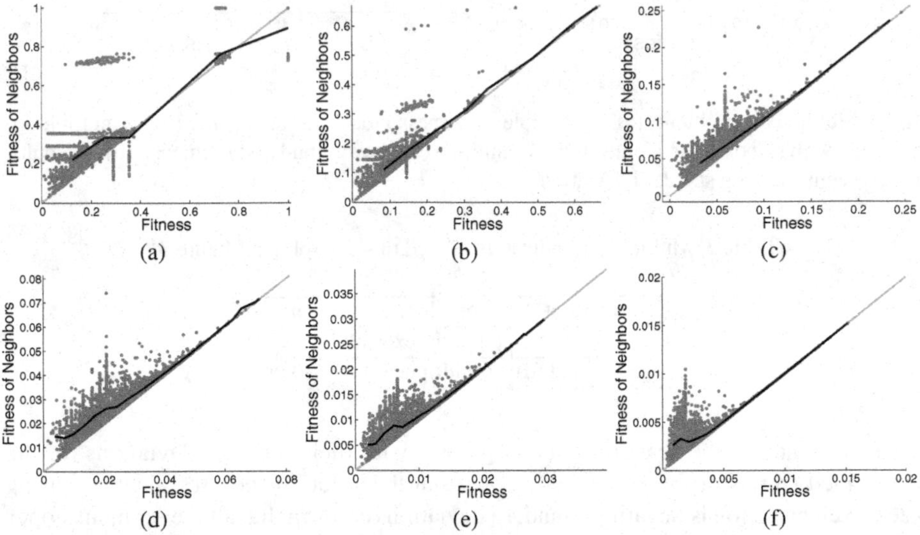

Fig. 5. Royal tree problem. Fitness clouds with segments. (a): $\mathcal{F} = \{A,B\}$. (b): $\mathcal{F} = \{A,B,C\}$. (c): $\mathcal{F} = \{A,B,C,D\}$. (d): $\mathcal{F} = \{A,B,C,D,E\}$. (e): $\mathcal{F} = \{A,B,C,D,E,F\}$. (f): $\mathcal{F} = \{A,B,C,D,E,F,G\}$. Note the change in the axis scale as the $\mathcal{F}$ set increases in size.

of possible function nodes, the problem becomes difficult (since performance is equal to zero, as shown by the last three rows of table 5). Consistently, the nsc becomes more and more negative for these instances of the problem. Figures 5(d), 5(e) and 5(f) show scatterplots and segments for these three instances and figures 6(d), 6(e) and 6(f) show

Table 5. Royal trees. Some data related to scatterplots of figure 5.

scatterplot	root	p	*nsc*
Fig. 5(a)	B	1	0
Fig. 5(b)	C	0.91	0
Fig. 5(c)	D	0.72	0
Fig. 5(d)	E	0	-0.17
Fig. 5(e)	F	0	-0.21
Fig. 5(f)	G	0	-0.32

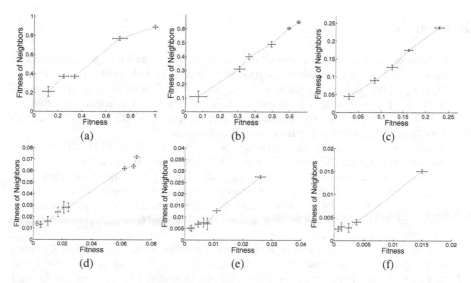

Fig. 6. Royal tree problem. Segments with standard deviations. (a): $\mathcal{F} = \{A,B\}$. (b): $\mathcal{F} = \{A,B,C\}$. (c): $\mathcal{F} = \{A,B,C,D\}$. (d): $\mathcal{F} = \{A,B,C,D,E\}$. (e): $\mathcal{F} = \{A,B,C,D,E,F\}$. (f): $\mathcal{F} = \{A,B,C,D,E,F,G\}$. Note the change in the axis scale as the $\mathcal{F}$ set increases in size.

the respective standard deviations. Once again, *nsc* values correctly indicate the relative order of GP problem hardness.

6   Conclusions and Future Work

The negative slope coefficient (*nsc*) is *not* a reliable measure of problem hardness if the fitness cloud is partitioned into segments in an arbitrary way. In this paper, a new way of partitioning fitness clouds, called size driven bisection, has been presented. It represents a suitable tradeoff between the size of segments and the density of points in the partitions. The *nsc* using size driven bisection gave reliable indications about the hardness of two instances of the multiplexer problem, the intertwined spirals problem and six instances of the royal trees problem. Furthermore, the *nsc* using size driven bisection gave reliable indications on some other typical GP benchmarks (such as the artificial ant on the Santa Fe trail, the even parity and one particular instance of the symbolic regression) and on trap functions (these results have not been shown here for lack of space. They are presented in [17]). These results encourage us to continue the study of *nsc*, with further tests on more "real life" GP problems. This paper leaves some open problems: first of all, it is based on statistical samplings of the search space and thus counterexamples can surely be built for this measure. Furthermore, and even more importantly, no technique has been found yet to normalize *nsc* values into a given range, in order to enable comparisons between the difficulties of two or more problems of different nature. Only the hardness of different instances of the same problem can be calculated using *nsc*, as defined here.

References

1. L. Altenberg. The evolution of evolvability in genetic programming. In K. Kinnear, editor, *Advances in Genetic Programming*, pages 47–74, Cambridge, MA, 1994. The MIT Press.
2. M. Clergue, P. Collard, M. Tomassini, and L. Vanneschi. Fitness distance correlation and problem difficulty for genetic programming. In *et al.* W. B. Langdon, editor, *Proceedings of the Genetic and Evolutionary Computation Conference, GECCO'02*, pages 724–732, New York City, USA, 2002. Morgan Kaufmann, San Francisco, CA.
3. K. Deb and D. E. Goldberg. Analyzing deception in trap functions. In D. Whitley, editor, *Foundations of Genetic Algorithms*, 2, pages 93–108. Morgan Kaufmann, 1993.
4. S. Forrest and M. Mitchell. What makes a problem hard for a genetic algorithm? some anomalous results and their explanation. *Machine Learning*, 13:285–319, 1993.
5. J. Horn and D. E. Goldberg. Genetic algorithm difficulty and the modality of the fitness landscapes. In D. Whitley and M. Vose, editors, *Foundations of Genetic Algorithms, 3*, pages 243–269. Morgan Kaufmann, 1995.
6. T. Jones. *Evolutionary Algorithms, Fitness Landscapes and Search*. PhD thesis, University of New Mexico, Albuquerque, 1995.
7. K. E. Kinnear Jr. Fitness landscapes and difficulty in genetic programming. In *Proceedings of the First IEEEConference on Evolutionary Computing*, pages 142–147. IEEE Press, Piscataway, NY, 1994.
8. J. R. Koza. *Genetic Programming*. The MIT Press, Cambridge, Massachusetts, 1992.
9. W. B. Langdon and R. Poli. *Foundations of Genetic Programming*. Springer, Berlin, Heidelberg, New York, Berlin, 2002.
10. N. Madras. *Lectures on Monte Carlo Methods*. American Mathematical Society, Providence, Rhode Island, 2002.
11. B. Manderick, M. de Weger, and P. Spiessens. The genetic algorithm and the structure of the fitness landscape. In R. K. Belew and L. B. Booker, editors, *Proceedings of the Fourth International Conference on Genetic Algorithms*, pages 143–150. Morgan Kaufmann, 1991.
12. M. Mitchell, S. Forrest, and J. Holland. The royal road for genetic algorithms: fitness landscapes and ga performance. In F. J. Varela and P. Bourgine, editors, *Toward a Practice of Autonomous Systems, Proceedings of the First European Conference on Artificial Life*, pages 245–254. The MIT Press, 1992.
13. B. Naudts and L. Kallel. A comparison of predictive measures of problem difficulty in evolutionary algorithms. *IEEE Transactions on Evolutionary Computation*, 4(1):1–15, 2000.
14. W. Punch. How effective are multiple populations in genetic programming. In J. R. Koza, W. Banzhaf, K. Chellapilla, K. Deb, M. Dorigo, D. B. Fogel, M. Garzon, D. Goldberg, H. Iba, and R. L. Riolo, editors, *Genetic Programming 1998: Proceedings of the Third Annual Conference*, pages 308–313, San Francisco, CA, 1998. Morgan Kaufmann.

15. P. F. Stadler. Fitness landscapes. In M. Lässig and Valleriani, editors, *Biological Evolution and Statistical Physics*, volume 585 of *Lecture Notes Physics*, pages 187–207. Springer, Berlin, Heidelberg, New York, 2002.

16. M. Tomassini, L. Vanneschi, P. Collard, and M. Clergue. A study of fitness distance correlation as a difficulty measure in genetic programming. *Evolutionary Computation*, 13(2): 213–239, 2005.

17. L. Vanneschi. *Theory and Practice for Efficient Genetic Programming*. Ph.D. thesis, Faculty of Science, University of Lausanne, Switzerland, 2004. Downlodable version at: http://www.disco.unimib.it/vanneschi.

18. L. Vanneschi, M. Clergue, P. Collard, M. Tomassini, and S. Vérel. Fitness clouds and problem hardness in genetic programming. In K. Deb *et al.*, editor, *Proceedings of the Genetic and Evolutionary Computation Conference, GECCO'04*, volume 3103 of *Lecture Notes in Computer Science*, pages 690–701. Springer, Berlin, Heidelberg, New York, 2004.

19. L. Vanneschi, M. Tomassini, M. Clergue, and P. Collard. Difficulty of unimodal and multimodal landscapes in genetic programming. In Cantú-Paz, E., *et al.*, editor, *Proceedings of the Genetic and Evolutionary Computation Conference, GECCO'03*, LNCS, pages 1788–1799, Chicago, Illinois, USA, 2003. Springer, Berlin, Heidelberg, New York.

20. L. Vanneschi, M. Tomassini, P. Collard, and M. Clergue. Fitness distance correlation in genetic programming: a constructive counterexample. In *Congress on Evolutionary Computation (CEC'03)*, pages 289–296, Canberra, Australia, 2003. IEEE Press, Piscataway, NJ.

21. S. Vérel, P. Collard, and M. Clergue. Where are bottleneck in nk-fitness landscapes ? In *CEC 2003: IEEE International Congress on Evolutionary Computation. Canberra, Australia*, pages 273–280. IEEE Press, Piscataway, NJ, 2003.

22. E. D. Weinberger. Correlated and uncorrelated fitness landscapes and how to tell the difference. *Biol. Cybern.*, 63:325–336, 1990.

Population Clustering in Genetic Programming

Huayang Xie, Mengjie Zhang, and Peter Andreae

School of Mathematics, Statistics and Computer Science,
Victoria University of Wellington, P.O. Box 600, Wellington, New Zealand
{Huayang.Xie, Mengjie.Zhang, Peter.Andreae}@vuw.ac.nz

Abstract. This paper proposes an approach to reducing the cost of fitness evaluation whilst improving the effectiveness in Genetic Programming (GP). In our approach, the whole population is first clustered by a heuristic called fitness-case-equivalence. Then a cluster representative is selected for each cluster. The fitness value of the representative is calculated on all training cases. The fitness is then directly assigned to other members in the same cluster. Subsequently, a clustering tournament selection method replaces the standard tournament selection method. A series of experiments were conducted to solve a symbolic regression problem, a binary classification problem, and a multi-class classification problem. The experiment results show that the new GP system significantly outperforms the standard GP system on these problems.

1   Introduction

Fitness evaluation in Evolutionary Computation (EC) is the most time consuming operation [1, 2]. Reducing the fitness evaluation cost is key to improving the efficiency of EC and has attracted an increasing amount of interest in both Genetic Algorithms (GAs) and Genetic Programming (GP).

There have been quite a few approaches in GAs aiming at reducing the cost of fitness evaluation. Sastry *et al* [3] introduced fitness inheritance and showed some very promising results for OneMax problems. Kim and Cho [4] used a k-means algorithm to cluster the whole population and used Euclidean distance to estimate the fitness values of other cluster members from the fitness value based on the cluster representative. Their method was tested on the Griewangk function, the De Jong functions, the Rastrigin function and the Schwefel function. Jin and Sendhoff [5] also used a k-mean algorithm to cluster the whole population. Only the chromosome closest to the cluster centre was evaluated. Fitness values of other chromosomes were estimated by a neural network ensemble. Their approach was tested on the Ackley function, the Rosenbrock function, and the Sphere function. Ziegler and Banzhaf [2] used a meta-model of the fitness function to replace the time consuming evaluations during tournament selection in analysing evolving walking patterns for quadruped robots.

However, in GP, previous methods for reducing fitness evaluation cost have been limited to fitness case selection. Altenberg and Tackett [6, 7] used a small fraction of training fitness cases to evaluate a large number of offspring produced by their brood recombination crossover operator. Giacobini et al [1] used a statistical method to select a fraction of all fitness cases to evaluate programs in

P. Collet et al. (Eds.): EuroGP 2006, LNCS 3905, pp. 190–201, 2006.

order to reduce the computational cost. They introduced the use of a concept called *entropy* in their study and concluded that once the number of fitness cases is greater than the entropy, a normal convergence behaviour can be observed in their boolean function and discrete step function problems.

Recently, Jackson [8] introduced a fitness evaluation avoidance method to avoid evaluating offspring generated by so-called fitness-preserving crossover. In his method, all nodes in a program are initially marked as *not-visited*. When a fitness case is fed to a fitness function and causes a node of the program to be evaluated, the node is then marked as *visited*. If a program P_1 is selected for crossover and the root of a sub-tree from another program P_2 replaces a not-visited node of P_1, then the generated child cannot act differently from its parent P_1, as the inserted sub-tree will never be executed. Therefore, there is no need to re-evaluate the fitness of the offspring. The method's effectiveness depends on the fraction of nodes in the programs that are not evaluated for any of the fitness cases. For the boolean function set that Jackson used, this fraction is high; for function sets with no *if* or short-circuited boolean operators, the fraction would be low, and other techniques for fitness evaluation are needed. This paper describes a technique based on clustering.

Since clustering a population and estimating cluster fitness values based on cluster representatives have been well tested on GAs, we hypothesised that these may also be applicable to GP. However, given the high diversity, complexity, and flexibility of program presentations, clustering programs may not be as straightforward as in GAs.

1.1 Goals

The goal of this study is to develop an approach to clustering the whole population in GP that can be used to reduce the fitness evaluation cost. A side-effect of clustering the population is that the clusters also enable alternative approaches to selecting programs for crossover and mutation. A secondary goal of this study is to investigate the effect of using these clusters to improve the selection operator for crossover. The critical research questions are the following:

- What measurement can be used for generating the clusters from the whole population?
- How can the fitness value of the members in the cluster be estimated?
- How will this approach affect the system performance?

2 Our Approach

Figure 1 gives an overview of our approach and shows the relationships between the major components, especially 1) population clustering; 2) fitness evaluation and assignment; and 3) clustering tournament selection for crossover. Other standard components of GP are not detailed in the figure.

The central idea of our approach is based on the observation that two programs that are equivalent (in the sense that they compute the same function of

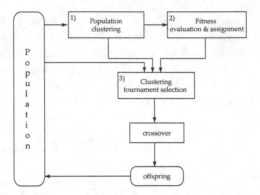

Fig. 1. Overview and relationship between the major components in this approach

their inputs) must necessarily have the same fitness value. If we could identify clusters of equivalent programs, then it would only be necessary to evaluate the fitness of one program in each cluster, and use the same fitness value for all the other programs in the cluster, avoiding the cost of evaluating the fitness of the other programs in the cluster.

In fact, it is sufficient that the programs in the cluster compute the same output values on all the training fitness cases, regardless of their output values on other inputs, since the fitness of a program depends only on its outputs on the fitness cases. We call such programs *"fitness-case-equivalent"*. *"fitness-case-equivalence"* is actually more useful than true equivalence since the clusters may be larger, and therefore generate greater saving.

The problem with this idea is that the obvious way of determining fitness-case-equivalence requires evaluating all the programs on all the fitness cases, which is the very time consuming computation that we are trying to avoid. Instead, we use a heuristic estimate of fitness-case-equivalence, based on evaluating programs on a small number of the fitness cases, making the heuristic assumption that programs that generate the same output values on a small random set of the fitness cases are likely to be equivalent on all fitness cases. The determination of the clusters is woven into the fitness evaluation so that no unnecessary fitness evaluations are performed.

Once the fitness of each cluster has been computed, a cluster-based tournament selection method replaces the standard tournament selection method to select programs for crossover.

Since clustering is the key aspect of the new approach, we refer to it as the *clustered GP system* (CGP). The rest of this section describes the details of CGP.

2.1   Population Clustering

At each generation during the evolutionary process, the algorithm starts by treating the entire population as a single cluster. Then it feeds the first training case into the programs and partitions the cluster into new clusters based on the program outputs. For each newly formed cluster, the partitioning process is applied again with the next fitness case until no new cluster is formed. The algorithm currently assumes that it has seen enough training cases to determine a cluster once all the programs in a cluster have the same output in two successive training cases. To reduce the chance of premature stopping where a cluster contains non-fitness-case-equivalent programs, the algorithm presents the training cases in a different random order in each generation.

The population clustering algorithm is outlined in Figure 2 and illustrated below using a simple one-variable symbolic regression example.

- *initialisation:* Treat the initial population consisting of 6 programs as one big cluster and randomise the order of the fitness cases.
- *Iteration 1:* Feed the first fitness case x=2 to each program. The program outputs are 4, 4, 4, 1, 1, and 1 respectively, which leave us with two sub-clusters, one with the program output of 4 and the other with 1. The initial cluster is replaced by the two sub-clusters.

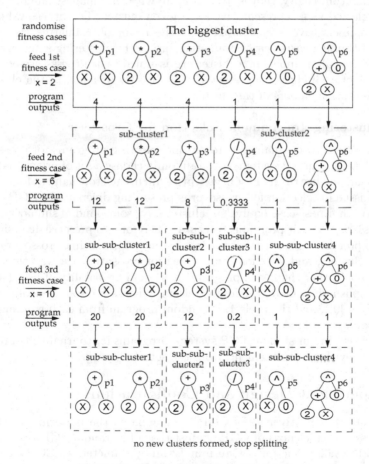

Fig. 2. Population clustering algorithm

- *Iteration 2:* Feed the second fitness case x=6 to the programs in each sub-cluster. The outputs of programs in sub-cluster1 are 12, 12, and 8. There-fore, the sub-cluster is further partitioned into two sub-sub-clusters, one with programs with output value 12, the other holding a program with an output value of 8. Similarly, sub-cluster2 is partitioned into two new sub-sub-clusters. Now we have four clusters (sub-sub-clusters1, 2, 3, 4).
- *Iteration 3:* Feed the third fitness case x=10 to programs in each sub-sub-cluster. According to the program outputs, the same set of clusters remains. As no new cluster is formed, the partitioning process completes.

2.2   Fitness Evaluation and Assignment

Upon completing the population clustering, we progress to the fitness evaluation stage. For each cluster, the program with the least program complexity is chosen as the cluster representative. In this study, the number of nodes is used as a proxy for program complexity, that is, the program with the smallest number of nodes will be selected as a representative for a given cluster. The fitness value of the cluster representative is calculated from the result of evaluating the program on all the training cases (cases evaluated during the clustering stage are not re-evaluated). As all members in a cluster are assumed to be fitness-case-equivalent, the fitness of each cluster representative is directly assigned to the cluster and to all the other members of the cluster.

2.3   Clustering Tournament Selection for Crossover

We use a standard tournament process for selecting programs for crossover. A standard method in GP systems is to randomly choose a set of programs for each tournament, and use the highest fitness program in each tournament for crossover.

A key issue in selection for crossover is preserving diversity. In CGP, the pro-grams in each fitness-case-equivalent cluster have some kind of similarity, though not necessarily in their program structure. Therefore, to preserve diversity in the crossover process, we ensure that the two parent programs in a crossover are from different clusters, and we choose programs for crossover in a way that ensures each cluster (rather than each program) has equal probability of being selected. To accomplish this, CGP randomly selects clusters for tournaments (without replacement [9]), and then selects a random program from each winning cluster for crossover.

In contrast, in our standard GP system, programs for tournaments are chosen at random, without replacement, from the set of all programs.

3   Experiment Design and Configuration

To evaluate the effectiveness of CGP, we compared the performance (both ef-fectiveness and efficiency) of CGP against that of a standard GP system (SGP) that had the same function set, terminals, and parameters as CGP except that it did not cluster the population of programs. We applied both systems to three different tasks in different domains.

3.1   Data Sets

We used three problems of increasing difficulty: a regression problem, a binary classification problem, and a multi-class classification problem.

The symbolic regression problem (SR) is shown in equation (1). We generated 100 fitness cases by choosing 100 values for x from (-10,10] with step 0.2.

$$f(x) = \begin{cases} x^2 - x & , x \geq 0 \\ sin(x) + \frac{1}{x} & , x < 0 \end{cases} \tag{1}$$

The binary classification problem (BC) is to classify two texture classes. A texture data set maintained by the Signal & Image Processing Institute at the University of Southern California (`http://sipi.usc.edu/services/database/`) is used in this example. We chose the two texture images, *wood grain,* and *herringbone weave* (see figure 3) from the texture data set because they are quite similar in many aspects and characters, and therefore harder to distinguish. The images are both 512×512 pixels and monochrome. We extracted 80×80 pixel cutouts from each image, taken every at 30 pixel steps, giving a total of 450 samples.

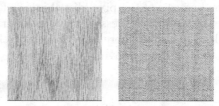

a) Wood Grain   b) Herringbone Weave

Fig. 3. Sample images in the texture data set

The multi-class classification problem (MC) is to classify distorted English letter images. A letter image data set from [10] was used for this problem. The image data set was generated by randomly distorting pixel images of the 26 upper case English letters from 20 different commercial fonts, including script, italic, serif, and Gothic. In this study, the four letters B, D, E, and R were selected from the data set because these letters were particularly difficult for humans to distinguish. All instances of the chosen letters were extracted from the original database: 766 samples for letter B, 805 samples for letter D, 768 samples for letter E, and 758 samples for letter R, giving 3097 samples in total. More information about the letter image data can be found in [10].

For BC and MC, the data sets were randomly partitioned into equal sized training and test sets.

3.2   Function Sets

The function set used for all three problems is

$$\{+, -, *, /, abs, sqrt, sin, if\} \tag{2}$$

The first four operators are the standard arithmetic binary operators, except that the / operator represents "protected" in which a divide by zero gives a result of zero. *abs*, *sqrt*, and *sin* are the standard real-valued unary operators. The *if* function takes three arguments and returns its second argument if the first argument is positive, and returns its third argument otherwise. All functions return zero if they encounter an invalid argument.

3.3   Terminal Sets

We have three terminal sets, one for each problem. Each terminal set includes real valued constants in the range [-1.0, 1.0], but the probability assigned to the whole range of constants when constructing or mutating programs, is equal to the probability assigned to each of the other discrete terminals.

The terminal set for SR consists of the single variable x, in addition to the range of constant values.

The terminal set for BC includes four pixel statistics as features: mean(μ), standard deviation(σ), *skew*, and *kurt*. The skewness of the pixel distribution of an image is used to characterise the degree of asymmetry of the pixel distribution around its mean and the kurtosis of the pixel distribution of an image is used to measure the relative peakedness or flatness of the pixel distribution. Equation 3 lists the formulas to calculate them, where x_i is the ith pixel value and N is the total number of pixels, in a training image.

$$skew(x) = \frac{\sum_{i=1}^{N}(x_i-\mu)^3}{N\sigma^3} \qquad kurt(x) = \frac{\sum_{i=1}^{N}(x_i-\mu)^4}{N\sigma^4} \qquad (3)$$

The terminal set used in MC includes the same 16 primitive numerical features of a letter image used in [10].

3.4   Fitness Function

The fitness function in the symbolic regression problem is the RMS error of the outputs of a program relative to the expected outputs for each fitness case. The fitness function for the classification problems is the classification error rate on the training data set. The classification error rate of a program is the fraction of fitness cases that are incorrectly classified by the program as a proportion of the total number of fitness cases in the training data set. In all three problems, the best fitness value is zero.

For the texture binary classification problem, the program classifies the fitness case as *wood grain* if the output of the program is negative, and *herringbone weave* otherwise. For the letter multi-class classification problem, we use the following classification rule:

$$class = \begin{cases} letter \text{ B} , \ output \geq 8 \\ letter \text{ D} , \ 4 \leq output < 8 \\ letter \text{ E} , \ 2 \leq output < 4 \\ letter \text{ R} , \ output < 2 \end{cases} \qquad (4)$$

3.5   Genetic Parameters and Termination Criteria

The population size for SR is 200, for BC is 500 and for MC is 2000 according to the increasing difficulty. Table 1 lists some shared common genetic parameters for the three problems.

Table 1. Genetic parameters for problems

Creation type	ramped half and half	Crossover rate	85%
Min. depth for creation	3	Mutation rate	10%
Max. depth for creation	5	Reproduction rate	5%
Max. generations	200	Tournament size	4

The learning/evolutionary process is terminated when either the problem has been solved (there is a program with a fitness of zero) or the number of generations reaches the pre-defined maximum.

3.6   Experiment Configuration

We ran an experiment comparing CGP to SGP for each of the three problems. In each experiment, we repeated the whole evolutionary process 100 times for both CGP and SGP. Therefore there are 100 pairs of runs in each experiment and 300 pairs of runs in total.

We ran all experiments sequentially on a single Sun Ultra server with 2GB memory. Although slower than using a server/client computing network, this reduced the possible effects of hardware differences and other users on the performance measurements.

4   Results and Analysis

This section presents the experimental results of CGP and SGP on the three problems. We investigated the effectiveness and the efficiency of CGP using several measurements.

4.1   Effectiveness of CGP

In order to investigate the effectiveness of our approach, we first measured the fraction of runs that successfully returned an optimal solution within the given number of generations. Table 2 summarises the completion rate for all problems in both systems.

In terms of completion , CGP outperformed SGP by a factor of 2.7 for SR and a factor 1.8 for BC. We think these significant improvements are due to the well maintained population diversity that is implicitly affected by the new clustering tournament selection method.

Due to the difficulty of the MC problem, neither system produced any completed runs, so the classification error rate was used to compare the performance

Table 2. Completion rate(%)

	SR	BC	MC
CGP	55	29	0
SGP	20	16	0

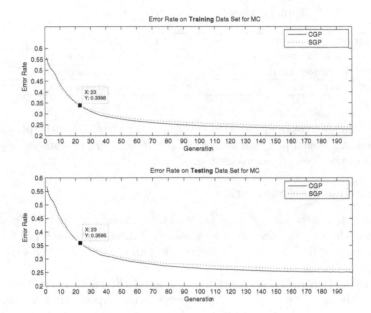

Fig. 4. Fitness for MC

of the two systems. Figure 4 demonstrates the patterns of average error rates of 100 runs for all generations. The patterns of both systems on both the training set (top panel) and the test set (bottom panel) are very similar. Except for a short period at the beginning, the error rate of CGP is consistently lower than that of SGP from the 23rd generation onwards, but the difference is quite small. Note that the error graphs do not have a 0 baseline.

The results suggest that using our heuristic estimate of fitness-case-equival ence to cluster does not reduce the accuracy or effectiveness of GP. On the contrary, when the clusters based on heuristic fitness-case-equivalence are used to select programs for crossover, the accuracy and effectiveness of GP is actually increased, quite significantly in the case of the two simpler problems.

4.2   Efficiency of CGP

The primary goal of the study was to increase efficiency of GP, without loss of effectiveness, by avoiding the need to evaluate all programs on all fitness cases.

Table 3 summarises the average number of programs evaluated in each system for each problem. The table shows that for all three problems, the number of programs evaluated in CGP are fewer than in SGP. For the two simpler problems,

Table 3. Average number of programs evaluated (1000's)

	SR	BC	MC
CGP	22 ± 9	72 ± 27	330 ± 15
SGP	36 ± 9	91 ± 23	400
Reduction:	39%	21%	17%

this reduction in the number of evaluations (39% and 21% respectively) is a result of two factors — avoiding evaluation on most fitness cases for all but the simplest program in each cluster, and the reduction in the total number of generations required. For the MC problem, all evolutionary runs took the maximum 200 generations, so the saving of approximately 17% is due entirely to the the evaluation avoidance.

The results clearly show that using the heuristic estimate of fitness-case-equivalence to cluster a population can efficiently reduce the number of programs that need to be evaluated.

To identify roughly how much of the reduction in program evaluations resulted from the reduction in the number of generations, Table 4 summarises the average number of generations used for each of the first two problems in each systems. These results suggest that around half of the saving is due to the reduction in generations, and half the saving is due to the program evaluation avoidance.

It is also of interest that as the problem difficulty increases, the reduction in the number of program evaluations decreases. We suspect that this may be related to the impact of the real-valued constants in programs — more constants in programs will reduce the chance of programs being fitness-case-equivalent. The particular symbolic regression problem in SR does not require any real-valued constants for an optimal solution, which may increase the number of fitness-case-equivalent programs compared to the BC and MC problems that require more real-valued constants.

Table 4. Average number of generations used

	SR	BC
CGP	145 ± 63	164 ± 62
SGP	179 ± 47	184 ± 47
Reduction:	19%	11%

However, the number of program evaluations is not the whole story on efficiency. For example, there is some overhead in performing and recording the clustering. Therefore, we also measured the average CPU time, to investigate whether this overhead was worthwhile. Table 5 summarises the average CPU time used for each problem with each system.

The results were surprising: there is some reduction in CPU time (about 12%) for the SR problem, but only a negligible reduction for BC and MC. Although our implementation of the clustering has not been highly optimised, it was hard to

Table 5. Average CPU time used (second)

	SR	BC	MC
CGP	7.2 ± 4.1	73 ± 29	3,600 ± 1,000
SGP	8.2 ± 3.5	74 ± 22	3,600 ± 650
Reduction:	39%	21%	17%

see how the overhead of the clustering could have swamped the quite significant reduction in number of program evaluations (usually the most expensive part of the GP process) in this way. We need to do further investigation to identify the cause, but preliminary analysis of the actual programs generated in the two systems suggests that the CGP system is creating larger and more complex programs than the standard system, presumably because of the greater diversity that the clusters are preserving. This may be part of the explanation of the increased effectiveness of CGP, but may also explain the lack of reduction in CPU time — larger programs have a higher evaluation cost than smaller programs, so that a smaller number of larger programs may require the same evaluation time as a larger number of smaller programs.

5   Conclusions and Future Work

The paper has discussed our method for reducing the fitness evaluation cost and improving the effectiveness using a clustering approach in GP. Our clustered GP system is compared with the standard GP system on three problems of increasing difficulty. The results showed that CGP is more effective than SGP, and reduces the number of program evaluations significantly. CGP was more efficient than SGP on the simplest task, but the saving in CPU time was negligible for the more complex tasks.

We have successfully demonstrated that using the heuristic estimate of fitness-case-equivalence is effective for clustering programs in GP and that the fitness values of cluster representatives can be directly used for other cluster members without any further manipulations. Clusters can also be used to improve the tournament selection for crossover, and sequentially to effectively maintain the population diversity.

We are currently investigating the reason for the negligible saving in CPU time to determine whether this is simply due to the overhead in our unoptimised implementation of the clustering algorithm, or whether it is due to a change in the programs that CGP generates.

A limitation of the current system is the weak heuristic criteria for determining when the clustering algorithm has considered sufficient training cases to be confident that the programs in a cluster are fitness-case-equivalent. We will investigate a statistical measures that are less dependent on the order of presentation of the training cases.

Acknowledgment

We would like to thank Neale Ranns for his wonderful GP package (Gouda), his endless technical support and useful discussions.

References

1. Giacobini, M., Tomassini, M., Vanneschi, L.: Limiting the number of fitness cases in genetic programming using statistics. In: PPSN VII: Proceedings of the 7th International Conference on Parallel Problem Solving from Nature, London, UK, Springer-Verlag (2002) 371–380
2. Ziegler, J., Banzhaf, W.: Decreasing the number of evaluations in evolutionary algorithms by using a meta-model of the fitness function. In Ryan, C., et al, eds.: Genetic Programming, Proceedings of EuroGP'2003. Volume 2610 of LNCS., Springer-Verlag (2003) 264–275
3. Sastry, K., Goldberg, D.E., Pelikan, M.: Don't evaluate, inherit. In Spector, L., et al, eds.: Proceedings of the Genetic and Evolutionary Computation Conference, San Francisco, California, USA, Morgan Kaufmann (2001) 551–558
4. Kim, H.S., Cho, S.B.: An efficient genetic algorithms with less fitness evaluation by clustering. In: Proceedings of IEEE Congress on Evolutionary Computation, IEEE (2001) 887–894
5. Jin, Y., Sendhoff, B.: Reducing fitness evaluations using clustering techniques and neural networks ensembles. In: Genetic and Evolutionary Computation Conference. Volume 3102 of LNCS., Springer (2004) 688–699
6. Altenberg, L.: Emergent phenomena in genetic programming. In Sebald, A.V., Fogel, L.J., eds.: Proceedings of the Third Annual Conference on Evolutionary Programming, World Scientific (1994) 233–241
7. Tackett, W.A.: Recombination, selection, and the genetic construction of computer programs. PhD thesis, University of Southern California, Los Angeles, CA, USA (1994)
8. Jackson, D.: Fitness evaluation avoidance in boolean GP problems. In Corne, D., et al, eds.: Proceedings of the 2005 IEEE Congress on Evolutionary Computation. Volume 3., Edinburgh, UK, IEEE Press (2005) 2530–2536
9. Xie, H.: Diversity control in GP with ADF for regression tasks. In: The 18th Australian Joint Conference on Artificial Intelligence. Volume 3809 of LNAI., Springer-Verlag (2005) 1253–1257
10. Frey, P.W., Slate, D.J.: Letter recognition using Holland-style adaptive classifiers. Machine Learning 6 (1991) 161–182
11. Jin, Y., Hüsken, M., Olhofer, M., Sendhoff, B.: Neural networks for fitness approximation in evolutionary optimization. In Jin, Y., ed.: Knowledge Incorporation in Evolutionary Computation. Springer, Berlin (2004) 281–305
12. Salami, M., Hendtlass, T.: The fast evaluation strategy for evolvable hardware. Genetic Programming and Evolvable Machines 6 (2005) 139–162

Projecting Financial Data Using Genetic Programming in Classification and Regression Tasks

César Estébanez, José M. Valls, and Ricardo Aler

Universidad Carlos III de Madrid,
Avda. de la Universidad, 30, 28911, Leganés (Madrid), Spain
{cesteban, jvalls, aler}@inf.uc3m.es

Abstract. The use of Constructive Induction (CI) methods for the generation of high-quality attributes is a very important issue in Machine Learning. In this paper, we present a CI method based in Genetic Programming (GP). This method is able to evolve projections that transform the dataset, constructing a new coordinates space in which the data can be more easily predicted. This coordinates space can be smaller than the original one, achieving two main goals at the same time: on one hand, improving classification tasks; on the other hand, reducing dimensionality of the problem. Also, our method can handle classification and regression problems. We have tested our approach in two financial prediction problems because their high dimensionality is very appropriate for our method. In the first one, GP is used to tackle prediction of bankruptcy of companies (classification problem). In the second one, an IPO Under-pricing prediction domain (a classical regression problem) is confronted. Our method obtained in both cases competitive results and, in addition, it drastically reduced dimensionality of the problem.

1 Introduction

The idea of projecting data spaces into other, more relevant, spaces in order to improve classification tasks has been widely used under many names. For instance, Support Vector Machines implicitly project data into a high number of dimensions (even infinite) by means of kernel functions, so that they are more easily separable [1]. In other cases, projections are used to reduce the number of dimensions, and in many cases, to improve classification accuracy (Fisher Linear Discriminant [2], Principal Component Analysis, ...). Similarly, projections can construct relevant attributes from low-level attributes or to reformulate the pattern recognition problem by constructing more relevant features (feature induction or constructive induction [3, 4, 5]). These new features can be either added to the original attribute set, or replace them.

However, most projections are closed-forms (linear, polynomial, ...). It would be interesting to obtain the most appropriate projection for the case at hand, given a set of primitives. In this paper, we have used Genetic Programming to

P. Collet et al. (Eds.): EuroGP 2006, LNCS 3905, pp. 202–212, 2006.

do so [6]. Genetic Programming is a stochastic population-based search method devised in 1992 by John R. Koza. It is inspired in Genetic Algorithms, being the main difference with them the fact that in the later, chromosomes are used for encoding possible solutions to a problem and making them evolve until converging to a valid solution. GP, nevertheless, proposes the idea of evolving whole computer programs. Within the scope of Evolutionary Algorithms, it exists a main reason for using GP in this problem: A projection is, in essence, a mathematical formula and so, its size and structure are not defined in advance. Thus, finding a codification that can fit a GA is a difficult problem. GP, nevertheless, does not impose restrictions to the size of evolved structures. There is another reason for using GP: their results are sometimes surprising, and may find some projection a human programmer might not think about. Finally, an advantage of GP is that some domain knowledge can be injected by selecting relevant primitives, whereas other Machine Learning methods use a predefined, non-modifiable set (ANN, attribute comparisons in ID3, ...).

In this paper, we present a GP-based method for finding projections that increase, leave equal, or decrease the data space dimensions, so that prediction in the projected space is improved. In classification tasks, fitness is determined by computing the degree of linear separation of data in the projected space. This has been implemented as a linear perceptron. We believe that, although more powerful classification methods (like C4.5 [7] , SVM, or NN) could be used, choosing a predictor with few degrees of freedom is an important decision: if GP is able to evolve any projection, and then a powerful classification scheme can separate the projected data using complex surfaces, there is a large risk of overfitting. Of course, there are other ways of preventing overfitting, both in GP and in the classification method, but we prefer to try simplest approach first. In addition, using simple methods means that fitness computation will be fast, which is important in evolutionary computation. Also, other simple classification methods (like nearest neighbor) could be used, and will be tested in the future. In regression tasks, we use a similar idea: a linear regression model is built for the projected data and NMSE error is used as fitness measure.

The structure of the rest of the paper is as follows. Section 2 describes the approach. Section 3 introduces two important financial domains: the bankruptcy prediction and the IPO underpricing predicion. Then, Section 4 applies the method to these financial domains. Next, Section 5 reports on the related work. And finally, Section 6 draws some conclusions and describe possible future research directions.

2   Description of the Method

We will learn from a set E of n examples expressed in a space U of N dimensions. Our objective is to be able to represent the examples in the space V, of P (projected) dimensions, and in which the examples will be linearly separable. Or, if the goal is numerical prediction (i.e. regression), then our aim is to project data so that they can be approximated by a linear regression. To include both cases, we will talk about linear behavior. P can be larger, equal, or smaller than N.

Anyway, the use of projections does not exclude the possibility of using this method with a set of examples expressed in a space U in which they already exhibit linear behavior. In this case, our method can generate projections that take the examples to a space V of a smaller number of dimensions than U but maintaining linear behavior. Thus, our method can have two different applications: on one hand, the improvement of prediction tasks by means of a transformation of the data set (towards higher, equal, or lower dimensionality); on the other hand, the reduction of dimensionality by constructing new attributes that are as good, at least, as the original ones. Of course, any combination of both applications fits our approach.

Our method uses standard GP to evolve individuals made of P subtrees (as many of dimensions of the projected space V). Fitness is computed by measuring the degree of linear behavior after applying the individual to the original data (in fact, projecting from U to V). The system stops if a 100% linear behavior has been achieved or if the maximum number of generations is reached. Otherwise, the system outputs the individual that predicted better the training data.

For the implementation of our application, we have used Lilgp 1.1 [8].

2.1 Terminal and Function Set

In our problem, terminal set will be formed by the attributes of the problem expressed in coordinates of U $(u_0, u_1 ..., u_N)$, and by the so-called Ephemeral Random Constants, which are randomly generated numerical constants that the program can use.

The set of functions to use is difficult to determine: it must be sufficient for, along with the set of terminals, being able to express the solution to the problem, but they must not be too many as for uselessly increase the search space. Of course, for different domains, different terminal and function sets will be more appropriate. We consider that the fact that they can be choosen is an advantage of GP over other methods. At this point, we have tested some generic sets, appropriate for numerical attributes:

- Basic arithmetical functions: +, -, *, and /
- Square and square root.

2.2 GP Individuals

Instead of having individuals that work with vectorial data and return a vector of P dimensions, every individual will contain P subtrees, using the same set of functions and terminals, that will be run independently. Thus, a projection is going to consist of a series of trees labelled $(v_0, v_1 ..., v_M)$ that represent combinations of all the terminals $(u_0, u_1 ..., u_N)$ and functions. Actually, we use the lil-gp mechanism for ADF (Automatically Defined Functions). That is, an individual is made of P ADF's and no main program. It is the fitness function that calls each one of the independent (non-hierarchical) ADFs. It is important to remark this issue because crossover is homologous, in the sense that subtree v_i from individual a will cross with subtree v_i of individual b. This makes sense, because if different features in V are independent and even orthogonal, subtrees in v_i will not be useful for subtrees in v_j, and vice versa. If it is suspected that different features migh share some code, the standard ADF approach (i.e. ADFs common to the P main subtrees) would be more efficient [9]. We will test the ADF approach in the future, but we believe that it is better to separate both approaches conceptually and experimentally.

2.3   The Fitness Function

We already have introduced the basic mechanism of the fitness function. It takes the examples expressed in space U, project them using the GP individual, and obtain a point in space V with P coordinates. Next, the degree of linear behavior must be determined. If the task is classification, a Simple Linear Perceptron (SP), Adaline or a Fisher linear discriminant could be applied to determine the degree of linear separability. In this paper, a SP has been used because it is very fast. We have preferred to use simple classification schemes in order to avoid overfitting: if both GP projections and the classification scheme have a lot of degrees of freedom, overfitting should be expected. The perceptron is run for 500 cycles (experimentally we have checked that this is enough). If the SP converges, the projection would be producing a linear separation of the data and it would be the solution to the problem. If the SP does not converge, the fitness assigned to the individual is the number of examples that the SP has been able to correctly classify in the best cycle: if projected data is not linearly separable, the SP will oscillate. Storing the best value guarantees stability of the fitness value. This way, fitness measure is gradual enough and has the resolution necessary to be able to exert a real selective pressure.

In case the goal is a regression task, a simple linear regression algorithm will be used to determine linearity. In particular, we use the normalized mean square error of the projected data.

3   Description of the Financial Domains

The bankruptcy prediction and the IPO underpricing prediction are two important financial problems that we tackle in this work. The high dimensionality of both problems makes them very suitable for testing our method. In this section we will describe these domains.

3.1   Bankruptcy Prediction

Predicting when a company is facing bankruptcy is a difficult and interesting problem that requires a good knowledge of the company [10]. This problem has traditionally been faced by experts applying heuristic rules. More recently, automatic approaches have been used; Some effort have been done in applying Artificial Neural Networks (ANN) to this kind of prediction problems [11, 12, 13]. These approaches take advantage of the capacity of ANNs to find non-linear relationships between variables of the problem. In [14] a training algorithm for classifying high dimensional data using Multilayer Perceptrons is applied to this problem. In [12], they use a model based on Genetic Algorithms for extracting rules that are easy to understand by users.

Our model also uses an Evolutive Computing approach. By means of a Genetic Programming engine, it generates projections that transform data into a new coordinate system. In this new space, data can be more easily treated, simplifying the classification task. This transformation of the data usually will imply a variation in the number of dimensions of the problem. Thus, our approach tries to improve the prediction rates and reduce the dimensionality of the problem at the same time. We explained our method more deeply in Section 2.

3.2   IPO Underpricing Prediction

An IPO is the first public stock offering of a company. It has been documented for many years the existence of important variations on the price of the IPOs in the first day of trading. This variations usually come as price gains, which means that the price of an IPO at the end of the first trading day is usually greater than the initial price [15]. The problem for the company is that it is very difficult to accurately price an IPO: the company has little or no information about demand, acceptance, competitive response and many other factors that should influence in the IPO pricing. Once the issue price is selected, the company is committed to maintain this price for the entire offering. If the final price is significantly over or under the IPO issue price, company will suffer important losses in the form of underpricing or overpricing (for more information about underpricing/overpricing looses, reader can refer to [10]). Thus, it is vital that the company and its investment bankers price the IPO as closely as possible to the final price.

This has been the motivation of a vast amount of Academic Work contributed in the last 30 years. Most of the proposed approaches consists in statistical methods such as multiple linear regression. Jain and Nag apply in [16] an Artificial Neural Network model to IPO underpricing prediction.

Here, we use an Evolutionary Computation approach to perform transformations of the data set. These transformations make easier to adjust data to a classic regression model and they also reduce the number of attributes of the problem. Thus, the prediction task is improved and the dimensionality of the problem is reduced.

4   Application to Financial Domains

In this work we have tested our method against two different problems: first, we confronted the problem of bankruptcy prediction, second, we worked in IPO Underpricing prediction domain. Also, in order to verify the correct operation of our method and to make it more comprehensible, we have decided, as a previous step, to apply it to a toy domain. In this domain, the direct solution is known and the solution given by our method can be easily verified.

4.1   Synthetic Domain

This domain is composed of two datasets: Ellipse and EllipseRT. Both are two-class classification problems with 1000 two-dimensional points. In dataset Ellipse, the examples belonging to class 0 are situated inside an ellipse centered in the origin, whose focuses are placed at points (-10,0) and (10,0). Class 1 instances are situated outside the ellipse. Dataset ElipseRT is similar, but the ellipse has been rotated and translated, being its focuses located at points (10, -10) and (1,7).

We ran our application on the data set Ellipse with the following parameters: Maximum number of generations (G) = 500; population size (M) = 5000; function set = {+, -, *, /, SQR, SQRT}. The number of dimensions selected for the projected space V is 2 in this case, due to considering them sufficient for a so simple problem.

The graphical representation (not shown here) shows an almost perfect linear separability of projected data. A Simple Perceptron on the projected data obtains 100% accuracy.

The same process was followed with dataset ElipseRT. Parameters for the execution stay the same, but this time the dimension of the projected space is 3. A Simple Perceptron applied to it obtains 99,9% accuracy, which means that data has also been separated almost linearly. Figure 1 displays the projected data. Points belonging to the inside of the elipse appear blacker and in the bottom of the valley-like figure, whereas points belonging to the outside appear grey, in the rest (upwards) of the figure.

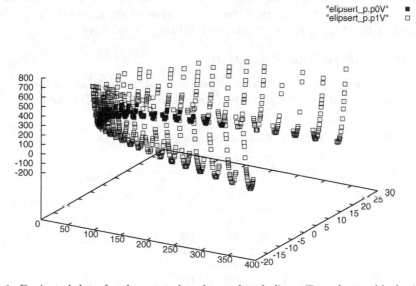

Fig. 1. Projected data for the rotated and translated elipse. Two classes: black circles and grey squares.

4.2   Bankruptcy Prediction Experiments

In this paper, we have applied the approach to a bankruptcy prediction problem. We use a data set provided and described by [17]. This data set studies the influence of several financial and economical variables on the financial health of a company.

We have applied our method to a data set formed by 1158 companies, half of which are in a bankruptcy situation (class 0) and the rest have a good financial health (class 1). Companies are characterized by 40 numerical attributes as described in [17]. For validation purposes, we have divided the data set into a training and a test set, containing 1048 (90%) and 118 (10%) instances respectively.

Our method will project the data from its original forty-dimension space to a new three-dimensional one. GP was run 10 times. The population size (G) was equal to 100 in all GP runs. Each experiment started from a different random seed. Table 1 shows other parameters used in each GP run. The first column shows the population size (M); Also, we introduced a limitation to the size of the individuals in some GP runs. The second column of Table 1 shows the maximum number of nodes allowed per individual. An experiment with a "–" in this column does not impose any limitation to the size of individuals. Classification accuracy obtained by each GP-run is shown in Table 2.

It can be seen that in both experiment 5 and 9, our method achieves 85.59% in test. In order to qualify our results, we ran a support vector machine (SMO) and the Simple Logistics algorithm from the Weka tool [18], two methods that perform very well on these data. Standard parameters were used. Results are displayed in Table 3.

We can see that our method compares well to other well-performing methods. In addition, it has to be remarked that the number of attributes of the problem has been reduced from 40 to 3, while maintaining competitive results.

4.3   IPO Underpricing Prediction

For this problem we use a sample provided by David Quintana and that is widely documented in [19]. The sample is composed by 1000 companies going

Table 1. Parameters used in each GP run

Exp.	M	max. nodes
1	1000	–
2	1000	–
3	500	–
4	500	–
5	500	150
6	500	150
7	500	100
8	500	100
9	500	75
10	500	75

Table 2. Classification Results on the Bankrupctcy Prediction Data Set

Exp.	Testing accuracy (%)
1	83.05
2	80.51
3	84.75
4	83.05
5	85.59
6	77.12
7	74.58
8	81.36
9	85.59
10	81.36

Table 3. Results obtained by Weka on the Bankrupctcy Prediction Data Set

Algorithm	Testing Accuracy (%)
SMO	81.35
Simple Logistics	83.89
Best GP Individual	84.75

Table 4. Regression error results on the IPO Underpricing Prediction Data Set

Exp.	NMSE Test
1	0.845798
2	0.861909
3	0.733960
4	0.858842
5	0.834267
6	0.857676

into the US Stock Market for the first time, between April 1996 and November 1999. Each company is characterized by seven explicative variables: underwriter prestige, price range width, price adjustment, offer price, retained stock offer size and relation to tech sector.

For validation purposes, we have divided the data set into a training and a test set, containing 800 (80%) and 200 (20%) instances respectively. The quality of the regression is measured by means of the Normalized Mean Square Error (NMSE).

Our method will project the data from its original seven-dimensional space to a new three-dimensional one. Six GP-runs (experiments 1 to 6) were carried out using the data set as input. Each GP-run was fed with a different random seed. All the experiments used a population size of 1000 individuals. Regression accuracy obtained by each GP-run is shown in Table 4. In experiment 3, it can be seen that an individual with 0.73 NMSE was obtained.

Our method managed to obtain a 0.733960 NMSE in experiment 3. In [19], a 0.92302 NMSE has been reported as the best result achieved in their experiments using classic linear regression. If 20 outliers are removed from the data set, a 0.77238 NMSE is obtained.[1] Thus, our method is able to obtain results that are comparable with classic linear regression models, while reducing the number of variables from seven to three.

5   Related Work

There are many different Constructive Induction algorithms that use a vast number of different approaches. Here we only discuss works that use GP or any other evolutionary strategy.

In [20], the authors use typed GP for building feature extractors. Functions are arithmetic and relational operators. Terminals are the original (continuous) attributes of the original data set. Every individual is an attribute and the fitness function uses the info gain ratio. Testing results, using C4.5, show some improvements in some UCI domains. Our approach differs in that our individuals contain as many subtrees as new attributes to be constructed and that the fitness function measures the degree of linear separation in the training data.

[21] follows a similar approach to ours, where every individual contains several subtrees, one per feature. C4.5 is used to classify in feature-space. Their work allows to crossover subtrees from different features, whereas we use homologous crossover. Also, we demonstrate the approach in a regression problem.

In [22] authors discuss the importance of applying GA as a global search strategy for CI methods and the advantages of using these strategies instead of classic greedy methods. Also, they present MFE2/GA: a CI method that uses GA to search through the space of different combination of attributes subsets and functions defined over them. MFE2/GA uses a non-algebraic form of representation to extract complex interactions between the original attributes of the problem. There are obviously great differences between this work and our approach, but it is still a very interesting application of evolutionary approaches to the generation of CI methods.

In [23] authors present the GCI system. GCI is a CI method based in GP. It is similar to our method in the facts that it uses basic arithmetic operators and that the fitness is computed measuring the performance of a MLA (a quick-prop net) using the generated attributes. However, each individual represents a new attribute instead of a new attribute set. This way, GCI can only generate new attributes that are added to the original ones, thus increasing the dimensionality of the problem. The possibility of reducing the number of attributes of the problem is only mentioned as a possible and very interesting future work.

In [24] Y. Hu Introduces another CI method based in Genetic Programming: GPCI. As in GCI, in GPCI each individual represents a new generated attribute. The fitness of a individual is evaluated by combining two different functions: an absolute measure and a relative measure. The absolute measure evaluates the quality

---

[1] Their paper also presents a rule-based method that obtains good results, but cannot be directly compared to ours.

of a new attribute using gain ratio. The relative measure evaluates the improvement of the attribute over its parents. Function set is formed by two Boolean operators: AND and NOT. GPCI is proved in twelve UCI domains and against two other CI methods, achieving some competitive results. While the basic scheme of GPCI is similar to our method, there are important differences including the function set, the representation of the attributes and the fitness function.

Finally, an important contribution of our work is the fact that we do not restrict our method to classification problems. Instead, we have used our CI to improve prediction rates in regression problems.

6   Conclusions

In this paper we have presented a Genetic Programming approach to project data from an original highly dimensional input space to a target space with fewer dimensions. The goal is to be able to approximate linear behavior in the final space, so that classification or regression can be more easily achieved by linear methods (linear separation or linear regression). We have applied our method to two very relevant financial domains: Bankruptcy prediction and IPO Underpricing Prediction. The first one is a classification problem which consists on predicting whether a company is facing bankruptcy. The second one is a regression problem since the goal is to predict the variations on the price of the IPOs in the first day of trading. In both cases, we have obtained results that are comparable to those of methods reported in the literature. In addition, we have managed to drastically reduce dimensionality: from 40 to 3 in the first problem, and from 7 to 3 in the second one.

Acknowledgements

This article has been financed by the Spanish founded research MCyT project TRACER, Ref:TIC2002-04498-C05-04M.

References

1. N. Cristianini and J. Shawe-Taylor. *An introduction to Support Vector Machines (and other kernel-based learning methods)*. Cambridge University Press, 2000.
2. T. Hastie, R. Tibshirani, and J. Friedman. *The elements of statistical learning*. Springer Series in Statistics. Springer-Verlag, New York, 2001.
3. T. Fawcett and P. Utgoff. A hybrid method for feature generation. In *Proceedings of the Eighth International Workshop on Machine Learning*, pages 137–141, Evanston, IL, 1991.
4. S. Kramer. Cn2-mci: A two-step method for constructive induction. In *Proceedings of ML-COLT'94*, 1994.
5. B. Pfahringer. Cipf 2.0: A robust constructive induction system. In *Proceedings of ML-COLT'94*, 1994.
6. John R. Koza. *Genetic Programming: On the Programming of Computers by Means of Natural Selection*. MIT Press, Cambridge, MA, USA, 1992.

7. J. R. Quinlan. *C4.5 – Programs for Machine Learning*. The Morgan Kaufmann series in machine learning. Morgan Kaufman Publishers, 1993.
8. Douglas Zongker and Bill Punch.   lil-gp 1.1 www homepage: http:// garage.cps.msu.edu/software/lil-gp/, September 1998.
9. John R. Koza. *Genetic Programming II: Automatic Discovery of Reusable Programs*. MIT Press, Cambridge Massachusetts, May 1994.
10. E.I. Altman. Business failure prediction models: An international survey. *Journal of Banking Accounting and Finance*, 8:171, 1984.
11. K.Y. TAM and M.Y. Kiang. Managerial applications of neural networks: the case bank failure predictions. *Management Science*, 38:926–947, 1992.
12. I. Han, H. Jo, and K. S. Shin. The hybrid systems for credit rating. *Journal of the Korean Operations Research and Management Science Society*, 22(3):163–173, 1997.
13. D. Fletcher and E. Goss. Forecasting with neural networks: An application using bankruptcy data. *Information and Management*, 24(3):159–167, 1993.
14. A. Vieira and N. Bas. A training algorithm for classification of high-dimensional data. *Neurocomputing*, 50:461–472, 2003.
15. J.R. Ritter and I. Welch. A review of ipo activity, pricing, and allocations. *Journal of Finance*, 57:1795–1828, 2002.
16. B. A. Jain and B. N. Nag. Artificial neural network models for pricing initial public offerings. *Decision Sciences*, 26:283–299, 1995.
17. Armando Vieira, Bernardete Ribeiro, and Joao C. Neves. A method to improve generalization of neural networks: Application to the problem of bankruptcy prediction. In *Springer Verlag series on Adaptative and Natural Computing Algorithms. Proceeding of 7th International Conference on Adaptive and Natural, Computing Algorithms. ICANNGA 2005*, volume 1, page 417, 2005.
18. Ian H. Witten and Eibe Frank. *Data Mining: practical machine learning tools and techniques with java implementations*. Morgan Kaufmann, 2000.
19. D. Quintana, C. Luque, and P. Isasi. Evolutionary rule-based system for ipo underpricing prediction. In *Proceedings of the Genetic and Evolutionary Computation Conference GECO 2005*, volume 1, 2005.
20. Fernando E. B. Otero, Monique M. S. Silva, Alex A. Freitas, and Julio C. Nievola. Genetic programming for attribute construction in data mining. In Conor Ryan, Terence Soule, Maarten Keijzer, Edward Tsang, Riccardo Poli, and Ernesto Costa, editors, *Genetic Programming, Proceedings of EuroGP'2003*, volume 2610 of *LNCS*, pages 389–398, Essex, 14-16April 2003. Springer-Verlag.
21. Krzysztof Krawiec. Genetic programming-based construction of features for machine learning and knowledge discovery tasks. *Genetic Programming and Evolvable Machines*, 3(4):329–343, December 2002.
22. Leila Shila Shafti and Eduardo Pérez. Constructive induction and genetic algorithms for learning concepts with complex interaction. In *GECCO*, pages 1811–1818, 2005.
23. Ibrahim Kuscu. A genetic constructive induction model. In *1999 Congress on Evolutionary Computation*, pages 212–217, Piscataway, NJ, 1999. IEEE Service Center.
24. Yuh-Jyh Hu. A genetic programming approach to constructive induction. In John R. Koza, Wolfgang Banzhaf, Kumar Chellapilla, Kalyanmoy Deb, Marco Dorigo, David B. Fogel, Max H. Garzon, David E. Goldberg, Hitoshi Iba, and Rick Riolo, editors, *Genetic Programming 1998: Proceedings of the Third Annual Conference*, pages 146–151, University of Wisconsin, Madison, Wisconsin, USA, 22-25July 1998. Morgan Kaufmann.

Solving Sudoku with the GAuGE System

Miguel Nicolau and Conor Ryan

Biocomputing and Developmental Systems Group,
Department of Computer Science and Information Systems,
University of Limerick, Ireland
{Miguel.Nicolau, Conor.Ryan}@ul.ie

Abstract. This paper presents an evolutionary approach to solving Sudoku puzzles. Sudoku is an interesting problem because it is a challenging logical puzzle that has previously only been solved by computers using various brute force methods, but it is also an abstract form of a timetabling problem, and is scalably difficult. A different take on the problem, motivated by the desire to be able to generalise it, is presented. The GAuGE system was applied to the problem, and the results obtained show that its mapping process is well suited for this class of problems.

1 Introduction

The GAuGE system (Genetic Algorithms using Grammatical Evolution) [14] is a genetic algorithm that uses a position independent representation of fixed-length genotype strings which, through a mapping process, generate fixed-length phenotype strings, which are neither under- nor over-specified. By position independent it is meant that each phenotypic variable is encoded into the genotype string along with an associated phenotypic position; that leads to a simultaneous evolution of both the structure and the contents of the genotype strings.

This simultaneous evolution has the potential to learn linear relationships (or dependencies) between variables; as the structure of genotype strings can adapt, more important (or salient) variables can be grouped together, boosting the exchange capability of the crossover operator. Due to its specific mapping process, GAuGE also allows phenotypic variables to exchange places, thus searching the space of permutations of such variables in the phenotype strings. Although not always a desirable effect, certain problem domains possess characteristics that make this permutation search a welcome feature [14, 9].

The Sudoku puzzle seems to require that characteristic. The game is composed of a $n \times n$ board, and the objective is to fill it with numbers, following a set of simple constraints (see Section 3). Although there exist many algorithms that solve these puzzles in a matter of seconds, in this work a different problem is solved: a sequence of instructions is evolved and applied to the board, and a fitness reward is given back. The objective is therefore to provide a sequence of instructions that solves the puzzle, and that is human-readable; to that effect, a number of logical instructions are available to the algorithm, which mimic the

P. Collet et al. (Eds.): EuroGP 2006, LNCS 3905, pp. 213–224, 2006.
© Springer-Verlag Berlin Heidelberg 2006

way a human solves this kind of puzzle. Moreover, Sudoku is analogous to many scheduling and timetabling problems, and a system that can not only provide a timetable, but also the logical steps used in deriving it can be a powerful tool.

The results obtained show that GAuGE is able to solve this problem, if a sufficient function set is available. Also, a fair degree of temporal saliency clearly helps the system to restructure individuals at the genotypic level, leading to the discovery of better individuals as evolution progresses.

This paper is structured as follows: Section 2 presents the GAuGE system, and Section 3 presents the Sudoku game. Section 4 presents the practical issues of the experiments performed, and Section 5 analyses the results obtained.

2   GAuGE

The GAuGE system shares many of the biologically inspired features of Grammatical Evolution (GE) [13], the main ones being a genotype-to-phenotype mapping process, a functional dependency between genes, and the use of degeneracy.

In GE, a population of binary strings is evolved. When an evaluation is required, these are first converted into integer strings, and the integers are then used to choose productions from a given grammar, creating a phenotype string.

In GAuGE, a similar process is employed. When a binary string is to be evaluated, it is first converted into an integer string; these integers are then interpreted as a sequence of (*position*, *value*) pairs, to create a phenotype string.

In GE, there is a functional dependency between each gene and all the genes that precede it. This is because the grammar production chosen by a given gene affects the context of the following genes; as a result, the set of productions available for each gene is dependent on the context created by previous choices.

A similar effect is observed in GAuGE, regarding each position specification at the genotypic level. The phenotypic position corresponding to that specification affects the context of the following specifications, as the set of available positions in the phenotype string changes; as a result, each specification is dependent on the context created by previous specifications.

Finally, the use of degenerate code plays an important role in GE: by using the *mod* operator to map an integer to a choice of productions from a grammar rule, neutral mutations can take place, creating a many-to-one mapping between the search and solution spaces, and introducing variety at the genotypic level.

In GAuGE, this feature is also present, as a direct result of the mapping process employed. It has also been shown that the explicit introduction of degeneracy can reduce structural bias at the genotypic level [10].

2.1   Background

Many systems have been developed using similar techniques to the ones employed in GAuGE. Bagley [1] used fixed-length strings of (*position*, *value*) specifications, and an inversion operator to move those specifications around in the chromosome strings; both Frantz [3] and Holland [7] extended some of that work, and similar operators were later designed, with the same purpose [12].

The messy genetic algorithms [4, 5] are also based on the idea of a separate encoding of the position and the value of each phenotypic variable. They dealt with the problem of over-specification with a system of "first come, first served" basis, whereas under-specification was dealt with the use of an evolved template.

More recently, Harik [6] applied the principles of functional dependency to the Linkage Learning Genetic Algorithm, in which a chromosome is expressed as a circular list of genes, with the functionality of a gene being dependent on a chosen interpretation point, and the genes between that point and itself.

2.2   GAuGE Mapping

A formal description of the mapping process can be found elsewhere [10]; in this work, a practical approach is presented. As an example, consider a simple problem composed of four phenotypic variables ($\ell = 4$), ranging between the values 0 and 7. The length of each individual depends on a chosen position field size (pfs) and a value field size (vfs). As there are four variables, a value of $pfs = 2$ has been chosen, as that is the minimum number of bits required to encode four positions; for the value fields, a value of $vfs = 4$ has been chosen, to introduce degeneracy (the minimum value required for vfs is 3). The required length for each binary string is therefore $L = (pfs + vfs) \times \ell = (2 + 4) \times 4 = 24$.

For example, take the following individual as an example genotype string:

$$001001101101110100010010$$

By using the pfs and vfs parameters, an integer string is created:

$$(0, 9), (2, 13), (3, 4), (1, 2)$$

These values are then interpreted as a sequence of ($position, value$) pairs: for each one, the $position$ is mapped to the number of positions available in the phenotype string, and the $value$ is mapped to the range of the phenotypic variables (8). For the first pair, the $position$ becomes ($0 \bmod \ell$) = ($0 \bmod 4$) = 0, as at this stage no positions have been specified yet; the $value$ becomes ($9 \bmod 8$) = 1. The phenotype string can thus begin to be constructed, by placing $value$ 1 into $position$ 0 (that is, the first **available** position in the phenotype string):

$$1, ?, ?, ?$$

The second pair is decoded in the same way: the $position$ becomes ($2 \bmod 3$) = 1 (as there are now only 3 positions available in the phenotype string), and the $value$ becomes ($13 \bmod 8 = 5$). The $value$ 5 can then be placed into $position$ 1 (the second currently available position in the phenotype string):

$$1, ?, 5, ?$$

The third pair is processed in the same way: $position$ = ($3 \bmod 2$) = 1, and $value$ = ($4 \bmod 8$) = 4, so $value$ 4 is placed in the second available position:

$$1, ?, 5, 4$$

Finally, after processing the last pair, the phenotype string becomes:

$$1, 2, 5, 4$$

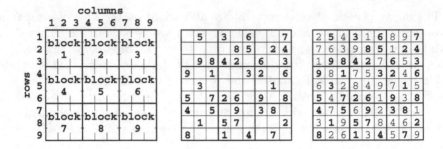

Fig. 1. Example Sudoku boards. The referencing system used is shown on the left, an example board in the middle, and its solution in the right.

3 Sudoku

The *Sudoku* game is a logic-based placement puzzle. It originated in the United States in 1979, under the name *Number Place*; in 1984, it was slightly changed in Japan, and quickly gained popularity. In November 2004, the British newspaper "The Times" first published a Sudoku puzzle; since then, many newspapers followed suit, and its popularity in the western world has increased immensely.

Traditionally, the puzzle consists of a 9×9 grid, made up of 3×3 *blocks*, for a total of 81 *cells* (Fig. 1, left). The objective of the puzzle is to place the numbers 1 through 9 in each cell, such that the following rule set holds:

1. Each row must contain the numbers 1 through 9 only once;
2. Each column must contain the numbers 1 through 9 only once;
3. Each block must contain the numbers 1 through 9 only once.

Each puzzle comes with a set of numbers already placed (called *givens*). It is considered *well-formed* if it has only one solution, and it can be solved using logic (that is, no guessing is required to place any of the numbers). Fig. 1 shows an example of a well-formed Sudoku puzzle, along with its (only) solution.

Although numbers have traditionally been used, any set of symbols can be used in Sudoku (such as letters, shapes or colours). Also, although the 9×9 size grid is the most common, other variants exist, such as 16×16 and 25×25.

There are clear parallels between Sudoku and scheduling problems, such as timetabling. Each row can be viewed as a time slot, each column a room and each number a course. All courses must be scheduled in each room exactly once per day, and no class can be scheduled in two different rooms at the same time.

3.1 Solving Sudoku with Computers

The problem of solving Sudoku puzzles on $n^2 \times n^2$ boards of $n \times n$ blocks is known to be NP-complete [20]; this gives an indication of why solving Sudoku puzzles can be difficult. However, due to the finite size of the puzzle, it can be solved by a deterministic finite automaton that knows the entire game tree [19].

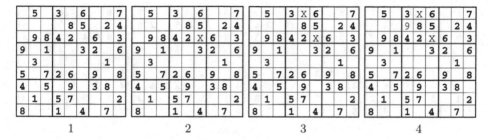

Fig. 2. Applying slice and dice to place number 9 in block 2. Starting with the left board, slice finds a 9 in the third row, so 9 cannot be placed anywhere else in that row (relevant cells are marked with an X in the second board). Dice finds a 9 in the fifth column, so 9 cannot be placed anywhere else in that column (third board). This results in only one cell being available to place 9 in block 2 (last board).

A different approach is to base each number-placing action purely on logic. This technique is limited to well-formed puzzles, but has the advantage of producing a list of logical actions, which can be easily reproduced by a human. Most Sudoku software packages tend to use a mix of logic and brute force computation.

3.2   Logical Operations

There are many logical operations that can be used when solving Sudoku puzzles; below are some of the most common (and simpler) techniques:

Last Remaining. This is a simple logic operation, that can be applied to any kind of region (row, column or block). It simply checks if that region has already eight numbers placed, in which case it places the remaining one.

Slice and Dice. This is a combination of two operations, *slice* and *dice* [17], and can be applied when trying to place number n in block b. Slice looks for n in each row passing through b; if it contains n, then the three cells intersecting with b cannot contain n. Dice works with columns instead. If, after applying slice and dice, only one cell is available, then it must contain n. Fig. 2 shows an example.

Column Fill. This technique tries to place number n in column c. It looks for n in all rows and blocks passing through c; if a row or block contain n, then the cell(s) corresponding to the intersection of that region and column c cannot contain n. If after checking all rows and blocks there is only one cell available in column c, then that cell must contain n. Fig. 3 shows an example.

Row Fill. This technique tries to place the number n in row r, and works in the same way as Column Fill, but going through all the columns instead.

Raising Numbers. This technique tries to place the number n in block b, by checking each empty cell in b to see if n is the only number that can be placed in that cell; Fig. 4 shows an example.

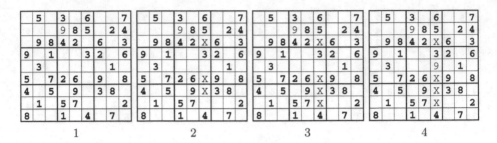

Fig. 3. Applying Column Fill to place number 9 in column 6. By searching through all rows in the left board for the number 9, a set of cells can be marked as being unsuitable to receive that number (second board); then looking through blocks 2, 5 and 8 (the blocks that intersect column 6) another unsuitable cell is discovered (third board); finally, only one cell is available in column 6, so it must contain 9 (last board).

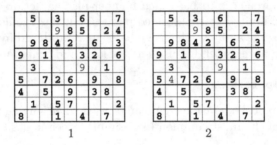

Fig. 4. Applying Raising Numbers to place number 4 in block 4. By analysing the left board, there are four empty cells in block 4, and the numbers 2, 4, 6 and 8 are missing. Through Slice and Dice operations, the set of possible numbers for each of the empty cells can be deduced: the leftmost empty cell can receive the numbers $\{2, 6\}$, the center top cell can receive $\{4, 6, 8\}$, the rightmost one $\{2, 4, 6\}$, and the bottom center $\{4\}$. Since this last cell can only receive the number 4, it is placed there (right board).

Sometimes different operations can be used to place the same number in the same cell; other times only a specific one will do. Note also that often an operation can only be applied if a previous one has placed a specific number. In other words, there are many *logical sequences* when using these logical operations.

3.3   Blind Sudoku

In this work, a variation of the original Sudoku puzzle is solved, which is termed *Blind Sudoku*. All the same rules and constraints of the original puzzle still apply; the difference lies on the way in which it is solved. A sequence of logic instructions is applied to a puzzle, and a measure of goodness is returned to the algorithm; in other words, the puzzle is never available to the algorithm, neither is a measure of goodness for each individual logic instruction. Once a sequence of instructions has been evaluated, the puzzle is reset to its original composition.

This way of solving Sudoku puzzles is not dissimilar to the Santa Fe Ant Trail problem [8], in which a sequence of instructions is given to an ant in a toroidal grid world, and the number of food objects caught by the ant is returned as the fitness measure.

Objective Function. As the number of cells in a 9×9 Sudoku board is always 81, that is used as the size of a sequence of instructions; this allows that sequence to be applied to any puzzle, regardless of the number of givens. The fitness of a sequence of instructions is simply the sum of the fitness of all its instructions; the fitness of each single instruction is

$$f_i = \begin{cases} k \times (82 - i) & \text{if successful} \\ coverage - 9 & \text{if unsuccessful} \end{cases}$$

where k is a constant, and *coverage* is a measure of how many cells were ruled out when unsuccessfully trying to place a number in a region (the X marks)[1]. If the puzzle is completed before using up all the instructions, all remaining instructions are considered neutral, and their fitness is $f_i = 0$.

The fitness function heavily rewards successful instructions, and punishes unsuccessful ones. A linear decreasing reward is also applied to each successful instruction: the earlier it is executed, the bigger the reward. This temporal saliency is regulated by the k parameter; the higher its value, the higher the reward (in these experiments, a value of $k = 81$ was used).

This problem has interesting characteristics, and can be compared to a class of scheduling problems. There is a clear temporal dependency between each phenotypic variable, as certain instructions can only be successful if a set of numbers has been placed before their execution. The negative score applied to unsuccessful instructions can be seen as an effort factor.

The GAuGE system seems adequate to solving this kind of problem. It allows for successful instructions, which have already been discovered, to change their phenotypic location (by mutating their position specification at the genotypic level), allowing them to be moved to the start of the phenotype string, thus possibly maximising their contribution to the fitness of the set of instructions.

4 Experiments

4.1 Practical Issues

In these experiments, GAuGE was used to evolve sequences of 81 instructions, from the set {SliceDice, RowFill, ColFill, RaisingNumbers}. If an instruction is successful, the LastRemaining instruction is tried on the corresponding region (as it is a fast instruction), and if successful the remaining number is placed.

---

[1] Note that the Raising Numbers technique does not mark any cells as unsuitable, and thus if it is unsuccessful its fitness is always -9; this is judged to be fair, as it is a slightly more expensive technique then all others.

Also, the logic instructions are mapped onto the original board. For example, if the algorithm tries to execute the instruction *SliceDice(2,8)* (place number 8 in block 2 using SliceDice) on the board from Fig. 1, that instruction is translated to *SliceDice(2,9)*, as 8 already exists in block 2. This is only applied to the original board: if a subsequent instruction is also *SliceDice(2,8)*, then it is considered unsuccessful, as number 9 has already been successfully placed in block 2.

The test set for these experiments consisted of puzzles taken from Carol Vorderman's How to do Sudoku [17] (pp. 178–187). These were taken from the "Difficult" section, and the first ten puzzles were picked (#111 to #120).

4.2   GAuGE Encoding

As there are 81 instructions in each sequence, the pfs parameter (size of position fields) needs to be at least 7 (as $2^7 = 128$). In these experiments, degeneracy is used to soften the biases of the *mod* operator [10], so the value chosen is $pfs = 8$.

The vfs parameter is more complex. Each variable encodes three choices:

1. which instruction to use (out of 4 instructions);
2. which region to apply it to (out of 9 regions, be it blocks, rows or columns);
3. which number to attempt to place (out of 9 numbers).

To encode an instruction, 2 bits are sufficient. To encode a region and a number, the minimum number of bits is 4 ($2^4 = 16$); as with the pfs parameter, degeneracy is used, and 5 bits are used for each of these encodings, so $vfs = 2 + 5 + 5 = 12$. This means that the length of each GAuGE string is:

$$L = (pfs + vfs) \times \ell = (8 + 12) \times 81 = 1620 \text{ bits}$$

4.3   Parameters

Table 1 shows the parameters used in these experiments. The mutation probabilities are in a *per-bit* basis; the following rough formulae were used to set those probabilities, to limit mutation events on each field to 1 per individual:

$$P_{\text{mut}}(pos) = \frac{1}{(8 \times \ell)} = \frac{1}{648} \approx 0.0015 \qquad P_{\text{mut}}(val) = \frac{1}{(12 \times \ell)} = \frac{1}{972} \approx 0.001$$

As a replacement strategy the Minimal Generation Gap model (MGG) [15] was used; previous tests, both published [11] and not, suggest that it is appropriate for GAuGE, as it maintains diversity at the early stages of evolution, and also keeps the population from stagnation at the later stages. It works as follows:

1. Two random parents are selected from the population;
2. The crossover operator is applied;
3. The two generated offspring are mutated and evaluated;
4. The best of the four individuals (both parents and offspring) is selected to replace the first parent in the population;
5. A roulette wheel is used to select another individual from all four to replace the second parent in the population.

Table 1. Experimental setup

Replacement strategy:	MGG
Crossover operator:	1-point
Problem length (ℓ):	81
Population size (N):	100
Max. number of generations:	800
Position field size (pfs):	8 bits
Value field size (vfs):	12 bits
Crossover probability:	0.5
Position field mutation probability:	0.0015
Value field mutation probability:	0.001

Table 2. Results obtained for all puzzles. For each one, the average numbers placed (over the total missing numbers) are shown, along with the average generation at which those placements were achieved, and the number of successful runs (out of 30).

Puzzle	#111	#112	#113	#114	#115	#116	#117	#118	#119	#120
Avg. placements	53/53	51/51	53/53	53/53	51/51	21/53	13/53	54/54	51/51	51/51
Avg. generation	238	181	166	210	123	55	14	301	188	135
Successful runs	30	30	30	30	30	0	0	30	30	30

5 Analysis

5.1 Results

Table 2 shows the results obtained in all puzzles; all runs for each puzzle (apart from puzzles #116 and #117) were successful. The average number of generations required to complete a puzzle can be seen as a rough measure of its difficulty: notice how for puzzle #118, which required 54 numbers to be placed, a higher number of generations were required for all runs to be successful.

Puzzles #116 and #117 were never solved. Close analysis of these puzzles showed that the function set available to the system was not sufficient to solve them: a brute force search with the available logical functions was performed, and a result could not be reached. Also, the maximum amount of numbers placed for each puzzle with the brute force search method was 21 and 13 respectively, which were the results obtained with GAuGE.

5.2 Sample Run and Solution

Figure 5 shows results from a sample run (puzzle #111, first run). It illustrates a behaviour observed in all runs: as evolution progresses, the phenotypic strings are rearranged, with successful instructions being placed at the start, due to fitness pressure, and through GAuGE's flexible genotypic representation. As these instructions are forced towards the left side, more instructions are discovered in the right side, which are then moved to the left as well.

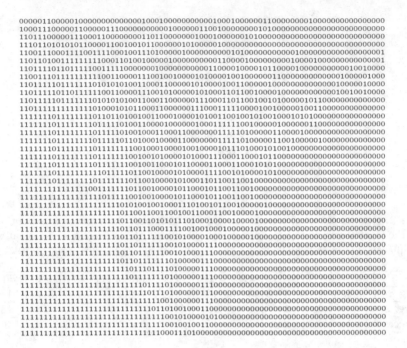

Fig. 5. Best individual found, every 20 generations (from sample run). Strings represent sequences of instructions: a 0 signals an unsuccessful instruction, and a 1 a successful one. As evolution progresses, successful instructions are moved towards the start, due to GAuGE's disassociation between position and value specifications, and fitness pressure.

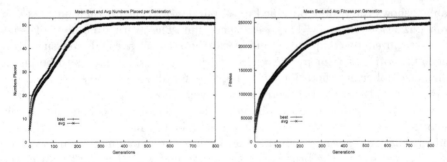

Fig. 6. Results for puzzle #111, averaged across 30 runs. The graph on the left shows the mean maximum and average number of successful instructions, and the graph on the right the mean best and average fitness scores. Notice how around generation 350 all numbers have already been placed on all runs, but yet the fitness score continues to raise, due to the nature of the fitness score used in the experiments.

Clearly, the scaled fitness measure used in these experiments, which highly rewards individuals with successful instructions at the start of their instruction sequence, is the major reason for the restructuring of individuals. However,

		6			5			
				8	9	4		
			2		7	6		
3			7	4				6
	9	7				1	8	
6				9	5			2
	2	6		5				
	7	4	2					
	5				6			

sliceDice(3,2); rowFill(8,6); colFill(2,6); colFill(7,5); rowFill(5,5); sliceDice(7,3); sliceDice(5,8); rowFill(4,9); sliceDice(4,2); sliceDice(9,5); sliceDice(5,6); rowFill(2,2); raisingNumbers(4,1); sliceDice(4,8); rowFill(6,7); rowFill(5,2); rowFill(9,2); colFill(1,7); rowFill(1,4); rowFill(2,7); raisingNumbers(1,5); raisingNumbers(2,1); colFill(6,7); colFill(1,4); colFill(4,5); sliceDice(2,9); colFill(3,9); colFill(8,3); sliceDice(8,1); colFill(2,3); raisingNumbers(3,8); raisingNumbers(3,2); sliceDice(3,8); raisingNumbers(4,4); rowFill(9,7); colFill(4,9); sliceDice(9,4); colFill(9,7); rowFill(7,1); sliceDice(9,6); sliceDice(4,8); rowFill(8,9); rowFill(9,1); rowFill(5,3); rowFill(6,3); sliceDice(9,3); colFill(6,3); rowFill(2,6); sliceDice(5,6); sliceDice(7,1); colFill(7,5); colFill(3,5); raisingNumbers(7,8); rowFill(6,3); sliceDice(7,8); sliceDice(5,2); raisingNumbers(2,9); rowFill(6,1); raisingNumbers(7,8); rowFill(3,3); sliceDice(1,2); sliceDice(9,2); rowFill(6,7); colFill(4,1); raisingNumbers(8,7); raisingNumbers(9,4); sliceDice(4,2); raisingNumbers(1,2); rowFill(7,9); colFill(3,3); colFill(1,9); colFill(8,3); colFill(3,8); sliceDice(9,7); raisingNumbers(1,8); rowFill(3,8); raisingNumbers(4,2); rowFill(3,8); raisingNumbers(6,9); rowFill(5,2); sliceDice(1,4);

Fig. 7. Puzzle #111 and a sample solution found for it

this would not be possible without a disassociation between position and value specifications at the genotypic level, which the GAuGE representation allows for.

Notice also how, after discovering a solution, evolution continues. This is again due to the way the fitness function rewards earlier successful instructions. This can also be seen in Figure 6, which shows graphs averaged across 30 runs for puzzle #111: at generation 361, all runs have been successful, but best and average fitness continue to grow until the maximum number of generations.

Figure 7 shows a sample solution for puzzle #111.

6 Conclusion

This paper presented an evolutionary approach to solving Sudoku puzzles. The problem introduced, "Blind Sudoku", is an interesting challenge to the field, and the variety of Sudoku puzzles available (there are 6,670,903,752,021,072,936,960 different Sudoku grids [2]) allow for a high degree of difficulty ranges.

The characteristics of the problem make it easily translated to real-world problems, such as timetabling, where variables exhibit a degree of temporal saliency, and potential dependency. It has the added bonus that the solution is not known in advance (and not required for the evaluation of solutions), so each evolved solution is potentially unique.

The GAuGE system, when supplied with suitable logical instructions, is able to solve the problem, and does so by producing a list of the logical steps taken. This could be invaluable when tackling real world scheduling problems, as the list of steps provides an audit trail, so the solutions produced are *provably correct*.

Future work will consider increasing the number of operators made available to the system, to make it possible to solve more difficult puzzles, although this will increase the search space. We will also examine real world scheduling problems with this system, which, particularly in the case of timetabling problems, can be viewed as special cases of Sudoku.

References

1. Bagley, J. D.: The Behaviour of Adaptive Systems which Employ Genetic and Correlation Algorithms. PhD Thesis, University of Michigan. (1967)
2. Felgenhauer, B., and Jarvis, F.: Enumerating Possible Sudoku Grids. Technical Report. (2005) http://www.shef.ac.uk/ pm1afj/sudoku/
3. Frantz, D. R.: Non-linearities in Genetic Adaptive Search. PhD Thesis, University of Michigan. (1972)
4. Goldberg, D. E., Korb, B., and Deb, K.: Messy genetic algorithms: Motivation, analysis, and first results. Complex Systems, Vol. 3, number 5. (1989) pp. 493–530
5. Goldberg, D. E., Deb, K., Kargupta, H., and Harik, G.: Rapid, Accurate Optimization of Difficult Problems Using Fast Messy Genetic Algorithms. In Forrest, S. (Ed.): Proceedings of the Fifth International Conference on Genetic Algorithms. Morgan Kaufmann Publishers. (1993) pp. 56–64
6. Harik, G.: Learning Gene Linkage to Efficiently Solve Problems of Bounded Difficulty Using Genetic Algorithms. Doctoral Dissertation, University of Illinois (1997)
7. Holland, J. H.: Adaptation in Natural and Artificial Systems (Second Edition). University of Michigan Press. (1992)
8. Koza, J. R.: Genetic Programming: On the Programming of Computers by Means of Natural Evolution. MIT Press. (1992)
9. Nicolau, M. and Ryan, C.: How Functional Dependency Adapts to Salience Hierarchy in the GAuGE System. In: Ryan et al, (eds.): Proceedings of EuroGP-2003. Lecture Notes in Computer Science, Vol. 2610. Springer-Verlag. (2003) pp. 153–163
10. Nicolau, M., Auger, A., and Ryan, C.: Functional Dependency and Degeneracy: Detailed Analysis of the GAuGE System. In: Liardet et al, (eds.): Proceedings of Évolution Artificielle 2003. Lecture Notes in Computer Science, Vol. 2936. Springer-Verlag. (2003) pp. 15–26
11. Ohnishi, K. Sastry, K., Chen, Y.-P., and Goldberg, D.: Inducing Sequentiality Using Grammatical Genetic Codes. In: Deb et al, (eds.): Genetic and Evolutionary Computation - GECCO 2004. Lecture Notes in Computer Science, Vol. 3102. Springer. (2004) pp. 1426–1437
12. Oliver, I. M., Smith, D. J., and Holland, J. R. C.: A Study of Permutation Crossover Operators on the Travelling Salesman Problem. In Grefenstette, J. J. (Ed.): Proceedings of the Second International Conference on Genetic Algorithms. Lawrence Erlbaum Associates. (1987) pp. 224–230
13. O'Neill, M. and Ryan, C.: Grammatical Evolution - Evolving programs in an arbitrary language. Kluwer Academic Publishers. (2003)
14. Ryan, C., Nicolau, M., and O'Neill, M.: Genetic Algorithms using Grammatical Evolution. In: Foster et al, (eds.): Proceedings of EuroGP-2002. Lecture Notes in Computer Science, Vol. 2278. Springer-Verlag. (2002) pp. 278–287
15. Satoh, H., Yamamura, M., and Kobayashi, S.: Minimal Generation Gap Model for GAs Considering Both Exploration and Exploitation. In: Proceedings of the 4th International Conference on Fuzzy Systems, Neural Networks and Soft Computing (vol. 2). World Scientific, Singapore. (1996) pp. 494–497
16. Sudoku Bulletin Board. http://www.setbb.com/phpbb/?mforum=sudoku
17. Vorderman, C.: Carol Vorderman's How To Do Sudoku. Ebury Press. (2005)
18. Websudoku. http://websudoku.com
19. Wikipedia: Sudoku. http://en.wikipedia.org/wiki/Sudoku
20. Yato, T., and Seta, T.: Complexity and Completeness of Finding Another Solution and its Application to Puzzles. IEICE Transactions on Fundamentals of Electronics, Communications and Computer Sciences, Vol. 86, No. 5. (2003) pp. 1052–1060

The Halting Probability in Von Neumann Architectures

W.B. Langdon and R. Poli

Department of Computer Science, University of Essex, UK

Abstract. Theoretical models of Turing complete linear genetic programming (GP) programs suggest the fraction of halting programs is vanishingly small. Convergence results proved for an idealised machine, are tested on a small T7 computer with (finite) memory, conditional branches and jumps. Simulations confirm Turing complete fitness landscapes of this type hold at most a vanishingly small fraction of usable solutions.

1 Introduction

Recent work on strengthening the theoretical underpinnings of genetic programming (GP) has considered how GP searches its fitness landscape [1, 2, 3, 4, 5, 6]. Results gained on the space of all possible programs are applicable to both GP and other search based automatic programming techniques. We have *proved* convergence results for the two most important forms of GP, i.e. trees (without side effects) and linear GP [1, 7, 8, 9, 10]. As remarked more than ten years ago [11], it is still true that few researchers allow their GP's to include iteration or recursion. Indeed there are only about 50 papers (out of 4631) where loops or recursion have been included in GP. Without some form of looping and memory there are algorithms which cannot be represented and so GP stands no chance of evolving them.

We extend our results to Turing complete linear GP machine code programs. We analyse the formation of the first loop in the programs and whether programs ever leave that loop. Mathematical analysis is followed up by simulations on a demonstration computer. In particular we study how the frequency of different types of loops varies with program size. In the process we have executed programs of up to 16 777 215 instructions. These are perhaps the largest programs ever (deliberately) executed as part of a GP experiment. (beating the previous largest of 1 000 000 [12]). Results confirm theory and show that, the fraction of programs that produce usable results, i.e. that halt, is vanishingly small, confirming the popular view that machine code programming is hard.

The next two sections describe the T7 computer and simulations run on it, whilst Sections 4 and 5 present theoretical models and compare them with measurement of halting and non-halting programs. The implications of these results are discussed in Section 6 before we conclude (Section 7).

P. Collet et al. (Eds.): EuroGP 2006, LNCS 3905, pp. 225–237, 2006.

Table 1. T7 Turing Complete Instruction Set

Instruction	#operands	operation	
			v set Every ADD operation either sets or
ADD	3	A + B→C	v clears the overflow bit v.
BVS	1	#addr→pc if v=1	LDi and STi, treat one of their argu-
COPY	2	A→B	ments as the address of the data. They
LDi	2	@A→B	allow array manipulation without the
STi	2	A→@B	need for self modifying code. (LDi and
COPY_PC	1	pc→A	STi data addresses are 8 bits.)
JUMP	1	addr→pc	To ensure JUMP addresses are legal,
			they are reduced modulo the program
			length.

2 T7 an Example Turing Complete Computer

To test our theoretical results we need a simple Turing complete system. Our seven instruction CPU (see Table 1) is based on the Kowalczy F-4 minimal instruction set computer http://www.dakeng.com/misc.html, cf. appendix of [13]. T7 consists of: directly accessed bit addressable memory (there are no special registers), a single arithmetic operator (ADD), an unconditional JUMP, a conditional Branch if oVerflow flag is Set (BVS) jump and four copy instructions. COPY_PC allows a programmer to save the current program address for use as the return address in subroutine calls, whilst the direct and indirect addressing modes allow access to stacks and arrays.

Eight bit data words are used. The number of bits in address words is just big enough to be able to address every instruction in the program. E.g., if the program is 300 instructions, then BVS, JUMP and COPY_PC instructions use 9 bits. These experiments use 12 bytes (96 bits) of memory (plus the overflow flag).

3 Experimental Method

There are simply too many programs to test all of them. Instead we gather representative statistics about those of a particular length by randomly sampling programs of that length. Then we sample those of another length and so on, until we can build up a picture of the whole search space.

To be more specific, one thousand programs of each of various lengths (30...16 777 215 instructions) are each run from a random starting point, with random inputs, until either they reach their last instruction and stop, an infinite loop is detected or an individual instruction has been executed more than 100 times. (In practise we can detect almost all infinite loops by keeping track of the machine's contents, i.e. memory and overflow bit. We can be sure the loop is infinite, if the contents is identical to what it was when the instruction was last executed.) The programs' execution paths are then analysed. Statistics are gathered on the number of instructions executed, normal program terminations, type of loops, length of loops, start of first loop, etc.

4   Terminating Programs

The introduction of Turing completeness into GP raises the halting problem, in particular how to assign fitness to a program which may loop indefinitely [14]. We shall give a lower bound on the number of programs which, given arbitrary input, stop, and show how this varies with their size.

The T7 instruction set has been designed to have as little bias as possible. In particular, given a random starting point a random sequence of ADD and copy instructions will create another random pattern in memory. The contents of the memory is essentially uniformly random. I.e. the overflow v bit is equally likely to be set as to be clear, and each address in memory is equally likely. (Where programs are not exactly a fraction of a power of two long, JUMP and COPY_PC addresses cannot completely fill the number of bits allocated to them. This introduces a slight bias in favour of lower addresses.) So, until correlations are introduced by re-executing the same instructions, we can treat JUMP instructions as being to random locations in the program. Similarly we can treat half BVS as jumping to a random address. The other half do nothing. We will start by analysing the simplest case of a loop formed by random jumps. First we present an accurate Markov chain model, then Section 4.2 gives a less precise but more intuitive mathematical model. Section 4.3 considers the run time of terminating programs.

4.1   Markov Chain Model of Non-looping Programs

The Markov chain model predicts how many programs will not loop and so halt. This means it, and the following segments model, do not take into account

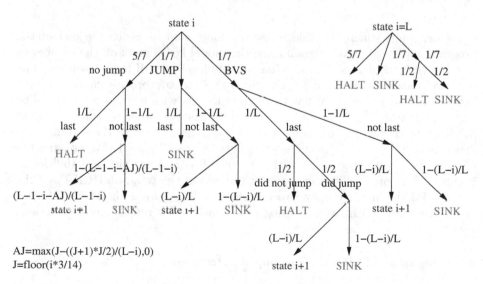

Fig. 1. Probability tree used to create Markov model of the execution of random Turing complete programs. HALT indicates a terminating program, while SINK means the start of a loop.

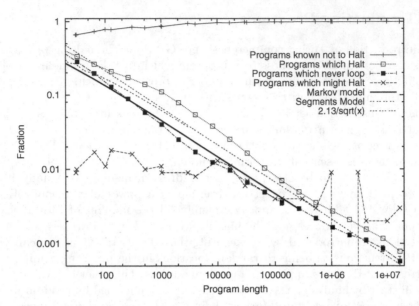

Fig. 2. Looping + and terminating (□ ■) T7 programs To smooth these two curves, 50 000 to 200 000 samples taken at exact powers of two. (Other lengths lie slightly below these curves). Solid diagonal line is the Markov model of programs without any repeated instructions. This approximately fits ■, especially if lengths are near a power of two. The other diagonal line is the segments model and its large program limit, $2.13\,\mathrm{length}^{-\frac{1}{2}}$. The small number of programs which did not halt, but which might do so eventually, are also plotted ×.

those programs which are able to escape loops and do reach the end of the program and stop. As a program runs, the model keeps track of: the number of new instructions it executes, if it has repeated any, and if it has stopped. The last two states are attractors from which the Markov process cannot escape. State i means the program has run i instructions without repeating any. The next instruction will take the program from state i either to state $i + 1$, to SINK or to HALT. In our model the probabilities of each of these transitions depends only on i and the program length L, see Figure 1. We construct a $(L + 2) \times (L + 2)$ Markov transition matrix T containing the probabilities in Figure 1. The probabilities of reaching the end of the program (HALT) or the looping (SINK) are given by two entries in T^L. Figure 2 shows our Markov chain describes the fraction of programs which never repeat any instructions very well.

4.2   Segment Model of Non-looping Programs

As before, we assume half BVS instructions cause a jump. So the chance of program flow not being disrupted is 11/14. Thus the average length of uninterrupted random sequential instructions is $\sum_{i=1}^{L/2} i\,(11/14)^{i-1}\,3/14$. We can reasonably replace the upper limit on the summation by infinity to give the geometric distribution (mean of $14/3 = 4.67$ and standard deviation $\sqrt{14^2/3^2 \times 11/3} = 8.94$).

For simplicity we will assume the program's L instructions are divided into $L/4.67$ segments. Two thirds end with a JUMP and the remainder with an active BVS (i.e. with the overflow bits set). The idea behind this simplification is that if we jump to any of the instructions in a segment, the normal sequencing of (i.e. non-branching) instructions will carry us to its end, thus guaranteeing the last instruction will be executed. The chance of jumping to a segment that has already been executed is the ratio of already executed segments to the total. (This ignores the possibility that the last instruction is a jump. We compensate for this later.)

Let i be the number of instructions run so far divided by 4.67 and $N = L/4.67$. At the end of each segment, there are three possible outcomes: either we jump to the end of the program (probability $1/N$) and so stop its execution; we jump to a segment that has already been run (probability i/N) so forming a loop; or we branch elsewhere. The chance the program repeats an instruction at the end of the ith segment is

$$= \frac{i}{N}(1 - \frac{2}{N})(1 - \frac{3}{N}) \ldots (1 - \frac{i}{N})$$

I.e. it is the chance of jumping back to code that has already been executed (i/N) times the probability we have not already looped or exited the program at each of the previous steps. Similarly the chance the program stops at the end of the ith segment is

$$\frac{1}{N}(1 - \frac{2}{N})(1 - \frac{3}{N}) \ldots (1 - \frac{i}{N}) = \frac{1}{N^i}\frac{(N-2)!}{(N-i-1)!} = \frac{(N-2)!}{N^{N-1}}\frac{N^{N-1-i}}{(N-i-1)!}$$

$$= (N-2)!N^{1-N}e^N \mathrm{Psn}(N-i-1, N)$$

Where $\mathrm{Psn}(k, \lambda) = e^{-\lambda}\lambda^k/k!$ is the Poisson distribution with mean λ.

The chance the program stops at all (ignoring both the possibility of leaving the first loop and of other loops for the time being) is simply the sum of all the ways it could stop

$$\sum_{i=1}^{N-1} (N-2)!N^{1-N}e^N \mathrm{Psn}(N-i-1, N) = (N-2)!N^{1-N}e^N \sum_{j=0}^{N-2} \mathrm{Psn}(j, N)$$

For large mean ($N \gg 1$) $\sum_{j=0}^{N-2} \mathrm{Psn}(j, N)$ approaches $1/2$ (see Figure 3). Therefore the chance of long programs not looping is (using Gosper's approximation $n! \approx \sqrt{(2n + 1/3)\pi}\, n^n e^{-n}$ and that for large x $(1 - 1/x)^x \approx e^{-1}$):

$$\approx 1/2(N-2)!N^{1-N}e^N \approx 1/2\sqrt{2\pi/N}\left(1 + \frac{37}{12N}\right)$$

That is (ignoring both the possibility of leaving the first loop and of other loops for the time being) the probability of a long random T7 program of length L

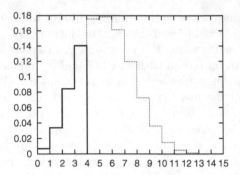

Fig. 3. Poisson distribution, with mean=5. Note region 0 to mean-2 corresponding to the segments model of non-looping programs.

stopping is about $1/2\sqrt{2\pi 14/3L}\left(1 + \frac{37\times 14}{36L}\right) = \sqrt{7\pi/3L}\,(1+259/18L)$. As mentioned above, we have to consider explicitly the $3/14$ of programs where the last instruction is itself an active jump. Including this correction gives the chance of a long program not repeating any instructions as $\approx 11/14\sqrt{7\pi/3L}\,(1+259/18L)$. Figure 2 shows this $\sqrt{\text{length}}$ scaling fits the data reasonably well.

4.3   Average Number of Instructions Run Before Stopping

The average number of instructions run before stopping can easily be computed from the Markov chain. This gives an excellent fit with the data (Figure 4). However, to get a scaling law, we again apply our segments model.

The mean number of segments evaluated by programs that do halt is: $\frac{\sum_{i=1}^{N-1} i/N\ \prod_{j=2}^{i}(1-j/N)}{\sum_{i=1}^{N-1} 1/N\ \prod_{j=2}^{i}(1-j/N)}$.Consider the top term for the time being

$$= 1/N \sum_{i=1}^{N-1} i \exp\left(\sum_{j=2}^{i} \log(1 - j/N)\right) < 1/N \sum_{i=1}^{N-1} i \exp\left(\sum_{j=2}^{i} -j/N\right)$$

$$= 1/N \sum_{i=1}^{N-1} i \exp\left(-\frac{i(i+1)-2}{2N}\right) < 1/N e^{\frac{1}{N}} e^{-\frac{1}{2N}} \sum_{i=1}^{N-1} i \exp\left(-\frac{i^2}{2N}\right)$$

$$\approx e^{\frac{1}{2N}} 1/N \int_{1/2}^{N-1/2} x e^{-x^2/2N}\,dx = e^{\frac{1}{2N}}\left[e^{-x^2/2N}\right]_{N-1/2}^{1/2} \approx e^{\frac{3}{8N}}$$

Dividing $e^{\frac{3}{8N}}$ by the lower part (the probability of a long program not looping) gives an upper bound on the expected number of segments executed by a program which does not enter a loop $\approx \dfrac{e^{3/8N}}{1/2\sqrt{2\pi/N}\left(1+\frac{37}{12N}\right)}$ $\approx (1 + \frac{3}{8N})(1 - \frac{37}{12N})\sqrt{2N/\pi} \approx (1 - \frac{65}{24N})\sqrt{2N/\pi}$. Replacing the number of segments N ($N = 3L/14$) by the the number of instructions L gives, to first order, $14/3 \times \sqrt{2 \times (3L/14)/\pi} = \sqrt{28L/3\pi} = 1.72\sqrt{L}$. Figure 4 shows, particularly

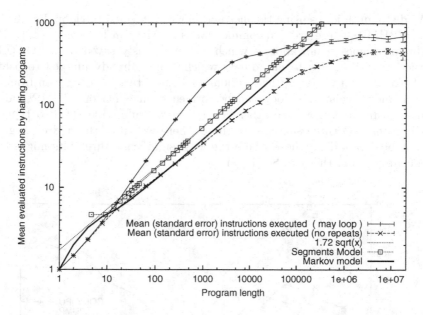

Fig. 4. Instructions executed by programs which halt. Std dev≈mean suggests geometric distribution. As Fig. 2, larger samples used to increase reliability. Models ok for short programs. However as random programs run for longer, COPY_PC and JUMP derandomise the 96 bit memory, so easing looping.

for large random programs, this gives a good bound for the T7 segments model. However, as Figure 2 confirms, the segments model itself is an over estimate.

Neither the segments model, nor the Markov model, take into account derandomisation of memory as more instructions are run. This is particularly acute since we have a small memory. JUMP and COPY_PC instructions introduce correlations between the contents of memory and the path of the program counter. These make it easier for loops to form.

5   Loops

5.1   Code Fragments Which Form Loops

If a BVS or an unconditional JUMP instruction jumps to an instruction that has been previously obeyed, a loop is formed. Unless something is different the second time the instruction is reached (e.g. the setting of the overflow flag) the program will obey exactly the same instruction sequence as before, including calculating the same answers, and so return to start of the loop again. Again, if nothing important has changed, the same sequence of instructions will be run again and an infinite loop will be performed. Automated analysis can, in most cases, detect if changes are important and so the course of program execution might change, so enabling the program to leave the loop.

We distinguish loops using the instruction which formed the loop. I.e. the last BVS or JUMP. There are two common ways JUMP can lead to a loop: either the program goes to an address which was previously saved by a LOAD_PC instruction or it jumps to an address which it has already jumped to before. E.g. because the two JUMP instructions take their target instruction from the same memory register. A loop can be formed even when one JUMP address is slightly different from the other. Therefore we subdivide the two types of JUMP loops into three sub-classes: those where we know the address register has not been modified, those where the least significant three bits might have been changed, and the rest. See Figure 5.

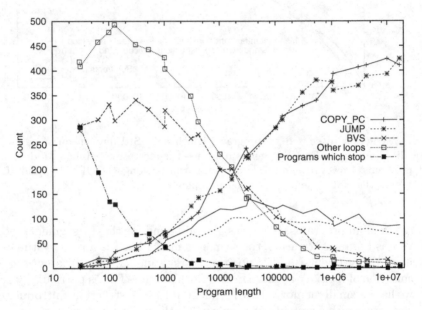

Fig. 5. Types of first loop in T7 random programs. In large programs most loops have a last branch instruction which is either COPY_PC (+) or JUMP (∗) with unsullied target addresses. In a further 20–30% of programs, the lower three bits of the target address may have been modified (plotted as solid and dashed lines). Since BVS (×) jumps to any address in the program, it is less likely to be responsible for loops as the program gets larger. Mostly, the fraction of unclassified loops (□) also falls with increasing program size.

5.2   Number of Instructions Before the First Loop

Since we are stopping on the first loop there is competition between the different types of loop and only the fastest to form are observed. So the observed mean number of instructions before a loop is formed is pretty much independent of loop type (cf. Figure 5). With bigger programs, BVS loops get longer and so might be expected to appear later in a program's execution. This apparent contradiction is resolved by noting BVS loops become a smaller fraction of first loops.

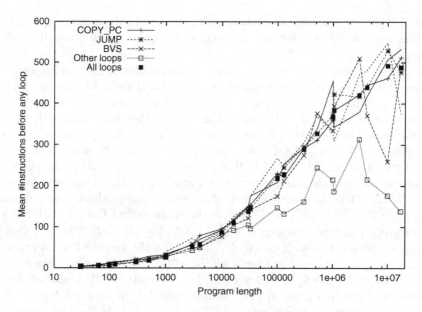

Fig. 6. Number of instructions before the first loop in T7 programs

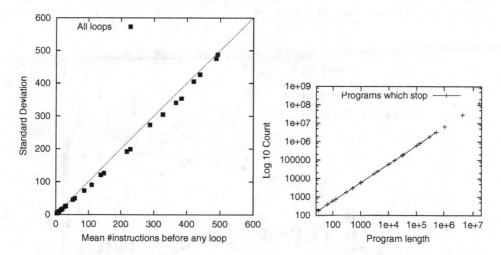

Fig. 7. Mean and std dev of the number of T7 instructions before the first loop. In a geometric distribution the mean and std dev are ≈ equal (dotted line).

Fig. 8. The number of Halting programs rises exponentially with length despite getting increasingly rare as a fraction of all programs. Note log log vertical scaling.

5.3   COPY_PC and JUMP Loops

As Figure 5 shows, almost all long programs get trapped in either a COPY_PC or a JUMP loop. We can approximately model the lengths of both types of loops. In both cases very short loops are predicted. We would expect, since there is less chance to disrupt memory, tight loops to be more difficult to escape.

Let $M = \#\text{bits} = 96$, A = size of program address, D = data size = 8. Assume the chance of a loop containing i instructions = chance appropriate JUMP $\times$ (chance loop not already formed and memory not disturbed)$^{i-1}$. It is very difficult to calculate the probability of another loop forming before the one of interest. Instead we will just model the random disruption of the address stored in memory by a COPY_PC instruction. There are seven instructions, four of which write D bits and COPY_PC which writes A bits. The effect of a random update not changing overwritten data, is as if the target was shrunk to $\approx A - 2$ bits. Thus the chance of a random instruction modifying the address is $(4(A + D - 3) + 2A - 3))/7M$. Therefore the chance of a COPY_PC-JUMP loop being exactly i instructions long is $\approx \frac{1}{7M}\left(1 - (6A + 4D - 15)/7M\right)^{i-1}$. This is a geometric distribution, with mean $7M/(6A + 4D - 15)$. For the longest programs $A = 24$, suggesting the mean length will be $161/672 = 4.17$. In fact, we measure 4.74 ± 0.16, cf. Figure 9. The mean length for JUMP-JUMP loops will be one less (lower curve in Figure 9). The simple model is quite good but does not fully capture the competition between different loops. Note the vast majority of programs in the whole search space (which is dominated by long programs) fall into loops with fewer than 20 instructions.

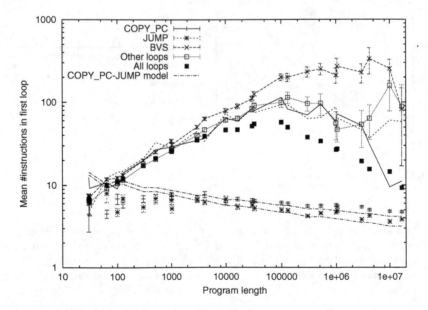

Fig. 9. Length of the first loop. Note the average (■) initially tracks "other" (□), BVS (×) etc. but as the number of these types of loop, cf. Figure 6, falls the mean begins to resemble the length of first loops created by unsullied COPY_PC (+) and JUMP (∗) instructions. The theoretical curves lie close by.

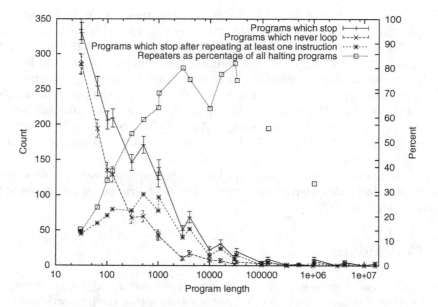

Fig. 10. Number of T7 programs (out of 1000) which escape the first loop and subsequent loops and then terminate successfully. Error bars are standard errors, indicating the measured differences (∗) and percentages (□) become increasingly noisy with programs longer than 3000. Nevertheless the trend for terminating programs to loop but escape from the loop can be seen.

6   Discussion

Of course the undecidability of the Halting problem has long been known. More recently work by Chaitin [15] started to consider a probabilistic information theoretic approach. However this is based on self-delimiting Turing machines (particularly the "Chaitin machines") and has lead to a non-zero value for Ω [16] and postmodern metamathematics. Our approach is firmly based on the von Neumann architecture, which for practical purposes is Turing complete. Indeed the T7 computer is similar to the linear GP area of existing Turing complete GP research.

While the numerical values we have calculated are specific to the T7, the scaling laws are general. These results are also very general in the sense that they apply to the space of all possible programs and so are applicable to both GP and any other search based automatic programming techniques.

Section 4 has accurately modelled the formation of the first loops in program execution. Section 5 shows in long programs most loops are quite short but we have not yet been able to quantitatively model the programs which enter a loop and then leave it. However we can argue recursively that once the program has left a loop it is back almost where it started. That is, it has executed only a tiny fraction of the whole program, and the remainder is still random with respect to its current state. Now there may be something in the memory which makes it to easier to exit loops, or harder to form them in the first place. For example, the overflow flag not being set. However, it may also contain previous values of the program counter (PC), which would tend to make it easier to form a new loop. Also initial studies indicate the memory and flag will become nearly random almost immediately. That is having left one loop, we expect the chance of entering another to be much the same as when the program started, i.e. almost one. Thus the program will stumble from one loop to another until it gets trapped by a loop it cannot escape. As explained in Section 5, we expect, in long programs, it will not take long to find a short loop from which it is impossible to escape.

Real computer systems lose information (converting into heat) [9]. We expect this to lead to further convergence properties in programming languages with recursion and memory.

7   Conclusions

Our models and simulations of a Turing complete linear GP system based on practical von Neumann computer architectures, show that the proportion of halting programs falls towards zero with increasing program length. However there are exponentially more long programs than short ones. In absolute terms the number of halting programs increases (cf. Figure 8) but, in probabilistic terms, the Halting problem is decidable: von Neumann programs do not terminate with probability one.

In detail: the proportion of halting programs is $\approx 1/\sqrt{\text{length}}$, while the average and standard deviation of the run time of terminating programs grows as $\sqrt{\text{length}}$. This suggests a limit on run time of, say, 20 times $\sqrt{\text{length}}$ instruction cycles, will differentiate between almost all halting and non-halting T7 programs. E.g. for a real GHz machine, if a random program has been running for a single millisecond that is enough to be confident that it will never stop.

Acknowledgements. We thank Dave Kowalczy and EPSRC GR/T11234/01.

References

1. W. B. Langdon and R. Poli. *Foundations of Genetic Programming*. 2002.
2. N. F. McPhee and R. Poli. Using schema theory to explore interactions of multiple operators. In W. B. Langdon, *et al.*, eds., *GECCO 2002*, pp853–860.
3. J. Rosca. A probabilistic model of size drift. In R. L. Riolo and B. Worzel, eds., *Genetic Programming Theory and Practice*, pp119–136. Kluwer, 2003.
4. K. Sastry, U-M O'Reilly, D. E. Goldberg and D. Hill. Building block supply GP. In *Genetic Programming Theory and Practice*, pp137–154. Kluwer, 2003.
5. B. Mitavskiy and J. E. Rowe. A schema-based version of Geiringer's theorem for nonlinear genetic programming with homologous crossover. In A. H. Wright, *et al.*, eds., *Foundations of Genetic Algorithms 8, LNCS 3469*, pp156–175. 2005.

6. J. M. Daida, A. M. Hilss, D. J. Ward, and S. L. Long. Visualizing tree structures in genetic programming. *Genetic Programming and Evolvable Machines*, 6(1):79–110
7. W. B. Langdon. Convergence rates for the distribution of program outputs. In W. B. Langdon, *et al.*, eds., *GECCO 2002*, pp812–819, New York, 9-13 July 2002.
8. W. B. Langdon. How many good programs are there? How long are they? In K. A. De Jong, *et al.*, eds., *FOGA 7*, pp183–202, Morgan Kaufmann. Published 2003.
9. W. B. Langdon. The distribution of reversible functions is Normal. In *Genetic Programming Theory and Practise*, pp173–188. Kluwer, 2003.
10. W. B. Langdon. Convergence of program fitness landscapes. In E. Cantú-Paz, *et al.*, eds., *GECCO 2003, LNCS 2724*, pp1702–1714. Springer-Verlag.
11. A. Teller. Turing completeness in the language of GP with indexed memory. In *1994 IEEE World Congress on Computational Intelligence*, pp136–141.
12. W. B. Langdon. Quadratic bloat in genetic programming. In D. Whitley, *et al.*, eds., *GECCO 2000*, pp451–458.
13. W. B. Langdon and R. Poli. On Turing complete T7 and MISC F-4 program fitness landscapes. Technical Report CSM-445, University of Essex, UK, 2005.
14. S. R. Maxwell III. Experiments with a coroutine model for genetic programming. In *1994 IEEE World Congress on Computational Intelligence*, pp413–417a.
15. G. J. Chaitin. An algebraic equation for the halting probability. In R. Herken, ed., *The Universal Turing Machine A Half-Century Survey*, pp279–283. OUP, 1988.
16. C. S. Calude, M. J. Dinneen and C-K Shu. Computing a glimpse of randomness. *Experimental Mathematics*, 11(3):361–370, 2002.

Using Subtree Crossover Distance to Investigate Genetic Programming Dynamics

Leonardo Vanneschi[1], Steven Gustafson[2], and Giancarlo Mauri[1]

[1] Dipartimento di Informatica,
Sistemistica e Comunicazione (D.I.S.Co.),
University of Milano-Bicocca, 20126 Milan, Italy
[2] School of Computer Science & IT,
University of Nottingham,
Jubilee Campus, Wollaton Rd. Nottingham,
NG81BB, United Kingdom

Abstract. To analyse various properties of the search process of genetic programming it is useful to quantify the distance between two individuals. Using operator-based distance measures can make this analysis more accurate and reliable than using distance measures which have no relationship with the genetic operators. This paper extends a recent definition of a distance measure based on subtree crossover for genetic programming. Empirical studies are presented that show the suitability of this measure to dynamically calculate the fitness distance correlation coefficient during the evolution, to construct a fitness sharing system for genetic programming and to measure genotypic diversity in the population. These experiments confirm the accuracy of the new measure and its consistency with the subtree crossover genetic operator.

1 Introduction

Tree-based genetic programming (GP) uses transformation operators on tree structures [1] to carry out search. These operators define a neighbourhood structure over the trees. To analyse various dynamics of the GP search process, it is useful to quantify the distance between two trees in this topological space. For example, the distance between trees is useful if we want to monitor population diversity (see for instance [2, 3, 4, 5, 6, 7]) or if we want to calculate well-known measures of problem hardness such as fitness distance correlation (FDC) (see among others [8, 9, 10, 11]). Operator-based distance measures can make calculating distance and the analysis of the search process more accurate [10, 11, 2, 3, 4, 5]. The difficulty in defining operator-based distance measures was highlighted in [12]. Defining a distance measure, or a measure of similarity, that is, in some sense "bound" to (or "consistent" with) the genetic operators informally means that if two trees are *close* to each other, or similar, one can be transformed into the other in a few applications of the operator(s). Mutation-based distance measures for GP have been defined, the most common being some variations on the Levenshtein edit distance [3] and the structural distance [7]. In [12], Gustafson and Vanneschi first defined the notion of a subtree crossover based pseudo-distance

P. Collet et al. (Eds.): EuroGP 2006, LNCS 3905, pp. 238–249, 2006.

measure. In this paper, we extend and generalise that definition and we experimentally show the usefulness of this new distance measure to analyse some properties of the search process.

2 Subtree Crossover Distance

Following the same notation as in [12], let P be a population of trees, T_1 be the tree we want to compute a distance from (or the parent tree), T_2 be the tree which we would like to transform T_1 into, and let "T_1/T_2" be the "difference" of these two trees. By definition, this difference operator produces a pair of subtrees (s_{T_1}, s_{T_2}), where subtree $s_{T_2} \in T_2$ must replace $s_{T_1} \in T_1$ to make $T_1 = T_2$. Supposing that $T_1 \in P$, the subtree crossover distance (SCD from now on) between T_1 and T_2 depends on the ability to select s_{T_2} from some tree in P. Thus, the SCD[1] between T_1 and T_2 also depends on the population P. One possibility to define the SCD is to consider it as being equal to 1 in case $s_{T_2} \in P$, since it is possible to transform T_1 into T_2 in just one crossover application. On the other hand, if $s_{T_2} \notin P$ then it will require more than one application of subtree crossover to make $T_1 = T_2$. In that case, calculating the distance would mean counting all these possible applications. This definition of the SCD clearly has some problems: we would need to consider all the necessary next populations or, at least, to approximate them. Creating all the necessary future populations for a particular application of the SCD is clearly computationally infeasible. We might create the future expected populations using calculations similar to the ones found in the schema theorems for GP [13]. However, finding the future expected populations is also costly, essentially requiring a similar amount of computation as actually running the GP algorithm. Furthermore, we have assumed that the distance between T_1 and T_2 is equal to 1 if one crossover application to T_1 can build T_2. However, when we actually execute our algorithm, it is not certain that this particular application will occur. Therefore it may be useful to know the likelihood of creating a particular tree T_2 in the next generation. To overcome the difficulty of defining a multiple operator distance, and to incorporate the stochastic properties of the algorithm, Gustafson and Vanneschi [12] introduced the possibility of considering operator-distance in terms of the probability of correctly applying the operator once. That is, if one tree is in the neighbourhood of another, how likely is it that this neighbour will be found. Since we know (or we can easily calculate) the values of parameters like the selection probability of trees and the frequency of all subtrees in the current population, we could assign a probability to the selection of all subtrees in the next population. If we know what subtree is required to make two trees equal, then we may approximate distance in terms

---

[1] The subtree crossover distance that we consider in this paper is a probability and thus it is clearly not a metric. Furthermore it is not just a function of two trees, but also of the population they belong to and in general it does not respect the properties of metrics (like for instance the triangle inequality). Thus, the term "pseudo-distance" (in the sense that it indicates how "far apart" the two items are) would be more appropriate than the term distance. In some senses, we could say that our measure is more like a similarity/dissimilarity measure than a proper distance (Euclidean) metric: it conveys information about how likely it is to make two trees equal, which does largely depend on their similarity. Nevertheless, we use the term distance for the sake of brevity.

of the probability of selecting this subtree. Thus, given the subtree crossover operator V, Gustafson and Vanneschi defined the distance function by the following pseudo-code:

$$
\begin{aligned}
&\text{func distance}(T_1, T_2, V, P)\{ \\
&\quad (s_{T_1}, s_{T_2}) = T_1/T_2 \\
&\quad ps1 = probSelecting(s_{T_1}, T_1) \\
&\quad ps2 = probCreating(s_{T_2}, P) \\
&\quad return\ (1 - ps1 * ps2) \\
&\}
\end{aligned}
$$

Given the subtree s_{T_2} that needs to replace $s_{T_1} \in T_1$, the distance is defined in terms of the probability of selecting s_{T_1} in T_1 and the probability of creating (or selecting) s_{T_2} from P. Both functions, *probSelecting()* and *probCreating()*, require knowledge of the selection probabilities used in the algorithm. Finding s_{T_1} and s_{T_2} and determining the probability of selecting $s_{T_1} \in T_1$ can be done in linear time in the size of T_1 and T_2. The *probSelecting()* function can be defined for subtree crossover based on the node selection probability. Given uniform node selection, selecting the subtree $s_{T_1} \in T_1$ has the probability of $\frac{1}{|T_1|}$. The *probCreating()* function for subtree crossover can be defined to consider all the occurrences of the subtree s_{T_2} in the population and their probability of selection. That is, for a tree that contains s_{T_2}, we may want to know how likely that tree will be selected by a selection method. We will then want to know the probability of selecting s_{T_2}. Since evolutionary algorithms use fitness-based selection to implement solution competition, not all trees have the same likelihood of being selected. Gustafson and Vanneschi [12] used this fact to provide an effective way of reducing complexity of this operator distance while preserving the utility of the measure: they only considered those trees and their subtrees that are *likely* to be selected. However, the distance used in [12] presents one major limitation: in that definition, in case a tree T_2 cannot be obtained from a tree T_1 with one crossover, the distance between T_1 and T_2 was the probability of selecting the root of T_1 as crossover point and a subtree equal to T_2 from the population. The likelihood of this event was considered to be very small and thus it was approximated to zero (and thus the distance was set to one, i.e. the maximum possible distance). In other words, the distance between two trees T_1 and T_2 was equal to one if T_1 and T_2 differed in more than one subtree. In some cases, this approximation may be too coarse, thus compromising the accuracy of the measure (for instance when using the SCD for calculating the FDC). In this paper, we extend that definition admitting that the distance between two trees T_1 and T_2 differing in more than one subtree can have a smaller value than one and thus overcoming this limitation. The new subtree crossover distance can be defined as follows: we define a new operator *diff*(T_1, T_2) which returns the *set* $S = \{(s_{T_1}^1, s_{T_2}^1), (s_{T_1}^2, s_{T_2}^2), ..., (s_{T_1}^n, s_{T_2}^n)\}$ such that $\forall i \in [1, n]$ if we replace $s_{T_1}^i$ with $s_{T_2}^i$ in T_2 we obtain T_1; *diff*(T_1, T_2) returns the empty set if T_1 and T_2 share no genetic material. Now, the new SCD can be defined by the following algorithm:

```
func SCD(T₁,T₂,P ){
    S = diff(T₁,T₂)
    res = 0
    for i = 1 to cardinality(S) do
        ps1 = probSelecting(s^i_T₁,T₁)
        ps2 = probCreating(s^i_T₂,P)
        res = res + (ps1 * ps2)
    endfor
    return(1 − res)
}
```

The main difference between this new definition and the one in [12] is that the returned value is a sum of probabilities, each of which is the product between the probability of selecting one subtree $s^i_{T_1}$ and the probability of creating one subtree $s^i_{T_2}$. The paper [12] contains a detailed discussion on the computational complexity of the old definition of crossover distance. The complexity of this new definition is not much higher than the complexity of the old one: the most expensive step is storing in a hash table all the subtrees in the population at each generation (and it was done also in the old version). Once it has been done, the cost of building the S set differs from the cost of generating only two subtrees s_{T_1} and s_{T_2} (eventually selecting the root of T_1 and $s_{T_2} = T_2$, as in the old definition) of a linear factor. This new distance measure will be used in the next section for analysing some properties of the GP search process.

3   Experimental Results

The goal of this section is to show the suitability of the new definition of SCD for monitoring various properties of the GP search process. In particular, Section 3.1 shows how this distance can be used to calculate fitness distance correlation (FDC) inside the population during the search process, Section 3.2 shows results of fitness sharing using SCD and Section 3.3 shows how the SCD can be used to measure genotypic diversity of populations.

3.1   Fitness Distance Correlation

FDC was first proposed as a difficulty measure for GAs in [8]. It is defined as follows: given a sample $F = \{f_1,f_2,...,f_n\}$ of n individual fitnesses and a corresponding sample $D = \{d_1,d_2,...,d_n\}$ of the n distances to the nearest global optimum, $FDC = C_{FD}/(\sigma_F\sigma_D)$, where: $C_{FD} = \frac{1}{n}\sum_{i=1}^{n}(f_i - \overline{f})(d_i - \overline{d})$ is the covariance of F and D and σ_F, σ_D, $\overline{f}$ and $\overline{d}$ are the standard deviations and means of F and D. In [8], Jones proposed that GAs problems may be partitioned into three classes, depending on the value of the FDC coefficient: *misleading* (if the FDC is positive, and thus fitness increases as the distance to the global optimum increases), *straightforward* (if FDC is negative, and thus fitness increases as individuals approach the global optimum) and *difficult* (if the there is no correlation between fitness and distance). In [9, 10, 11], Vanneschi *et al.* showed the suitability of FDC as a measure of problem hardness for tree based GP. In particular, they used systems with single-node altering transformation operators (like single-node mutation) and they employed the well known structural distance [7] (which they proved to be bound to this operator) to accurately calculate the FDC. They also showed that FDC calculated using structural distance is a reasonable indicator of problem hardness for GP systems using subtree crossover. Nevertheless, given that no bound was proven between subtree crossover and structural distance, they used large samples of individuals (and not just the individuals composing the population) to calculate FDC. On the other hand, the study of the trend of the FDC in the population during the evolution would be very interesting, since this study would be more *dynamic* than studying the FDC once for all on a single large sample of individuals. In fact, this investigation would allow us to study how the FDC gets modified during the evolution and this information could allow us to draw some conclusions on the dynamics of the GP search process. In particular, we could imagine that if the FDC value decreases during the evolution and it tends towards -1, the population is converging towards the global optimum (individuals are approaching the global optimum as fitness is improving). On the other hand, if the FDC value increases during the evolution, or it remains static at some initial positive level or at zero, this probably means that the population is converging towards a local optimum (fitness is improving, but the distance to the global optimum is not decreasing). The following experiments have been done to confirm this hypothesis and to test the suitability of SCD to calculate the FDC.

Syntactic Trees

In the syntactic trees problem, as used in [12], trees are represented using the set of functions $\mathcal{F} = \{N\}$, where N is a binary operator (N stands for "Non-terminal") and the set of terminal symbols $\mathcal{T} = \{L\}$ (L stands for "Leaf"). No "content" is associated with the nodes and fitness is simply equal to the edit distance (ED from now on) to a fixed global optimum. The global optimum of an instance is generated using a random tree growing algorithm described in [12]. The definition of ED used here is the same as in [3]. Figure 1(a) shows the tree chosen as optimum for the experiments in Figure 2, and Figure 1(b) shows the tree chosen as optimum for the experiments in Figure 3.

These experiments have been performed using the following set of parameters: generational GP, population size of 30 individuals, standard subtree crossover as the only genetic operator, tournament selection of size 5, ramped half-and-half initialisation,

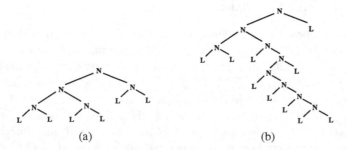

(a)   (b)

Fig. 1. (a) The tree used as optimum for the experiments in Figure 2. (b) The tree used as optimum for the experiments in Figure 3.

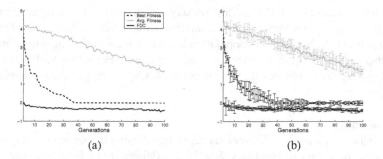

(a)   (b)

Fig. 2. Syntactic Trees Problem. Average values (a) and average values with their standard deviations (b) of average fitness, best fitness and FDC in the population against generations over 50 independent GP runs. In all these runs the optimum has been found before generation 100. The tree used as optimum in these experiments was the tree in Figure 1(a).

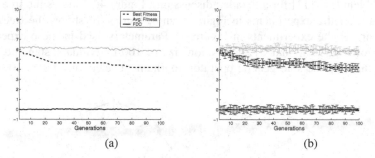

(a)   (b)

Fig. 3. Syntactic Trees Problem. Average values (a) and average values with their standard deviations (b) of average fitness, best fitness and FDC in the population against generations over 50 independent GP runs. In all these runs the optimum has *not* been found before generation 100. The tree used as optimum in these experiments was the tree in Figure 1(b).

maximum depth of individuals for the initialisation phase equal to 4, maximum depth of individuals for crossover equal to 8. All the runs have been stopped at generation 100. Figure 2 reports the average values (with their standard deviations in Figure 2(b)) of the best fitness, the average fitness and the FDC (calculated using SCD) in the population (against generations) over 50 independent GP runs in which the global optimum has been found before generation 100 (*successful runs*). Producing 50 successful runs has been easy, probably for the very simple shape of the tree that we have used as optimum (shown in Figure 1(a)). The method that we have used to collect 50 successful runs was simply to execute a sequence of GP runs until 50 successful ones were found. It has been sufficient to execute 52 runs to get 50 successful ones. Figure 3 reports the same information, but this time for 50 *unsuccessful runs*. Collecting 50 unsuccessful runs has been easy, probably for the particular shape of the tree that has been used as optimum, shown in Figure 1(b) (over 61 runs, 50 were successful). These figures show that, in case of success, the FDC decreases until the global optimum is found and than remains negative until the end of the run. In case of unsuccessful runs, the FDC value always stays around zero, independently from the fact that fitness is slightly improving. Our interpretation is that, in this last case the evolutionary process in "leading" the population towards a local optimum, which probably has a rather large crossover distance from the global one. For successful runs the fact that FDC is negative indicates that evolution is "leading" the population towards the global optimum.

Trap Functions
We now define a problem where trees are represented using the same syntax as in [14], i.e. by means of the set of functions $\mathcal{F} = \{B,C\}$ (where B is a binary operator and C has arity $= 3$) and the set of terminal symbols $\mathcal{T} = \{X\}$. The fitness of each tree is a function of its structural distance (as defined in [7]) to a fixed global optimum and it is not defined here for lack of space (see for instance [11] for a formal definition). In this paper, it is sufficient to remember that the fitness definition for trap functions depends on two parameters (called b and r), which can be used to tune the difficulty of the problem (see [11] for a detailed discussion). Figure 4(a) shows the tree chosen as optimum for the experiments in Figure 5 and Figure 4(b) shows the tree chosen as optimum for the experiments in Figure 6. Parameters used in these experiments are as follows: generational GP, population size of 100 individuals, standard subtree crossover used as the sole genetic operator, tournament selection of size 10, ramped

(a)   (b)

Fig. 4. (a) The tree used as optimum for the experiments in Figure 5. (b) The tree used as optimum for the experiments in Figure 6.

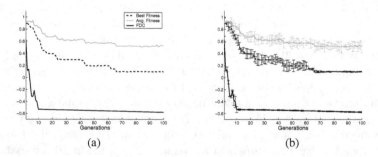

(a)   (b)

Fig. 5. Trap Functions. Average values (a) and average values with their standard deviations (b) of average fitness, best fitness and FDC in the population against generations over 50 independent GP runs. In all these runs the optimum has been found before generation 100. The tree used as optimum in these experiments was the tree in Figure 4(a).

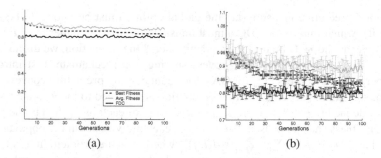

Fig. 6. Trap Functions. Average values (a) and average values with their standard deviations (b) of average fitness, best fitness and FDC in the population against generations over 50 independent GP runs. In all these runs the optimum has *not* been found before generation 100. The tree used as optimum in these experiments was the tree in Figure 4(b).

half-and-half initialisation, maximum depth of individuals for the initialisation phase equal to 6, maximum depth of individuals for crossover equal to 10. Here, we have used larger trees than in the case of the syntactic tree problem discussed in the previous section (arity 3 nodes and deeper trees have been considered). The reason is that we wanted to test our hypotheses in different conditions. Figure 5 reports the average values (with their standard deviations in Figure 5(b)) of the best fitness, the average fitness and the FDC (calculated using SCD) in the population (against generations) over 50 independent successful GP runs. The method used to collect 50 successful runs was the same as the one discussed in the previous section. In these experiments, we have set the b and r trap functions parameters as follows: $b = 0.9$ and $r = 0.1$. In this way, the fitness landscape is easy to search for GP [11] and thus it is easy to have successful runs. Figure 6 reports the same information as Figure 5, but for 50 independent unsuccessful GP runs. In this case, the b parameter was set to 0.1 and the r parameter to 0.9 in order to make the fitness landscape difficult to search for GP [11]. The method used to collect 50 unsuccessful runs was the same as the one discussed in the previous section. In Figure 3(b), the scale on the ordinates axis has been restricted in order to enlarge the graph and to make it clearer and more readable. These figures show that for successful runs the FDC decreases until the global optimum is found and than remains negative until the end of the run, while in case of failure the FDC is always positive. Here the phenomenon is even more marked than in the case of syntactic trees. In fact, for successful runs FDC rapidly stabilises to approximately -0.6, while for unsuccessful runs FDC always remains approximately equal to 0.8. Once again, our conclusion is that the value of FDC in the population (calculated using the SCD) is a good indicator of the "direction" the search process is "leading" the population: negative values of the FDC mean that the search is moving towards a global optimum, while positive values of the FDC mean that the search is moving towards local ones.

3.2 Fitness Sharing

In the previous section, we have shown that SCD can appropriately be used to dynamically calculate the population FDC during the evolution. However, as discussed in [11],

FDC is not a predictive measure (i.e. the global optima must be known to be able to calculate it), which makes the FDC almost unusable in practice. Other than a measure for diversity, can the SCD be useful for practitioners? In this section, we discuss *fitness sharing*, calculated using the SCD. Fitness sharing is a mechanism, first introduced by Goldberg and coworkers [15] for GAs, for counteracting premature convergence of populations. With this scheme, the fitness function is modified to incorporate a sharing function s, defined to determine the degree of sharing of each individual in the population. When fitness sharing is used, the fitness of each individual i in the population P is calculated as $f_s(i) = f(i)/\sum_{j \in P \wedge j \neq i} s(d(i,j))$, where f is the problem fitness function and d is a distance measure between genotypes. In this section, we compare the performance of two different fitness sharing systems using the SCD and the ED as distance d with standard GP systems. For the s function, we have simply used $s(x) = 1 - x$, after normalizing ED values into the set $[0,1]$ (there is no need of normalising SCD values, since they are probabilities, and thus they are already included into $[0,1]$). Experiments have been done on a problem which is the same as the syntactic tree problem described in Section 3.1, except for the fitness of an individual i is equal to the sum of the differences of the number of nodes of i and the ones of a fixed global optimum for each level in the trees. This is the same fitness used in [12]. In this way, the global optimum is not unique, which is a case in which using fitness sharing may be appropriate [15]. GP parameters are the same as the ones used for syntactic trees in Section 3.1. Results are shown in Figure 7, where two experiments, with two different global optima, are considered. These two optima were two different randomly generated trees (whose structure

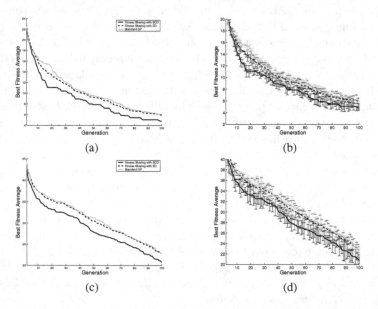

Fig. 7. Average best fitness values against generations (Figures (a) and (c)) and average best fitness values with their standard deviations (Figures (b) and (d)) over 50 independent GP runs using standard GP (gray curves) and fitness sharing (black curves). Figures (a) and (b) differ from Figures (c) and (d) for the particular tree chosen as optimum.

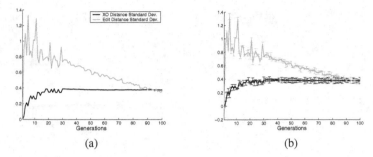

(a)   (b)

Fig. 8. Average values (a) and average values with their standard deviations (b) of population's diversity against generations over 50 independent runs. In all these runs the optimum has been found before generation 100.

is not shown here for lack of space). Curves in Figure 7(a) and 7(c) show the average values of the best fitness in the population against generations over 50 independent GP runs for the two cases where the two different randomly generated trees have been used as optima. Figures 7(b) and 7(d) show standard deviations of the curves in Figures 7(a) and 7(c) respectively. As these figures show, the fitness sharing system using the SCD finds, on average, better quality solutions than standard GP and than fitness sharing systems using the ED for both the cases studied, even though standard deviations bars may slightly overlap in some cases[2]. We hypothesise that the better results achieved by the SCD occur because SCD is bound to the genetic operator used by GP and thus more accurate than ED in directing the evolutionary search process.

3.3 Diversity

In this section, we compare results of population genotypic diversity calculated by the SCD with the ones obtained using the ED. In both cases, diversity has been measured as the standard deviation of the distance of the individuals in the population to a fixed optimal tree. The problem and GP parameters used in this section are the same as the syntax trees problem described in Section 3.1, with the only difference that the tree chosen as optimum has been randomly generated at the beginning of each GP run (and thus it changes from one run to the other). Figure 8 shows average values (with their standard deviations, which are reported in Figure 8(b)) of diversity against generations over 50 independent successful GP runs The method used to collect 50 successful runs was the one presented in section 3.1. Figure 9 reports analogous results for 50 independent runs in which the optimum has *not* been found before generation 100. Also the method used to collect 50 unsuccessful runs was the one presented in section 3.1. First of all, we remark that the behavior of SCD diversity is rather different from the one of ED diversity: ED diversity is, in general, very "unstable", in particular at the beginning of the runs. On the other hand, SCD diversity has much smaller variations during the evolution.

---

[2] In particular, the bars of the fitness sharing system using the ED and the ones of the standard GP system always overlap. On the other hand, the bars of the fitness sharing system using SCD and the ones of the other two systems only slightly overlap in some cases.

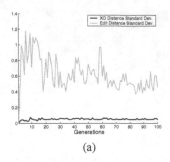 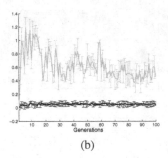

(a)   (b)

Fig. 9. Average values (a) and average values with their standard deviations (b) of population's diversity against generations over 50 independent runs. In all these runs the optimum has been found before generation 100.

Furthermore, while ED diversity curves are always decreasing and tend towards zero, the SCD diversity tends to stabilise on a certain value and to constantly maintain this value until the end of the runs. Finally, we observe that in the unsuccessful runs, SCD diversity tends to stabilise towards zero. This happens because in those cases, after a certain number of generations, all the individuals in the population tend to have a SCD to the optimum equal to zero: it becomes more and more difficult to find trees that can be transformed into the global optimum by simply swapping some of its subtrees with some other in the population. On the other hand, in the successful runs, SCD diversity values remain approximately equal to a value that, although not very large, is always larger than zero. In those cases, producing the optimum by means of crossover from trees in the population is possible.

4   Conclusions

This paper has two main goals: extending the definition of subtree crossover distance (SCD) given in [12] and empirically showing that this new measure is useful to investigate some properties of the GP search process. Results that have been presented show that (1) the SCD is appropriate to study the trend of fitness distance correlation (FDC) of populations during the evolution; (2) the SCD is also appropriate for fitness sharing, producing better results than standard GP and than fitness sharing systems using edit distance (ED); (3) if we use the SCD standard deviation to quantify population diversity, we obtain different results and we capture different properties than if we use ED standard deviation. We hypothesise that the reason for these results is that the SCD appropriately models subtree crossover. Future work includes exploring other definitions of operator-based measures and the tradeoffs involved with reducing their complexity.

References

1. J.R. Koza. *Genetic Programming: On the Programming of Computers by Means of Natural Selection*. MIT Press, Cambridge, MA, USA, 1992.
2. S. Gustafson, A. Ekárt, E.K. Burke, and G. Kendall. Problem difficulty and code growth in genetic programming. *Genetic Programming and Evolvable Hardware*, 5(3):271–290, 2004.

3. S. Gustafson. *An Analysis of Diversity in Genetic Programming*. PhD thesis, School of Computer Science and Information Technology, University of Nottingham, Nottingham, England, February 2004.
4. E.K. Burke, S. Gustafson, and G. Kendall. Diversity in genetic programming: An analysis of measures and correlation with fitness. *IEEE Transactions on Evolutionary Computation*, 8(1):47–62, 2004.
5. N.F. McPhee and N.J. Hopper. Analysis of genetic diversity through population history. In W. Banzhaf et al., editors, *Proceedings of the Genetic and Evolutionary Computation Conference*, pages 1112–1120, FL, USA, 1999. Morgan Kaufmann.
6. M. Tomassini, L. Vanneschi, F. Fernández, and G. Galeano. A study of diversity in multipopulation genetic programming. In *6th International Conference on Evolutionary Computation EA'03*, pages 69–81, 2003.
7. A. Ekárt and S. Z. Németh. Maintaining the diversity of genetic programs. In J. A. Foster *et al.*, editor, *Genetic Programming, Proceedings of the 5th European Conference, EuroGP 2002*, volume 2278 of *LNCS*, pages 162–171. Springer-Verlag, 2002.
8. T. Jones and S. Forrest. Fitness distance correlation as a measure of problem difficulty for genetic algorithms. In L. Eshelman, editor, *Proceedings of the Sixth International Conference on Genetic Algorithms*, pages 184–192, San Francisco, CA, 1995. Morgan Kaufmann.
9. M. Tomassini, L. Vanneschi, P. Collard, and M. Clergue. A study of fitness distance correlation as a difficulty measure in genetic programming. *Evolutionary Computation*, 13(2):213–239, 2005.
10. L. Vanneschi, M. Tomassini, P. Collard, and M. Clergue. Fitness distance correlation in structural mutation genetic programming. In C. Ryan et al., editors, *Genetic Programming, Proceedings of the European Conference*, volume 2610 of *LNCS*, pages 459–468, Essex, 14-16 April 2003. Springer-Verlag.
11. L. Vanneschi. *Theory and Practice for Efficient Genetic Programming*. Ph.D. thesis, University of Lausanne, Switzerland, 2004.
12. S. Gustafson and L. Vanneschi. Operator-based distance for genetic programming: Subtree crossover distance. In Keijzer, M., *et al.*, editor, *Genetic Programming, 8th European Conference, EuroGP2005*, Lecture Notes in Computer Science, LNCS 3447, pages 178–189. Springer, Berlin, Heidelberg, New York, 2005.
13. R. Poli and N.F. McPhee. General schema theory for genetic programming with subtree-swapping crossover: Part i. *Evolutionary Computation*, 11(1):53–66, 2003.
14. B. Punch, D. Zongker, and E. Goodman. The royal tree problem, a benchmark for single and multiple population genetic programming. In P. Angeline and K. Kinnear, editors, *Advances in Genetic Programming 2*, pages 299–316, Cambridge, MA, 1996. The MIT Press.
15. D. E. Goldberg. *Genetic Algorithms in Search, Optimization and Machine Learning*. Addison-Wesley, 1989.

Characterizing Diversity in Genetic Programming

Bart Wyns, Peter De Bruyne, and Luc Boullart

Department of Electrical Energy,
System and Automation Ghent University,
Technologiepark 913, 9052 Zwijnaarde, Belgium
Bart.Wyns@UGent.be

Abstract. In many evolutionary algorithms candidate solutions run the
risk of getting stuck in local optima after a few generations of optimization. In this paper two improved approaches to measure population diversity are proposed and validated using two traditional test problems
in genetic programming literature. Code growth gave rise to improve
pseudo-isomorph measures by eliminating non-functional code using an
expression simplifier. Also, Rosca's entropy to measure behavioral diversity is updated to cope with problems producing a more continuous
fitness value. Results show a relevant improvement with regard to the
original diversity measures.

1 Introduction

In many evolutionary algorithms candidate solutions run the risk of getting stuck
in local optima after a few generations of optimization. As evolution progresses,
more and more individuals grow towards those high-scoring (deceptive) solutions,
eliminating possibly useful genetic material. The population isn't able to escape
from the local optima and hence converges. This paper elaborates on the issue of
measuring diversity in the context of tree-based genetic programming (GP).

In GP there are two major types of diversity. We can either look for structural diversity (differences in the tree structure) or diversity based on behavior
(fitness). The simplest way to obtain the former measure in a standard genetic
programming population, is by counting the number of structurally unique individuals, programs or trees (variety). The GP tree structure could also be checked
for graph isomorphism. However, verifying if both trees are isomorph is very
time consuming and the computational effort needed increases dramatically as
the trees grow bigger (due to the properties of some tree nodes: associativity,
etc.). Rather than trying to find out if two trees are identical twins or isomorphs,
determine if there is a *possibility* that they are isomorph. This is done by calculating a set of simple characteristics such as tree depth, the number of terminals
and the number of functions. If these properties match, both individuals are
called *pseudo*-isomorph. Burke et al. [1] mention that pseudo-isomorphs are as
informative as the number of structurally unique individuals (variety). This is
an extra reason to choose for the latter, more simpler measure.

P. Collet et al. (Eds.): EuroGP 2006, LNCS 3905, pp. 250–259, 2006.

Besides basing diversity measures solely on the parse tree itself or some derived characteristics of this tree, it is also useful to have some measures based on its behavior. The easiest way of measuring such diversity, is by counting the number of distinct fitness values. This measure gives an idea of how scattered the individuals are inside the solution space. Also, the distribution of the fitness values (depicted in histograms) can return useful information [2]. In [3] the entropy, denoting the amount of disorder in the population, was introduced. First fitness values are divided into several partitions. Then entropy is calculated as $-\sum_k p_k \cdot \log p_k$ with p_k the proportion of the population occupied by partition k. Rosca observed that plateaus or monotonic decreases in entropy over an increased number of generations were associated to plateaus in best fitness plots. Moreover, entropy decreases indicated loss of population diversity. More advanced structural and behavioral diversity measures exist. A detailed explanation is beyond the scope of this paper but an excellent overview and comparison are given in [4].

An important problem with GP genomes is that, while evolution proceeds, programs contain more and more non-functional code (called code growth [5]). Many diversity measures don't take non-functional code into account when calculating structural diversity of the population. Also, in many real-life problems there exists an almost infinite amount of possible fitness values (see quartic regression, section 2). When putting each fitness value in a different partition (= standard definition of entropy), the entropy remains high while often (some) behavioral convergence is seen. To overcome both difficulties two improved diversity measures are presented in this paper. A *structural* method based on the functional size of an individual 's parse tree and a *behavioral* method that is an extension of Rosca's entropy [3]. The rest of the paper is organized as follows. In the following section the two test cases used in this study and the GP software are briefly explained. A detailed explanation of both improved diversity measures is given in section 3 while results are presented in section 4. Finally section 5 summarizes the experimental findings and draws some conclusions.

2 Problem Set-Up

This section will describe two test cases that were used to test and validate the effect of both enhanced diversity measures. Also, a description of the GP system used in this study is given here.

2.1 Quartic Regression

The regression problem is to evolve a function $g(x)$ that matches sample points taken from a function $f(x)$. The target function chosen is $f(x) = x^4 + x^3 + x^2 + x$; x ranging from -1 to +1. Candidate solutions are tested against 20 uniformly distributed points ranging over the same interval. Fitness F_{reg} is defined as follows:

$$F_{reg} = \frac{1}{1 + \sum_{i=1}^{n} |A_i - P_i|}$$

with P_i the predicted value, A_i the actual (real) output and n the number of fitness cases (=20). The function set has 5 members which are: $\times, \div$ (returns 1 when dividing by 0), $-, +, \log(|number|)$ ($\log 0 = 1$). The terminal set has two members: the input value x, and a random constant in the range $[-1, 1]$ whose value, once generated, is fixed during the rest of the evolutionary run.

2.2 The Artificial Ant

The artificial ant can be viewed as a miniature robot that has to follow a trail of food pellets distributed over some grid. Here the Santa-Fe trail is chosen with 89 food pellets spread over a grid of 32 by 32 positions [6]. The robot generates a path by walking through this map. It is allowed to run for 500 time-steps after which fitness is measured by the number of food pellets "run over" or consumed. Each terminal costs one time-step to evaluate; each function on the other hand takes no time. The function set has three members. The first is IF-FOOD-AHEAD, which has two arguments — one to be performed if there is food in front of the ant, the other otherwise. The remaining two functions are PROGN2 and PROGN3, each taking 2 and 3 arguments respectively. Each of these functions simply executes its children from left to right. The terminal set has three members: MOVE, which moves the ant one step forward. LEFT, which turns the ant left, and RIGHT, turning the ant right. Fitness is given by the number of food pellets eaten divided by the total amount of food on the trail.

2.3 GP Engine

The same standard GP system was used for both test problems. The GP is generational and is run for 50 generations. The ramped half-and-half technique is used to generate the initial population containing 500 individuals. The initially generated programs are evenly distributed (ramped) between depths of 2 and 4. As in [1] only crossover is used (no mutation). No additional depth/node limit is placed on the programs. The GP system continues running even when an optimal solution (100% correct) has been discovered. All results are averaged over 100 independent runs (each time with a different random seed). The GP software is a modified version of the Lil-gp package developed by Punch and Zongker [7].

3   Enhanced Diversity Measures

As mentioned in the introduction, pseudo-isomorphs are fast to calculate because they require a set of simple tree characteristics. Entropy on the other hand appears to be a promising alternative combining the expressive power of fitness histograms and unique fitness values. In this section, both measures are enhanced to give a more accurate view on population diversity.

3.1   Structural Measures: The Code Growth Issue

An important problem with variable length tree structures is that they tend to grow without a corresponding increase in fitness. While evolution proceeds, programs contain more and more non-functional code [5]. In that way they occupy a lot of memory, reduce speed and make the programs harder to read by humans.

Many diversity measures don't take non-functional code into account when calculating structural diversity of the population. In this paper an enhanced approach is proposed eliminating non-functional code when calculating structural diversity. The algorithm comprises two important steps: (A) simplification of the program tree and (B) calculating pseudo-isomorphism based on the simplified tree. To help implementing the first step, an expression simplifier is used to get rid off all redundant (non-functional) code, keeping only the functional part. The simplifier uses a set of reduction rules, tailored to the problem at hand. Some examples:

- for the regression problem:
  - if one of the operands of a multiplication, addition or substraction is a constant valued zero (or one), the tree is replaced by the result. Example: $X \times 0 = 0$, $X \times 1 = X$, $X + 0 = X$ and $X - 0 = X$ and vice versa.
  - if both operands of $+, -, \times, \div$ are constants, the tree is replaced by the result. The same applies to log.
  - if both operands of a substraction (division) are equal, the result will be zero (one) and the subtree is replaced with a constant. Some special properties (associativity, commutativity, etc.) are not taken into account due to computational complexity.
- for the artificial ant:
  - if the first child (or the second) of the function IF-FOOD-AHEAD is also an IF-FOOD-AHEAD node then only the first subtree (or second) will be executed and hence, the tree can be reduced.
  - The successive execution of LEFT and RIGHT with no other functions/terminals executed in between has no relevant effect. Therefore, redundant pairs like (LEFT, RIGHT) and (RIGHT, LEFT) statements are removed from the parse tree.

Depending on the problem (see section 4) there are many more terminals and functions in traditional trees while there are less in simplified ones. After pruning the tree structure, the 3-tuple <program depth, terminal nodes, function nodes> is calculated (which we will call functional pseudo-isomorphs). If the number of terminals, functions and the depth are smaller in pruned trees then there are fewer combinations, which lead to distinct 3-tuples. Therefore, it is expected that the number of functional pseudo-isomorphs is smaller than the number of pseudo-isomorphs.

3.2   Phenotypical Measures: The Entropy

In many real-life problems there exists an almost infinite amount of possible fitness values. The regression problem as described in the previous section is a good example of this. Here, fitness values are floating point numbers, scaled between 0.0 and 1.0. Inherently, two individuals with exactly the same fitness value hardly ever occur and so, the entropy will generally remain high because fitness values that are very close to each other, are put in different partitions. For example: if the population contains 500 individuals and all fitness values are different then the entropy will be $-\sum_{k=1..500} p_k \cdot \log p_k = -500 \times \frac{1}{500} \times \log(\frac{1}{500}) \approx 2.70$.

Specifically for the symbolic regression problem, the calculation of Rosca's entropy is changed. Instead of assigning a unique partition to each fitness value (as is usually done), the range of possible fitness values is divided in a number of equally sized intervals. Different settings have been tried: #intervals= 10, 20, 40, 60, 100 and 200. In the artificial ant problem, the maximum number of different fitness values is given by 90 since there are only 89 food pellets and fitness is zero if no food is collected. Therefore in that problem there is no explicit need to use a different entropy measure and the original definition [3] applies.

4   Results and Discussion

Figure 1b shows mean and best fitness for both test cases. As can be noticed, fitness rapidly increases during the first few generations. The population is evolving from an initially random (bad fitness) situation to a more optimized form. After a few generations, however, *best* fitness improvement slows down and hardly changes. From this point onwards, it seems that further optimizing (i.e. evolving) the population has almost no effect on *best* fitness and is a waste of computational effort[1]. This critical point was around generation 15 for the quartic regression problem and slightly sooner for the artificial ant (generation 11). In this section we investigate if the usage of both original and enhanced diversity measures, could provide more information on why this slowdown occurs.

4.1   Functional Pseudo-isomorphs

Figure 2 shows results of original and functional pseudo-isomorphic diversity measures on the symbolic regression and artificial ant problem. On both graphs (left and right) it is shown that the number of unique pseudo-isomorphic 3-tuples is small in the beginning of the evolutionary run. Because the initial population is generated using small depths (depth ramp between two and four), individuals will have a limited program size (=small number of terminals and functions) and inherently fewer pseudo-isomorphic combinations, which lead to distinct 3-tuples, exist. However, from the initial population onwards — due to the unrestricted search space — individuals will start to grow (compare with Fig. 1a). Although pseudo-isomorphs are based on more general characteristics of program trees instead of exact resemblance, this will lead to an increased number of distinct pseudo-isomorphic 3-tuples (original definition of pseudo-isomorphs). In both test cases, the number of unique pseudo-isomorphic 3-tuples increases until the maximum (= population size) is reached, indicating that continuously structurally new individuals are created. In what follows, it is shown that *functional* pseudo-isomorphs will give a more accurate description of the population's state.

---

[1] Please note that *mean* fitness in the regression problem is still improving, even at generation 50.

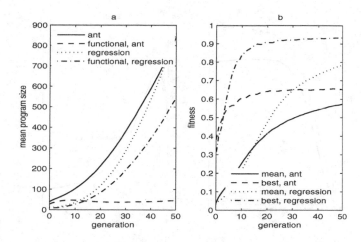

Fig. 1. On the left: mean (functional) program size for both test cases. On the right: mean and best fitness for the artificial ant and the regression problem.

Figure 1, the artificial ant problem, shows a large gap between original and functional program size. The obtained reduction is huge, indicating that the ant problem is very vulnerable to introns. When eliminating large portions of non-functional code (using the expression simplifier), it is expected that a lot of individuals —although possibly structurally different— will fall in the same class of functional pseudo-isomorphs thereby reducing the number of distinct 3-tuples. This effect will be more obvious when the overhead becomes bigger. This is confirmed in Fig. 2 (right). At first the number of distinct functional pseudo-isomorphic 3-tuples increases rapidly, reaching a maximum at generation four, and decreases from that point onward. Crossover will produce tree structures resembling the fitter-than-average ones. There are various ways to create such program trees. For example, nested IF-FOOD-AHEAD statements are an ideal hangout for code which can be easily removed by the expression simplifier (see section 3). This will result in fewer unique functional pseudo-isomorphs (decreased diversity), a slowdown in best fitness and an increase in mean fitness (as can be seen in fig. 1b). With regard to the ant problem, functional pseudo-isomorphs indicate structural convergence towards a (sub)optimal solution.

It is remarkable that when comparing these findings with the original pseudo-isomorphs, the latter continues to (slowly) increase. According to this result, structurally different solutions continue to be generated by crossover while from previous discussion it is clear that the opposite is true.

The regression problem shows a different situation (Fig. 2, left). Both the original and functional pseudo-isomorphic measures rise quickly in the beginning and slow down around generation 20. From that point onwards, the original pseudo-isomorphs continue to increase (but very slowly) while the functional pseudo-isomorphs slowly decrease. The gap in absolute value between both curves is probably due to the difference between program size and functional

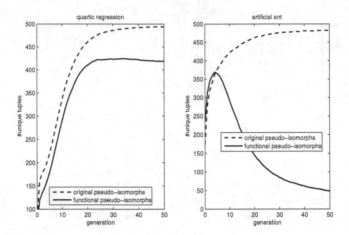

Fig. 2. Traditional and enhanced pseudo-isomorphs applied to the quartic regression problem (left) and the artificial ant (right)

program size as shown in Figure 1. This difference in program size is much smaller compared to the artificial ant problem. In contrast with the ant problem, there is no steep descent after generation 20. Using commutativity, associativity and by the nature of the problem definition there exist many (structurally) different trees approximating the target function. In combination with the inclusion of various extraneous functions (only $x, +$ and $\times$ are necessary to build the target function) the already unrestricted search space is further enlarged. We assume that the large offer of fit but structurally different solutions provides an explanation of why populations in the quartic regression problem don't (or very slowly) seem to converge structurally. This is also confirmed in [8] where the authors state that relatively easy problems have a lot of structurally different solutions resulting in high structural diversity.

4.2   Standard and Enhanced Entropy

In problems with a discrete and limited set of possible fitness values such as the ant problem, program fitness in the initial population is expected to be low (situated around 0) with few unique fitness values. After a few rounds of optimization and combining better than average subtrees, fitness values are spread over a larger range of possible values (so probability of having more unique values increases). Near the end of an evolutionary run —when optimal solutions arise more often— individuals tend to gather around these optima, again leading to a decrease in unique fitness values. This is seen in Fig. 3 (left): an increase during the first few generations followed by a decrease. Entropy produces similar results because it is strongly related to the number of unique fitness values (= number of partitions). Besides it gives an idea of how fitness is distributed. Entropy reaches its maximum a few generations before the number of unique fitness values does. When entropy decreases (suppose the number of

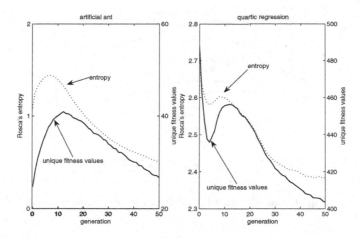

Fig. 3. Rosca's entropy (dashed line) and the number of unique fitness values (solid line) for the artificial ant problem (left) and the quartic regression (right)

partitions is fixed), fitness values are less uniformly spread over the different intervals.

Problems, having a more continuous output generally show the same behavior (although during the first few generations there is a decrease immediately followed by a sharp increase), but the number of unique fitness values is usually much larger (Fig. 3 right). Also, changes in entropy are more subtle compared to the artificial ant problem (smaller scale). Since fitness is a floating point number between 0 and 1, an almost infinite amount of possible fitness values exists (initially almost 500 different fitness values exist, a count equal to the population size) and as a consequence the standard entropy will remain high. Especially the inclusion of an constant in the terminal set adds to an increased number of phenotypically different solutions. After all, constants are floating point numbers between -1 and 1 (continuous), and the smallest difference between two constants could generate a different fitness value.

To overcome these problems (initial fluctuation and subtle changes) fitness was split up into a number of equally-sized partitions. Example: when using 10 intervals, fitness was divided into 10 groups with fitness values ranging from 0 to 0.1, from 0.1 to 0.2 and so on. Figure 4 shows results of the entropy using intervals. In general, the lower the number of intervals, the lower the entropy since it resembles the amount of disorder in the population. Less intervals (categories) means more order and less chaos. By transforming the continuous fitness space into a discrete one, similarly shaped curves as in the artificial ant problem are generated. Initially the number of non-empty intervals will be very low since the individuals' fitness is very low. Looking at Fig. 1b (mean fitness regression) we don't expect to find a lot of fitness values above 0.3 (and if so, center of distribution will be situated around low fitness). Inherently also the entropy will be very low (in an extreme case the entropy is zero when all fitness values settle in the

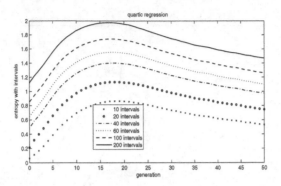

Fig. 4. Entropy with intervals in the regression problem

same interval, for example when using 10 intervals). After the initial generation the fitness values are dispersed over a larger number of intervals. This trend continues until the maximum entropy is reached. From then on, the population will optimize towards higher fitness values and the entropy starts to decrease again (opposite effect). To conclude, in the regression problem behavioral convergence is seen (although slower compared to the ant).

5   Conclusion

Premature convergence together with the loss of diversity is a problem with many evolutionary optimization methods. Candidate solutions get stuck in local optima and often no further improvement in fitness is noticed. In this paper two new approaches to accurately measure diversity are proposed. Code growth gave rise to improve pseudo-isomorph measures by eliminating non-functional code using an expression simplifier. Results show that this newly founded measure more accurately indicates the amount of genotypical diversity in the artificial ant problem. Also the standard entropy to measure phenotypic diversity is updated to cope with problems producing a more continuous fitness value such as the regression problem. Fitness is first clustered into a limited number of intervals. Afterwards the entropy is calculated. Results show a relevant improvement with regard to the original entropy.

Recently, the authors developed a local optimization operator based on subtree fitness to control code growth in genetic programming [9]. As with many multi-objective methods [10], the GP search suffers from premature convergence when using this growth reducing operator. The authors assume that this is due to a fixed setting of the probability with which the operator is applied. Using both diversity measures explained in this paper the authors first hope to confirm this hypothesis. Second, the authors wish to use these diversity measures in an adaptive controller scheme, making the probability setting dependent on the amount of growth and the diversity in the population (as in [11]).

References

1. Burke, E., Gustafson, S., Kendall, G.: A survey and analysis of diversity measures in genetic programming. In et al., W.L., ed.: Proceedings of the Genetic and Evolutionary Computation Conference, Morgan Kaufmann (2002) 716–723
2. Rosca, J.P.:   Genetic programming exploratory power and the discovery of functions. In McDonnell, J.R., Reynolds, R.G., Fogel, D.B., eds.: Evolutionary Programming IV Proceedings of the Fourth Annual Conference on Evolutionary Programming. (1995) 719–736
3. Rosca, J.P.: Entropy-driven adaptive representation. In Rosca, J., ed.: Proceedings of the Workshop on Genetic Programming: From Theory to Real-World Applications, Tahoe City, California (1995) 23–32
4. E. Burke, S.G., Kendall, G.: Diversity in genetic programming: An analysis of measures and correlation with fitness. IEEE Transactions on Evolutionary Computation 8 (2004) 47–62
5. Soule, T., Foster, J.: Effects of code growth and parsimony pressure on populations in genetic programming. Evolutionary Computation 6 (1998) 293–309
6. Koza, J.R.: Genetic Programming: On the Programming of Computers by Means of Natural Selection. MIT Press, Cambridge, MA (1992)
7. Punch, B., Zongker, D.: Lilgp 1.01 user's manual. Technical report, Michigan State University, Michigan, USA (1996)
8. Gustafson, S., Ekárt, A., Burke, E.: Problem difficulty and code growth in genetic programming. Genetic programming and Evolvable Machines 5 (2004) 271–290
9. Wyns, B., Sette, S., Boullart, L.: Self-improvement to control code growth in genetic programming. In Liardet, P., Collet, P., Fonlupt, C., Lutton, E., Schoenauer, M., eds.: Artificial Evolution, Proceedings of the 6th International Conference, selected papers. Volume 2936 of Lecture Notes in Computer Science., Springer-Verlag (2004) 256–266
10. Ekárt, A., Németh, S.: Selection based on the pareto nondominance criterion for controlling code growth in genetic programming. Genetic Programming and Evolvable Machines 2 (2001) 61–73
11. de Jong, E., Pollack, J.: Multi-objective methods for tree size control. Genetic Programming and Evolvable Machines 4 (2003) 211–233

Complexity and Cartesian Genetic Programming

John R. Woodward

The University of Birmingham, Birmingham B15 2TT, UK
http://www.cs.bham.ac.uk/~jrw/

Abstract. Genetic Programming (GP) [1] often uses a tree form of a
graph to represent solutions. An extension to this representation, Automatically Defined Functions (ADFs) [1] is to allow the ability to express
modules. In [2] we proved that the complexity of a function is independent of the primitive set (function set and terminal set) if the representation has the ability to express modules. This is essentially due to the
fact that if a representation can express modules, then it can effectively
define its own primitives at a constant cost.

Cartesian Genetic Programming (CGP) [3] is a relative new type of
representation used in Evolutionary Computation (EC), and differs from
the tree based representation in that outputs from previous computations
can be reused. This is achieved by representing programs as directed
acyclic graphs (DAGs), rather than as trees. Thus computations from
subtrees can be reused to reduce the complexity of a function. We prove
an analogous result to that in [2]; the complexity of a function using a
(Cartesian Program) CP representation is independent of the terminal
set (up to an additive constant), provided the different terminal sets can
both be simulated. This is essentially due to the fact that if a representation can express Automatic Reused Outputs [3], then it can effectively
define its own terminals at a constant cost.

1 Introduction

GP is a test-and-generate paradigm where a representation is chosen to express
programs, and programs are generated and tested against a set of test cases.
A broad variety of representations have been used in GP, e.g. lists, trees and
graphs. Research in EC involves choices about the fitness function, representation and genetic operators, however in this paper we are only concerned with
representation. Typically, GP is supplied with a function set and a terminal set
and new functions are created by stringing together these primitives so the output of one is fed into another. The choice of representation determines how new
functions can be created from the primitive set. In standard tree style GP, each
time a new 'sub-function' is needed it must be represented again as a new subtree. ADFs, on the other hand, can arbitrarily define new functions which can
be reused as and when needed. CGP, which we now introduce, lies somewhere
between these two types of representation in terms of the type of reuse allowed.

In CGP, a Cartesian Program (CP) representation is evolved. In a CP a set
of function nodes are placed on a 2D grid arranged in rows and columns (see
figure 1). The inputs to the CP are fed in from the left and the outputs are

P. Collet et al. (Eds.): EuroGP 2006, LNCS 3905, pp. 260–269, 2006.

taken from the right. There can be one output or many. Information flows from left to right through the representation. Each function node can take its input from the output of any of the function nodes to the left of it. The functions at each location in the grid and the connectivity of the function nodes (i.e. which function node is connected to which other function node) are evolved. It maybe that some function nodes are not connected at some point during the evolution. For example, the function nodes in the final column could be directly connected to the inputs and so no intermediate computation takes place. While the overall structure has fixed size (effectively the number of rows times the number of columns, as there is a function node at each point in the grid), the 'actual' size may be much smaller as some function nodes are not connected. For example, in figure 1, the middle node in the first column is not connected (i.e. its output, labelled 5, is not used).

There are a number of important points which can be made about this representation. Firstly, large parts of the representation may not be connected to the rest of the program, and so a single mutation may connect in large 'subprograms' allowing 'large jumps' in the search space. Secondly, as information flows from left to right through this representation, the output of a computation (i.e the output value at some point in the 2D grid) can be used multiple times by any function nodes appearing to the right of it. This is in contrast to tree based GP where no reuse occurs. It is this second point which concerns us in this paper.

CGP has been applied to a variety of problems including function regression and boolean problems. A CP typically has more than one output. Mathematically a function has only a single output (i.e. an element in one set maps to an element in a second set). However, we can think of a CP representing a number of functions (which may share parts of the same representation). For example, the CP may be used to control a robot with two wheels, the two outputs controlling each of the wheels. This is similar to artificial neural networks, where there are typically multiple outputs.

In the remainder of this paper, we look at related work using DAGs as a representation in section 2. In section 3 we introduce CP, and in section 4 we examine reuse in different types of representation. Before proving the main results of this paper in section 6 we provide some preliminary definitions in section 5. We end with a section summarising and concluding.

2   Related Work

Handley [4] uses a DAG to store a population of trees, rather than a forest of trees (i.e. a set of trees). This has a two benefits. Firstly, identical subtrees (down to the leaves) only need to be represented once. Miller [3] does this within an individual, but Handley [4] does this across the whole population. While there may not be identical subtrees within an individual program, there may be identical subtrees in individuals in the population. Secondly, time is saved by caching the value for each subtree for each fitness case. This information is copied to the next generation so values only need to be computed once. Handley's method achieves good improvements in the amount of space needed and the run time of a GP algorithm.

Keijzer [5] continues Handley's [4] work using minimal DAGs to store a population. Roberts [6] also applies this method of representing a population as a DAG to a medical imaging problem. He identifies a trade off between the time to find a subtree in the cache and the time to evaluate the subtree. The method is developed by introducing ways to add and remove subtrees from the cache. One interesting point common to both of these works is that as time increases (i.e. the number of evaluations), the accumulated number of evaluations increases *linearly*, whereas uncached versions climb much more steeply.

CGP represents programs as DAGs, rather than as trees. As a CP has a number of outputs, a CP could be considered as representing a population of programs. The same idea of representing duplicate subtrees once by referring to an index of a subtree is the same in CP as it is with storing a population as a DAG.

3   Cartesian Genetic Programming

In CGP the genotype is a string. User defined parameters set the number of rows and columns. In this example (see figure 1), we have 3 rows and 3 columns. Each node is described by 3 integers, the first two are the inputs and the third is which function from the function set is to be placed at the location. The first 3x3 integers thus describe the function nodes found in the first column of the CP. For example, the function set $\{+, -, *, /\}$ is represented by the integers $\{1, 2, 3, 4\}$ respectively. Each of these functions has arity 2, i.e. takes two inputs. The inputs to the whole program are labelled 1, 2 and 3 which are listed on the left. An example of a genotype is the following integer string; (We have put commas in to make the list more readable, but do not appear in the genotype). The interpretation of this string is shown in figure 1.

$$2\ 1\ 3,\ 3\ 2\ 1,\ 2\ 3\ 2,\ 6\ 6\ 3,\ 4\ 2\ 4,\ 2\ 6\ 3,\ 2\ 2\ 2,\ 7\ 8\ 1,\ 7\ 9\ 3$$

The outputs of each function node are labelled incrementally, starting with the top right node with output labelled 4 (as we have program inputs 1, 2, 3) and the final node, bottom right has output labelled 12. The integer string is interpreted in groups of 3 integers. Consider the first set of 3 integers from the genotype, namely 2 1 3. The first two numbers describe the input to the function, in this case inputs 2 and 1. The next number, 3, is the function this node performs, in this case multiplication ($*$). There are 3 outputs from this program. Some nodes are not connected e.g. the middle node in the first column (function node with output 5). There is reuse, the output from the bottom node in the first column (labelled output 6) is used 3 times by function nodes in the middle column. Note that in the proof and in figure 3, we represent a CP as a tree with overlapping subtrees (i.e. we are only concerned with the connected nodes). The number of leaves in a CP never needs to exceed the number of terminals as function nodes in the program can refer directly to the terminals.

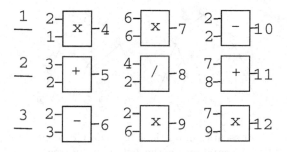

Fig. 1. Visual representation of a CP

4 Reuse in Different Types of Representations

Some representations allow reuse of component parts, other representations do not. In this section we contrast three different types of representation used in the evolution of programs. Each have increasing flexibility in the type of reuse which is allowed. In the first type of representation, tree based, no reuse is supported at all. In the second type, CP, reuse of previously expressed subtrees (down to the leaves) is permitted. In the third type of representation, ADFs, arbitrary subtrees may be reused. The ability of reuse has effects on the complexity of a function expressed with each representation.

To describe these representations the following terminology is used. The node at the top is called the root node. A tree has a single root node. A CP may have more than one root node as it may have more than one output. The nodes at the bottom are called leaf nodes. The remaining nodes in the 'body' of the tree are called non-terminal nodes. The root node is a special case of a non-terminal node. The leaf nodes correspond to terminals from the terminal set and the non-terminals correspond to functions from the function set.

In a tree there is no reuse (see figure 2). Each node in a tree is executed once or not at all. There are two ways a tree representation may be executed, top down or bottom up. In the bottom up case, each of the leaf nodes would

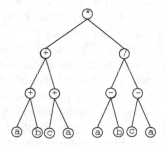

Fig. 2. A function represented as a tree. Each node may be executed once during a single computation and no reuse is permitted.

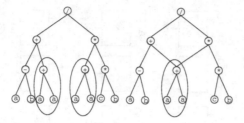

Fig. 3. A tree based representation on the left and a CP of the same function on the right. In tree based representation on the left, two subtrees down to the roots are identical (both are circled by ellipses). On the right, in a CP representation identical subtrees can be represented once (shown by a single subtree circled by an ellipse).

be assigned a value and these are passed up the tree to the nodes above which makes their calculation and pass the output value up to non-terminal nodes above. Eventually a value emerges from the root node. Each node is executed exactly once. In the top down case, we start at the top and evaluate downwards. The important difference between top down and bottom up evaluation can be illustrated with the following example. If a node represents the logical function AND, and the left hand subtree evaluates to $false$, time can be saved by not evaluating the right hand branch as we can already determine the value of this computation ($false$). Similarly if a node represents an IF-THEN-ELSE function, once the condition part of the subtree is evaluated, we do not need to evaluate both the THEN and ELSE subtrees as only one of the computations is required depending on the condition of the IF subtree. In the top down case each node may be evaluated once or not at all, whereas in the bottom up case each node is evaluated exactly once. If we were to trace out the path from a leaf node to the root node, there would only be one path.

Given a function expressed as a tree using a given primitive set, what happens to the complexity of the function when we express it as a tree in terms of a different primitive set. The depth is bounded by a multiplicative constant and the number of nodes may potentially increase exponentially.

In order to illustrate the similarities and distinctions of CP with tree based data structures and ADFs, we represent them in a similar fashion. Instead of information entering from left and leaving on the right (as in figure 1) we rotate the diagram so information flows from bottom to top. We also remove the grid and only show the connected nodes. Thus we drop the left-to-right grid based representation of figure 1 and represent CPs as trees with overlapping subtrees (where the overlap is all the way down to the terminals) (as in figure 3).

As data enters at the leaf nodes, it is processed and passed further up the tree. Any node further up the tree may make use of any output further down the tree. In [3] this is referred to as 'Automatic Re-used Outputs' (AROs), where the point is made, "A potential disadvantage is that AROs are not as general as ADFs as they can only re-use an output *with the same inputs*." Indeed, it is at the heart of the proof that ADFs *with the same inputs* (i.e. terminals) is the reason why complexity is invariant with respect to the terminal set.

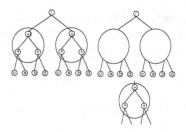

Fig. 4. A tree based representation on the left and a program with an ADF on the right. Two identical subtrees on the right, are represented once on the left but referred to twice. The module contains 3 nodes and takes 4 arguments.

If we were to trace out the path between a leaf node and an output node, we would find that there could be multiple paths between an input and an output node (see figure 3). If two paths overlap, they must overlap all the way down to the leaf node. CPs can be evaluated from the bottom up or top down.

With ADFs, arbitrary subtrees can be defined as modules and an ADF can take different arguments as inputs. This is in contrast to CPs, where subtrees can be reused, but must be subtrees down to the leaf nodes. On the left of figure 4 is a tree, with two subtrees which are identical, indicated by the ellipses. In a representation capable of expressing modules, arbitrary repeated structures can be defined once, and called when needed with the appropriate arguments. On the right, the same function is represented, but the identical structures in the previous tree based representation are represented once (in the ellipse), and is referred to twice in the main tree.

The main difference between CP and ADFs is that 'modules' defined in CP do not take any arguments (and are therefore modules with zero arity i.e. terminals). ADFs are modules which may have non-zero arity, and are therefore modules that can be called with *different* arguments each time.

If we trace a path down from the root node in an ADF representation, two paths may overlap. If the do overlap, there is no guarantee that they will terminate at the same leaf node (essentially as ADFs can be called with different arguments). This is in contrast to CP, where if paths do overlap, they are guaranteed to end at the same leaf node.

In summary, ADFs are the vehicle for reuse. Arbitrary functions can be defined (using the operation of composition and a predefined set of primitives), and can be used as if they are new primitives, i.e. called when needed with different arguments each time. With CGP, a new set of terminals can effectively be defined and this set can be called when needed. A terminal is effectively a function with no input (i.e. arity zero). Trees, on the other hand, have no mechanism for reused.

5   Preliminary Definitions

In this section we give a number of definitions which are similar in nature to those in [2]. These definitions are needed for the proof in the following section.

Definition 1 (terminal set, function set, primitive set). *The terminal set t is the set of inputs to the program. These are typically problem variables and/or constants. The function set f is the basic functions GP uses to construct more complex functions. The primitive set p is the union of the function set f and the terminal set f, i.e* $p = t \cup f$. *These definitions are taken from [1] (section 5.1).*

Definition 2 (size). *The size of the instance of a CP representation is the number of nodes it contains.*

Note that under this definition, if nodes are not connected in to the overall representation then they still contribute to the size. Alternatively we could have defined size to be the number of connected nodes, but this makes no difference when we consider complexity which is defined in terms of the minimum size.

Definition 3 (equally expressive). *Two primitive sets are equally expressive if they can express the same set of functions in finite size.*

For example, the sets $\{NAND\}$ and $\{NOT, AND, OR\}$ are logically complete (i.e. can express all logical functions) and are therefore equally expressive. The programming languages Java and C are both Turing Equivalent and are therefore equally expressive. While this definition tells us if two primitive sets are equally expressive or not, we need to know how to construct a function in a new primitive set given the function expressed in an old primitive set. This is done using a special CP we call a dictionary.

Definition 4 (dictionary). *A dictionary, $D_{t1,t2}$, is the CP which takes the inputs t1 and has outputs t2, where t1 and t2 are terminal sets. The function nodes are from the primitive set f. The size of the dictionary must be finite.*

Each member of the set $t1$ can be expressed in terms of $p2 = t2 \cup f$. In this paper we are not concerned with switching function sets, only terminal sets. The existence of the pair of dictionaries $D_{t1,t2}$ and $D_{t2,t1}$ is a necessary and sufficient condition to imply that $p1$ $(= t1 \cup f)$ and $p2$ $(= t2 \cup f)$ are equally expressive.

Definition 5 (complexity). *The complexity, C, of a function (or set of functions) f under the CP representation, with respect to a fixed primitive set p, is the size of the smallest CP which can represent the function (or set of functions), denoted by $C_p(f)$.*

Definition 6 (complexity of a dictionary). *The complexity of a dictionary $D_{t1,t2}$ is the size of the smallest dictionary which expresses the set of terminals t_2 in terms of a CP using primitive set p1 $(= t1 \cup f)$. We write $K_{t1,t2}$ for the complexity of dictionary $D_{t1,t2}$.*

Strictly, this definition is not necessary as it is implied by the previous two definitions of dictionary and complexity. However, we make this definition explicit as it is made use of in the proofs.

Definition 7 (translate terminal set). *Given a function expressed in terms of one primitive set, p1 (= t1 ∪ f), we can express the same function in terms of a second primitive set, p2 (= t2 ∪ f). As the function sets are the same we need only consider the terminal sets. The process of re-expressing the function in terms of p2 is called translation of terminal set from p1 to p2.*

6   Complexity

We present 3 theorems regarding the complexity of a function when expressed using a CP representation. We prove that the complexity of a function is invariant under translation of terminal set, if the two primitive sets are equally expressive. We then go onto prove the tightest upper and lower bounds on the complexity of an arbitrary function when expressed using primitive sets with a different terminals sets but the same function set.

Theorem 1 (complexity). *The complexity of a function under the CP representation is invariant under translation of terminal set, within a constant $K_{t1,t2}$ (the complexity of the dictionary $D_{t1,t2}$) provided the primitive sets are equally expressive.*

$$C_{t2}(f) \leq C_{t1}(f) + K_{t1,t2} \ (eq. \ 1)$$

Note, strictly we should talk about complexity with respect to a primitive set, but as the function set remains fixed here we drop reference to it.

Proof. Given that the two primitive sets are equally expressive (i.e. $p1 = t1 \cup f$ and $p2 = t2 \cup f$), we can simulate the set of terminals $t2$ using the dictionary $D_{t1,t2}$. As $p1$ and $p2$ are equally expressive, the dictionaries $D_{t1,t2}$ and $D_{t2,t1}$ both exist. These are represented as subtrees of the new CP. As we are using a CP, we only need to represent the new set of terminals once. We illustrate this graphically (see figure 5).

Theorem 2 (smallest bound). $K_{t_2 t_1}$ *is the smallest bound.*

Proof. Some functions will not depend on all of the terminals in a given terminal set, therefore these terminals do not need to be translated and do not need to

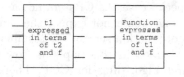

Fig. 5. A visualization of the proof. The box on the right is a CP expressed in terms of a primitive set $f \cup t_1$. The program has 2 outputs and 3 inputs. The box on the left is the CP expressing the set of functions t_1 in terms of $f \cup t_2$. Hence, the combination of CPs expresses the function in terms of $f \cup t_2$ without any reference to t_1.

be expressed by the dictionary. However in the worst cases, all of the terminals are required to be translated and the complete dictionary is needed. Therefore the smallest size of the bound is the complexity of the dictionary (i.e. the size of the smallest dictionary which translates all of the terminals).

Theorem 3 (lower bound). $C_{t2}(f) \geq C_{t1}(f) - K_{t2,t1}$

Proof. Consider the above equation (eq. 1). Consider the translation from terminal set $t2$ to terminal set $t1$, i.e. $C_{t1}(f) \leq C_{t2}(f) + K_{t2,t1}$ then rearrange the equation $C_{t1}(f) - K_{t2,t1} \leq C_{t2}(f)$ We can also say this is the tightest lower bound by an identical argument to that in the previous proof.

We can combine the above results into a single expression

$$C_{t1}(f) - K_{t2,t1} \leq C_{t2}(f) \leq C_{t1}(f) + K_{t1,t2}$$

and say that these bounds are the tightest obtainable.

7   Summary and Conclusions

CP uses a DAG to represent programs, rather than using trees which are typically used in GP. DAGs allow some reuse of subtrees, and this reuse has an affect on the complexity of a function when expressed using a DAG. In contrast, a tree representation offers no reuse as each branch of the computation must be represented explicitly, even if subtrees are identical.

We proved that the complexity of a function, when expressed by a CP, is independent of the terminal set (within an additive constant), provided the primitive sets are equally expressive. This was essentially done with a simulation argument. We also proved that the tightest upper bound on the complexity is the complexity of the set of functions (i.e. the complexity of the dictionary) corresponding to the new terminal set. We also proved the tightest lower bound on complexity is symmetric to this. Thus the complexity of a function is sandwiched symmetrically between the complexity of the function with reference to a different terminal set.

In [2] we proved that the complexity of a function is independent (within an additive constant) of the function set and terminal set provided the sets are equally expressive and the representation is capable of expressing modules (i.e. ADFs). The results in this paper are completely analogous to those in [2], and can be thought of as a special case. As CPs are not as flexible as ADFs in the amount of reuse allowed, one would not expect the same degree of robustness regarding the translation of function set and/or terminal set.

What we have not addressed in this paper is how to use these results to design more efficient search algorithms for CGP. There are two benefits from representing a program as a DAG; the amount of space needed to express a given function is reduced and also the amount of time needed to compute a function for a given input is reduced. We also believe that similar results regarding complexity exist for Binary Decision Diagrams and Artificial Neural Networks as there is the possibility of reuse in these representations.

References

1. Banzhaf, W., Nordin, P., Keller, R.E., Francone, F.D.: Genetic Programming – An Introduction; On the Automatic Evolution of Computer Programs and its Applications. Morgan Kaufmann, dpunkt.verlag (1998)
2. Woodward, J.R.: Modularity in genetic programming. In: Genetic Programming, Proceedings of EuroGP 2003, Essex, UK, Springer-Verlag (2003)
3. Miller, J.F., Thomson, P.: Cartesian genetic programming. In Poli, R., Banzhaf, W., Langdon, W.B., Miller, J.F., Nordin, P., Fogarty, T.C., eds.: Genetic Programming, Proceedings of EuroGP'2000. Volume 1802 of LNCS., Edinburgh, Springer-Verlag (2000) 121–132
4. Handley, S.: On the use of a directed acyclic graph to represent a population of computer programs. In: Proceedings of the 1994 IEEE World Congress on Computational Intelligence, Orlando, Florida, USA, IEEE Press (1994) 154–159
5. Keijzer, M.: Efficiently representing populations in genetic programming. In Angeline, P.J., Kinnear, Jr., K.E., eds.: Advances in Genetic Programming 2. MIT Press, Cambridge, MA, USA (1996) 259–278
6. Roberts, M.E.: The effectiveness of cost based subtree caching mechanisms in typed genetic programming for image segmentation. In Raidl, G.R., Cagnoni, S., Cardalda, J.J.R., Corne, D.W., Gottlieb, J., Guillot, A., Hart, E., Johnson, C.G., Marchiori, E., Meyer, J.A., Middendorf, M., eds.: Applications of Evolutionary Computing, EvoWorkshops2003: EvoBIO, EvoCOP, EvoIASP, EvoMUSART, EvoROB, EvoSTIM. Volume 2611 of LNCS., University of Essex, UK, Springer-Verlag (2003) 444–454

Design of Robust Communication Systems Using Genetic Algorithms

Chien-Min Ou[1], Wen-Jyi Hwang[2,*], and Hung-Chuan Yung[1]

[1] Department of Electronics Engineering,
Ching Yun University, Chungli, Taiwan 320, ROC
cmou@cyu.edu.tw, M9311020@mail.cyu.edu.tw
[2] Graduate Institute of Computer Science and Information Engineering,
National Taiwan Normal University, Taipei, Taiwan 117, ROC
whwang@ntnu.edu.tw

Abstract. This paper presents a novel genetic algorithm for jointly optimizing source and channel codes. The algorithm uses a channel-optimized vector quantizer for the source code, and a rate-punctured convolutional code for the channel code. The genetic algorithm enhances the robustness of the rate-distortion performance of the channel-optimized vector quantizer, and reduces the computational time for finding the best rate-punctured convolutional code. Numerical results show that the algorithm attains near optimal performance while having low computational complexity.

Keywords: Vector Quantization, Genetic Algorithm, Error Correct Coding.

1 Introduction

The objective of designing a robust communication system is to minimize the end-to-end average distortion of the system over a noisy channel. The basic techniques for the design can be classified into three classes: the channel-optimized source coding, the source-optimized channel coding, and the combination of these two classes. The channel-optimized source coding techniques design source codes of the communication system optimally matched to a given noisy channel. Typical examples are the source-optimized vector quantization (COVQ) [1] and its variants. The source-optimized channel coding techniques usually construct unequal error protection (UEP) schemes best matched to a given source code. Some variable-rate channel codes such as rate-compatible convolutional codes (RCPCs) [3] have been found to be effective for the implementation of the UEP. The application of RCPCs to UEP is realized by a bit allocation process, which determines the degree of error protection to different locations of the binary channel indices representing VQ codewords.

The combination of channel-optimized source coding and source-optimized channel coding may further improve the performance of the joint design. An

---

* Corresponding author.

P. Collet et al. (Eds.): EuroGP 2006, LNCS 3905, pp. 270–279, 2006.

iterative procedure optimizing source code and channel code one at a time has been employed to realize this combination [2]. Although the iterative scheme is effective, it has two major drawbacks. First, its source code at each iteration is designed using the COVQ, which usually falls into a poor local optimum. Therefore, the results of the iterative scheme may also be a local optimal solution. Second, each iteration of the scheme consists of the design of both source and channel codes. Its computational complexity is higher than the algorithms designing only source or channel codes. In addition, the full-search bit allocation scheme is used for the UEP, which may require high computational time for long binary channel indices [4].

One way to prevent the joint design from getting trapped in a poor local optimum is to adopt the stochastic optimization. An extensively used algorithm for the stochastic optimization is the genetic algorithm (GA) [6], which has been found to be effective for various vector quantizer (VQ) design algorithms [5]. With less computational complexity, the GA-based bit allocation scheme for UEP [4] can also attain comparable performance to that of the full-search bit allocation scheme. Therefore, an iterative scheme based on the COVQ and the UEP with GA may achieve better performance as compared with that of the iterative scheme [2] without GA. Nevertheless, since there are two GA optimizations in each iteration with one for the COVQ and the other for the UEP, the long computational time may still be necessary.

In light of the facts stated above, the objective of this paper is to present a novel algorithm for the joint design of source and channel codes, which attains a near global optimal performance while having low computational complexity. Instead of using the iterative approach, this algorithm employs the GA-based concurrent scheme for the optimization of source and channel codes. The concurrent design requires only one GA optimization so that the algorithm may have lower computational complexity as compared with its iterative counterpart.

To use the GA in our design, each genetic string has two segments. The first segment consists of the codewords of the VQ. The second segment contains a possible bit allocation for UEP. The fitness function for regeneration is the weighted sum of the end-to-end average distortion and the total number of redundancy bits. The weight of the redundancy bits in the fitness function determines the degree of overall error protection. To accelerate the speed of convergence of the GA, the VQ codewords of each genetic string are optimized further using the COVQ after the completion of each generation. The results of the COVQ design are then used for the evolution of the next generation.

2 Problem Formulation

Consider a full-search VQ with N codewords $\mathbf{y}_1, ..., \mathbf{y}_N$. Each codeword $\mathbf{y}_i$ is represented by a binary index c_i with length n, where $n = \log N$. Let $c_i(m), m = 1, ..., n$, be the m-th bit of c_i. Suppose the noisy channel is a binary symmetric channel (BSC) with bit error rate (BER) ϵ. In addition, the RCPC is used for the error correction of binary indices. The set of channel code rates from Table 1 in [3] (denoted by $\mathcal{C}$) are used to obtain our RCPC candidates. We represent each candidate code by a vector with dimension n, where the m-th element in the vector is the channel code rate applied to $c_i(m)$. For example, suppose $n = 3$. The RCPC code $\{1/2, 2/3, 2/3\}$ applies the convolutional code with rate $1/2$ to $c_i(1)$, and the convolutional code with rate $2/3$ to $c_i(2)$ and $c_i(3)$. The average transmission rate of the VQ is defined as the average number of bits representing each source vector after the channel encoding process. Consequently, for a RCPC code $\{s_1, ..., s_n\}$, the average transmission rate is given by $\sum_{m=1}^{n} \frac{1}{s_m}$.

Let $P_{k/i}$ be the probability that the binary index c_i delivered by VQ encoder is received as c_k by the VQ decoder because of channel errors. We call $P_{k/i}, i, k = 1, ..., N$, the index crossover probabilities, which are functions of RCPC and the bit error rate (BER) of the BSC. Given source codewords and index crossover probabilities, the average end-to-end distortion, D, is given by

$$D = \frac{1}{wt} \sum_{j=1}^{t} \sum_{k=1}^{N} P_{k/\alpha(\mathbf{x}_j)} d(\mathbf{x}_j, \mathbf{y}_k), \tag{1}$$

where w is the vector dimension, $\{\mathbf{x}_j\}_{j=1}^{t}$ are source vectors, $\alpha(\mathbf{x}_j)$ is the source encoder, and $d(\mathbf{u}, \mathbf{v})$ is the squared distance between vectors $\mathbf{u}$ and $\mathbf{v}$. The goal of joint design is then equivalent to the following optimization problem:

$$\min_{\substack{(\mathbf{y}_1, ..., \mathbf{y}_N) \\ (s_1, ..., s_n)}} \frac{1}{wt} \sum_{j=1}^{t} \sum_{k=1}^{N} P_{k/\alpha(\mathbf{x}_j)} d(\mathbf{x}_j, \mathbf{y}_k), \quad \text{subject to} \sum_{m=1}^{n} \frac{1}{s_m} \leq R, \tag{2}$$

where R is the constraint on the average transmission rate. To solve this problem, the Lagrangian method with cost function J can be used, where

$$J = \frac{1}{wt} \sum_{j=1}^{t} \sum_{k=1}^{N} P_{k/\alpha(\mathbf{x}_j)} d(\mathbf{x}_j, \mathbf{y}_k) + \lambda \sum_{m=1}^{n} \frac{1}{s_m}, \tag{3}$$

and $\lambda > 0$ determines the resulting transmission rate after the optimization.

3   The Algorithms

In this section, four joint design algorithms are presented: the GA-based COVQ (G-COVQ) algorithm, the GA-based UEP (G-UEP) algorithm, the iterative combination of G-COVQ and G-UEP (GA-based iterative) algorithm, and the GA-based concurrent design algorithm.

3.1   G-COVQ Algorithm

We first introduce the COVQ algorithm, which is the basic channel-optimized source coding technique. In the COVQ design, we assume that the BER ϵ of the BSC channel and RCPC rates $\{s_1, ..., s_n\}$ are fixed. The index crossover probabilities $P_{k/i}, i, k = 1, ..., N$, thereby are also fixed. Consequently, the minimization of J given in eq.(3) is simply equivalent to the minimization of D. Hence, the objective of the COVQ design can be stated as finding a set of VQ codewords $\mathbf{y}_k, k = 1, ..., N$ minimizing D. It can be shown that, given codewords $\mathbf{y}_k, k = 1, ..., N$, the optimal source encoder α minimizing D should satisfy

$$\alpha(\mathbf{x}_j) = \arg \min_{1 \leq l \leq N} \sum_{k=1}^{N} P_{k/l} d(\mathbf{x}_j, \mathbf{y}_k), \tag{4}$$

In addition, given α, the optimal codewords $\mathbf{y}_k, k = 1, ..., N$, minimizing D can be evaluated as

$$\mathbf{y}_k = \frac{\sum_{j=1}^{t} P_{k/\alpha(\mathbf{x}_j)} \mathbf{x}_j}{\sum_{j=1}^{t} P_{k/\alpha(\mathbf{x}_j)}} \tag{5}$$

The COVQ algorithm is based on an iterative procedure where source encoder α and codewords $\mathbf{y}_k, k = 1, ..., N$ are optimized one at a time using eqs.(4) and (5), respectively. The major disadvantage of the COVQ is that its performance is sensitive to the selection of initial codewords, which can be solved by the G-COVQ algorithm.

Suppose there are G strings in the algorithm. Each string $\mathbf{g} = \{\mathbf{y}_1, ..., \mathbf{y}_N\}_{\mathbf{g}}$ is a set of VQ codewords. Let $\mathcal{G}(q)$ be the set of G strings after the execution of the q-th evolution. Let $\mathbf{g}^*$ be the *current optimal* string during the course of the GA. We set the initial $\mathbf{g}^*$ as null. In addition, the VQ codewords in $\mathcal{G}(0)$ are formed by randomly selecting source vectors in $\{\mathbf{x}_j\}_{j=1}^{t}$. Now, suppose the $(q - 1)$-th evolution is completed, and the execution of the q-th evolution is to be done. We then perform the following genetic operations sequentially on the strings in $\mathcal{G}(q - 1)$.

Reproduction of G-COVQ: Since each string in $\mathcal{G}(q - 1)$ contains VQ codewords, their corresponding D can be computed using eq.(1). The inverse of D is used as a fitness function for each string. There are G reproduction strings created by the roulette-wheel technique.

Crossover of G-COVQ: On each regeneration string $\mathbf{g}$, $\{\mathbf{y}_1, ..., \mathbf{y}_N\}_{\mathbf{g}}$, the crossover operation is applied with probability P_c. Out of the total population, a partner string $\mathbf{g}'$, $\{\mathbf{y}_1', ..., \mathbf{y}_N'\}_{\mathbf{g}'}$, is randomly chosen. Then an integer random number b between 1 and n is generated. Both strings are cut into two portions at position b, and the portions $\{\mathbf{y}_{b+1}, ..., \mathbf{y}_N\}$ and $\{\mathbf{y}_{b+1}', ..., \mathbf{y}_N'\}$ are mutually exchanged.

Mutation of G-COVQ: For each string $\mathbf{g}$, mutation is performed on each element of $\mathbf{y}_k, k = 1, ..., N$, with a small probability P_m. Suppose $\mathbf{y}_k$ is determined to be mutated. One of the w components of $\mathbf{y}_k$ is then selected at random. A random number, taking binary values b or $-b$, is generated, and is added to the selected component.

COVQ optimization of G-COVQ: After the regeneration, crossover and mutation operations, the COVQ algorithm is applied to each string $\mathbf{g}$. The initial codewords and index crossover probabilities for the COVQ design are obtained from the VQ codewords and RCPC rates of that string, respectively. The resulting codewords after the COVQ design will replace the original VQ codewords in that string. The G strings after the COVQ design are then the strings of the set $\mathcal{G}(q)$.

Test for convergence of G-COVQ: After the completion of the COVQ optimization, The D value of each string in $\mathcal{G}(q)$ is computed for updating D^* and $\mathbf{g}^*$. This completes the execution of q-th evolution of our genetic programming algorithm. In the algorithm, the evolution continues until the observation of I consecutive evolutions yielding identical D^* value.

3.2   G-UEP Algorithm

The G-UEP algorithm can be used to reduce the computational complexity of the UEP [4]. Let S_i be the cluster such that $S_i = \{\mathbf{x}_j : \alpha(\mathbf{x}_j) = i\}$, and $\mathbf{z}_i$ be the centroid of S_i. We can rewrite eq.(1) as

$$D = \frac{1}{wt} \sum_{j=1}^{t} d(\mathbf{x}_j, \mathbf{y}_{\alpha(\mathbf{x}_j)}) + \frac{1}{N} \sum_{i=1}^{N} \sum_{k=1}^{N} P_{k/i} d(\mathbf{y}_i, \mathbf{y}_k). \tag{6}$$

Note that, the first term in eq.(6) depends only on the VQ codewords $\mathbf{y}_i$ and source vectors $\mathbf{x}_j$. Therefore, this term does not change as a function of RCPC code. The optimal RCPC code only minimizes the second term of eq.(6): $\frac{1}{N} \sum_{i=1}^{N} \sum_{k=1}^{N} P_{k/i} d(\mathbf{y}_i, \mathbf{y}_k)$. Since the first term requires higher computational complexity, given a set of VQ codewords $\{\mathbf{y}_1, ..., \mathbf{y}_N\}$, the objective function J in eq.(3) for UEP design can be simplified into

$$L = \frac{1}{N} \sum_{i=1}^{N} \sum_{k=1}^{N} P_{k/i} d(\mathbf{y}_i, \mathbf{y}_k) + \lambda \sum_{m=1}^{n} s_m^{-1}. \tag{7}$$

The problem of the UEP therefore is equivalent to find a set of RCPC rates $\{s_1, ..., s_n\}$ minimizing the cost function L given in eq.(7) for a fixed set of VQ codewords. Suppose there are G strings. Each string $\mathbf{s} = \{s_1, ..., s_n\}_\mathbf{s}$ is a set of RCPC rates. Let $\mathcal{S}(q)$ be the set of G strings after the execution of the q-th evolution, where each evolution consists of regeneration, crossover and mutation operations. Let $\mathbf{s}^*$ be the *current optimal* string during the course of the GA, and L^* be its L value. We set the initial $\mathbf{s}^*$ and L^* as null and ∞, respectively. In addition, the strings in $\mathcal{S}(0)$ is formed by randomly selecting channel rates in $\mathcal{C}$. Now, suppose the $(q-1)$-th evolution is completed, and the execution of the q-th iteration is to be done. We then perform the following genetic operations sequentially on the strings in $\mathcal{S}(q-1)$.

Reproduction of G-UEP: Each string in $\mathcal{S}(q-1)$ in fact is a RCPC code. Hence, their corresponding L can be computed using eq.(7). The inverse of L is used as a fitness function for each string. There are G regeneration strings created after the regeneration operation.

Crossover of G-UEP: This process is similar to that of the G-COVQ with crossover probability P_c for each string $\mathbf{s}$.

Mutation of G-UEP: Mutation is performed on each element $s_m, m = 1, ..., n$, of each string with a small probability P_m. Suppose s_m is determined to be mutated, then a rate selected at random from $\mathcal{C}$ is used to replace s_m.

Test for convergence of G-UEP: The G strings after these operations are the strings of $\mathcal{S}(q)$. The L value of each string in $\mathcal{S}(q)$ is computed for updating the $\mathbf{s}^*$ and L^*. This completes the execution of q-th evolution of G-UEP algorithm.In the G-UEP algorithm, the evolution continues until the observation of I consecutive evolutions yielding identical L^* value.

3.3   GA-Based Iterative Algorithm

In the iterative algorithm, each iteration executes the G-COVQ and G-UEP sequentially. Let $\{\mathbf{y}_1^f, ..., \mathbf{y}_N^f\}$ and $\{s_1^f, ..., s_n^f\}$ be the set of VQ codewords and RCPC rates after the design of the f-th iteration, respectively. Now, suppose the $(f-1)$-th iteration is completed, and the design of the f-th iteration is to be done. Each iteration contains two steps, which correspond to G-COVQ and G-UEP design, respectively.

Step 1: Given $\{s_1^{f-1}, ..., s_n^{f-1}\}$, the objective at this step is to design $\{\mathbf{y}_1^f, ..., \mathbf{y}_N^f\}$ using the G-COVQ algorithm. The set of RCPC rates $\{s_1^{f-1}, ..., s_n^{f-1}\}$ is used to determine the index crossover probabilities $P_{k/i}, i, k = 1, ..., N$, for the computation of D given in eq.(1). The VQ codewords $\{\mathbf{y}_1^f, ..., \mathbf{y}_N^f\}$ at the iteration f is then set to be the final current optimal string $\mathbf{g}^*$ after the completion of G-COVQ.

Step 2: Using the G-UEP, this step finds the RCPC rates $\{s_1^f, ..., s_n^f\}$ best matched to the VQ codewords $\{\mathbf{y}_1^f, ..., \mathbf{y}_N^f\}$ designed at the previous step. The VQ codewords are used to compute the first term in L shown in eq. (7)(i.e., $\frac{1}{N} \sum_{i=1}^N \sum_{k=1}^N P_{k/i} d(\mathbf{y}_i, \mathbf{y}_k)$) for the execution of the G-UEP. The RCPC rates $\{s_1^f, ..., s_n^f\}$ at the iteration f is then set to be the final current optimal string $\mathbf{s}^*$ after the completion of G-UEP.

Test for convergence of the iterative algorithm: Let J^f be the value of J after the completion of the f-th iteration. Since each execution of G-COVQ and G-UEP reduces the J value [5], the iteration algorithm will continue until the convergence of the sequence $\{J^f\}$.

3.4   GA-Based Concurrent Algorithm

In the GA-based concurrent algorithm, each string $\mathbf{g}$ in the algorithm can be divided into two segments: the VQ codewords segment $\{\mathbf{y}_1, ..., \mathbf{y}_N\}_{\mathbf{g}}$ and the RCPC rates segment $\{s_1, ..., s_n\}_{\mathbf{g}}$. Let $\mathcal{G}(q)$ be the set of G strings after the execution of the q-th evolution, where each evolution consists of regeneration, crossover, mutation and COVQ optimization operations. Let $\mathbf{g}^*$ be the *current optimal* string during the course of the GA and J^* be its J value. We set the initial $\mathbf{g}^*$ as null, and initial $J^* = \infty$. In addition, the VQ codewords and RCPC rates of each string in $\mathcal{G}(0)$ are formed by randomly selecting source vectors and channel rates in $\{\mathbf{x}_j\}_{j=1}^t$ and $\mathcal{C}$, respectively. Now, suppose the $(q-1)$-th evolution is completed, and the execution of the q-th evolution is to be done.

Reproduction of GA-based concurrent algorithm: We use the inverse of J given in eq.(3) as the fitness function for each string in $\mathcal{G}(q-1)$. There are G regeneration strings created after the regeneration operation.

Crossover of GA-based concurrent algorithm: On each regeneration string $\mathbf{g}$ the crossover operation is applied with probability P_c. Out of the total population, a partner string $\mathbf{g}'$ is randomly chosen. Then two integer random numbers b_1 (between 1 and N) and b_2 (between 1 and n) are generated. The VQ codewords segment and RCPC rates segment of both strings are cut into two portions at positions b_1 and b_2, respectively. Portions of each segment of strings $\mathbf{g}$ and $\mathbf{g}'$ are mutually exchanged. The resulting strings are then given by

$$\mathbf{g} = \{\mathbf{y}_1, ..., \mathbf{y}_{b_1}, \mathbf{y}'_{b_1+1}, ..., \mathbf{y}'_N, s_1, ..., s_{b_2}, s'_{b_2+1}, ..., s'_n\}_{\mathbf{g}},$$
$$\mathbf{g}' = \{\mathbf{y}'_1, ..., \mathbf{y}'_{b_1}, \mathbf{y}_{b_1+1}, ..., \mathbf{y}_N, s'_1, ..., s'_{b_2}, s_{b_2+1}, ..., s_n\}_{\mathbf{g}'}.$$

Mutation of GA-based concurrent algorithm: For each string $\mathbf{g}$, mutation is performed on each element of $\mathbf{y}_k, k = 1, ..., N$, and $s_m, m = 1, ..., n$, with a small probability P_m. Suppose $\mathbf{y}_k$ is determined to be mutated. One of the w components of $\mathbf{y}_k$ is then selected at random. A random number, taking binary values b or $-b$, is generated, and is added to the selected component. For each s_q determined to be mutated, a rate is first selected at random from $\mathcal{C}$, and s_q is then replaced by the rate.

COVQ optimization of GA-based concurrent algorithm: After the regeneration, crossover and mutation operations, the COVQ algorithm is applied to each string $\mathbf{g}$. The initial codewords and index crossover probabilities for the COVQ design are obtained from the VQ codewords and RCPC rates of that string, respectively. The resulting codewords after the COVQ design will replace the original VQ codewords in that string. The G strings after the COVQ design are then the strings of the set $\mathcal{G}(q)$.

Test for convergence of GA-based concurrent algorithm: After the completion of the COVQ optimization, the J value of each string in $\mathcal{G}(q)$ is computed for updating $\mathbf{g}^*$ and J^*. This completes the execution of q-th evolution of GA-based concurrent algorithm. The evolution continues until the observation of I consecutive evolutions yielding identical J^* value.

4   Simulation Results

This section presents some simulation results of various algorithms for the joint design of source and channel codes. The vector dimension is $w = 8$ for all the experiments. The BER of the BSC channel is 0.01. The Gauss-Markov sequences (84000 samples) with $\rho = 0.9$ are used for both training and performance measurement.

Figure 1 elaborates the dependence of the GA-based concurrent algorithm on the population size G for $\lambda = 1$. The number of codewords is $N = 32$. Each

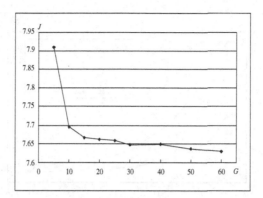

Fig. 1. The dependence of the GA-based concurrent algorithm on the population size G

Table 1. The mean, minimum, maximum and standard deviation values of cost J from 100 independent trials for various λ values

λ	GA-based Concurrent				GA-based Iterative			
	min	max	mean	variance	min	max	mean	variance
5	30.42	31.74	30.63	0.13	41.50	49.03	43.55	1.14
10	58.53	59.77	58.76	0.20	70.58	87.89	76.38	3.14
15	86.64	91.72	87.00	0.73	91.27	129.78	103.88	5.35

sample point in the figure is an average value over 100 independent executions using randomly chosen initial genetic strings. From the figure, we observe that the average J decreases as G increases. However, the reduction becomes negligible when $G \geq 15$. Since the computational time grows with G, we choose $G = 15$ for the subsequent experiments for attaining low computational complexity.

Table 1 compares the GA-based concurrent algorithm with its major counterpart, the GA-based iterative algorithm. The comparison includes the mean, minimum, maximum and standard deviation values of J from 100 independent trials of each algorithm for various λ values. It can be observed from the table that the GA-based concurrent algorithm has lower mean, minimum, maximum and standard deviation values for each λ as compared with the GA-based iterative algorithm. This implies that the GA-based concurrent algorithm provides robust solutions with superior performance. The GA-base iterative algorithm does not perform well because it optimizes source and channel codes one at a time iteratively. Poor source codes obtained from the first step of the algorithm will be used to design the channel codes at the second step. This may result in a poor local optimum solution.

Figures 2 and 3 show the rate-distortion performance of various algorithms having the same number of VQ codewords $N = 128$. It is not surprising to observe from Figure 2 that the GA-based concurrent algorithm significantly outperforms the COVQ, G-COVQ and G-UEP algorithms, which only design

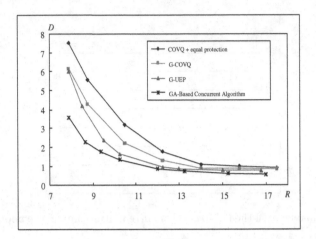

Fig. 2. The rate-distortion performance of COVQ, G-COVQ, G-UEP and GA-based concurrent algorithms

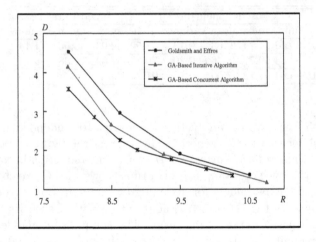

Fig. 3. The rate-distortion performance of Goldsmith and Effros, GA-based iterative and GA-based concurrent algorithms

either a source code or a channel code. In addition, as illustrated in Figure 3, the GA-based concurrent algorithm also has superior rate-distortion performance over the GA-based iterative algorithm and Goldsmith-Effros algorithm[2], which design both the source and channel codes iteratively. These observations are consistent with those shown in Table 1, where the concurrent algorithm attains lower cost for the optimization.

The average CPU time of various algorithms for the experiments shown in Figures 2 and 3 are included in Table 2. It can be observed from the table that the average CPU time of the GA-based concurrent algorithm is only 2.1 hrs. By contrast, because the Goldsmith-Effros algorithm uses the full-search scheme for

Table 2. The average CPU time (measured on 1.6G HZ Pentium IV) of various algorithms for the experiments shown in Figure 2 and 3

Algorithm	G-COVQ	GA-based Iterative	GA-based Concurrent	Goldsmith and Effros [2]
CPU time	1.9 hrs	7.3 hrs	2.1 hrs	60.3 hrs

finding the channel codes, it needs 60.3 hrs for the VQ design. All these facts demonstrate the effectiveness of the GA-based concurrent algorithm.

5   Conclusion

The GA-based concurrent optimization algorithm has been found to be effective for the joint design of source and channel codes. Experimental results show that the algorithm outperforms its iterative counterparts with lower CPU time. The algorithm therefore can be an effective alternative for the applications where both low computational complexity and high performance are desired for the design of robust transmission systems.

References

1. N. Farvardin and V. Vaishampayan, "On the performance and complexity of channel-optimized vector quantizers," *IEEE Trans. Information Theory*, Vol. 37, pp.155-160, 1991.
2. A.J. Goldsmith and M. Effros, "Joint design of fixed-rate source codes and multiresolution channel codes," *IEEE Trans. Commun.*, Vol.46, pp. 1301-1311, Oct. 1998.
3. J. Hagenauer, "Rate-compatble punctured convolutional codes (RCPC) codes and their applications," *IEEE Trans. Comm.*, Vol.36, pp.389-400, 1988.
4. W.J. Hwang, Y.C. Chen and C.C. Hsu, "Robust transmission based on variable-rate error control and genetic programming," *IEEE Communication Letters*, Vol.6, pp.25-27, 2002.
5. W.J. Hwang, C.M. Ou, C.C. Hsu and T.Y. Lo, "Iterative optimization for joint design of source and channel codes using genetic algorithms," *Journal of the Chinese Institute of Engineers*, Vol. 28, pp.803-810, 2005.
6. M. Srinivas and L.M. Patnaik, "Genetic algorithm: a survey," *IEEE Computer*, Volume 27, pp. 17 - 26, 1994.

Developmental Evaluation in Genetic Programming: The Preliminary Results

Robert Ian (Bob) McKay[1], Tuan Hao Hoang[2],
Daryl Leslie Essam[2], and Xuan Hoai Nguyen[3]

[1] School of Computer Science & Engineering,
College of Engineering, Seoul National University, San 56-1,
Sinlim-dong, Gwanak-gu, Seoul 151-744, Korea
rim@cse.snu.ac.kr
[2] School of ITEE, University of New South Wales,
@ Australian Defence Force Academy, Canberra, Australia
t.hao@adfa.edu.au,
daryl@cs.adfa.edu.au
[3] Vietnamese Military Technical Academy, Hanoi, Vietnam
nxhoai@gmail.com

Abstract. This paper investigates developmental evaluation in Genetic Programming (GP). Extant GP systems, including developmental GP systems, typically exhibit modular and hierarchical structure only to the degree it is built-in by the designer; by contrast, biological systems exhibit a high degree of organization in their genotypes. We hypothesise that even when GP systems are subject to changing environments, for which the adaptability arising from modular structure would be advantageous, the benefit is at the species rather than individual level, so that selection is very weak. By contrast, biological systems are selected repeatedly throughout their development process. We suggest that this difference is crucial; that if an individual is evaluated multiple times throughout its development, then modular structure can provide an adaptive advantage to that individual, and hence can be selected for by evolution. We investigate this hypothesis using Tree Adjoining Grammar Guided Genetic Programming (TAG3P) [1], which has good properties for supporting evaluation during incremental development. Our preliminary results show that developmental TAG3P outperforms both original TAG3P and standard tree-based GP on an appropriate problem, in ways which suggest that modular solutions may have been developed.

1 Introduction

Genetic Programming (GP) was developed by Koza [2] in 1992 It is an automatic programming methodology using simulation of evolution to discover functional programs to solve a problem. Genetic programming breeds a population of trial solutions using biologically inspired operators, which include reproduction, crossover (sexual recombination), mutation, and forms of natural selection. In essence, it uses

P. Collet et al. (Eds.): EuroGP 2006, LNCS 3905, pp. 280–289, 2006.
© Springer-Verlag Berlin Heidelberg 2006

evolutionary search methods to search for solutions to given problems within an in-principle unbounded space of expressions. However, the solutions found are generally poorly structured and highly disorganised, exhibiting no hierarchical or modular structure. An individual in a genetic programming system is generally expected to solve problems immediately, without the benefit of a developmental phase. By contrast, the natural evolutionary systems on which it is based are able to evolve hierarchical modular structure (e.g. the homeobox gene complex). Generating hierarchical, modular structures would greatly benefit GP, potentially dramatically increasing the scalability of GP applications, as well as the adaptability of GP solutions.

There have been a wide range of approaches to solving this problem in GP. For example, Angeline [3] developed a technique called Module Acquisition, which is based on the creation and administration of a library of modules for the automatic generation of subroutines. Other studies have investigated Automatically Defined Functions (ADF) [4], which is probably the most popular of the modularization methods used in GP. Rosca investigated an Adaptive Representation [5], which is based on the discovery of useful building blocks of code. This approach greatly improved search efficiency on the problem's considered. However, all these approaches involve some level of programmer intervention, thus imposing a level of modularity that nature has been able to evolve for itself.

Recently, interest in developmental approaches in Evolvable Hardware has begun to increase. Haddow et al. [6] used Lindenmayer systems for digital circuit design, while Miller [7] developed Cartesian Genetic Programming for the automatic evolution of digital circuits, and attempted to evolve a cell that could construct a larger program by iteration of the cell's program.

Nevertheless, modular structure has not been clearly demonstrated in existing developmental GP systems. We argue that this is because modular structure, if used for a single evaluation as in most artificial developmental systems, only has adaptive advantages to entire species, not to particular individuals, and hence imposes very weak selection pressure in evolution. In developmental biological systems, on the other hand, evaluation is continuous throughout development (if the individual is insufficiently fit to survive at a particular stage of development, the fitness it would exhibit at later stages is immaterial). A modular structure, which allows biological sub-systems to develop in synchrony throughout development, can thus provide a selective advantage to the individual. Our working hypothesis is that, if the individual is evaluated on multiple problems at different stages of development, then modular structure can provide an adaptive advantage to that particular individual, and hence can be selected for by evolution. This hypothesis is investigated using the Tree Adjoining Grammar Guided GP (TAG3P) representation, which has ideal properties for supporting evaluation during incremental development. In particular, this representation has a feasibility property, allowing any expression tree to be evaluated, regardless of the detachment of any number of its sub-trees. This means that smaller sections of the tree can easily be tested on simpler problems, providing a straightforward way to test our hypothesis at relatively low implementation cost.

In these experiments, the developmental process is extremely naïve, consisting in effect of undirected growth of each individual (in implementation, we evolve the whole tree but evaluate increasing portions of it). We do not propose this as a serious

developmental model; we deliberately use a minimal developmental model to empha-
sise the crux of this paper, namely the effect of evaluation during development.

The paper outline is as follows. The next section briefly describes Tree Adjoining
Grammars (TAGs) and TAG based Genetic Programming. Section 3 introduces our
Developmental Evaluation method based on Tree Adjoining Grammar Guided
Genetic Programming (DEVTAG). Experimental setups are described in section 4.
Section 5 and 6 provide the results and discussion. Conclusions and future work are
laid out in the last section.

2   Tree Adjoining Grammar, TAG Based Genetic Programming

The following section gives a brief, somewhat intuitive introduction to TAG; a fuller
description of TAG may be found in [1].

2.1 Tree Adjoining Grammars (TAGs)

TAGs are tree-generating and analysis systems, first proposed by Joshi [8] for Natural
Language Processing (NLP) purposes.

The aim of TAG is to more directly represent the structure of natural languages
than is possible in Chomsky languages, and in particular, to represent the process by
which natural language sentences can be built up from a relatively small set of basic
linguistic units by inclusion of insertable sub-structures. Thus 'The cat sat on the mat'
becomes 'The black cat sat lazily on the mat' by the subsequent insertion of the elements 'black', and 'lazily'. In more detail, a tree-adjoining grammar comprises of a
quintuple (T, V, I, A, S), where:

- T is a finite set of terminal symbols.
- V is a finite set of non-terminal symbols ($T \cap V = \varnothing$).
- $S \in V$ is a distinguished symbol called the start symbol.
- I is a set of initial trees, characterised by all interior nodes being labeled by non-
  terminal symbols, while the nodes on the frontier are labeled by terminals.
- A are auxiliary trees, characterised by all internal nodes being labeled by non-
  terminal symbols, while nodes on the frontier are labeled by terminals, except
  for one special node called the foot node. A foot node must be labeled with the
  same non-terminal symbol as that labeling the tree's root node. The convention
  of marking the foot node with an asterisk (*) is followed here.

The trees in $E = I \cup A$ are called elementary trees. Initial trees and auxiliary trees
are indicated as α and β respectively. A tree with root labeled by non-terminal symbol
X is called an X-type elementary tree.

The key operation used with TAG is adjunction. Adjunction builds a new tree γ
from an auxiliary tree β and a tree α by inserting β into α at a specified place.
Adjunction is illustrated in Figure 1. More formally, if a tree α has an interior node
labeled A, and β is an A-type tree, the adjunction of β into α to produce γ is as follows:
Firstly, the sub-tree $\alpha 1$ rooted at A is temporarily disconnected from α (consider
Figure 1.a). Next, β is attached to α to replace the sub-tree α_1(1.b). Finally, the process
of building γ is completed when $\alpha 1$ is attached back to the foot node of β (1.c).

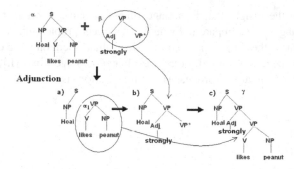

Fig. 1. An example of the Adjunction operator

2.2 TAG Based Genetic Programming

Tree Adjoining Grammar Guided Genetic Programming (TAG3P) [1] is a grammar guided genetic programming system. One of the most important of the TAG representation's properties is a feasibility property, namely that any rooted subtree of a valid TAG tree is also a valid TAG tree. Thanks to the feasibility property, in growing a derivation tree from the root, one can stop at any time and still have a valid derivation tree as well as a valid derived tree. For example, if a derivation tree consisted of β_1 adjoined to α (from figure 3), we could either stop at α before considering β_1, generating the derived tree x, or consider the entire tree and generate $x+x$.

3 Developmental Evaluation Based on TAG3P

The problem chosen for investigating our hypothesis is the symbolic regression problem with simple polynomials as target functions. This kind of symbolic regression problem is well-known for its increasing difficulty with polynomial degree [2, 9]. In particular we experimented with the series of polynomial functions as follows: F1 = X, F2 = X^2+ X, F3 = X^3+X^2+X, F4 = X^4+ X^3+X^2+X ... F9 = X^9+X^8+X^7+X^6+X^5+X^4+X^3+X^2+X. We expect this increasing difficulty could allow us to exploit the developmental evaluation approach.

To fulfil the requirement of tackling increasingly difficult problems throughout development, the individual is separated into multiple layers, with more of the individual being used for the more difficult fitness functions. Specifically, the individual is separated as below:

Depth 2 for function F1 = X
Depth 4 for function F2 = X^2+X
...
Depth 18 for function F9 = X^9+X^8+X^7+X^6+X^5+X^4+X^3+X^2+X.

We use tournament selection, which only requires a fitness ordering of individuals. For DEVTAG, we use a special multi-stage comparison to generate this ordering.

Corresponding to the insight that later-stage fitness is only important if the individual survives earlier stages, we compare individuals on simpler problems first; only if they are roughly equivalent on the simpler problems do we evaluate them on more complex ones.

We denote the fitness of an individual I evaluated at stage j by $F(I,j)$. For two individuals (I_1, I_2), the comparison process (for minimisation) is:

```
i := 1;
While |F(I₁, i) - F(I₂, i)| < ε
    i := i + 1;
if (F(I₁, i) < F(I₂, i))
    then I₁ wins
    else I₂ wins
```

An example of this algorithm is shown in Figure 2, comparing the individuals I_1 and I_2 with fitness value arrays (corresponding to the 9 different stages), I_1(10.05, 14.67..., 20.35), and I_2 (10.06, 14.66, ... , 10.35). In this case, I_2 would be chosen for evolution.

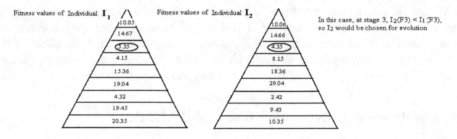

Fig. 2. An example of comparing two individual in DEVTAG

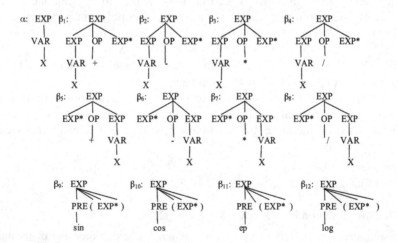

Fig. 3. Elementary trees for G_{lex}

The context-free grammar G for this problem has a function set including unary and binary operators {+, - ,*, /, sin, cos, log, EXP}. The terminal set is X. Formally:

G = (N,T,P,S}
S = EXP – the start symbol
N = {EXP, PRE, OP, VAR}
T = {X, sin, cos, lg, ep, +, -, *, /},   (ep is exponential, lg is log function)

The corresponding LTAG G_{lex} is shown overleaf
G_{lex}= {N={EXP, PRE, OP,VAR},T={X, sin, cos, log, ep,+, -, *, /, (,)}, I, A) where
I∪ A is as in Figure 3.

4 Experimental Setups

To investigate the effect of developmental evaluation on TAG3P, three experimental settings have been used with different population sizes (POPSIZE = 100, 250, 500 and 1000), with the maximum generation size (MAXGEN) changing correspondingly to keep a constant budget of 229,500 (9x51x500) function evaluations:

1. **DEVTAG:** using developmental evaluation, as described above
2. **GP:** A standard Koza-style tree-based GP run for evolving F9, using population size POPSIZE, evolving until the evaluation budget is used.
3. **TAG:** This treatment is designed to address a potential issue, that any differences might arise from differences in representation. The GP experiment is repeated using TAG representation, but otherwise a standard tree-based GP algorithm (the TAG3P system).

Table 1. Parameter settings for the symbolic regression problem

Objective	Find a function that exactly fits a given sample of 20 (xi, yi) data points.
Success Predicate	Sum of errors over 20 points < ε = 0.01
Terminal sets	X - the independent variable
Operators(Function set)	+,-,*,/, sin, cos, exp, log
Fitness Cases	The sample of 20 points in the interval [-1..+1].
Fitness	Sum of the errors over 20 fitness cases.
Genetic Operators	Tournament selection(3), sub-tree crossovers and sub-tree mutations using on TAG3P, normal standard crossovers and muations using on GP
Parameters	The crossover probability is 0.9. The mutation probability is 0.1.
Min/Max initial zise on TAG3P	2 to 1000
Max depth using for GP	20

5   Results

Table 2 shows the absolute number of successful runs out of 100 for each of the three treatments and four different population sizes. Note that the 0 entries mean that the GP runs were never successful.

Table 2. Successful runs (from 100 runs)

	POPSIZE=100	POPSIZE=250	POPSIZE=500	POPSIZE=1000
DEVTAG	13	33	27	3
TAG	3	8	9	4
GP	0	0	0	0

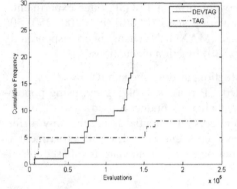
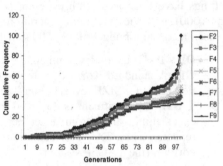

Fig. 4. Cumulative success frequency of DEVTAG and TAG against number of function evaluations

Fig. 5. Cumulative success frequency of DE-VTAG on each of the 9 problems

Figure 4 shows the cumulative probability of success of the two successful treatments (for the setting where the population size is 250), plotted against the number of function evaluations used in the evolution. To help in understanding how incrementally DEVTAG solves the problems, figure 5 shows the cumulative probability of success of DEVTAG, for all 9 symbolic regression problems, for the particular case of population size 250.

6   Discussion

From table 2, it is clear that developmental evaluation is very effective at finding exact or near-exact solutions to the problem, over a wide range of population size settings (for population size 1000, the very short number of generations – 26 – gives DEVTAG no realistic chance of finding all nine functions, F1 through F9). At population size 250, DEVTAG's probability of success was 33%, well above that achieved by the other treatments. It is also clear that this is an extremely difficult task for standard GP.

It is worth noting that DEVTAG gives us solutions to all the other eight functions, at no additional computational cost.

From Figure 4, we see that it takes DEVTAG some time to find solutions at all, but once it does so, it rapidly finds more. We interpret this as DEVTAG needing a number of evaluations to get evolution running well at the lower levels, but once it does, solutions to F9 follow rapidly. We note that the stepped evaluation method of DEVTAG means that many of the higher functions do not need to be evaluated in the earlier generations, so that DEVTAG does not actually use its whole budget of evaluations. This is why the DEVTAG plot stops early in figure 4.

In fact, the contrast in total computational cost is even greater than these figures suggest. TAG3P generates far larger individuals than DEVTAG. For example, the average size of the phenotype of the best-of-run individual for the TAG3P runs (i.e. what in Koza-style GP is known as the s-expression tree) with population 250 was 533.2 nodes, while that for DEVTAG was 31.88 nodes Since the computational cost of evaluating an s-expression is generally proportionate to the number of nodes evaluated, it is already clear that DEVTAG has much lower computational cost, per evaluation, than TAG3P (or GP). Yet even so, DEVTAG has a further computational cost advantage. An individual is only ever fully evaluated if it has near-identical function values for the lower level functions with some individual that it meets in a tournament. Since this is an unusual occurrence in the dynamic phases of evolution, most individuals will only ever be partially evaluated, reducing the computational cost still further. These parsimony issues will be investigated in greater detail in later papers, where we hope to present detailed results on the number of nodes actually evaluated in a run. They also raise interesting issues regarding optimal tournament size and diversity mechanisms for DEVTAG, which we plan to investigate in future work.

Figure 5 appears to confirm our interpretation, of gradually finding lower-level solutions, with the solutions of higher complexity following fairly rapidly. More detailed analyses, which we have insufficient room to present in detail here, show that DEVTAG virtually never finds a solution to function F_i without previously having found a solution to F_{i-1}. Further, there is a strong suggestion from the very closeness of the curves, that once DEVTAG has found building blocks for lower-level solutions, they are quickly assembled to form higher-level solutions. We conjecture that DEVTAG is achieving this by replicating building blocks and creating modularity; testing this hypothesis primarily awaits our determining an adequate empirical test for modularity. At the very least, the results strongly support the view that incremental learning of a family of increasingly difficult functions has been demonstrated.

7 Conclusions and Future Works

The results of developmental evaluation using TAG representation clearly demonstrate a form of problem-driven incremental learning. DEVTAG has been provided with a family of related problems of increasing difficulty, and it has proceeded to solve them incrementally. We believe this is a landmark in itself.

The computational cost of the approach is also worth noting (though it is not the primary focus of this work), DEVTAG being much less expensive than the other approaches in computational cost, as well as yielding much more (a family of functions rather than just one) in return for that computational investment.

Equally important, the results strongly suggest that developmental evaluation has promoted the evolution of modular structure, and this is certainly our impression on viewing the evolved genotypes. Confirming it is primarily a matter of developing an operational measure for modularity applicable to the TAG representation. Hornby [10] has recently considered this question, but his metrics are based on an assumption of explicit representation of modularity, hence it is not easy to see how to extend them to our work. Finding an appropriate metric for modularity and code re-use is our primary short-term goal.

The work reported here is primarily a pilot study for a larger-scale approach with a more sophisticated developmental process. The TAG representation is crucial to this, because it removes any difficulty in ensuring that intermediate developmental stages can be evaluated. We plan to replace DEVTAG's trivial developmental process with a more sophisticated approach based on a TAG analogue to L-systems. We aim to apply this system to a range of problems, and to analyse its behaviour, particularly in terms of the modularity and complexity of evolved solutions.

References

1. Nguyen, Xuan Hoai, McKay, R. I. and Abbass, H. A.: Tree Adjoining Grammars, Language Bias, and Genetic Programming. In Ryan, C., Soule, T., Keijzer, M., Tsang, E. P. K., Poli, R. and Costa, E. (eds): Proceedings of EuroGP2003, Lecture Notes in Computer Science, Vol. 2610, Springer-Verlag (2003), pp. 335-344.
2. Koza John R. Genetic Programming: On the Programming of Computers by Means of Natural Selection. MIT Press, Cambridge, MA, USA,1992.
3. Angeline, P.J "Evolutionary Algorithms and Emergent Intelligence", PhD thesis, Computer Science Department, Ohio State University, 1994.
4. Koza. John R. Genetic Programming II: Automatic Discovery of Reusable Programs, MIT Press, Cambridge Massachusetts, May 1994.
5. Rosca, Justinian P. and Ballard, Dana H.: Hierarchical Self- Organization in Genetic Programming. In Rouveirol, C. and Sebag, M. (eds): Proceedings of the Eleventh International Conference on Machine Learning, Morgan Kaufmann, 1994.
6. Haddow, P.C., Tufte G., and van Remortel P,: Shrinking the genotype: L-systems for Evolvable Hardware. In Liu, Y., Tanaka, K., Iwata, M., Higuchi, T. and Yasunaga, M. (eds): Evolvable Systems: From Biology to Hardware, 4th International Conference, ICES 2001, Lecture Notes in Computer Science, Vol. 2210, Springer-Verlag, Berlin – Heidelberg – New York (2001) 128 –139.
7. Miller J.F and Thomson, P.: A Developmental Method for Growing Graphs and Circuits. In Tyrrell, A.M., Haddow, P.C. and Torresen, J. (eds): 4th International Conference on Evolvable Systems: From Biology to Hardware, LNCS 2210, Springer-Verlag (2003), 93 – 104
8. Joshi, A.K., Levy, L. S., and Takahashi, M.: Tree adjunct grammars, *Journal of Computer and System Sciences*, 21(2) (1975), 136 – 163.
9. Nguyen Xuan Hoai, McKay, R.I., Essam, D.L. and Chau, R.: Solving the Symbolic Regression Problem with Tree Adjunct Grammar Guided Genetic Programming: The Comparative Results.. In Yao, X. (ed): Congress on Evolutionary Computation (CEC2002), IEEE Press, 2002, vol. 2, 1326-1331.

10. Hornby, Gregory S.: Measuring, Enabling and Comparing Modularity, Regularity and Hierarchy in Evolutionary Design. In Beyer, H.-G., O'Reilly, M., Arnold, D. V., Banzhaf, W., Blum, C., Bonabeau, E.W., Cantu-Paz, E., Dasgupta, D., Deb, K., Foster, J.A., de Jong, E., Lipson, H., Llora, X., Mancoridis, S., Pelikan, M., Raidl, G.R., Soule, T., Tyrrell, A.M., Watson, J.-P. and Zitzler, E.: Proceedings of the 2005 Genetic and Evolutionary Computation Conference (GECCO'05) ACM Press (2005) Vol.2, 1729-1736

Evolving Noisy Oscillatory Dynamics in Genetic Regulatory Networks

André Leier[1], P. Dwight Kuo[2], Wolfgang Banzhaf[3], and Kevin Burrage[1]

[1] Advanced Computational Modelling Centre,
University of Queensland, Brisbane, QLD 4072, Australia
{leier, kb}@acmc.uq.edu.au
[2] Department of Bioengineering, University of California,
San Diego, La Jolla, CA 92093-0412, USA
pdkuo@ucsd.edu
[3] Dept. of Computer Science, Memorial University of Newfoundland,
St. John's, NL A1B 3X5, Canada
banzhaf@cs.mun.ca

Abstract. We introduce a genetic programming (GP) approach for evolving genetic networks that demonstrate desired dynamics when simulated as a discrete stochastic process. Our representation of genetic networks is based on a biochemical reaction model including key elements such as transcription, translation and post-translational modifications. The stochastic, reaction-based GP system is similar but not identical with algorithmic chemistries. We evolved genetic networks with noisy oscillatory dynamics. The results show the practicality of evolving particular dynamics in gene regulatory networks when modelled with intrinsic noise.

1 Introduction and Background

In recent years, there has been significant interest in synthetic biology and the engineering of genetic circuits [1,2,3,4,5,6,7]. To this end, efforts have been made to construct small constituent subnetworks or "modules" for general use in larger genetic circuits [1,6]. Typically, synthetic genetic circuits [1] are either designed by hand or by using the directed evolution paradigm *in vivo* [7]. This process is both time–consuming and expensive. Alternatively, evolutionary approaches *in silico* have shown that regulatory networks can be evolved to display certain dynamical characteristics (e.g. as bistable switches or oscillators) [5,8,9]. Essentially, these approaches differ in the specific formalism describing genetic networks (e.g. piece–wise linear differential equations augmented by Boolean functions [5], differential equations corresponding to deterministic rate equations [8], artificial regulatory network model with dynamics derived from differential equations [9]). In this contribution, we introduce a genetic programming (GP) approach for evolving biochemical reaction networks based on simple enzyme kinetics which demonstrate sustained (noisy) oscillations when *simulated* as *discrete stochastic models*.

Stochasticity (or noise) is a fundamental phenomenon in many biological systems such as gene regulatory systems [10,11,12,13]. Although noise can adversely

P. Collet et al. (Eds.): EuroGP 2006, LNCS 3905, pp. 290–299, 2006.

affect cell function, it is also considered a source of robustness and stability, signal amplification, and selection of signalling pathways. Stochasticity originates from the fact that the relative statistical uncertainty for the system state is inversely proportional to the square root of the system size, i. e. the number of elements or molecules. As a result, with smaller numbers of interacting molecules, fluctuations become increasingly noticeable. Due to the uncertainty of knowing when a reaction occurs and which reaction it might be, this form of stochasticity is also called *intrinsic* stochasticity, as opposed to *extrinsic* stochasticity which results from environmental effects. Here, only intrinsic stochasticity is considered.

In order to model intrinsic noise, we use the stochastic simulation algorithm (SSA) of Gillespie [14]. The SSA represents a nonlinear discrete Markov process, $X(t)$, whose elements represent the number of molecules of molecular species in a well-mixed system at time t (see Sec. 3). Since the dynamical behaviour of chemical systems can be very different in the ODE regime (where we deal with very large numbers of molecules neglecting the stochastic nature of their interactions) from the SSA regime, it is important to see how certain dynamical behaviour can evolve when there are only small numbers of certain key molecules. By taking this stochastic nature into account, this can be considered to be a more realistic scenario. Examples of different dynamical behaviours between deterministic continuous and stochastic discrete versions of a model can be found in [6,15]. Specifically, the deterministic model of blood testosterone levels in [15] shows a globally stable fixed point while its discrete stochastic counterpart shows sustained oscillations. The repressilator designed in [6] behaves in an oscillatory fashion in both regimes. However, stochastic simulations of this system exhibit large variabilities in oscillations. These and other studies confirm the relevance of considering stochasticity in modelling and analysis of biochemical systems.

In this contribution genetic networks are modelled as reaction systems. The underlying model is explained in the following section.

2   The Reaction Model

In this reaction model inspired by the work of François and Hakim [8], a genetic network is defined by a set of species (genes, mRNAs, proteins and complexes such as gene-protein bindings or protein complexes) and *elementary, irreversible* chemical reactions (first–order reactions, second–order reactions and homodimer formations) governing their interactions. That is, each reaction has associated reaction substrates, products and the specific rate constant. One or more elementary reactions are combined in *master* reactions which constitute the building blocks of the genetic network and correspond to biologically meaningful processes (cf. Table 1). The following seven biological (master) reactions are modelled:

1. Transcription and translation: a new gene, its mRNA, and the corresponding protein are added to the genetic network model. Elementary reactions for the basal transcription, translation, mRNA degradation, and protein degradation are generated. Unlike the reaction model in [8], transcription and translation are modelled as separate reactions.

Table 1. Set of master reactions that are the building blocks of the genetic networks. Lowercase letters followed by two underscores, such as $a\_\_$, represent genes with unbound regulatory sites. The corresponding mRNA is indicated such as in a_{mRNA}. The associated capitalized letters (A,B, etc.) represent the proteins produced by the associated genes. Protein complexes are represented using colons (i.e. a protein complex composed of proteins A and B is represented by $A{:}B$). When a promoter P is bound to an unbound gene $a\_\_$ the binding is denoted $aP\_$. The case of a repressor R bound to $aP\_$ is denoted as aPR. Each reaction is specified by a reaction rate constant that is ignored in this representation.

No.	Master Reaction	Single Reactions
1	Transcription and translation	$a\_\_ \rightarrow a\_\_ + a_{\mathrm{mRNA}}$ $a_{\mathrm{mRNA}} \rightarrow a_{\mathrm{mRNA}} + A$ $a_{\mathrm{mRNA}} \rightarrow \emptyset$ $A \rightarrow \emptyset$
2	Regulation	$a\_\_ + P \rightarrow aP\_$ $aP\_ \rightarrow a\_\_ + P$ $aP\_ \rightarrow aP\_ + a_{\mathrm{mRNA}}$ $aP\_ + R \rightarrow aPR$ $aPR \rightarrow aP\_ + R$
3	Protein modification	$A \rightarrow A^*$ $A^* \rightarrow \emptyset$
4	Dimerization	$A + B \rightarrow A{:}B$ $A{:}B \rightarrow A + B$
5	Partial degradation	$A{:}B \rightarrow A$
6	Catalytic degradation	$A + B \rightarrow A$
7	Partial cat. degradation	$AB + C \rightarrow A$

2. Regulation: transcriptional regulation is based on Goutsias' simplified model of transcriptional regulation of the bacteriophage λ repressor protein [16]. Each gene has two regulatory binding sites, R_1 and R_2. Binding of a transcription factor at R_1 activates transcription for every non-zero reaction rate, whereas binding at R_2 excludes any transcriptional activity and hence, represses transcription. In addition, binding of a transcription factor at R_2 requires R_1 to be occupied by another factor.
3. Protein modification: a single protein or protein complex reacts leading to an altered version of the original species (e.g. phosphorylation).
4. Dimerization: two proteins / protein complexes form a compound product.
5. Partial degradation: a protein complex degrades such that a constituent protein is the degradation product.
6. Catalytic degradation: one protein / protein complex catalyses degradation of another protein / protein complex.
7. Partial catalytic degradation: in the case of protein complexes, this reaction is a catalytic degradation where one of the proteins (or sub–complexes) being part of the complex is also the reaction product.

3 Stochastic Simulation

To analyse and evaluate the dynamics of regulatory networks given in the reaction model described above, we use Gillespie's stochastic simulation algorithm [14]. This is a method for *exact* simulation of biochemical systems that are assumed to be homogeneous and well-mixed within a constant volume.

In the following we briefly describe the functioning of the SSA according to [17]: Let the biochemical system consist of $N \geq 1$ molecular species $\{S_1, \ldots, S_N\}$ that chemically interact through $M \geq 1$ reaction channels $\{R_1, \ldots, R_M\}$. The system state at time t is described by a vector $X(t) \equiv (X_1(t), \ldots, X_N(t))^T$ where $X_i(t)$ is the number of molecules of species i at time t. Let $X(t_0) = X_0$ be the initial state. For each $j = 1, \ldots, M$ we can define the *propensity function* a_j for reaction R_j such that $a_j(X)dt$ is the probability that given $X(t) = X$, one reaction R_j will occur somewhere in the system in the next infinitesimal time interval $[t, t + dt)$. The *state-change* or *stoichiometric vector* ν_j specifies the update of the system state when reaction R_j occurred. This is defined by ν_{ji} for $i = 1, \ldots, M$, which is the change in the number of S_i molecules produced by one R_j reaction. Our SSA implementation simulates the time evolution of a system according to the *direct method*: two independent samples r_1 and r_2 of the uniform random variable $\mathbf{U}(0, 1)$ are drawn consecutively. The length of the time interval $[t, t + \tau)$ is given by

$$\tau = \frac{1}{a_0(X(t))} \ln(\frac{1}{r_1}),$$

where

$$a_0(X(t)) = \sum_{j=1}^{M} a_j(X(t))$$

is the sum of all propensities. The specific reaction R_j occurring in $[t, t + \tau)$ is determined by the index j satisfying

$$\sum_{j'=1}^{j-1} a_{j'}(X(t)) < r_2 a_0(X(t)) \leq \sum_{j'=1}^{j} a_{j'}(X(t)).$$

Table 2 specifies the propensity functions and non-zero entries of the state-change vectors for the three elementary reaction types: the first and second order reaction and homodimer formation (cf. Sec. 2). As the SSA becomes computationally intensive for systems with a large number of reaction channels and/or fast reactions due to large reaction rates and/or large numbers of molecules, we limit our model to small numbers of species with small population size. In fact, we keep the number of genes/mRNA/protein creations fixed and limit the number of reactions creating new species. In addition, in order to avoid "unending" calculations, the algorithm stops simulation if the reciprocal value of the summed propensities (a_0) falls below a predefined threshold (e. g. 10^{-8}). Methods to accelerate the SSA while maintaining a reasonable accuracy such as the τ-leap method, the midpoint-τ-leap method [17] or binomial leap methods [18]

Table 2. For the three types of elementary reactions we determine the propensity functions and non-zero entries of the state-change vectors for the present state $X(t) = X$. c_j is the reaction rate constant of the respective reaction.

Reaction	Propensity Function	Stoichiometric Coefficients
First order reaction $S_k \xrightarrow{c_j} S_l$	$a_j = c_j * X_k$	$\nu_{jk} = -1, \nu_{jl} = 1$
Second order reaction $S_k + S_l \xrightarrow{c_j} S_m$ with $S_k \neq S_l$	$a_j = c_j * X_k * X_l$	$\nu_{jk} = \nu_{jl} = -1, \nu_{jm} = 1$
Homodimer formation $S_k + S_k \xrightarrow{c_j} S_l$	$a_j = c_j * X_k * (X_k - 1)/2$	$\nu_{jk} = -2, \nu_{jl} = 1$

are not used as they allow all the reaction channels to fire within each time step with a certain frequency.

4   The GP System

Here we use a GP–based algorithm to evolve genetic networks that obtain sustained oscillations in an arbitrarily chosen protein or mRNA. Typical GP algorithms use tree–based encodings [19,20]. This allows an individual solution to be parsed into an equation where order of operations is important. However, this encoding is inappropriate for this application since the order in which reactions are triggered is chosen randomly. Instead, we choose a set–based encoding scheme where each individual is represented by a set of biochemical reactions. This *reaction-* or *set-based* GP approach is very similar (but not equivalent) to a GP-approach based on algorithmic chemistries [21] which, unlike our approach acts on instruction multisets and aims to create functioning algorithms.

Each individual initially starts with two gene (+ mRNA + protein) creation reactions (reaction 1) and three other master reactions. This is not essential for evolution but complies with our intention of studying small regulatory systems consisting of two genes. The individual master reactions (2 to 7) listed in Section 2 are added to an individual through subsequent mutation steps. Reactions of type 1 cannot be added to genetic circuits during evolution. When a reaction is added to the network this may introduce a new product. Therefore, its list of species, i.e. proteins and bindings, is updated. Reaction rates are uniformly drawn between 0 and 1 and reactants are randomly chosen from the list of suitable reactants while avoiding the generation of duplicate reactions. Other mutation operations involve deletions of reactions and modification of reaction rates. The deletion of a reaction eventually includes the deletion of the product introduced by this reaction and of all other reactions using the product as a substrate. Reaction rates are modified by multiplication with a random number from $U[0, 2]$. At the beginning of each evolutionary run, the initial concentrations of proteins and protein complexes are randomly chosen from $\{1, 2, \ldots, 10\}$ and remain fixed for the entire evolution.

Recognizing sustained oscillations from noisy signals is the crucial point in our evolution. The individual's fitness is calculated by simulating the corresponding reaction system over a predefined simulation time using the SSA. In a second step, the resulting trajectory of length N for a specified species is assessed according to its oscillatory behaviour. This is accomplished by applying the Fast Fourier Transform. A rather simple and coarse indicator for oscillatory behaviour is the ratio of the summed magnitude over the first $N/2 + 1$ Fourier values, M_{sum}, to the maximum magnitude within a predefined frequency range (e.g. $1/N \ldots 1/4$), M_{max}. In summary, the fitness value is calculated as $1 - M_{max}/M_{sum} + 1/M_{max}$.

Stochasticity in the outcome of the fitness evaluation is a problem that must be dealt with: a trajectory (resulting from an SSA run) may show a certain behaviour but another simulation may be different due to the different stochastic path. To get a reliable result we perform several simulations. Calculating an "average" trajectory from the resulting single trajectories and performing fitness evaluation on this mean behaviour would be misleading since the average trajectory might not match any single trajectory. Therefore, we calculate the mean fitness over all SSA runs.

The selection method driving evolutionary dynamics is a simple $(\mu + \mu)$ strategy: each individual generates one offspring by performing two mutations on its own copy; the best μ out of 2μ individuals build the new generation. The generational GP algorithm is implemented as a synchronous parallel GP using MPI (message passing interface). Evolution is terminated if the number of generations without fitness improvement exceeds a certain threshold. Table 3 lists the most important parameters and their values used in evolutionary runs.

Table 3. These are some exemplary parameter settings of our GP system. With these settings we evolved the genetic network shown in Fig. 1.

Parameter	Value
no. of SSA runs (for each individual)	20
length of (SSA) simulation (in time units)	2048
GP termination threshold (in generations)	100
population size	100
max. no. of master reactions:	
gene/mRNA/protein creation	2
regulation	2
protein modification	2
dimerization	3
partial degradation	2
catalytic degradation	2
partial catalytic degradation	2
mutation probabilities:	
add reaction	0.1
delete reaction	0.1
modify rate constant	0.5

5   Preliminary Results

Here we present two evolved genetic networks showing noisy oscillatory dynamics. They are good representatives of other evolved networks featuring noisy oscillatory behaviour resulting from a total of 50 GP runs. So far, we have not focused on the performance of the evolution itself. However, the evolved solutions were usually generated in the first 150 generations. Figure 1(a) shows a regulatory genetic network that utilizes the regulation (master) reaction (cf. Table 1). This exerts negative feedback on the transcription and translation of gene a whenever protein A binds to the regulatory site R_2, thus repressing the transcription activated by the binding of dimer AB at R_1. The Figures 2(a) and 2(b) show the resulting dynamics for a single simulation run.

A second genetic regulatory network is depicted in Figure 1(b). This network generates a less regular form of oscillation in the concentration of protein A

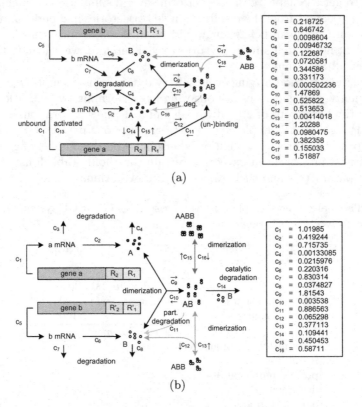

(a)

(b)

Fig. 1. Schematic representation of two evolved genetic networks exhibiting noisy oscillatory dynamics. (a) A core element in this genetic network that shows a regular, sustained oscillation in protein A concentration (cf. Fig. 2(a)) is the negative autoregulation of gene a. (b) This network comes without the regulation reaction but still shows some form of oscillatory dynamics in the concentrations of protein A (cf. Fig. 2(c)). Apparently, post-translational modifications are sufficient for generating pulsed signals.

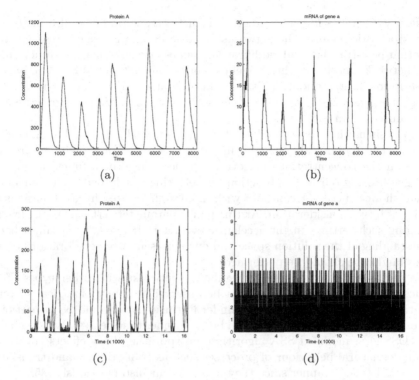

Fig. 2. Simulation results showing the concentration dynamics of protein A and a mRNA of the genetic regulatory networks in Figure 1(a) (a,b) and 1(b) (c,d)

(cf. Figure 2(c)). It does so without utilizing any direct regulation reactions (cf. Table 1) but by solely using post-translational modifications. A similar network based only on post-translational reactions that exhibits a sustained oscillation in the ODE model was also reported in [8]. In this model, however, one protein complex is constantly produced without being consumed. The Figures 2(c) and 2(d) depict the concentration dynamics of protein A and a mRNA. The dynamics of protein A are controlled by only a few other molecules that occasionally initiate the production of protein A. This leads to a short burst in the molecular concentration that appears quite regular. Note that all evolved networks were simulated several times to verify sustained oscillatory behaviour. Moreover, the corresponding ODE models of the networks in Figure 1 do not show oscillatory behaviour which underpins the necessity of stochastic simulation.

6   Discussions and Suggestions for Future Work

In this contribution, we present a GP approach for evolving genetic regulatory networks. Unlike others evolutionary approaches [5,8] we model those networks as sets of elementary reactions based on simple enzyme kinetics and simulate the network using Gillespie's exact SSA. We showed that evolution of noisy oscillatory dynamics in genetic regulatory networks is practical also in the discrete, stochastic regime. The networks found in [8] and the ones presented here show that post-translational modifications can be crucial to network function. As such, network function in this model cannot be understood by focusing only on transcriptional interactions. This is an important consideration for researchers in the bioinformatics community since such post-translational interactions are often omitted from such models.

In our simulations, the number of genes was fixed but can be changed to evolve specific dynamical behaviour in larger networks. For evolving desired dynamics in the concentrations of several species, the fitness function must be redesigned. Using our fitness function for detecting oscillatory behaviour in one protein showed success. Evolutions with more sophisticated fitness functions are worthy of future consideration. At this point, parameter settings are heuristics. Changing such settings might accelerate evolution. In order to obtain a better understanding of the solution space and our representation, explorations on the fitness landscape should be performed.

We also plan to evolve genetic regulatory networks with other types of dynamics. Since bistable behaviour can be observed in many biological systems, evolution of genetic toggle switches under intrinsic noise would be of particular interest [22]. An additional step would be to consider time delays. By using delay-SSA (DSSA), a modified SSA algorithm incorporating delay effects [23,24], we can model natural behaviour of processes such as transcription and translation in a more detailed manner since they do not occur instantaneously [25].

This contribution shows how methods from evolutionary computation can be used to achieve improved models of genetic regulatory networks, a better understanding of regulation in cells, the finding of functional design principles and the search for novel genetic networks.

Acknowledgements

KB would like to thank the Australian Research Council for funding via his Federation Fellowship. DK was supported by the National Science and Engineering Research Council of Canada PGS-D3. WB has been supported by NSERC under grant RGPIN 283304-04.

References

1. Kobayashi, H., Kaern, M., Chung, K., Gardner, T.S., Cantor, C.R., Collins, J.J.: Programmable cells: Interfacing natural and engineered gene networks. Proc. Natl. Acad. Sci. **101(22)** (2004) 8414–8419
2. Isaacs, F.J., Hasty, J., Cantor, C.R., Collins, J.J.: Prediction and measurement of an autoregulatory genetic module. Proc. Natl. Acad. Sci. **100**(13) (2003) 7714–7719
3. Gardner, T.S., Cantor, C.R., Collins, J.J.: Construction of genetic toggle switch in *escherichia coli*. Nature **403**(6767) (2000) 339–342
4. Guet, C.C., Elowitz, M.B., Hsing, W., Leibler, S.: Combinatorial synthesis of genetic networks. Science **296** (2002) 1466–1470

5. Mason, J., Linsay, P.S., Collins, J.J., Glass, L.: Evolving complex dynamics in electronic models of genetic networks. Chaos **14(3)** (2004) 707–715
6. Elowitz, M.B., Leibler, S.: A synthetic oscillatory network of transcriptional regulators. Nature **403**(6767) (2000) 335–338
7. Yokobayashi, Y., Weiss, R., Arnold, F.H.: Directed evolution of a genetic circuit. Proc. Natl. Acad. Sci. **99**(26) (2002) 16587–16591
8. François, P., Hakim, V.: Design of genetic networks with specified functions by evolution *in silico*. Proc. Natl. Acad. Sci. **101**(2) (2004) 580–585
9. Kuo, P.D., Banzhaf, W., Leier, A.: Network topology and the evolution of dynamics in an artificial genetic regulatory network model created by whole genome duplication and divergence. BioSystems (2006) In press.
10. McAdams, H.H., Arkin, A.: Stochastic mechanisms in gene expression. Proc. Natl. Acad. Sci. **94**(3) (1997) 814–819
11. Arkin, A., Ross, J., McAdams, H.H.: Stochastic kinetic analysis of developmental pathway bifurcation in phage λ–infected Escherichia coli cells. Genetics **149**(4) (1998) 1633–1648
12. Elowitz, M.B., Levine, A.J., Siggia, E.D., Swain, P.S.: Stochastic gene expression in a single cell. Science **297**(5584) (2002) 1183–1186
13. Hasty, J., Collins, J.J.: Translating the noise. Nature Genetics **31**(1) (2002) 13–14
14. Gillespie, D.T.: Exact stochastic simulation of coupled chemical reactions. J. Phys. Chem. **81**(25) (1977) 2340–2361
15. Heuett, W.J., Qian, H.: A stochastic model of oscillatory blood testoterone levels. To appear in Bulletin for Mathematical Biology (2005)
16. Goutsias, J.: Quasiequilibrium approximation of fast reaction kinetics in stochastic biochemical systems. J. Chem. Phys. **122**(184102) (2005) 1–15
17. Gillespie, D.T.: Approximate accelerated stochastic simulation of chemically reacting systems. J. Chem. Phys. **115**(4) (2001) 1716–1733
18. Tian, T., Burrage, K.: Binomial leap methods for simulating stochastic chemical kinetics. J. Chem. Phys. **121**(21) (2004) 10356–10364
19. Koza, J.R.: Genetic Programming. MIT press (1992)
20. Banzhaf, W., Francone, F.D., Keller, R.E., Nordin, P.: Genetic programming: an introduction. Morgan Kaufmann (1998)
21. Lasarczyk, C.W.G., Banzhaf, W.: An algorithmic chemistry for genetic programming. In Keijzer, M., Tettamanzi, A., Collet, P., Tomassini, M., van Hemert, J., eds.: Proceedings of the 8th European Conference on Genetic Programming. Volume 3447 of LNCS., Springer (2005) 1–12
22. Tian, T., Burrage, K.: Stochastic models for regulatory networks of the genetic toggle switch. Proc. Natl. Acad. Sci. (2005) Submitted.
23. Barrio, M., Burrage, K.: Oscillatory regulation of hes1: Discrete stochastic delay modelling and simulation. PLoS Computational Biology (2005) Submitted.
24. Bratsun, D., Volfson, D., Tsimring, L.S., Hasty, J.: Delay-induced stochastic oscillations in gene regulation. Proc. Natl. Acad. Sci. **102**(41) (2005) 14593–14598
25. Monk, N.A.M.: Oscillatory expression of Hes1, p53, and NF-kappaB driven by transcriptional time delays. Curr. Biol. **13**(16) (2003) 1409–1413

Information-Dependent Switching
of Identification Criteria in a Genetic
Programming System for System Identification

Thomas Buchsbaum and Siegfried Vössner

Department of Engineering and Business Informatics,
Graz University of Technology, Kopernikusgasse 24/III,
A-8010 Graz, Austria
{Buchsbaum, Voessner}@tugraz.at
http://www.mbi.tugraz.at

Abstract. Genetic Programming (GP) can be used to identify the non-linear differential equations of dynamical systems. If, however, the fitness function is chosen in a classical way, the optimization will not work very well. In this article, we explain the reasons for the failure of the GP approach and present a solution strategy for improving performance. Using more than one identification criterion (fitness function) and switching based on the information content of the data enable standard GP algorithms to find better solutions in shorter times. A computational example illustrates that identification criteria switching has a bigger influence on the results than the choice of the GP parameters has.

1 Introduction

System identification is about building models from experimental data [8], [11]. The system identification loop includes the design of experiments, data collection, definition of a model set, selection of a criterion of fit, and the calculation and validation of the model. Prior knowledge can be incorporated to improve the efficiency of each step. GP can be utilized for identifying models ranging from black-box symbolic regression models up to strongly-typed, dimensionally aware expressions [9].

Rodriguez-Vazquez et al. used GP to identify structure, model order, and parameters of a NARMAX (Nonlinear AutoRegressive Moving Average with eXogenous inputs) model [13]; Koza [10] showed that GP is able to find solutions to ordinary differential equations (ODEs). Burgess [2] also investigated approaches for ODE solutions. Gray et al. [6] used a GP approach to identify a symbolic expression, which was part of the ODE system of a coupled water tank system and which had physical significance. Babovic et al. [1] used GP for ecological modeling. Time series approximation using GP generated ODEs was another worthwhile application of Evolutionary Computation [3].

Our focus is the identification of mechanical systems, for example, aircrafts. Mechanical systems are commonly and very efficiently represented by means of

P. Collet et al. (Eds.): EuroGP 2006, LNCS 3905, pp. 300–309, 2006.

differential equations. However, available GP methodologies do not seem to be sophisticated enough to handle complex problems with sufficient performance. There are still problems and open questions: Babovic et al. [1] showed that for complex systems a simple output error criterion does not allow the GP algorithm to find a good solution. They could improve the performance by incorporating a measure of mutual sensitivity.

In our approach, we generalize this idea: by applying different identification criteria, performance can be increased dramatically even if the data which the criteria work on are not available from the data sets and have to be approximated from other data.

In section 2 we will give an overview of time-domain identification criteria. Section 3 explains the reasons for GP's failure and introduces a system identification concept for GP. In section 4 we will present conditions for automated identification criterion switching. The computational example in section 5 will serve as a proof of concept. A conclusion follows.

2   Time-Domain Identification Criteria

Consider the following 2nd order system:

$$\dot{y} = v$$
$$\dot{v} = a = f(y, v, u) \,, \tag{1}$$

where $\dot{}$ means differentiation with respect to the time t. The variables y and v are called *altitude* and *velocity*. The variable $u(t)$ is a time-dependent *control* variable (control input). The function f could also depend on t explicitly in the more general case. Now we are seeking an approximation to the acceleration $a(y, v, u)$, called $\hat{a}$, given a set of (noisy) measurement data.

Given some initial conditions (taken from the first records of the data sets) and a specific control input u, a velocity $\hat{v}$ and an altitude $\hat{y}$ can be computed using numerical ODE integration methods. Following the *output error approach*, the model output is compared to the system's output:

$$\left\| \tilde{y} - \iint \hat{a} dt^2 \right\| \,, \tag{2}$$

where $\tilde{y}(t_i) = y(t_i) + \varepsilon(t_i)$ is the discrete-time data used to run the identification process (noisy (preprocessed) measurement data). As function norm the summation over all squared errors for the whole data set or the mean square error could be used. A disadvantage of the altitude output error approach is its algorithmic complexity: there is a high computational cost for solving the ODE numerically stable and with sufficient precision.

If velocity variables are used to compare model output with system data, algorithmic complexity is reduced:

$$\left\| \tilde{v} - \int \hat{a} dt \right\| \,, \tag{3}$$

where $\tilde{v}(t_i)$ is either measured (and preprocessed) or calculated from $\tilde{y}(t_i)$ by means of numerical differentiation, denoted by $\Delta\tilde{y}/\Delta t$.

Following the *equation error approach*, the modeled acceleration, $\hat{a}$, is directly compared to the system's acceleration values, $\tilde{a}(t_i)$, which are measured or approximated (numerical differentiation of $\tilde{v}(t_i)$):

$$\|\tilde{a} - \hat{a}\| \ . \tag{4}$$

Using this identification criterion, no ODE solving is required at all.

3   Identification Concept for a Genetic Programming System

In a GP system, two problems arise from using the output error approach: There are high computational costs for solving the ODEs and there is high sensitivity of the phenotype to modifications in the genotype. As an example, consider an acceleration a that leads to a trajectory y. Let D be a simple constant disturbance. The resulting trajectory is

$$\iint (a + D)dt^2 = y + \iint Ddt^2 = y + \frac{Dt^2}{2} \ . \tag{5}$$

Therefore, small changes in the acceleration may lead to big changes in the trajectories, especially if time periods are long. Oscillations, on the other hand, are filtered. The search space topology depends on the chosen identification criterion. A good evolutionary step towards a good –but not yet perfect– model structure may lead to a bad fitness value and is therefore eliminated from the population with high probability.

This problem can be avoided by using the equation error approach. If data (in our case: acceleration data) is not available, it can be produced by numerical differentiation of velocity or altitude data. In this case, systematic errors are induced because of the finite time intervals. Noise may be amplified and signal-to-noise ratio may be reduced, depending on the chosen differentiation method. As a result, the signal contains less information than the original (for example, altitude) signal. A second derivative decreases the information content further.

3.1   Reasoning for Switching the Identification Criterion

Using the results from above, a strategy for choosing the most appropriate identification criterion can be formulated: Because of reduced computational complexity, the equation error criterion is preferred to the velocity output criterion, which itself is preferred to the altitude (or trajectory) output error criterion. When the information content of the data used with a certain criterion is exploited and further training would only lead to approximating noise (over-fitting), the criterion needs to be changed. The system identification algorithm has to switch to a criterion which works on data with better signal-to-noise ratio (higher information content), if such data is available.

3.2   Algorithm

Based on the argumentation, the basic concept for the algorithmic structure looks like the following:

1. Select criterion/data with least computational costs with respect to optimization (algorithmic complexity)
2. Use it for model building as long as there is useful information content
3. If stopping criterion is fulfilled: stop identification procedure
4. If not: Select other criterion/data with more information content and lowest possible algorithmic complexity
5. Continue with step 2.

4   The Switching Criterion

In this paper we present a switching criterion based on an approach adopted from neural network learning theory: the *early stopping method* [7], [12].

Early stopping can be applied when iterative optimization methods are used to estimate models from noisy data. Instead of performing training (or evolution) until convergence, training is stopped before over-fitting occurs. A validation set is used to monitor the current solution's (or population's) generalization capability. A performance drop on the validation set indicates a drop in generalization and the possible onset of over-fitting.

During GP evolution the following statistical cross-validation data is used: average validation fitness, population's best validation fitness, and the validation fitness of the best (with respect to the training fitness) individual. They will be referred to as *validation variables* in the following. An indicator for stagnation of the evolution (with respect to the expected test performance) is computed using the following approach, which is applied from an early generation on:

1. Calculate the slopes of the linear regressions based on the five most recent values of each of the validation variables
2. If all (three) slopes are smaller than or equal to zero, increase the indication counter
3. When the indication counter reaches the value two, switch to a criterion that uses more informative data

These rules were derived from data analysis of GP runs with different realizations of noise and different GP parameters. The use of regression is necessary since the validation variables tend to oscillate during evolution.

5   Computational Example

5.1   The Parachute Model

For creating measurement date, we consider a simple model of a sky diver with a parachute falling through the air. The force of gravity accelerates the parachute towards earth. On the other hand, air resistance causes a drag force acting in the opposite direction of the velocity. The drag force is assumed proportional to the parachutes squared speed. The size of this drag force can be controlled using a control input u, which can be thought of changing the parachute's cross section area A. The considered differential equation is the following:

$$\dot{y} = v$$
$$\dot{v} = a = -g + \frac{1}{2m}c_w \rho u A v^2 \,, \tag{6}$$

where y is the object's altitude and v its velocity; m is the mass of the sky diver and parachute, g is the acceleration of gravity, ρ the air's density, c_w is the shape dependent drag coefficient, A is the cross-section area normal to the velocity, and v the parachute's velocity. The equation is valid as long as v is negative (parachute moves towards earth).

5.2   Training, Validation, and Test Sets

Given a set of time-varying input signals $u(t_i)$ the response of the parachute model (altitude $y(t_i)$) is calculated using a forth order Runge-Kutta method with 20 iterations per data interval. For training and validation sets Gaussian white noise is added to the altitude values, see Table 1. Altitude data is differentiated numerically using quadratic regression of five data points (*smoothed local differentiation*) to generate approximated velocity information. Numerical differentiation of the velocity gives an approximation of the acceleration acting on the sky diver. The model parameters used are: $m = 80$ kg, $g = 9.81$ m/s^2, $\rho = 1$ kg/m^3, $A = 25$ m^2, $c_w = 0.34$. Fig. 1 shows the resulting GP input data.

Table 1. Standard errors (in m) of the stationary Gaussian white noise (zero mean) used to generate the training and validation cases

Signal	Standard error (σ) of noise
Training case C, altitude	0.01
Training case D, altitude	0.1
Training case F, altitude	0.08
Validation case A, altitude	0.01
Validation case G, altitude	0.1

5.3   Experiments and Experimental Settings

Six experiments are performed with 30 runs each. Two experiments use the altitude output criterion; two experiments use the acceleration equation error approach, and two experiments use the criterion switching approach. Acceleration equation error, velocity output error, and altitude output error criteria are utilized for the switching runs. The GP system is run with two different GP

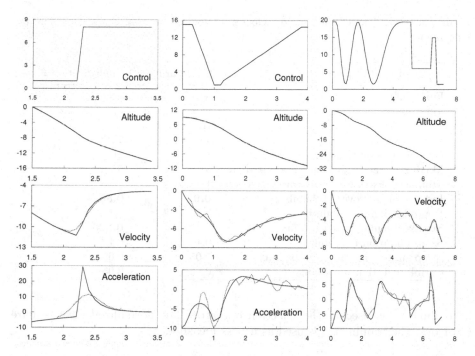

Fig. 1. The GP training set consists of three cases C, D, and F (from left to right), which depend on the control input $u(t)$ (first row). There is noise added to the system's outputs (solid lines) to generate altitude values $\tilde{y}(t)$ (dotted lines, second row). Velocities $\tilde{v}(t)$ (third row) and accelerations $\tilde{a}(t)$ (forth row) are computed from the noisy altitude by smoothed local differentiation.

Table 2. Identification criteria used for the computational experiments

Experiments	Identification Criterion
Altitude	$\left\| \tilde{y} - \iint \hat{a}\,dt^2 \right\|$
Acceleration	$\left\| \frac{\Delta^2 \tilde{y}}{\Delta t^2} - \hat{a} \right\|$
Switching	all identification criteria

parameter sets (see parameters section below). Whenever ODE integration is necessary, a forth order Runge-Kutta is used (10 iterations/interval). See section 4 for details about the applied switching criterion. Table 2 gives an overview of the utilized identification criteria.

Genetic Programming, Parameter Settings, and Fitness Function. For running the experiments, Open BEAGLE [4], [5] –a C++ Evolutionary Computation (EC) framework– is used. A tree representation is used to encode forces. Acceleration values are calculated by dividing the forces by the mass. Any experiment consists of 30 runs with different random number seed values. The major GP settings are shown in Table 3. Tournament selection (seven

Table 3. Overview of the major Genetic Programming settings used for the experiments

Name of the GP parameter	Configuration 1	Configuration 2
Function set	$+, -, *$	$+, -, *$
Terminal set	$u, x, v, m, g,$	$u, x, v, m, g,$
	$A, c_w, 1/2$	$A, c_w, 1/2$
Population size	**1000**	**7750**
Maximum allowed depth of trees	**8**	**10**
Maximum depth for newly initialized trees	5	5
Minimum depth for newly initialized trees	1	1
Individual crossover probability	**0.9**	**0.85**
Reproduction probability	0.1	0.1
Standard mutation probability	**0**	**0.325**
Swap mutation probability	0.1	0.1
Swap subtree mutation probability	0.05	0.05
Shrink mutation probability	0.05	0.05

individuals) was used as the selection operator. The normalized mean square error over the training set is used as fitness measure.

5.4   Results

Fig. 2 shows the performance of the population's best individuals on the test set. The fitness values of the altitude runs increase very slowly. Acceleration runs improve very fast in the beginning but stagnate afterwards because of low information content in the training data. The switching concept outperforms

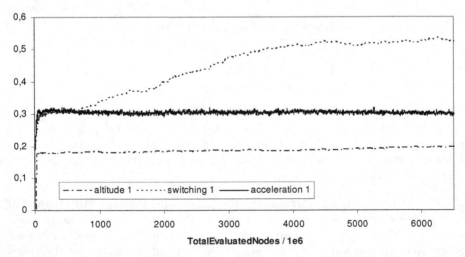

Fig. 2. Test performance: Average of the population's maximum test fitness values over 30 runs using GP Configuration 1

Table 4. Mean values, standard errors, and significance measures for altitude runs and switching runs, configuration 1

Evaluated nodes / 1e6	2,000	10,000	80,000
Altitude 1 average	0.184	0.206	0.276
Altitude 1 std.-error	0.019	0.096	0.191
Switch 1 average	0.399	0.536	0.669
Switch 1 std.-error	0.142	0.168	0.161
T-test p-value	3.20E-09	3.70E-12	7.90E-12

Table 5. Mean values, standard errors, and significance measures for acceleration runs and switching runs, configuration 1

Evaluated nodes / 1e6	2,000	10,000	17,000
Acceleration 1 average	0.295	0.301	0.299
Acceleration 1 std.-error	0.040	0.046	0.048
Switch 1 average	0.399	0.536	0.599
Switch 1 std.-error	0.142	0.168	0.147
T-test p-value	3.19E-04	1.34E-08	2.23E-12

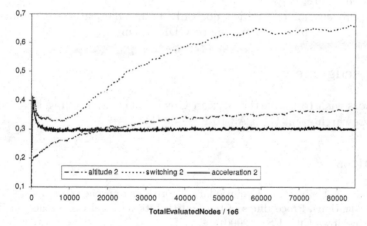

Fig. 3. Test performance: Average of the population's maximum test fitness values over 30 runs using GP Configuration 2. Above 2000e6 evaluated nodes, all differences (t-test) are significant.

altitude-only and acceleration-only criteria significantly. Applying GP Configuration 2, similar results were obtained; see Fig. 3 for a plot.

6   Conclusion

In this article we introduced the idea of criteria switching for (evolutionary) system identification. For the automated switching procedure the necessary switching conditions were developed. It was shown that the application of the criterion switching influenced the system identification performance significantly. Although the applied switching condition was rather simple, the approach led to great results.

In the computational example, performance on the validation set was measured every generation. The frequency of these evaluations could be reduced to lower computation time. Evaluation speed could be optimized further using sophisticated switching criteria. For example, characteristics of the training fitness could be considered and specialized time series methods could be applied. We currently investigate conditions which use the validation value of the best (with respect to the training fitness) individual only and which do not need validation information of the whole population.

If prior knowledge is available about the accuracy of the signals (information content, systematic and statistical errors ...), this information can be used for defining switching events. In these cases, no validation computations would be necessary at all.

The better the quality of the acceleration signal is, the longer can the acceleration equation error criterion be used. Better differentiation methods (e.g., taking the control signal into account) and signal filtering could improve the approximation of unknown identification signals a lot and may be investigated separately in future.

This approach can be applied not only to mechanical systems but to any application that requires integrating or ODE solving.

Acknowledgements

The authors wish to thank the Styrian Government for funding this project as part of a research grant (GZ: A3-10 F 59-04/1).

References

1. Babovic, V., Keijzer, M.: Evolutionary algorithms approach to induction of differential equations. Proceedings of the Fourth International Conference on Hydroinformatics. Iowa City, USA (2000)
2. Burgess, G.: Finding Approximate Analytic Solutions To Differential Equations Using Genetic Programming. Salisbury, SA, 5108, Australia (1999)
3. Cao, H., Kang, L., Chen, Y.: Evolutionary Modeling of Ordinary Differential Equations for Dynamic Systems. Proceedings of the Genetic and Evolutionary Computation Conference. 2. Morgan Kaufmann, Orlando, Florida, USA (1999) 959-965
4. Gagne, C., Parizeau, M.: Open BEAGLE: A New C++ Evolutionary Computation Framework. (2002)
5. Gagne, C., Parizeau, M.: Open BEAGLE: A New Versatile C++ Framework for Evolutionary Computations. (2002)
6. Gray, G.J., Murray-Smith, D.J., Li, Y., Sharman, K.C., Weinbrenner, T.: Nonlinear model structure identification using genetic programming. Control Engineering Practice, 6. (1998) 1341-1352

7. Haykin, S.: Neural Networks - A Comprehensive Foundation. Second Edition. Prentice Hall International Inc., (1999) 215-217
8. Juang, J.N.: Applied system identification. Prentice-Hall, Inc., Upper Saddle River, NJ, USA (1994)
9. Keijzer, M., Babovic, V.: Dimensionally Aware Genetic Programming. Proceedings of the Genetic and Evolutionary Computation Conference. 2. Morgan Kaufmann, Orlando, Florida, USA (1999) 1069-1076
10. Koza, J.R.: Genetic programming: On the programming of computers by natural selection. MIT Press, Cambridge, Mass. (1992)
11. Ljung, L.: System Identification: Theory for the User (Second Ed.). Prentice-Hall, Inc., Upper Saddle River, NJ, USA (1998)
12. Nelles, O.: Nonlinear System Identification. Springer, Berlin (2001) 182-184
13. Rodriguez-Vazquez, K., Fonseca, C.M., Fleming, P.J.: Multiobjective Genetic Programming: A Nonlinear System Identification Application. Late Breaking Papers at the 1997 Genetic Programming Conference. Stanford Bookstore, Stanford University, CA, USA (1997) 207-212

Invariance of Function Complexity Under Primitive Recursive Functions

John R. Woodward

The University of Birmingham, Birmingham B15 2TT, UK
http://www.cs.bham.ac.uk/~jrw/

Abstract. Genetic Programming (GP) [1] often uses a tree form of a graph to represent solutions. An extension to this representation, Automatically Defined Functions (ADFs) [1] is to allow the ability to express modules. In [2] we proved that the complexity of a function is independent of the primitive set (function set and terminal set) if the representation has the ability to express modules. This is essentially due to the fact that if a representation can express modules, then it can effectively define its own primitives at a constant cost. This is reminiscent of the result that the complexity of a bit string is independent of the choice of Universal Turing Machine (UTM) (within an additive constant) [3], the constant depending on the UTM but not on the function.

The representations typically used in GP are not capable of expressing recursion, however a few researchers have introduced recursion into their representations. These representations are then capable of expressing a wider classes of functions, for example the primitive recursive functions (PRFs). We prove that given two representations which express the PRFs (and only the PRFs), the complexity of a function with respect to either of these representations is invariant within an additive constant. This is in the same vein as the proof of the invariants of Kolmogorov complexity [3] and the proof in [2].

1 Introduction

In much of Machine Learning, we aim to learn the underlying function given some sampled data points in an attempt to generalise from these observations in order to make predictions about novel data points [1, 3, 4]. If there are regularities in the data, then it can be compressed (i.e. represented in less space than the raw data). Some researchers equate compressing observed data with learning the underlying function [4].

To achieve function regression we need a representation to express the target function (e.g. a neural network or a polynomial). The choice of model is important and is guided by heuristics like Occam's Razor and minimum description length [3, 4]. Once we have picked a representation, the parameters of the model need to be found (i.e. the weights of the neural network or the coefficients of the polynomial). In some cases this can be done with analytic techniques, but where computationally tractable methods do not exist a different approach is needed.

P. Collet et al. (Eds.): EuroGP 2006, LNCS 3905, pp. 310–319, 2006.

GP is a method of searching the space of a given type of representation, where solutions are represented typically as tree structures (though other data structures have been used e.g. graphs, forests). For example, we could choose as our function set $\{x, x^2, ...x^n\}$. Alternatively we could choose

$$\{sin(x), sin(2x), ...sin(nx), ... cos(x), cos(2x), ...cos(nx)\}.$$

The choice of function set can prove critical to the performance of GP. We now consider expressing an arbitrary function using different function sets.

Polynomials. Given a set of data points we can represent them with a polynomial [5]. A polynomial of degree n is defined as $f_n^{poly}(x) = a_0 x^0 + a_1 x^1 + ... + a_{n-1} x^{n-1} + a_n x^n$ where x is the variable and a_is are coefficients, some of which may be zero. Ideally the polynomial will be a close fit to the data, and provide a good estimate of unseen data points, i.e. it provides close functional resemblance to the process which produced the data.

There are two extremes we need to be aware of when fitting data; under-fitting and over-fitting [4, 5]. If the polynomial is too simple, it will fail to capture the underlying function. Alternatively if the polynomial is too flexible, it can over-fit the data and learn the noise. A polynomial with n degrees of freedom can pass exactly through all n data points. Generally, the more degrees of freedom a polynomial has, the closer it can potentially fit the data.

Once we have decided the type of polynomial (e.g. $a_0 x^0 + a_1 x^1$), we can then calculate the values for a_0 and a_1, which best fit the data. It is an open question as to how to decide which model to fit the data. For example, how can we decide if $a_0 x^0 + a_1 x^1 + a_2 x^2$ is a better model than $a_{10} x^{10}$ for some given data?

Fourier series. Instead of choosing to represent our target function using polynomials, we could use a different basis. For example, one of the most common is to use trigonometric functions. Under certain conditions one can approximate a function $f(x)$ (we assume a period of 2π) $f_n^{trig}(x) = a_0/2 + a_1 sin(1x) + b_1 cos(1x) + ... + a_n sin(nx) + b_n cos(nx)$ where sin and cos are the trigonometric functions, x is the variable and a_i and b_i are coefficients. This sum is referred to as a trigonometric polynomial of degree n.

The problem is the following. If we are trying to approximate a function $f(x)$, it may be very easy to describe using $f^{poly}(x)$ in that it only requires a few coefficients. However if we use $f^{trig}(x)$, we may require many more coefficients, and the number of coefficients may affect how easy it is to learn the function.

For example representing the function sin only requires one coefficient if we are using a trigonometric basis. However, if we are using a polynomial basis this would require many terms depending on how closely we wanted to approximate the sin function. Conversely, there are functions which are easy to express using a polynomial basis, but difficult using a trigonometric basis.

The intuition behind the idea in this paper can be expressed with the following example. We may have a target function f we would like to approximate, $f(x) = 45sin(x) + 67cos(x)$. If we are using a trigonometric basis, this function is easy to express. However, if we wanted to express this function using a polynomial basis, this would require an infinite number of terms. We could begin writing this; $f(x) = 45(x - x^3/3! + x^5/5!...) + 67(1 - x^2/2! + x^4/4!...)$. If we are using standard tree based GP, we have no way to express this sort of regularity. In order to express this recursion is needed. We can express this as;

$$f(x) = 45s(x) + 67c(x) \text{ where}$$

$$s(x) = \sum_{i=0}^{n} x^{2i+1}/(2i+1)! \text{ and } c(x) = \sum_{i=0}^{n} x^{2i}/(2i)!$$

Now we can express the function f in a finite sized expression in terms of the polynomial basis, now we have the power to express iteration. In this way, any regularity that can be expressed in one basis is also expressible with another basis at constant cost of defining the functions which define the transformation from one basis to the other.

The outline of the remainder of this paper is as follows. In section 2 we review the literature regarding evolution of representations involving recursion. In section 3 we define the partial recursive functions and the PRFs. In section 4 we give some preliminary definitions used in section 5. We end the paper with a discussion and summary in sections 6 and 7.

2   Evolving Recursive Representations

In this section we review a number of papers which have used representations which use recursion. Some of the representations are equivalent to the PRFs and some are equivalent to the partial recursive functions.

Cramer [6], evolved a program to multiply two integers together. Initially he describes a language, PL, which consists of the following instruction set; INC v increments a variable v by 1. $ZERO$ v sets a var v to zero. $LOOP$ v $STAT$ performs the statement $STAT$ v times. $GOTO$ LAB jumps to the statement labelled LAB. While PL is Turing Equivalent, he is interested in a subset of PL, $PL - \{GOTO\}$ (i.e. PL without the $GOTO$ instruction). This new language, while no longer Turing Equivalent, is equivalent to the PRFs. He makes the point that programs written in this language are guaranteed to halt.

Brave [7] evolves programs with ADFs and a restricted form of recursion. He investigates the scalability of GP with programs with and without recursions and ADFs. He shows that as the size of the problem increases, the effort to find a solution with ADFs with recursion remains constant. Whereas basic GP scales linearly. We comment on this in section 6.

Koza [8] explored iteration with the Do Until DU operator. This operator takes two arguments; the first specifies what is to be iterated over, and the second specifies a condition which when satisfied will terminate the operation. He tackled a block stacking problem.

Yu [9] evolves modular recursive programs using a novel approach. She recognises the fact that, while recursion is a powerful reuse mechanism, it can loop forever and care must be taken (i.e. evolution may not give a base case which causes termination). She introduces implicit recursion where the terminating condition is incorporated into the expression so the computation will always terminate. She tackles the even-n-party problem and finds general solutions.

Spector [10] introduces a new language and acknowledges that *"it therefore usually makes sense to collect repeated code into subroutines that can be defined once and then used many times"*. A maximum runtime is placed on a computation to avoid the problem of non-terminating recursive code. Wong et. al [11], Yu [9] and Spector et. al [10] all evolve solutions to the even-n-parity problem.

Given a function represented by any of the representations described in section 2, we can guarantee that the complexity differs by at most a constant which depends on the representation but not on the function.

Work has also been done evolving representation which can express the partial recursive functions [12, 13]. See [14] for more references. One of the central themes of these works is the halting problem. We cannot tell ahead if a computation will halt or not. In all of these works an upper limit on the computation time is enforced, and if the program has not halted in this time, it is terminated.

3 Recursive Functions

It is constructive to consider recursive functions as this is the class of computable functions and therefore the class of functions which we can potentially evolve. An understanding of the theory of recursive functions may help us understand the evolution of Turing Equivalent representations better.

Functions made only from the basic operations and the operations of composition and recursion are called total recursive functions (i.e. they are total functions and therefore halt). Yu [9] and Cramer [6] evolved total recursive functions, (see section 2).

There are many models of computation which have been shown to be equivalent to Turing Machines. For example, see Cutland [15] (chapter 3, section 1) who lists 7 different approaches, including partial recursive functions, lambda definable functions and unlimited register machines. All of these models compute the class of functions called the partial recursive functions. Recursive functions can be expressed using three basic operations and three meta functions. The three basic function are successor (also known as increment), zero (also known as clear), and projection. The three meta functions are composition, recursion and minimisation, which can be used to construct new functions from previously defined functions. Functions made only from the basic operations of composition and recursion are called PRFs. A function is a total function if it has a defined output for all of its inputs. A function is a partial function if it has an undefined output for any of its inputs.

The basic operations are simple and consist of the following three operations: successor, zero and projection. The successor operation maps a number n to $n+1$ i.e. $S(n) = n+1$. The zero operation maps a number n to 0, i.e. $Z(n) = 0$. The projection is slightly different; given a list of n numbers and an integer i, we return the ith number in the list i.e. $P_i(x_1, ..., x_n) = x_i$ for $1 \le i \le n$.

Composition, also known as substitution, is a way of creating new functions. Given functions $f(x)$ and $g(x)$, a new function $h(x)$ can be constructed by composition $h(x) = f(g(x))$. This is the operation GP uses to build up more complicated functions from the function and terminal set. The composition of total functions results in a total function, i.e. if f and g are total then h is total.

In GP terminology, composition corresponds to ADFs [1]. We must be careful to distinguish between the situation in standard GP, which also uses composition, but each time a function $h(x) = f(g(x))$ is needed it must be defined again. Whereas, if ADFs are available $h(x)$ can be defined once and called when needed.

Given functions $f(x)$ and $g(x, y, z)$, a new function $h(x, y)$ can be constructed as follows; $h(x, 0) = f(x)$ (base case) and $h(x, y + 1) = g(x, y, h(x, y))$ (recursive case). The recursion of total functions results in a total function (i.e. if f and g are total then h is total). Hence given an algorithm written with the structure defined above, it is guaranteed to halt.

Given a function $f(x, y)$, the function $\mu y(f(x, y) = 0)$ is defined as the least y such that $f(x, z)$ is defined for all $z \leq y$, and $f(x, y) = 0$. Otherwise, if there is no such y it is undefined. It is due to the operation of minimisation that we encounter partial functions which correspond to non terminating programs.

4   Preliminary Definitions

In this section we give a number of definitions which are similar in nature to those in [2]. These definitions are needed for the proof in the following section.

Definition 1 (terminal set). *The terminal set t is the set of inputs to the program. These are typically problem variables and/or constants.*

Definition 2 (function set). *The function set f is the basic functions GP uses to construct more complex functions.*

In this set we assume two meta functions are present in the function set. The first is composition, C, the second is recursion, R. These are defined in section 3. These may be achieved by different implementations. There may be more than one of each of these primitives in a given primitive set, but we assume at least one of each. We also assume the base functions (or their equivalent) are present.

Definition 3 (primitive set). *The primitive set p is the union of the function set f and the terminal set f, i.e p = t ∪ f.*

These definitions are similar to those in [1] (section 5.1). The arity of a primitive is the number of inputs it takes. The only distinction between the function set and the terminal set is that all terminals have zero arity and functions have a non-zero arity. We will assume that the primitive sets can express the PRF class of functions.

Definition 4 (size). *The size of the instance of a PRF representation is the number of nodes it contains.*

Definition 5 (equally expressive). *Two primitive sets are equally expressive if they can express the same set of functions in finite size.*

Thus given two primitive sets p_1 and p_2, if each member of p_1 can be expressed in terms of p_2 and vice versa, then the two sets are equally expressive. In this paper we are only interested in primitive sets which express the PRFs.

While this definition tells us if two primitive sets are equally expressive or not, we need to know how to construct a given function in a new primitive set given the function expressed in an old primitive set. This is done using a dictionary.

Definition 6 (dictionary). *A dictionary is the collection of PRFs which express each member of p2 in terms of p1. The size of the dictionary must be finite.*

In other words, each member of the set $p1$ can be expressed in terms of $p2$. The existence of the pair of dictionaries $D_{p1,p2}$ and $D_{p2,p1}$ is a necessary and sufficient condition to imply that the primitive sets $p1$ and $p2$ are equally expressive.

Definition 7 (complexity). *The complexity of a function with respect to a PRF representation, is the size of the smallest PRF which can represent the function. The complexity of a function f with respect to a PRF primitive set p, is written as $C_p(f)$.*

Definition 8 (complexity of a dictionary). *The complexity of a dictionary $D_{p1,p2}$ is the size of the smallest dictionary which expresses the set of functions p_2 in terms of a PRF using primitive set p1. We write $K_{p1,p2}$ for the complexity of dictionary $D_{p1,p2}$. In general $K_{p1,p2} \neq K_{p2,p1}$.*

Definition 9 (translate primitive set). *Given a function expressed in terms of one primitive set p1, we can express the same function in terms of a second primitive set p2. The process of re-expressing the function in terms of p2 is called the translation of primitive set from p1 to p2.*

5 Theorems and Proofs

In this section we present 3 theorems regarding the complexity of a function when expressed using a PRF representation. We prove that the complexity of a set of functions is invariant under translation of primitive set, if we are using PRFs as our representation and the two primitive sets are equally expressive. We then go onto prove the tightest upper and lower bounds on the complexity of a function when expressed using a different primitive set.

Theorem 1 (complexity). *The complexity of a function under the PRF representation is invariant under translation of primitive set, within a constant $K_{p1,p2}$ (the complexity of the dictionary $D_{p1,p2}$) provided the primitive sets are equally expressive.*

$$C_{p2}(f) \leq C_{p1}(f) + K_{p1,p2}$$

Proof. Assume we have two primitive sets $p1 = \{f_1, f_2, ... f_n, C_1, R_1\}$ and $p2 = \{g_1, g_2, ... g_m, C_2, R_2\}$. where C_1 and C_2 are methods of expressing composition and R_1 and R_2 are methods of expressing recursion. Assuming $p1$ and $p2$ are equally expressive (i.e. they can express the PRF class of functions), the dictionaries $D_{p1,p2}$ and $D_{p2,p1}$ both exist. We can simulate the functions of one primitive set with the functions from the other primitive set. Thus, the set of functions $\{f_i\}$ (where i = 1 to n) can each be written in terms of primitive set $p2$, and the set of functions $\{g_j\}$ (where j = 1 to m) can each be written in terms of primitive set $p1$. We assume the sets of functions $\{f_i\}$ and $\{g_j\}$ are expressible as PRFs. As long as composition is a member of both of the primitive sets we can construct a primitive and refer to it when needed.

There are different ways of expressing iteration/recursion. For example, in $p1$, $C_1(n, f)$ could be the primitive `for(int i = 0; i < n; i++) {f}` while in $p2$, $C_2(n, f)$ could be the primitive `do n times {f}` And these can be shown to be equally expressive. Koza [8] uses a Do Until operator (DU (work) (predicate)).

In each of these primitive sets $p1$ and $p2$ we have only included one method of recursion, and one for composition. Other recursive methods could be included, but as long as we have one method of expressing recursion we can simulate other methods of expressing recursion at constant cost.

Given theorem 1, we can now ask ourselves if a smaller bound exists. We now show that a smaller constant does not exist.

Theorem 2 (tightest bound). $K_{p1,p2}$ *is the smallest bound we can place on the constant in theorem 1.*

Proof. Some functions will not depend on all of the primitives in a given primitive set, therefore these primitives do not need to be translated and do not need to be included in the dictionary. However in the worst cases, all of the primitives are required to be translated and the complete dictionary is needed. Therefore the smallest size of the bound is the complexity of the dictionary (i.e. the size of the smallest dictionary which translates all of the primitives).

Theorem 3 (lower bound). *Theorem 1 gives an upper bound. We can rearrange this equation to give a lower bound on complexity*

$$C_{p2}(f) \geq C_{p1}(f) - K_{p2,p1}$$

Proof. Consider the above equation (eq. 1). Consider the translation from primitive set $p2$ to primitive set $p1$ which gives the equation

$$C_{p1}(f) \leq C_{p2}(f) + K_{p2,p1}$$

then rearrange the equation

$$C_{p1}(f) - K_{p2,p1} \leq C_{p2}(f)$$

We can also say this is the tightest lower bound by an identical argument to that above. We can combine the above results into a single expression

$$C_{p1}(f) - K_{p2,p1} \leq C_{p2}(f) \leq C_{p1}(f) + K_{p1,p2}$$

and state that these bounds are the tightest obtainable.

6   Discussion

There are a number of interesting properties we can point out regarding PRFs. Let us take as an example the problem of expressing the solution to the even-n-parity problem as an illustration. A number of researchers have used this as a problem to test their systems [9, 10, 11]. If we use a traditional GP representation, each of the problem variables have to be addressed explicitly in the solution, i.e. $v_1, v_2, ..., v_n$, and these would appear as leaves on the tree of our solution. We would have to know at the start of the GP run how many variables we are dealing with. There is no way of addressing a general variable, i.e. the ith variable v_i. If, however, we have a system which can address this issue then we have the ability to express a general solution as we have in [9, 10, 11].

Another important point can also be addressed using the even-n-parity problem as an illustration. Imagine we were not interested in the general solution, but wanted to find the solution to the even-1000-parity problem. We could set up out GP system to learn to solve the problem with 1000 explicitly labelled inputs, i.e. $v_1, v_2, ..., v_{1000}$. Alternatively, we could learn the even-n-parity and learn on smaller instances of the problem e.g. even-2-parity and even-3-parity. This is precisely what Yu does, and manages to evolve a general solution using all $2^2 + 2^3$ test cases. Importantly, as Brave [7] points out, the minimal 'structural complexity' of solutions does not increase with problem size. This approach of evolving general solutions to a number of small sized instances of a problem in order to solve large instances of a problem is widely applicable (e.g. to image recognition problems or games).

In [2, 14] we proved that the complexity of a function is independent (within an additive constant) of the function set and terminal set provided the sets are equally expressive and the representation is capable of expressing modules (i.e. composition or ADFs). The constant does not depend on the function being expressed, only the primitive set being used. In [3] it is proved that the complexity of a bit string is invariant with respect to the model of computation (e.g an arbitrary UTM which is equivalent to the partial recursive functions). The complexity of a function and a bit string are analogous as a function is ultimately stored as a bit string in the computers memory. It therefore seems reasonable that a similar result should hold for PRFs. Indeed, in this paper we have proved that the complexity of a function is independent (within an additive constant) of the primitive set, provided it can express exactly the class of PRFs. Given these three results it would appear that if two representations are equally expressive, and have the ability to express composition (i.e. reuse of component parts), then this is a necessary and sufficient condition for the complexity of a function to be invariant, within an additive constant.

Brave [7] makes the point that small variations is the structure of a recursive program can lead to large changes in functionality and thus fitness. The fitness of an individual does not necessary reflect its proximity to a global solution. Teller [16] (appendix) also comments that the more expressive a representation is, in general, the more difficult it is to learn using that representation.

While the class of PRF is a proper subset of the class of computable functions (i.e. the partial recursive functions), this is still an important class. To quote Hartley [17] (page 8), *"Virtually all of algorithmic functions of ordinary mathematics can be shown to be primitive recursive"*. Whether it is also true of the problems we are likely to encounter in the domain of AI, this is not clear.

The complexity of a function with respect to a UTM is in general not computable. As the class of PRFs contain only total function, the complexity of a function with respect to a given representation of PRFs is computable and this may be helpful when constructing learning algorithms.

7   Summary

The PRFs is an important class of functions mathematically. Just as there are different representations of the partial recursive functions (e.g. Turing Machines and Unlimited Register Machines) there are many ways of representing the PRFs. Kolmogorov complexity [3] of a function is the minimum amount of computer memory needed to express the function. The Kolmogorov complexity of a function is independent of the model of computation used to express it. In this paper we have proved that if a function is a PRF, then the minimum amount of space needed to represent it is independent of the representation and depends only on the function. This is essentially due to the fact that the process of composition allows a representation to define arbitrary PRFs once and refer to them as needed. This result is analogous to that of Kolmogorov [3].

While a number of systems equivalent to PRFs have been evolved (see section 2), we could evolved expressions directly in the mathematical notation (see section 3). We question the utility of inventing new representations for the purpose of evolution in light of the fact that whatever new representation we care to produce, we can guarantee that the complexity of any function will be bound by a constant which is independent of the representation and only dependent on the function.

References

1. Banzhaf, W., Nordin, P., Keller, R.E., Francone, F.D.: Genetic Programming – An Introduction; On the Automatic Evolution of Computer Programs and its Applications. Morgan Kaufmann, dpunkt.verlag (1998)
2. Woodward, J.R.: Modularity in genetic programming. In: Genetic Programming, Proceedings of EuroGP 2003, Essex, UK, Springer-Verlag (2003)
3. Li, M., Vitanyi, P.M.B.: An Introduction to Kolmogorov Complexity and Its Applications. Springer-Verlag, Berlin (1993)
4. Grnwald, P.D., Myung, I.J., Pitt, M.A.: Advances in Minimum Description Length Theory and Applications. MIT press (2005)
5. Bishop, C.M.: Neural networks for pattern recognition. Oxford University Press, Oxford, UK, UK (1996)
6. Cramer, N.L.: A representation for the adaptive generation of simple programs. In: International Conference on Genetic Algorithms and Their Applications. (1985) 183–187

7. Brave, S.: Evolving recursive programs for tree search. In Angeline, P.J., Kinnear, Jr., K.E., eds.: Advances in Genetic Programming 2. MIT Press, Cambridge, MA, USA (1996) 203–220
8. Koza, J.R.: Genetic Programming: On the Programming of Computers by Means of Natural Selection. MIT Press (1992)
9. Yu, T.: Hierachical processing for evolving recursive and modular programs using higher order functions and lambda abstractions. Genetic Programming and Evolvable Machines 2(4) (2001) 345–380
10. Spector, L.: Simultaneous evolution of programs and their control structures. In Angeline, P.J., Kinnear, Jr., K.E., eds.: Advances in Genetic Programming 2. MIT Press, Cambridge, MA, USA (1996) 137–154
11. Wong, M.L., Leung, K.S.: Evolving recursive functions for the even-parity problem using genetic programming. In Angeline, P.J., Kinnear, Jr., K.E., eds.: Advances in Genetic Programming 2. MIT Press, Cambridge, MA, USA (1996) 221–240
12. Huelsbergen, L.: Learning recursive sequences via evolution of machine-language programs. In Koza, J.R., Deb, K., Dorigo, M., Fogel, D.B., Garzon, M., Iba, H., Riolo, R.L., eds.: Genetic Programming 1997: Proceedings of the Second Annual Conference, Stanford University, CA, USA, Morgan Kaufmann (1997) 186–194
13. Vallejo, E.E., Ramos, F.: Evolving turing machines for biosequence recognition and analysis. In Miller, J., Tomassini, M., Lanzi, P.L., Ryan, C., Tettamanzi, A.G.B., Langdon, W.B., eds.: Genetic Programming: 4th European conference. Volume 2038 of LNCS., Berlin, Springer (2001) 192–203
14. Woodward, J.R.W.: Algorithm Induction, Modularity and Complexity. PhD thesis, The School of Computer Science, The University of Birmingham (2005)
15. Cutland, N.J.: Computability, An introduction to recursive function theory. Cambridge University Press (1997)
16. Teller, A.: Algorithm Evolution with Internal Reinforcement for Signal Understanding. PhD thesis, School of Computer Science, Carnegie Mellon University, Pittsburgh, USA (1998)
17. Hartley Rogers, J.: Theory of recursive functions and effective computability. MIT Press, Cambridge, MA, USA (1987)

On the Locality of Grammatical Evolution

Franz Rothlauf and Marie Oetzel

Department of Business Administration and Information Systems,
University of Mannheim, 68131 Mannheim, Germany
rothlauf@uni-mannheim.de

Abstract. This paper investigates the locality of the genotype-phenotype mapping (representation) used in grammatical evolution (GE). The results show that the representation used in GE has problems with locality as many neighboring genotypes do not correspond to neighboring phenotypes. Experiments with a simple local search strategy reveal that the GE representation leads to lower performance for mutation-based search approaches in comparison to standard GP representations. The results suggest that locality issues should be considered for further development of the representation used in GE.

1 Introduction

Grammatical Evolution (GE) [1] is a variant of Genetic Programming (GP) [2] that can evolve complete programs in an arbitrary language using a variable-length binary string. In GE, phenotypic expressions are created from binary genotypes by using a complex representation (genotype-phenotype mapping). The representation selects production rules in a Backus-Naur form grammar and thereby creates a phenotype. GE approaches have been applied to test problems and real-world applications and good performance has been reported [1, 3, 4].

The locality of a genotype-phenotype mapping describes how well genotypic neighbors correspond to phenotypic neighbors. Previous work has indicated that a high locality of representations is necessary for efficient evolutionary search [5, 6, 7, 8, 9]. Until now locality has mainly been used in the context of standard genetic algorithms to explain performance differences.

The purpose of this paper is to investigate the locality of the genotype-phenotype mapping used in GE. The design of high-locality genotype-phenotype encodings is important to ensure high GE performance. We present experiments for standard GE test problems that show that the mapping used in GE has low locality leading to low performance of standard mutation operators. The study at hand is an example of how basic GA design principles can be applied to explain performance differences between different GP approaches and demonstrates current challenges in the design of GE-based systems.

2 Representations, Locality and Mutation Operators

When using a representation, every optimization problem f can be decomposed into a genotype-phenotype mapping f_g (representation), and a phenotype-fitness

P. Collet et al. (Eds.): EuroGP 2006, LNCS 3905, pp. 320–330, 2006.

mapping f_p (problem) [10]. Φ_g is the genotypic search space where the search operators are applied and Φ_p is the phenotypic search space. Consequently, we distinguish between phenotypes $x^p \in \Phi_p$ and genotypes $x^g \in \Phi_g$.

2.1   Metrics

When using search algorithms, a metric has to be defined on the search space Φ. Based on the metric, the distance d_{x_a, x_b} between two individuals $x_a \in \Phi$ and $x_b \in \Phi$ describes how different the two individuals are. The larger the distance, the more different two individuals are. Two individuals are neighbors if the distance between them is minimal.

If we use a representation f_g there are two different search spaces, Φ_g and Φ_p. Therefore, different metrics can be used for Φ_g and Φ_p. In general, the metric used on Φ_p is determined by the specific problem that should be solved. For GP approaches, common phenotypes are tree structures that describe programs or expressions and possible distances are tree edit distances. In contrast, the metric defined on Φ_g is not given a priori. Different GP variants use different types of genotypes. For example, GE uses linear bitstrings and standard GP [2] uses tree structures and applies search operators directly to trees.

2.2   Locality

The locality [5, 6, 10] of a representation describes how well neighboring genotypes correspond to neighboring phenotypes. The locality of a representation is high if all neighboring genotypes correspond to neighboring phenotypes. In contrast, the locality of a representation is low if some neighboring genotypes do not correspond to neighboring phenotypes.

We want to emphasize that the locality of a representation depends on the representation f_g and the metrics that are defined on Φ_g and Φ_p. f_g only determines which phenotypes are represented by which genotypes and says nothing about the similarity between solutions. To describe or measure the locality of a representation, a metric must be defined on Φ_g and Φ_p.

2.3   Locality and Mutation-Based Search

The metric defined on Φ_g and the functionality of the search operators depend on each other. In most search heuristics, mutation usually creates offspring that have a small or sometimes even minimal distance to their parents. As the metric used on Φ_g defines which genotypes are similar to each other, the used genotypic metric directly determines the mutation operator.

In mutation-based search approaches, mutation steps must be small and should result in similar solutions as larger search steps would result in a randomization of the search. Then, guided search around good solutions would become impossible as the mutation-based search algorithm would jump randomly around the search space. However, low-locality representations show exactly this behavior, as small changes in a genotype do not result in small changes of a phenotype. Therefore, for low-locality representations, guided search is no longer possible as local search steps in Φ_g result into random (large) search steps in Φ_p. This leads to a low performance of EA approaches when using low-locality encodings.

3   Grammatical Evolution

Grammatical evolution is a form of linear GP that employs linear genomes, uses a grammar in Backus-Naur form (BNF) to define the phenotypic structures, and performs an ontogenetic mapping from the genotype to the phenotype.

3.1   Functionality

GE is an EA variant that can evolve computer programs defined in BNF. In contrast to standard GP [2], the genotypes are not parse trees but bitstrings of a variable length. A genotype consists of groups of eight bits (denoted as codons) that select production rules from a BNF grammar. For the construction of the phenotype from the genotype, see Sect. 3.3.

The functionality of GE follows standard EA approaches using binary genotypes. As simple binary strings are used as genotypes, no specific crossover or mutation operators are necessary. Therefore, standard crossover operators like one-point or uniform crossover and standard mutation operators like bit-flipping mutation can be used. A common metric for measuring the similarity of binary strings (compare Sect. 2.1) is the Hamming distance. Therefore, the application of bit-flipping mutation creates a new solution with genotypic distance $d^g = 1$. For selection, standard operators like tournament selection or roulette-wheel selection can be used. Some GE implementations use steady state replacement mechanisms and duplication operators that duplicate a random number of codons and insert these after the last codon position. As usual, selection decisions are performed based on the fitness of the phenotypes.

GE has been successfully applied to a number of diverse problem domains such as symbolic regression [1, 3], trigonometric identities [4], symbolic integration [3], the Santa Fe trail [1], and others. The results indicate that GE can be applied to a wide range of problems and validates the ability of GE to generate multi-line functions in any language following BNF notation.

3.2   Backus-Naur-Form

In GE, the Backus-Naur form (BNF) grammar is used to define the grammar of a language as production rules. Based on the information stored in the genotypes, BNF-production rules are selected and form the phenotype. In BNF, it can be distinguished between terminals, which are equivalent to leaf nodes in trees, and non-terminals, which can be interpreted as interior nodes in a tree and can be expanded. A grammar in BNF is defined by the quadruple $\{N, T, P, S\}$, where N is the set of non-terminals, T is the set of terminals, P is a set of production rules that maps N to a set of elements of T and N, and $S \in N$ is a start symbol.

To apply GE to a problem, it is necessary to define the BNF grammar for the problem. The BNF grammar must be defined such that the optimal solution for a specific problem can be created from the elements defined by the grammar.

3.3   Genotype-Phenotype Mapping of Grammatical Evolution

In GE, a phenotype is created from binary genotypes in two steps. In a first step, integer values are calculated from codons of eight bits. Therefore, from a binary genotype $x^{g,bin}$ of length $8l$ we get an integer genotype $x^{g,int}$ of length l, where each integer $x_i^{g,int} \in \{0, \ldots, 255\}$, for $i \in \{0, \ldots, l-1\}$. Beginning with the start symbol $S \in N$, the integer value $x_i^{g,int}$ is used to select production rules from the BNF grammar. We denote with n_P the number of production rules in P. To select a rule, we calculate the number of the used rule as $x_i^{g,int} mod\ n_P$, where mod denotes the modulo operation. In this manner, the mapping process traverses the genome beginning from the left hand side $(x_0^{g,int})$ until one of the following situations arises:

- The mapping is complete. All non-terminals are transformed into terminals and a complete phenotype x^p is generated.
- The end of the genome is reached $(i = l - 1)$ but the mapping process is not yet finished. The individual is wrapped, the alleles are reused, and the reading of codons continues. As genotypic alleles are used several times with different meaning, wrapping can have a negative effect on locality. However, without mapping a larger number of individuals is incomplete and invalid.
- An upper threshold on the number of wrapping events is reached and the mapping is not yet complete. The mapping process is halted and the individual is assigned the lowest possible fitness value.

The mapping is deterministic, as the same genotype always results in the same phenotype. However, the interpretation of $x_i^{g,int}$ can be different if the genotype is wrapped and a different type of rule is selected. A more detailed description of the mapping process including illustrative examples can be found in [1, 3].

4   Test Problems

We investigate the locality and performance of GE for the Santa Fe Ant trail and symbolic regression problem. Both problems are standard for GP and GE.

4.1   Santa Fe Ant Trail

In the Santa Fe Ant trail problem, 89 Pieces of food are located on a discontinuous trail which is embedded in a 32 by 32 toroidal grid. The goal is to determine rules that guide the movements of an artificial ant and allows the ant to collect a maximum number of pieces of food in t_{max} search steps. In each search step, exactly one action can be performed. The ant can turn left (left()), turn right (right()), move one square forward (move()), or look ahead one square in the direction it is facing (food_ahead()). The BNF grammar for the Santa Fe ant trail problem is shown in Fig. 1(a).

N= {code,line,expr,if-stat,op},
T= {left(), right(), move(),
    food_ahead(), else, if, {,
     }, (,), ;},
S= code.
Production rules P:
```
<code>    ::= <line>
        |   <code><line>
<line>    ::= <expr>
<expr>    ::= <if-stat>
        |   <op>
<if-stat> ::= if(food_ahead())
              {<expr>} else
              {<expr>}
<op>      ::= left();
        |   right();
        |   move();
```
(a) Santa Fe Ant trail

N= {expr, op, pre_op}
T= {sin,cos,exp,log,+,-,/,*,x,1,(,)}
S= <expr>
Production rules P:
```
<expr>    ::= <expr><op><expr>
        |   (<expr><op><expr>)
        |   <pre-op>(<expr>)
        |   <var>
<op>      ::= +
        |   -
        |   /
        |   *
<pre-op>  ::= sin
        |   cos
        |   exp
        |   log
<op>      ::= x
        |   1
```
(b) symbolic regression

Fig. 1. BNF grammars for test problems

4.2 Symbolic Regression

In this example [2], a mathematical expression in symbolic form must be found that approximates a given set of 20 data points (x_i, y_i). The function that should be approximated is

$$f(x) = x^4 + x^3 + x^2 + x, \tag{1}$$

where $x \in [-1; 1]$. The used BNF grammar is shown in Fig. 1(b).

5 Locality of Grammatical Evolution

To measure the locality of a representation, we have to define a metric for Φ_g and Φ_p. For binary genotypes, usually the Hamming distance is used. It measures the number of different alleles in two genotypes x^g and y^g and is calculated as $d_{x^g,y^g}^g = \sum_i |x_i^g - y_i^g|$. A mutation (bit-flipping) of an individual x results in a neighboring solution y with distance $d_{x,y}^g = 1$.

5.1 Tree Edit Distance

It is more difficult to define appropriate metrics for phenotypes that are programs or expressions. In GE and GP, phenotypes can be described as expression trees. Therefore, edit distances can be used for measuring differences/similarities between different phenotypes. In general, the edit distance between two trees (phenotypes) is defined as the minimum cost sequence of elemental edit operations that transform one tree into the other. There are the following three elemental operations:

1. deletion: A node is removed from the tree. The children of this node become children of their parent.
2. insertion: A single node is added.
3. replacement: The label of a node is changed.

To every operation a cost is assigned (usually the same for the different operations). [11] presented an algorithm to calculate an edit distance where the operations insertion and deletion may only be applied to the leaves. [12] introduced an unrestricted edit distance and [13] developed a dynamic programming algorithm to compute tree edit distances.

In the context of GP, tree edit distances have been used as a measurement for the similarity of trees [14, 15, 16]. [17, 18] used tree edit distances for analyzing the causality of GP approaches.

5.2   Results

For investigating the locality of the genotype-phenotype mapping used in GE, we created 1,000 random genotypes. For the genotypes, we used standard parameter settings. The length of an individual is 160 bits, the codon size is 8, the wrapping operator is used, the upper bound for wrapping events is 10, and the maximum number of elements in the phenotype is 1,000. For each individual x, we created all 160 neighbors y, where $d_{x,y}^g = 1$. The neighbors differ in exactly one bit from the original solution. The locality of the genotype-phenotype mapping can be determined by measuring the distance $d_{x,y}^p$ between the phenotypes that correspond to the neighboring genotypes x and y. The phenotypic distance $d_{x,y}^p$ is measured as the edit distance between x^p and y^p.

For the GE genotype-phenotype mapping, we use the version 1.01 written by Michael O'Neill. The GE representation also contains the BNF Parser Gramma, version 0.63 implemented by Miguel Nicolau. For calculating the tree edit distance, we used a dynamic programming approach implemented by [13].

As the representation used in GE is redundant, some changes of the genotypes may not affect the corresponding phenotypes. We performed experiments for the Santa Fe Ant trail problem and the symbolic regression problem and found that either 81.98% (Santa Fe) or 94.01% of all genotypic neighbors are phenotypically identical ($d_{x,y}^p = 0$). Therefore, in about 90 % of cases a mutation of a genotype (resulting in a neighboring genotype) does not change the corresponding phenotype.

What is important for the locality of GE are the remaining neighbors that result in different phenotypes. The locality is high if the corresponding phenotypes are similar to each other. Figure 2 shows the frequency and cumulative frequency over the distance $d_{x,y}^p$ between expression trees for the two different

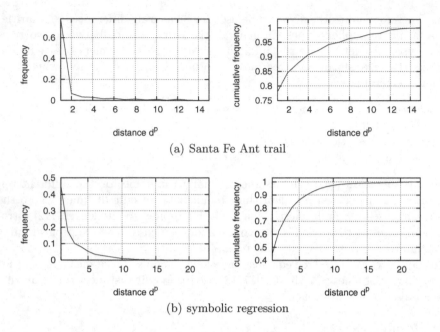

(a) Santa Fe Ant trail

(b) symbolic regression

Fig. 2. Distribution of tree edit distances $d^p_{x,y}$ for neighboring genotypes x and y, where $d^g_{x,y} = 1$. We show the frequency (left) and cumulative frequency (right) over $d^p_{x,y}$ for the Santa Fe Ant trail problem and the symbolic regression problem.

test problems. We only consider the case where $d^p_{x,y} > 0$. The results show that for the Santa Fe Ant trail problem, many genotypic neighbors are also phenotypic neighbors (about 78%). However, there are also a significant amount of genotypic neighbors where the corresponding phenotypes are completely different. For example, more than 8% of all genotypic neighbors have a tree edit distance $d^p_{x,y} \geq 5$. The situation is worse for symbolic regression. Only about 45% of all genotypic neighbors correspond to phenotypic neighbors and about 14% of all genotypic neighbors correspond to phenotypes where $d^p_{x,y} \geq 5$.

We see that the locality of the genotype-phenotype mapping used in GE is not perfect. For the two test problems, a substantial percentage of neighboring genotypes do not correspond to neighboring phenotypes. Therefore, we expect some problems with the performance of mutation-based GE search approaches in comparison to other approaches that use a high-locality encoding.

6   Influence of Locality on GE Performance

The previous results indicate some problems of GE with low locality. Therefore, we investigate how strong the low locality of the genotype-phenotype mapping influences the performance of GE. We focus the study on mutation only. However, we assume that the results for mutation are also relevant for crossover operators (compare [8, 6, 10]).

6.1   Experimental Setting

For the experiments, we want to make sure that we only examine the impact of locality on GE performance and that no other factors blur the results. Therefore, we implemented a simple local (1+1)-EA using only mutation as a search operator. The search strategy starts with a randomly created genotype and iteratively applies bit-flipping mutations to the genotypes. If the offspring has a higher fitness than the parent it replaces it. Otherwise the parent remains the actual solution. The (1+1)-EA behaves like a simple local search.

We perform experiments for both test problems and compare an encoding with high locality with the representation used in GE. In the runs, we randomly generate a GE-encoded initial solution and use this solution as the initial solution for both types of representations. For GE, a search step is the mutation of one bit of the genotype, and the phenotype is created from the genotype using the GE genotype-phenotype mapping process. Due to the low locality of the representation, we expect problems when focusing the search on areas of the search space where solutions with high fitness can be found. However, the low locality increases the evolvability of GE what often makes it easier to escape local optima. Furthermore, we should bear in mind that many genotypic search steps do not result in a different phenotype.

We compare the representation used in GE with a standard representation used in GP. We define the search operators in such a way that a mutation always results in a neighboring phenotype ($d^p_{x,y} = 1$). Therefore, the mutation operators are directly applied to the trees x^p. We use the following mutation operators:

- Santa Fe Ant trail
  - Deletion: A leaf node from the set of terminals T is deleted.
  - Insertion: A new leaf node from T is inserted.
  - Replacement: A leaf node (from T) is replaced by another leaf node.
- symbolic regression
  - Deletion: Either two nodes (a leaf node that contains x and a preceding node that contains sin, cos, exp, or log) or three nodes (two leaf nodes x or 1 and the common preceding node that contains +, -, *, or /) are replaced by a leaf node x.
  - Insertion: Either sin, cos, exp, or log or +, -, *, or / (plus an additional leaf node x or 1) are inserted at a leaf that contains x.
  - Replacement: +, -, *, and / are replaced by each other; sin, cos, exp, and log are replaced by each other; x and 1 are replaced by each other.

A mutation step (in the EA, the type of mutation operator is chosen randomly) always results in a neighboring phenotype and we do not need an additional genotype-phenotype mapping like in GE as we apply the search operators directly to the phenotypes.

Comparing these two different approaches, in GE, a mutation of a genotype results in most cases in the same phenotype, sometimes in a neighboring phenotype, but also sometimes in phenotypes that are completely different (compare the plots presented in Fig. 2). The standard GP representation is a high-locality

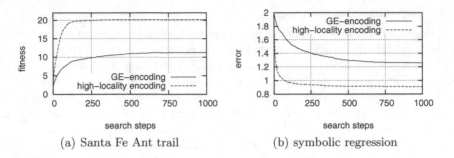

(a) Santa Fe Ant trail   (b) symbolic regression

Fig. 3. Performance of a mutation-based (1+1)-EA using either the GE encoding or a high-locality encoding for the Santa Fe Ant trail problem and the symbolic regression problem

representation as a mutation always results in a neighboring phenotype. Therefore, the search can be focused on promising areas of the search space but the search can never escape the local optima.

6.2 Performance Results

For the GE approach, we use the same parameter setting as described in Sect. 5.2. For both problems, we perform 1,000 runs of the (1+1)-EA using randomly created initial solutions. Each EA run is stopped after 1,000 search steps. Figure 3 compares the performance for the Santa Fe Ant trail (Fig. 3(a)) and the symbolic regression problem (Fig. 3(b)) over the number of search steps. Figure 3(a) shows the mean fitness of the found solution and Fig. 3(b) shows the mean error $1/20 \sum_{i=0}^{19} |f_j(x_i) - f(x_i)|$, where f is defined in (1) and f_j ($j \in \{0, \ldots, 1000\}$) denotes the function found by the search in search step j. The results are averaged over all 1,000 runs.

The results show that the (1+1)-EA using a high-locality representation outperforms a (1+1)-EA using the GE representation. Therefore, the low-locality of the encoding illustrated in Sect. 5 has a negative effect on the performance of evolutionary search. Although the low locality of the GE encodings allows a local search strategy to escape local optima, EAs using the GE encoding show lower performance than a high-locality encoding.

The presented results show that using the GE encoding prolongs search as more search steps are necessary to converge. This increase is expected as for the GE encoding a search step often does not change the corresponding phenotypes. However, the plots show that allowing the (1+1)-EA using the GE encoding to run for a higher number of search steps does not increase its performance.

7   Conclusions

Previous work has shown that the locality of the genotype-phenotype mapping (representation) is important for the success of EAs. This study analyzes the locality of the representation used in grammatical evolution (GE). GE differs from other GP approaches by using binary genotypes and constructing phenotypes by choosing construction rules in Backus-Naur form grammar.

The results show that the GE representation has some problems with locality as neighboring genotypes often do not correspond to neighboring phenotypes. Therefore, a guided search around high-quality solutions can be difficult. However, due to the lower locality of the representation, it is easier to escape from local optima. Comparing a simple $(1+1)$-EA using either the GE representation with a standard GP encoding with high-locality reveals that the low locality of the GE representation reduces the performance of local search.

The results of this study allow a better understanding of the functionality of GE and can deliver some explanations for problems of GE that have been observed in literature. We want to encourage GE researchers to consider locality issues for further developments of the genotype-phenotype mapping. We believe that increasing the locality of the GE representation can also increase the performance and effectiveness of GE.

References

1. O'Neill, M., Ryan, C.: Grammatical evolution. IEEE Transactions on Evolutionary Computation **5** (2001) 349–358
2. Koza, J.R.: Genetic programming: On the programming of computers by natural selection. MIT Press, Cambridge, Mass. (1992)
3. O'Neill, M., Ryan, C.: Grammatical Evolution: Evolutionary Automatic Programming in a Arbitrary Language. Volume 4 of Genetic Programming. Kluwer Academic Publishers (2003)
4. Ryan, C., O'Neill, M.: Grammatical evolution: A steady state approach. In: Late Breaking Papers, Genetic Programming 1998. (1998) 180–185
5. Rothlauf, F., Goldberg, D.E.: Tree network design with genetic algorithms - an investigation in the locality of the prüfernumber encoding. In Brave, S., Wu, A.S., eds.: Late Breaking Papers at the Genetic and Evolutionary Computation Conference 1999, Orlando, Florida, USA, Omni Press (1999) 238–244
6. Gottlieb, J., Raidl, G.: Characterizing locality in decoder-based eas for the multidimensional knapsack problem. In Fonlupt, C., Hao, J.K., Lutton, E., Ronald, E., Schoenauer, M., eds.: Proceedings of Artificial Evolution. Volume 1829 of Lecture Notes in Computer Science., Springer (1999) 38–52
7. Gottlieb, J., Raidl, G.R.: The effects of locality on the dynamics of decoder-based evolutionary search. In Whitley, D., Goldberg, D.E., Cantú-Paz, E., Spector, L., Parmee, L., Beyer, H.G., eds.: Proceedings of the Genetic and Evolutionary Computation Conference 2000, San Francisco, CA, Morgan Kaufmann Publishers (2000) 283–290
8. Gottlieb, J., Julstrom, B.A., Raidl, G.R., Rothlauf, F.: Prüfer numbers: A poor representation of spanning trees for evolutionary search. IlliGAL Report No. 2001001, University of Illinois at Urbana-Champaign, Urbana (2001)
9. Rothlauf, F., Goldberg, D.E.: Prüfernumbers and genetic algorithms: A lesson on how the low locality of an encoding can harm the performance of GAs. In Schoenauer, M., Deb, K., Rudolph, G., Yao, X., Lutton, E., Merelo, J.J., Schwefel, H.P., eds.: Parallel Problem Solving from Nature, PPSN VI, Berlin, Springer-Verlag (2000) 395–404

10. Rothlauf, F.: Representations for Genetic and Evolutionary Algorithms. 2 edn. Springer, Heidelberg (2006)
11. Selkow, S.M.: The tree-to-tree editing problem. Information Processing Letters **6** (1977) 184–186
12. Tai, K.C.: The tree-to-tree correction problem. Journal of the ACM **26** (1979) 422–433
13. Zhang, K., Shasha, D.: Simple fast algorithms for the editing distance between trees and related problems. SIAM Journal on Computing **18** (1989) 1245–1262
14. Keller, Banzhaf: Genetic programming using genotype-phenotype mapping from linear genomes into linear phenotypes. In Koza, J.e.a., ed.: Proceedings of First Annual Conference on Genetic Programming, MIT Press (1996) 116–122
15. O'Reilly, U.M.: Using a distance metric on genetic programs to understand genetic operators. In: Late breaking papers at the 1997 Genetic Programming Conference, Stanford University, CA (1997) 199–206
16. Brameier, Banzhaf: Explicit control of diversity and effective variation distance in linear genetic programming. In Tettamanzi, A.e.a., ed.: Genetic Programming, Proceedings of the 5th European Conference. Volume 2278 of LNCS., Springer (2002) 162–171
17. Igel, C.: Causality of hierarchical variable length representations. Proceedings of 1998 IEEE International Conference on Evolutionary Computation (1998) 324–329
18. Igel, C., Chellapilla, K.: Investigating the influence of depth and degree of genotypic change on fitness in genetic programming. In Banzhaf, W., Daida, J., Eiben, A.E., Garzon, M.H., Honavar, V., Jakiela, M., Smith, R.E., eds.: Proceedings of the Genetic and Evolutionary Computation Conference. Volume 2., Orlando, Florida, USA, Morgan Kaufmann (1999) 1061–1068

Optimizing the Initialization of Dynamic Decision Heuristics in DPLL SAT Solvers Using Genetic Programming

Raihan H. Kibria[1] and You Li[2]

[1] Computer Systems Lab,
Dept. of Electrical Engineering and Information Technology,
Darmstadt University of Technology, D-64283 Darmstadt, Germany
kibria@rs.tu-darmstadt.de
[2] sufei.lee@gmail.com

Abstract. The Boolean satisfiability problem (SAT) has many applications in electronic design automation (EDA) as well as theoretical computer science. Most SAT solvers for EDA problems use the DPLL algorithm and conflict analysis dependent decision heuristics. When the search starts, the heuristics have little or no information about the structure of the CNF. In this work, an algorithm for initializing dynamic decision heuristics is evolved using genetic programming. The open-source SAT solver MINISAT v1.12 is used. Using the best algorithm evolved, an advantage was found for solving unsatisfiable EDA SAT problems.

1 SAT

The *Boolean satisfiability problem (SAT)* is the seminal NP-complete problem described by S. Cook in 1971. Given a Boolean function $f(v_1, v_2, ..., v_n)$ in n variables, the SAT problem is the question if there exists an assignment to the variables $v_1, ..., v_n$ so that the function f evaluates to *true*, or if no such assignment exists, i.e. $f = false$. In the former case f is called *satisfiable*, in the latter *unsatisfiable*. A set of variable assignments that satisfies a Boolean expression is called a *model*.

SAT problems are usually given in *conjunctive normal form* (CNF), which is a product of sum-terms. Each sum-term or *clause* is the Boolean OR of a number of *literals*, which are variables or negated variables. Clauses which contain only one literal are called *unit-literal clauses*.

For a CNF to become satisfied, each clause must be satisfied (i.e. evaluate to *true*). This is the case if at least one literal in the clause evaluates to *true*. Unit-literal clauses can only be satisfied if their single literal evaluates to *true*; this forced assignment is called an *implication*. The implied assignment must be made in the entire CNF, possibly leading to further implications. Assigning implications until no further implications are present is called *Boolean constraint propagation (BCP)*.

P. Collet et al. (Eds.): EuroGP 2006, LNCS 3905, pp. 331–340, 2006.

If a variable occurs only in one polarity (negated or not negated), the literal can be assigned *true* without changing the satisfiability of the expression. This is the *pure literal rule*.

1.1   DPLL Algorithm

After the *Davis-Putnam* algorithm (*DP*), which suffered from rapid memory exhaustion, the *Davis(-Putnam)-Loveland-Logemann* algorithm (*DPLL* or *DLL*) [2] for solving SAT was invented. DPLL is a *complete* algorithm (can prove satisfiable and unsatisfiable) and operates on Boolean formulas in CNF. The basic concept of DPLL is a depth-first search of all possible variable assignments to find a model of the SAT problem. If no model can be found, then the problem is unsatisfiable.

Before the actual search starts, some preprocessing can be performed. This always consists at least of the application of BCP for all unit-literal clauses of the original CNF, but can also include application of the pure literal rule or other, more sophisticated algorithms. The search starts with a *decision* being made about an assignment, i.e. which variable should be assigned which value (*true* or *false*). Then, to prune the search space, all implications of the decision are propagated (BCP). The first decision and all its implications have the *decision level* 1, the second has level 2 etc. Decision level 0 refers to assignments made before the actual search.

After BCP, the CNF is either satisfied, unsatisfied or its value is undetermined. In the latter case, another decision must be made. If the CNF is satisfied, a model was found and the algorithm ends. If it is unsatisfied, then a *conflict* has occurred and *backtracking* is necessary.

In the original DPLL algorithm, backtracking is *chronological*. When a conflict is encountered, the algorithm inverts (*flips*) the value of the last decision assignment that was not flipped already. Many current DPLL SAT solvers use *non-chronological backtracking* (e.g. GRASP [6] and CHAFF [3]), which is achieved by learning new clauses during search and analyzing the CNF to find the lowest decision level at which the current conflict can be resolved. A CNF is found to be unsatisfiable if backtracking is not possible any more because the first decision was already flipped (classic DPLL) or if two conflicting unit-literal clauses have been learned (DPLL with learning). Non-chronological backtracking is usually more effective for EDA problems.

The learned clauses are computed each time a conflict has occurred. They encode assignment combinations that would lead to the same conflict, and are also called *conflict clauses*. More than one clause can be learned from a conflict. The conflict clauses are derived by analyzing an *implication graph (IG)* [6]. There are several schemes for the extraction of the conflict clauses from the IG.

1.2   Decision Heuristics

Decision heuristics can be classified as *static* or *dynamic*. *Static decision heuristics* compute a variable order before the search starts (e.g. during preprocessing) and never change that order. *Dynamic decision heuristics* take into account the current state of the CNF and the solver.

Conflict analysis dependent decision heuristics make use of learned clauses for decisions. The solver CHAFF uses the *Variable State Independent Decaying Sum (VSIDS)* heuristic, which attempts to satisfy recent conflict clauses. MINISAT, the solver used in this work, uses a slightly improved variant of VSIDS. Each variable has an *activity* associated with it, which is a double-precision floating-point value initialized with 0 (in VSIDS, each literal has its own activity; their initial values are the literal counts in the original CNF). When a decision has to be made, the variable with the highest activity is chosen (ties are broken randomly).

After each conflict, an increment value is added to the activities of the variables occurring in the conflict clause, and the increment value is multiplied with a constant greater than 1. This ensures that recently learned clauses have more influence on the activities. The activities have to be rescaled once in a while to prevent overflow. With a small probability, MINISAT sometimes chooses a random variable; this has been found to help solving some problems. Decision variables are always assigned the value *false* first.

2   Genetic Programming

Genetic programming (GP) as described in [1] is used in this work to evolve an initialization algorithm for DPLL dynamic decision heuristics. *Automatically Defined Functions (ADF)* were not used.

GP is a type of *evolutionary algorithm*. It evolves a population of individuals over a number of generations, where the individuals are LISP *S-expressions* (parse trees) composed of *terminals* and *functions*. The arguments and return types of functions have to be of the same type (e.g. floating-point numbers). Terminals are either numerical *constants* or *sensors*, which convey information about the environment. A *fitness measure* evaluates how well an individual solves a problem. Through a process similar to natural selection, a new population is created by copying, *mutation* or *crossover* of individuals of the previous generation.

2.1   Designing an Initialization Algorithm

As mentioned in Sect. 1.2, in the MINISAT heuristic the activities determining which variable to choose are initialized to 0. Therefore the first decision is quasi-random, because all activities are tied and some free variable will be chosen randomly. It is conjectured in this work that initializing the activities before the search starts, taking into account the structure of the CNF, can significantly improve solving time. Related works [8] have been successful in accelerating SAT by extracting an improved ordering of the variables from the structure of the CNF. The MINISAT heuristic will be the target for improvement. Let x be the variable for which its initial activity $a_0(x)$ is computed (Equation 1).

$$a_0(x) = \sum_{\substack{\text{clauses } C, \\ x \in C \lor \neg x \in C}} \left(\sum_{\substack{\text{literals } l \in C, \\ l \neq x \land l \neq \neg x}} f(x_p, x_n, l_p, l_n, C_s, ...) \right) \qquad (1)$$

$a_0(x)$ iterates over all clauses C containing x or $\neg x$, and in each clause C all literals l except x or $\neg x$ are examined. The total initial activity $a_0(x)$ is computed as a sum over the expression f, whose arguments are numerical values describing the CNF, e.g. x_p (the number of positive occurrences of the current x). f is the expression that will be described by the GP individuals; its arguments are implemented by sensor terminals.

2.2   Terminal and Function Sets

The return- and argument type of the functions as well as of the terminals is a double-precision floating-point number, so that the *closure* requirement [1] is satisfied. The terminal set (Table 1) consists of 11 different sensors with information about the current variable x, the current literal l, the clause C and the CNF itself, and additionally, randomly generated numerical constants.

A number of binary and unary functions (Table 2) are available. The arithmetic division operation ($\div$) is the special division commonly used in GP that allows division by 0, returning 0 in that case.

Table 1. Terminal set

Terminal	Meaning
x_n, l_n	# of negative literals of x and the variable of l in the CNF
x_p, l_p	# of positive literals of x and the variable of l in the CNF
x_c, l_c	# of occurrences of x and l in the CNF ($x_c = x_n + x_p, l_c = l_n + l_p$)
x_s, l_s	Polarity of x in clause C / current literal l (0 negative, 1 positive)
C_s	# of literals in current clause C
N_v, N_c	# of variables/clauses of the CNF
Constants	Real numbers between -10 and 10

Table 2. Function set

Function	Return value	Function	Return value
$a \{+, -, \times, \div\} b$		$\text{abs}(a)$	$|a|$
$a \text{ min } b$	$\text{minimum}(a, b)$	$\text{sqrt}(a)$	$\sqrt{|a|}$
$a \text{ max } b$	$\text{maximum}(a, b)$	$\text{sign}(a)$	$a < 0: -1, a = 0: 0, a > 0: 1$
$a \text{ if>0 } b$	$a > 0: b, a \leq 0: 0$	$\text{exp}(a)$	e^a
$a \text{ less } b$	$a < b: 1, a \geq b: 0$	$\text{inv}(a)$	$a \neq 0: \frac{1}{a}, a = 0: 0$
		$\text{neg}(a)$	$-a$

2.3   Fitness Measure

The fitness measure (to be minimized) is the accumulated run time in seconds of the SAT solver for a training set of SAT problems. The run time does not include the time needed for initializing the activities, which is ignored in this work. If the solver times out for a problem, then the fitness value to accumulate for that problem is set to twice the timeout limit in seconds as a penalty.

2.4   Creating a New Population

The default strategy implemented in the GP library [5] was used. Individuals exist in discrete generations (*generational GA*). The current generation's population is sorted by fitness, and the better half is copied unchanged into the next generation (*elitism*); the worse half is deleted. For the copied individuals the fitness does not have to be recomputed. The remaining individuals of the next generation are offspring of the better half. On each pair of current individuals ranked 1st and 2nd, 3rd and 4th etc. crossover is applied once, and the ensuing two offspring individuals enter the next generation. The best individual found always remains in the population. Mutation is not used.

3   Experimental Results

3.1   Implementation

C++ source code from [5] was used for the implementation of the GP functionality. The library provides the ability to create user-defined terminals and functions, and includes algorithms for initializing the population and the breeding strategy described in Sect. 2.4. MiniSAT v1.12, due to its high performance and well-documented source (also C++), was used as the SAT solver. The GNU C++ compiler was used to create the executable.

3.2   Preprocessing the Training Problems

SAT benchmark problems usually are published in a raw state containing unit-literal clauses etc. To remove as many interfering influences on the initialization algorithm as possible some preprocessing was applied on the problems.

Covered clauses are clauses that contain a superset of the literals of another, smaller clause. The larger clause can be removed without changing the Boolean function represented by the CNF.

The *resolution rule* creates a new clause (the *resolvent*) out of two clauses. The CNF consisting of the resolvent and the original clauses describes the same Boolean function as the original clauses. Given two clauses $c_1 = (r \vee L_1)$ and $c_2 = (\neg r \vee L_1 \vee L_2)$, where L_1 and L_2 are (sub-)clauses not having any literals in common, nor the complementary literals r and $\neg r$, the resolvent of c_1 and c_2 is the clause $c_r = (L_1 \vee L_2)$. c_2 is covered by c_r, therefore c_2 can be replaced by c_r. This limited form of resolution makes some of the constraints more strict.

The training problems were preprocessed with a separate self-made tool that applied BCP, the pure literal rule, removal of covered (and duplicate) clauses and limited resolution in a loop until no further change was possible. Due to the algorithm used, the clauses are also sorted by size in ascending order, which has no effect on the initialization algorithm but affects the solving time. The preprocessed SAT problems have the same satisfiability as the original ones.

3.3   Experiment Setup

The experiments were run on four PCs with different architectures. All fitnesses and solving times reproduced in the following have been normalized to the reference machine, a 2.4 GHz Pentium 4 PC running Linux.

The problems used for the training sets in this work were circuit verification problems taken from [7]. Two training problem sets were used, one with 9 problems ("large" set) and one with 3 problems ("small" set). All training problems were unsatisfiable.

3.4   Results

Given the population size P, number of training problems N, number of generations G and a timeout in seconds T, the maximum run time for the GP program is $T_m = PNT(1 + \frac{G-1}{2})$ (because the fitness of half of the individuals in each generation has been computed before). Very large values of P and G are usual in GP, but this was not possible for this work due to the large run times required.

18 runs of the small and 10 runs of the large training set were executed with varying parameters. The parameters, resulting f-expressions and best fitnesses of the best, one average and the worst run of both sets are shown in Table 3. The best f-expressions found for the two sets will be referred to as $f_{best,L}$ resp. $f_{best,S}$ in the following.

The f-expressions usually contained some amount of redundancy typical of GP (e.g. $abs(abs(x))$); they have been simplified for clarity. The syntax for the expressions is in the format of the program's output, e.g. the terminal l_n is written as Ln. Binary functions have their arguments left and right of their name, e.g. (Xc max Lp) for $max(x_c, l_p)$. Unary functions have their argument in brackets, e.g. e^(Xn) for e^{x_n}.

Table 3. Best, average and worst results for large and small training set

f-expression	Fitness	P	G	T
e^(-Lc) - Lp	228	64	16	60
7.055845 / abs(9.116130 - Xc)	261	64	16	90
-Ln	294	64	12	120
e^(Xp)/((sqrt((0.042679+Lp)/1.540332))-7.029679)	114	128	8	120
-7.187368	161	64	8	120
e^(2.068685/Nc)-2.068685	197	64	16	60

It is interesting that many of the resulting f-expressions always computed a *negative* initial activity for any reasonable CNF (in 8 of 18 runs of the small, and 9 of 10 runs of the large set). This might prevent some variables from being chosen early on, even after occurring in conflict clauses, when they start with large negative activities.

Table 4 shows the solving times for the best individuals of both sets: T_{orig} and T_{prep} for the original and preprocessed CNF with standard MINISAT, $T_{GP,L}$ using $f_{best,L}$ and $T_{GP,S}$ using $f_{best,S}$ (as reported by the GP program). Additionally, for counterchecking, the run times are given for solving preprocessed and original problems with a MINISAT solver modified to initialize the activities with $f_{best,L}$ (columns $T_{prep,L}$ and $T_{orig,L}$) and $f_{best,S}$ (columns $T_{prep,S}$ and $T_{orig,S}$). These times include the time for the computation of the initialization, which took up to ca. 4 seconds for the largest CNFs. Problems that timed out after 10 minutes are shown with a time of 1200 seconds.

The last row of Table 4 shows the average time required to solve the problems in the respective column. As can be seen, preprocessing almost doubled the average solving time. It is unknown if this is a coincidence for this particular training set, or if the preprocessing used here is always detrimental to the solving process.

Some of the solving times in the counterchecking columns differ strongly from the times reported by the GP program. It was found after some experimenting that even small changes of how the f-expression is computed in the source code, e.g. in the form $\frac{a+b}{c}$ as opposed to $\frac{a}{c} + \frac{b}{c}$, could result in large changes of the solving times. Also, small changes in the numerical constants strongly affect solving times. It is presumed that the reason why the times reported by the GP program and those by the countercheck solver using $f_{best,S}$ are so different is that the GP program reported the values of the constants only up to a certain number of decimal places; the very small differences to the actual, non-truncated values were enough to distort the solving times. Since $f_{best,L}$ contains no constants, this effect is less pronounced for it.

Table 4. Solving times of training sets with best initialization

Problem	T_{orig}	T_{prep}	$T_{GP,L}$	$T_{GP,S}$	$T_{prep,L}$	$T_{prep,S}$	$T_{orig,L}$	$T_{orig,S}$
3pipe_2_ooo	5	11	9	-	9	8	4	3
3pipe	6	10	3	-	4	3	3	9
4pipe_1_ooo	18	27	18	-	19	23	26	1200
4pipe_2_ooo	28	31	17	-	18	235	42	1200
4pipe_3_ooo	55	82	49	-	52	27	46	1200
4pipe_4_ooo	132	64	41	-	43	48	34	1200
engine_5_case1	24	23	19	-	29	131	21	192
4pipe_q0_k	38	306	36	30	38	54	29	18
engine_4	52	36	36	28	39	27	41	43
4pipe	113	325	-	57	200	42	125	521
Average	47.1	91.5	-	-	45.1	59.8	37.1	-

The best result for the large training set was $f_{best,L} = e^{-l_c} - l_p$. A qualitative analysis of this result will be attempted in the following. For the first term it is always true that $0 < e^{-l_c} < 1$, because the variable count $l_c > 0$. Therefore the dominant term is l_p with $l_p \geq 1$, so that $f < 0$. For an expression $g = l_p$, the initial activity would be highest for variables that occur often and in large clauses (then the outer and inner sums in Equation 1 have many iterations), where the clauses contain variables whose positive literal occurs often in the CNF (so the l_p themselves are large). Because $f \approx -l_p$, these variables have the lowest (i.e. negative) activity, therefore their opposite is chosen, i.e. variables occurring rarely, and in short clauses; the clauses should contain variables whose positive literals occur rarely. If a variable occurs mostly in short clauses, then assigning it is likely to create implications quickly (clauses are shortened where the literals are *false*) and relatively strong constraints are removed (clauses are satisfied by *true* literals). The significance of the l_p is not clear. It may have something to do with the fact that MINISAT assigns *false* to decision variables first. That the worst expression for the large training set was $-l_n$ is probably coincidence.

The best result for the small training set was $f_{best,S}$. This expression does not always compute a negative value. The effect of $f_{best,S}$ is not clear, but it is assumed that this result is strongly specialized on the 3 training problems.

Fig. 1 charts the best fitness value found in each generation for the 3 runs of both training sets presented in Table 3. It is noticeable that the worst run for the small training set experienced almost no improvement over the generations;

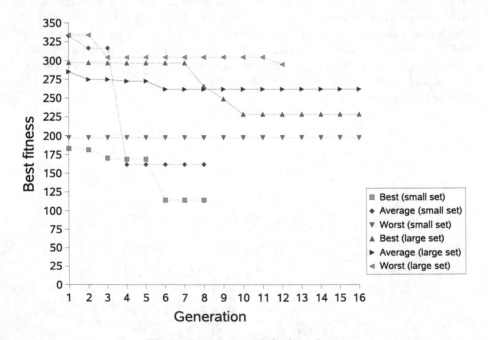

Fig. 1. Progression of the best fitness

Table 5. Solving time for problems not used in the training sets

Problem	$T_{std,orig}$	$T_{std,prep}$	$T_{init,orig}$	$T_{init,prep}$
5pipe_1_ooo	86	113	83	119
5pipe_2_ooo	108	116	165	142
5pipe_3_ooo	76	134	134	174
5pipe_4_ooo	1200	346	386	1200
5pipe_5_ooo	97	95	97	102
5pipe	55	131	45	147
6pipe_6_ooo	1200	1200	538	1200
7pipe_bug	1	1200	1200	1200
engine_4_nd	218	176	204	198
engine_5_nd_case1	102	109	104	104
engine_6_case1	438	273	329	275
5pipe_q0_k	278	1200	415	1200
6pipe_q0_k	210	189	144	341
Sum	4068	5281	3845	6403

it used the same population size (64) and timeout (60 sec.) as the best run for the large training set. Presumably the P parameters used in this work are too low, aggravating an effect known as *premature convergence* [1]. Another problem is the imprecision of the run time measurement, which could vary up to several seconds, so that small improvements can not be detected reliably.

Table 5 shows solving times in seconds for other problems from the benchmark suites [7] that were not used in the training sets (1200 for timing out after 10 minutes); not shown are problems that were not solvable by at least one configuration or took negligible solving time (less than 10 seconds). The indexes *std* and *init* mean standard MiniSAT or MiniSAT with initialization using $f_{best,L}$; *orig* and *prep* mean original or preprocessed problems. The last row of Table 5 contains the sum of the times, similar to the GP fitness measure. Solving the original problems with initialization has the best fitness, because it only times out once, for the problem 7pipe_bug. This may be because 7pipe_bug is the only satisfiable problem in [7], although preprocessing also makes it unproportionally harder to solve.

4   Conclusion and Future Work

An approach for optimizing the dynamic decision heuristics of DPLL SAT solvers was presented, in which the variable activities are initialized with values (once, before the search starts) which are dependent on the structure of the problem's CNF. A variable's activity is computed by examining all literals (except the variable's) in clauses that contain the variable, and calculating the sum over a function whose arguments are numerical values describing the literal, the variable or the CNF. The function is described by the individuals of genetic programming, which is used to evolve an optimal expression that minimizes solving time.

SAT problems from 3 different EDA benchmark suites were preprocessed to make the problems as compact and free of avoidable interference as possible for GP. A number of GP runs were executed using a small and a large training set of problems. Attempts to analyze the best evolved functions yielded unclear results. When the best initialization evolved for the large set was applied on the remaining problems of the benchmark suites, it was found that by using initialization on the original CNFs, rather than preprocessed ones, more problems could be solved with a timeout of 10 minutes than with the other configurations.

The population sizes and number of generations used in this work were untypically low for GP. One consequence of this was premature convergence, which was probably reinforced by the breeding strategy of the GP library. Higher GP parameters, larger training sets and a better breeding strategy may increase the chance to find a more efficient and more generally beneficial initialization.

The extent to which a single initialization of the variable activities can improve SAT solving is unknown. The presented approach may not be the most efficient to effectively analyze the CNF structure and compute generally beneficial initial activities. Using GP to describe more powerful programs, i.e. with memory operations, rather than a simple algebraic expression as in this work may yield a much better initialization.

References

1. J. R. Koza: Genetic Programming II: Automatic Discovery of Reusable Programs. MIT Press, Cambridge Massachusetts, 1994.
2. M. Davis, G. Logemann, D. Loveland: A machine program for theorem proving. Communications of the ACM, vol 5, 1962.
3. M. W. Moskewicz, C. F. Madigan, Y. Zhao, L. Zhang, S. Malik: Chaff: Engineering an Efficient SAT Solver. Proc. of the 38th Design Automation Conference, 2001.
4. N. Een, N. Sörensson: An Extensible SAT-solver. SAT 2003.
5. M. Hollick, H. Kuhlmann: Genetic Programming in C/C++. CSE99/CIS899 Final Report, May 1995. http://www.cis.upenn.edu/~hollick/genetic/paper2.html
6. J. P. Marques-Silva, K. A. Sakallah: GRASP - A New Search Algorithm for Satisfiability. ICCAD. IEEE Computer Society Press, 1996.
7. M. N. Velev, ENGINE-UNSAT.1.0, FVP-UNSAT.2.0, PIPE-UNSAT.1.1, Available from: http://www.ece.cmu.edu/~mvelev.
8. F. A. Aloul, I. L. Markov, K. A. Sakallah: MINCE: A Static Global Variable-Ordering Heuristic for SAT Search and BDD Manipulation. Journal of Universal Computer Science, vol. 10, no. 12 (2004), 1562-1596.

P-CAGE: An Environment for Evolutionary Computation in Peer-to-Peer Systems

Gianluigi Folino and Giandomenico Spezzano

Institute for High Performance Computing and Networking (ICAR)-CNR,
Via P. Bucci 41C - Rende(CS), Italy
{folino, spezzano}@icar.cnr.it

Abstract. Solving complex real-world problems using evolutionary computation is a CPU time-consuming task that requires a large amount of computational resources. Peer-to-Peer (P2P) computing has recently revealed as a powerful way to harness these resources and efficiently deal with such problems. In this paper, we present a P2P implementation of Genetic Programming based on the JXTA technology. To run genetic programs we use a distributed environment based on a hybrid multi-island model that combines the island model with the cellular model. Each island adopts a cellular genetic programming model and the migration occurs among neighboring peers. The implementation is based on a virtual ring topology. Three different termination criteria (*effort*, *time* and *max-gen*) have been implemented. Experiments on some popular benchmarks show that the approach presents a accuracy at least comparable with classical distributed models, retaining the obvious advantages in terms of decentralization, fault tolerance and scalability of P2P systems.

1 Introduction

Peer-to-peer (P2P) computing is attracting attention in research and industry, spurred also by the popularity of file sharing systems such as Napster, Gnutella, and Morpheus. Peers operate autonomously and asynchronously and perform well in a decentralized environment, as they reuse existing architecture, guarantee interoperability and can exploit the availability of networks resources. P2P networks are emerging as a new distributed computing paradigm for their potential to harness the computing power of the hosts composing the network and make their under-utilized resources available to others.

Genetic programming (GP) is an extension of genetic algorithms (GAs) that iteratively evolves a population of trees having variable size, by applying variation operators. Each individual encodes a candidate solution and is associated with a fitness value that measures the goodness-of-fit of that solution. The capability of GP in solving challenging problems, coming from different application domains, has been largely recognized, but for difficult problems GP requires large sizes of population and a sufficient number of generations. The necessity

P. Collet et al. (Eds.): EuroGP 2006, LNCS 3905, pp. 341–350, 2006.
© Springer-Verlag Berlin Heidelberg 2006

of high computational resources, both in terms of memory, to store large populations of trees, and in terms of time, to evaluate the fitness of the individuals in the population, may degrade GP performance drastically or make the algorithm inapplicable when it must cope with large difficult problems. The use of P2P resources may make large problems affordable for GP, by using large populations distributed around the network.

While P2P implementations of genetic algorithms are present in literature [10] [7], to the best of our knowledge, there are no P2P implementations of GP. Some efforts in this direction have already been made in the papers [2] [11] in which asynchronous and distributed GP models adapt to P2P implementations have been addressed. Other steps forward have been made in [5], in which some P2P problems are tackled to the aim of coping with wireless sensor networks.

We have devised a system, called P-CAGE (P2P CellulAr Genetic Environment), that is one of the first P2P implementation of GP. Our system has been developed using JXTA-J2SE libraries, the Java implementation of JXTA protocols [1] that guarantee interoperability, platform independence and ubiquity. JXTA technology is a set of open, generalized P2P protocols that allows any connected device (cell phone to PDA, PC to server) on the network to communicate and collaborate.

P-CAGE is based on a hybrid variation of the classic multi-island model that leads not only to a faster algorithm, but also to superior numerical performance. This hybrid model combines the island model with the cellular model. The island model is based on subpopulations, that are created by dividing the original population into disjunctive subsets of individuals, usually of the same size. Each subpopulation can be assigned to one processor and a standard (panmictic) GP algorithm is executed on it. Occasionally, a migration process between subpopulation is carried out after a fixed number of generations. For example, the k best individuals from one subpopulation are copied to the other subpopulations exchanging the genetic information among populations. Our hybrid model modifies the island model by substituting the standard GP algorithm with a cellular GP algorithm. In the cellular model each individual has a spatial location, a small neighborhood and interacts only within its neighborhood. The main difference in a cellular GP, with respect to a panmictic algorithm, is its decentralized selection mechanism and the genetic operators (crossover, mutation) adopted. In P-CAGE, to take advantage of the cellular model of GP, the cellular islands are not independently evolved, but the outmost individuals are asynchronously exchanged so that all islands can be thought as portions of a single population. P-CAGE distributes the evolutionary processes (islands) that implement the detection models over the network nodes using a virtual ring configuration. P-CAGE implements the hybrid model as a collection of cooperative autonomous islands running on the various hosts within a heterogeneous network that works as a P2P system. P-CAGE supports many advantages of P2P systems. It is asynchronous, scalable, fault tolerant and maintains the accuracy of other distributed approaches of GP.

The paper is organized as follows: in section 2, we provide a description of the architecture and give some details about the implementation of P-CAGE; section 3 presents the experimental results showing a comparison with other approaches and analyzing the scalability. Finally, section 4 concludes the paper and illustrates some directions for future works.

2   P-CAGE Architecture and Implementation

In this section we describe the implementation of P-CAGE and the algorithm executed by each peer to implement GP.

As showed in figure 1 P-CAGE is built on the top of JXTA services such as discovery and membership services and also supplies a graphical user interface. Peers are arranged on a self-configuring ring topology architecture, so they need to know only information on the left (previous) and right (next) neighbor. Each peer adopts the GP cellular approach described in [4] and performs the algorithm showed in figure 2.

In practice, first it discovers new peers, then it builds the virtual ring topology, conveniently choosing the left and right neighbor and connecting the neighboring peers by bidirectional channels. After the topology is established, each peer executes a certain number of iterations exchanging, at prefixed generations, the borders of the sub-population, in an asynchronous fashion, until a termination criterion is achieved. The general architecture of P-CAGE is showed in figure 3. In the following, the different phases of the algorithm are described in more detail.

Finding peers and building the ring: The ideas to build the virtual ring are inspired to the strategies described in [8]. The algorithm uses two parameters *min_peers* and *max_peers* to define respectively a minimum and a maximum number of peers forming the ring. At the beginning, each peer creates and joins a group called "GeneticProgramming" using the JXTA *membership service* and starts the search of peers belonging to this group (JXTA *discovery service*), until a timeout is expired or the maximum number of peers is reached. The time of discovery of each peer is stored. At this point, information is distributed to all the peers discovered and the peers are ordered by minimum time of discovery. The

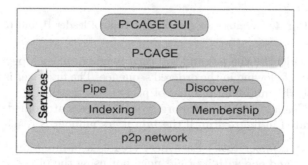

Fig. 1. P-CAGE application overview

```
find_peers(); build_ring(); build_pipes();
create_populations();
gen = 0;
while(!termination_criterion()){
        evolve_population(gen);
        evaluate_fitness();
        if(gen%gen_migration == 0)
                send_borders(); asinc_receive_borders();
        gen + +;
}
report_on_run();
```

Fig. 2. The pseudo code executed by each peer (termination criteria and fault tolerance strategy not reported)

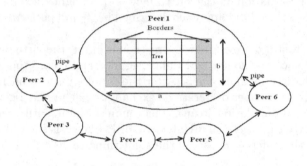

Fig. 3. Architecture of P-CAGE

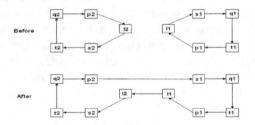

Fig. 4. Merging two groups by means of leader l1 and l2

order allows to identify the *left* and the *right* neighbor of each peer, respectively the previous and following in the ordered sequence. The first peer is named *leader* of the group. If the minimum number of peers is not reached, the leader tries to discover other leaders and two or more groups of peers are joined, following the schema illustrated in figure 4 until the *min_peers* number is reached.

Building pipe and finger table: Each peer creates a bi-directional channel with its left neighbor and one with its right neighbor using the pipe service of JXTA. To make the system robust a finger table is built storing k left and k right successors, where k typically assumes a value from 2 to 4. If a pipe falls down, the peer creates a new one using the information contained in the finger table, i.e. the table is checked until a peer is found and then linked with a pipe.

Evolving population: In the evolving phase, a population of trees with dimension $a \times b$ evolves on each peer, following the hybrid multi-island model adopted by P-CAGE (in practice, each peer represents an island adopting the cellular model as CAGE). Every k (gen_migration parameter) generations, the borders of the populations (the outside b trees on the left and on the right side) are exchanged among neighboring peers using the pipes, in an asynchronous fashion (i.e. if borders do not arrive to a peer before starting the computation, the peer goes on with the old trees).

Termination criteria: The algorithm terminates its execution, when a termination criterion is met, chosen among the following : *max-gen*, *time* and *effort*.

Using the first criterion, P-CAGE ends when each peer has reached the maximum number of generations. This criterion is easy to implement, but faster peers must wait slower ones. A timeout is introduced to avoid infinite waiting for peers that have gone down.

Using a time-based termination criterion, a maximum time is fixed and, when this time expires, all the peers must terminate. No synchronization is required, but it is difficult to estimate the right time, also considering the different loads and speeds of the computers involved in the computation. In fact, if we choose a time too short, the algorithm could not converge.

Last choice considers the effort, derived from the definition given in [3]. Let G be the number of generations, N the number of individuals of the population lying on each peer and AVG_LEN_p the average number of nodes per individual concerning peer p. Then the required effort in a particular generation n is:

$$\sum_{p=1}^{n} G \times N \times AVG\_LENGTH_p \tag{1}$$

Effort takes into account the overall effective computation carried out by the system. However, it requires an overhead necessary to compute the effort and to communicate the information; in fact, for each prefixed period of time, the total effort must be computed summing the efforts produced by each peer.

3   Experimental Results

In order to verify the goodness of our implementation, we compared, in terms of accuracy, our asynchronous hybrid multi-island model to a canonical sequential implementation of GP and to a parallel cellular implementation of GP.

We used sgpc1.1 [9] as the sequential implementation of genetic programming and CAGE [4] as the parallel cellular implementation of GP. The peer-to-peer experiments were conducted on the LAN of the CNR-ICAR Institute. All the experiments were run for 100 generations and averaged over 20 tries.

We have used the following problems as benchmark:

Symbolic Regression ([6] par. 7.3). The *symbolic regression* problem consists in searching for a non-trivial mathematical expression that, given a set of values x_i for the independent variable(s), always assumes the corresponding value y_i for the dependent variable(s) of a given mathematical function. In the first experiment, the target function was the polynomial $x^4 + x^3 + x^2 + x$. A sample of 20 data points (x_i, y_i) was generated by randomly choosing the values of the independent variable x in the interval [-1,1].

Discovery of Trigonometric Identities ([6] par. 10.1). In the second experiment, our aim was to discover a trigonometric identity for $cos2x$. 20 values x_i of the independent variable x were chosen randomly in the interval $[0,2\pi]$ and the corresponding value $y_i = cos2x_i$ computed. The 20 pairs (x_i, y_i) constituted the fitness cases. The fitness was then computed as the sum of the absolute value of the difference between y_i and the value generated by the program on x_i.

Symbolic Integration ([6] par. 10.5). The symbolic integration problem consists in searching for a symbolic mathematical expression that is the integral of a given curve. In this experiment the curve was $cosx + 2x + 1$ so the genetic program had to obtain $sinx + x^2 + x$, given 50 pairs (x_i, y_i) in the interval $[0,2\pi]$.

Even-4 Parity ([6] par. 20.4). The *Even-4 parity* problem consists in deciding the parity of a set of 4 bits. A Boolean function receives 4 Boolean variables and it returns TRUE only if an even number of variables is true. Thus the goal function to discover is $f(x_1, x_2, x_3, x_4) = x_1 x_2 x_3 x_4 \vee \overline{x_1} x_2 \overline{x_3} x_4 \vee \overline{x_1} x_2 x_3 \overline{x_4} \vee x_1 \overline{x_2} \overline{x_3} x_4 \vee x_1 \overline{x_2} x_3 \overline{x_4} \vee x_1 x_2 \overline{x_3} \overline{x_4} \vee \overline{x_1}\ \overline{x_2}\ \overline{x_3}\ \overline{x_4}$. The fitness cases explored were the 2^4 combinations of the variables. The fitness was the sum of the Hamming distances between the goal function and the solution found.

Even-5 Parity. The problem is the analogue of even-4 considering 5 bit instead of 4.

Ant Santa Fe ([6] par. 7.2). The *artificial ant* problem consists in finding the best list of moves that an ant can execute on a 32×32 matrix in order to eat all the pieces of food put on the grid. In this experiment we used the *Santa Fe trail* that contains 89 food particles. The fitness function was obtained by diminishing the number of food particles by one every time the ant arrived in a cell containing food. The ant can see the food only if it is in the cell ahead in its same direction (*IfFoodAhead* move); otherwise it can move randomly (*left* or *right*) for two (*Progn2*) or three (*Progn3*) moves.

This last problem is known to be difficult for distributed *GP*.

The parameters of the method are shown in table 1; functions and terminal symbols for each problem are tha same described in Koza's book [6]. For all the experiments, we used an overall population size of 3200, except for *Symbolic Regression*. For this problem, the size of the population was set to 800 individuals. In the parallel implementation, the population size was divided equally among the nodes and the same was made in the peer-to-peer implementation

Table 1. GP Parameters

Maximum number of generations	100
Probability of crossover	0.8
Probability of choosing internal points for crossover	0.1
Probability of mutation	0.1
Probability of reproduction	0.1
Generative Method for initial random population	Ramped
Maximum depth for a new tree	6
Max depth for a tree after crossover	17
Max depth of a tree for mutation	4
Parsimony factor	0.0

among the peers. In this two last cases the *Moore* neighborhood was adopted. For P-CAGE, we used 5 peers, migration occurred every 5 generations and the termination criterion was max-gen.

In the figures 5 a and b, 6 a and b and 7 a and b the results of our experiments are reported respectively for symbolic regression, discoveries of trigonometric identities, symbolic integration, ant Santa Fe and even 4 and 5 parity problems.

Observing these figures, we can notice that P-CAGE outperforms canonical GP for all the problems and it is better or at least comparable with the parallel cellular implementation. The P-CAGE accuracy is considerably better for the even 4 parity problem, it is lightly better for the discovery of trigonometric identities and the symbolic regression problem, and is lightly worst only for the Ant Santa Fe problem.

To study the scalability of our system, we ran our system, using the same parameters previously described, varying the number of peers (3, 5, 10) and maintaining the same overall population. As you can see in figures 8 a and b,9 a and b, 10 a and b, differences are not statistically significant or are minimal.

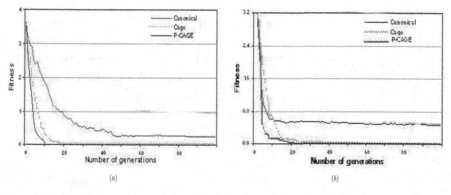

(a)   (b)

Fig. 5. Accuracy comparison for a) symbolic regression and b) discovery of trigonometric identities: Canonical GP, CAGE and P-CAGE

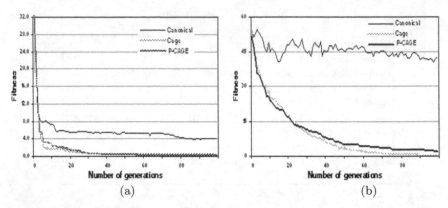

Fig. 6. Accuracy comparison for a) symbolic integration and b) Ant Santa Fe: Canonical GP, CAGE and P-CAGE

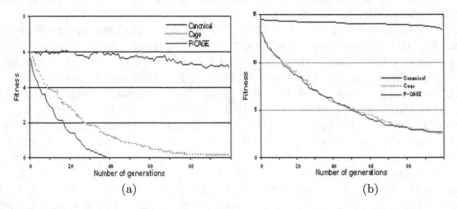

Fig. 7. Accuracy comparison for a) Even 4 parity and b) Even 5 parity: Canonical GP, CAGE and P-CAGE

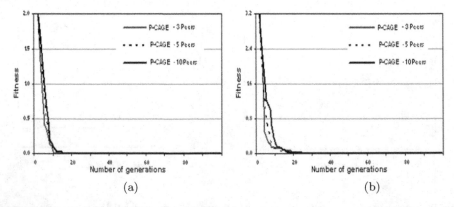

Fig. 8. Scalability for (a) symbolic regression and (b) discovery of trigonometric identities: 3, 5 and 10 peers

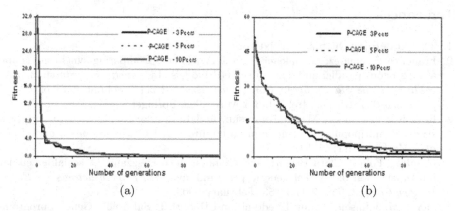

Fig. 9. Scalability for (a) symbolic integration and (b) Ant Santa Fe: 3, 5 and 10 peers

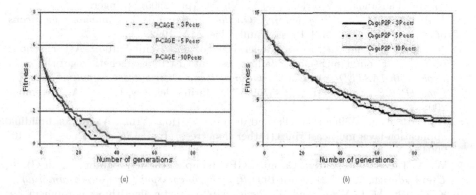

Fig. 10. Scalability for (a) Even 4 parity and (b) Even 5 parity: 3, 5 and 10 peers

4 Conclusions

In this paper the P-CAGE environment for the execution of genetic programs
in a P2P environment has been presented. Each peer adopts a cellular model
and the migration occurs among the neighboring peers, displaced in a
virtual ring topology. Experiments on a real network showed that P-CAGE
outperforms canonical GP implementation, as expected, and is at least comparable with parallel implementations of GP. Anyway, it exploits the advantages of P2P networks as it is fault tolerant, inexpensive and scalable in terms
of resources. Scalability is reached also in terms of accuracy, as showed by
the experiments, even if we used a number of peers that, in some cases, was
excessive for the difficulty of the problem. In the future, we are interested
in investigating the use of different topologies as small world and scale-free
networks.

References

1. The jxta project. http://www.jxta.org.
2. Francisco Fernandez, G. Galeano, and J. A. Gomez. Comparing synchronous and asynchronous parallel and distributed GP models. In *Genetic Programming, Proceedings of the 5th European Conference, EuroGP 2002*, volume 2278 of *LNCS*, pages 326–335, Kinsale, Ireland, 3-5 April 2002. Springer-Verlag.
3. Francisco Fernandez, Marco Tomassini, and Leonardo Vanneschi. An empirical study of multipopulation genetic programming. *Genetic Programming and Evolvable Machines*, 4(1):21–51, 2003.
4. Gianluigi Folino, Clara Pizzuti, and Giandomenico Spezzano. A scalable cellular implementation of parallel genetic programming. *IEEE Transactions on Evolutionary Computation*, 7(1):37–53, February 2003.
5. Derek M. Johnson, Ankur Teredesai, and Robert T. Saltarelli. Genetic programming in wireless sensor networks. In *Proceedings of the 8th European Conference on Genetic Programming*, volume 3447 of *Lecture Notes in Computer Science*, pages 96–107, Lausanne, Switzerland, 30 March - 1 April 2005. Springer.
6. J. R. Koza. *Genetic Programming: On the Programming of Computers by means of Natural Selection*. MIT Press, Cambridge, MA, 1992.
7. José Carlos Clemente Litrán, Xavier Défago, and Kenji Satou. Asynchronous peer-to-peer communication for failure resilient distributed genetic algorithms. In *Proc. 15th IASTED Int'l Conf. on Parallel and Distributed Computing and Systems (PDCS)*, volume II, pages 769–773, Marina del Rey, CA, USA, November 2003.
8. Ahmed Sobeih, William Yurcik, and Jennifer C. Hou. Vring: A case for building application-layer multicast rings (rather than trees). In *MASCOTS*, pages 437–446, 2004.
9. W. A. Tackett and Aviram Carmi. SGPC (simple genetic programming in C). *C Users Journal*, 12(4):121, April 1994,*ftp://ftp.io.com/pub/genetic-programming*.
10. K. C. Tan, M. L. Wang, and W. Peng. A p2p genetic algorithm environment for the internet. *Commun. ACM*, 48(4):113–116, 2005.
11. Marco Tomassini, Leonardo Vanneschi, Francisco Fernandez, and German Galeano. Experimental investigation of three distributed genetic programming models. In *Parallel Problem Solving from Nature - PPSN VII*, number 2439 in Lecture Notes in Computer Science, LNCS, pages 641–650, Granada, Spain, 7-11 September 2002. Springer-Verlag.

Positional Independence and Recombination in Cartesian Genetic Programming

Xinye Cai, Stephen L. Smith, and Andy M. Tyrrell

Department of Electronics, The University of York,
Heslington, York YO10 5DD, UK
{sls5, amt}@ohm.york.ac.uk

Abstract. Previously, recombination (or crossover) has proved to be unbeneficial in Cartesian Genetic Programming (CGP). This paper describes the implementation of an implicit context representation for CGP in which the specific location of genes within the chromosome has no direct or indirect influence on the phenotype. Consequently, recombination has a beneficial effect and is shown to outperform conventional CGP in the even-3 parity problem.

1 Introduction

Cartesian Genetic Programming (CGP) [1,2] is a form of Genetic Programming (GP) which adopts a cartesian arrangement of functional components, in contrast to convetional GP, which is based on a parse tree structure. CGP exhibits a number of benefits over traditional GP, the best known of which is avoidance of *bloat*, an uncontrolled expansion of the program during evolution.

A criticism of CGP (and GP in general) is that the location of genes within the chromosome has a direct or indirect influence on the resulting phenotype [6]. In other words, the order in which specific information regarding the definition of the GP is stored has a direct or indirect effect on the operation, performance and characteristics of the resulting program. Such effects are considered undesirable as they may mask or modify the role of the specific genes in the generation of the phenotype (or resulting program). Consequently, GPs are often referred to as possessing a direct or indirect context representation.

An alternative representation for GPs in which genes do not express positional dependence has been proposed by Lones and Tyrrell [3-7]. Termed *implicit context representation,* the order in which genes are used to describe the phenotype (or resulting program) is determined after their self-organised binding, based on their own characteristics and not their specific location within the genotype. The result is an implicit context representation version of conventional parse tree-type GP termed *Enzyme Genetic Programming.*

It is argued that important sources of evolvability include *positional independence, functional and structural redundancy, neutrality* and *implicit reuse* of components. CGP is an example of an indirect context representation and exhibits three of these properties. A summary of Lones' argument is provided below with particular regard to conventional CGP.

P. Collet et al. (Eds.): EuroGP 2006, LNCS 3905, pp. 351–360, 2006.
© Springer-Verlag Berlin Heidelberg 2006

Functional and structural redundancy: Components are only active in the final program if connections are specified by the genotype, otherwise, components are inactive. During the process of evolution, it is possible that some components will subsequently become active and others inactive. This is termed variation filtering and can be considered a characteristic of functional and structural redundancy. A number of researchers have reported improved performance when non-coding components of evolving solutions (commonly termed introns) are accommodated within genetic algorithms [8,9] and linear genetic programming [10,11], but detrimental for tree-based genetic programming [12].

Implicit reuse: As the components within CGP can have more than one output (and hence satisfy more than one input) implicit reuse of components is provided in a way that is not possible within a conventional parse tree representation of standard GP. Poli [13] and Miller and Thomson [1] report solutions utilising components with multiple outputs that supports the argument that implicit reuse (as with the biological equivalent, pleiotropy) encourages evolvability.

Neutrality: The functional and structural redundancy described above also permits neutrality to be exhibited in the form of evolving interconnections between components that aren't expressed in the current program. Subsequent single point mutations may lead to changes to the network that cause these previously redundant components to contribute to a fitter program.

However, CGP does not exhibit positional independence. The effect or meaning of a component in the evolved or resulting program is determined by its absolute or relative position in the program representation. The manner in which components are referenced in CGP is considered arbitrary as there is no correlation between a component's absolute coordinates and its behaviour. Therefore it can be argued that indirect context representation has no effect beyond describing the connectivity of a specific program. This is also the case when considering the behaviour of components in different programs. Components with the same functionality may have different coordinates and those with different functionality the same coordinates. Hence, any form of recombination, such as crossover is unlikely to be constructive in the evolutionary process and could explain why this has not been found to be useful in CGP [1]. A lack of positional independence also has an important effect on the relationship between genes that in combination effect good performance.

Recombination will not preserve the relationship of these genes, commonly referred to as building blocks, when conventional forms of crossover are employed. Various attempts have been adopted to minimise the destructive effect that such positional dependence in the representation by preserving building blocks that describe the beneficial relationship between particular genes. In GAs, this is termed linkage learning, and has been implemented by limiting the destructive effect of crossover operations by using special crossover templates [14,15]. However, this does not overcome the underlying problem which is associated with the program representation. A successful approach is the messy GA [16] which uses a floating representation to achieve linkage learning. This adopts a two stage solution of identifying building blocks and then reassembling them intact in the recombined program. However, the algorithm is complex and difficult to apply to a wide range of problem domains with good effect. An alternative proposed by Harik [17] called the linkage learning GA overcomes many of these shortcomings. Floating representations have also been applied to GPs, but with limited success [18] and hence the position dependent nature of CGP still needs addressing.

A further concern with an indirect context representation such as CGP is that when a component's input references are mutated, the resulting arrangement of components is in no way represents the degree of mutation applied and hence, cannot be varied in a gradual manner.

This paper describes the implementation of an implicit context representation of CGP which it is argued overcomes many of the disadvantages described above. Specifically, it provides positional independence and thus, supports recombination in a constructive manner.

2   Implicit Context Representation

As described above, CGP can be described as an *indirect context representation*; the position a particular gene occupies in the chromosome has an influence on the resulting phenotype. Ideally, the evolution of a system should be independent of the position of genes within the chromosome, but should still be a result of the values of those genes. This is termed an *implicit context representation* by Lones and Tyrrell [3], who have developed a form the conventional parse tree type GP that exploits this representation, called *Enzyme Genetic Programming* (EGP). The biological inspiration for Enzyme GP is the metabolic pathway, and the role of enzymes which express computational characteristics. Implicit context representation employs an enzyme model comprising a shape, activity and specificities (or binding sites) [6], as shown in Fig. 1.

Along with inputs and outputs, the enzyme model can be considered a program component from which a genetic program may be constructed. The shape describes how the enzyme is seen by other program components. Similarly, the binding sites determine the shape (and hence type) of program component the enzyme wishes to bind to. Finally, the activity determines the logical function the enzyme is to perform. A typical EGP will comprise a set number of inputs and outputs and a number of enzyme models or components. Values for each component's binding sites and logical function are initialized non-deterministically; the component's shape, however, is derived from a combination of its binding site's shapes and logical function as shown in Fig. 2. In this example the conventional GP parse tree is formed through binding of sub-trees whose shapes match the binding site shapes of the AND component. Consequently, the shape of the AND component now represents the functionality of the whole tree below it. Once initialized, components are bound together to form a network. The order in which components are bound is determined by the closeness of match between one component's binding site and another component's shape.

The best matching components are bound first and the process is repeated until a network has formed in which no further binding is possible.

Over time, components may evolve through mutation. Mutation is applied to the component's binding sites and logical function with a pre-determined probability. When this occurs, a new component shape is derived accordingly and may lead to different binding between components occurring. This in turn may result in a modified network.

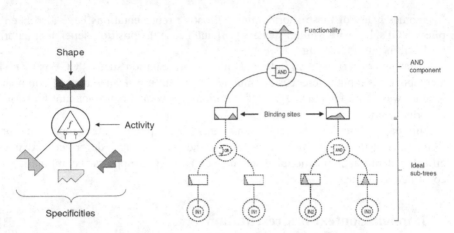

Fig. 1. Enzyme model illustrating shape, activity and specificities (binding sites) [6]

Fig. 2. Calculation of a component's shape from its binding site shapes and logical function [6]

3   Implementation of Implicit Context Representation in CGP

The aim of the work described here is to combine the benefits of an implicit context representation with CGP and, hence, address the undesirable positional dependence expressed by CGP.

The processing elements within the CGP are particularly suited to the implicit context representation. However, instead of employing a parse tree arrangement, the existing CGP Cartesian arrangement is maintained. There is also significant difference in the manner in which components are initialized, selected and interconnected within the representation.

3.1   Network Structure

A predetermined number of functional components are generated to form the network. Each component has the same (predetermined) number of binding sites, a function and a shape. The binding sites facilitate binding to other components and hence provide input values to which the selected function is applied. All shapes share a common format and consist of a number of dimensions which represent the different inputs and functions available within the network. For example, a network that has three inputs and a choice of four functions will employ a shape with seven dimensions for each component. Each dimension within the shape contains an integer value between 0 and 255 that represents the strength of that input or function expressed by the component. This is illustrated in Fig. 3.

The component's shape is derived from a combination of the component's binding sites' shapes and the component's function index (using a value of 255 in the relevant dimension) as shown in Fig. 4.

Formation of a component's shape in this way not only describes the functionality of the component itself, but also those components which the binding sites have a desire to bind to. In this way, a shape gives a description of the functionality of the desired network to be formed from this point onwards.

The problem to be addressed will normally dictate the number of input and output components that the representation will employ, e.g. even parity 3 will require three input components and one output component. Input components differ from others in that they have no need for binding sites or a function. They do, however, still have a shape which describes the respective input component. Conversely, output components have a binding site and function, but no shape.

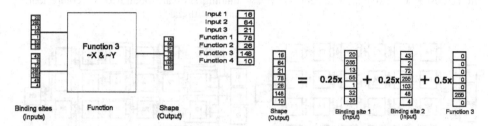

Fig. 3. Implicit context representation CGP component showing multidimensional shape and binding sites

Fig. 4. Derivation of the component's shape from the component's function and binding sites' shapes

3.2 Component Initialisation

All functional and output components have their binding sites initialised by assigning random values. A component's function is also assigned randomly from a predetermined set. Each component's shape is then derived from a combination of its function and binding sites' shapes as shown in Fig. 4.

3.3 Network Formation

Initialisation of the network is similar to that employed in conventional CGP. Components populate the specified Cartesian graph (e.g. four rows by six columns) and the shape of each component is initially bound randomly to the binding site of another component. However, it should be noted that as more than one component's shape may be bound to a single binding site, so it is not necessarily the case that every component's binding site is utilised. To encourage stability in the early evolution of the network, during the initialisation process, the dimension of a binding site is replaced with that of the shape to which it is bound, providing a perfect bind.

During evolution, formation of the network follows more closely that described in Section 2. Binding of components in the CGP network begins with the assignment of an output component that will ultimately provide the resulting value for the problem under consideration. The binding site of the output component is then made active and will bind to the component shape which exhibits the closest match. This is simply determined by summing the difference between each relative pair of dimensions within the vector for one component's binding site and another component's shape.

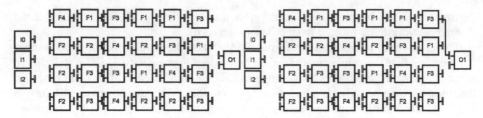

Fig. 5a. Components are arranged, unbound, in the desired Cartesian arrangement

Fig. 5b. Starting at the Output component, binding sites are bound to the component's shape with the "best fit"

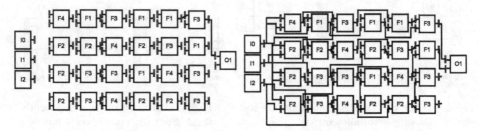

Fig. 5c. Binding sites for each component bound are then bound to further components on a "best-fit-first" basis

Fig. 5d. When no further binding can take place, the network can be evaluated

The combination of component shape and binding site that exhibits the smallest difference can be considered to be the "best fit".

Once bound, a component's binding sites will also become active and will bind in the same way to other components located in columns to the left. This continues until all components have been bound. A simple example is provided in Fig. 5.

The particular Cartesian arrangement specified constrains the manner with which the formation of the network takes place. Successful binding of a new component may only take place if it is within a set number of columns to the left of the existing component. If this is not the case, then binding with an existing, suboptimal fitting component will occur.

This follows the constraints imposed in the conventional GCP representation, specifically that any newly bound component must be placed to the left of the existing component. Additional constraints may also be applied, such as specifying a maximum distance between bound components, in terms of the number of columns separating them. Similarly, input components may also be constrained, if required, so they may only be bound to components a certain number of columns to their right in the representation, again to reflect the limitations of the target hardware infrastructure.

Once all possible binding has completed, a network description is generated which describes the network in the same manner as for conventional CGP and the fitness of the resulting network is calculated in the normal way.

The above process is repeated for each individual in the population and selection criteria for the next generation may be applied as required. Evolution of the selected individual, is however, different to that undertaken in conventional CGP. The concept of mutating both the connections and function of a component is maintained, but in the implicit context representation this is performed by mutating the component's binding sites and function in a non-deterministic manner.

As stated earlier, recombination is not usually undertaken in conventional CGP because it has not been found to improved performance, possibly because of arbitrary references that the indirect representation facilitates. However, now an implicit context representation has been adopted, recombination should, in theory, increase performance of the program; its implementation is described below.

Once mutation and recombination has been completed, the component's activity shape needs to be recalculated to represent any changes that have subsequently occurred. A new network can then be formed by rebinding components; again on a "best fit first" basis as previously described.

3.4 Mutation

Two separate mutation operations are performed according to predefined probabilities: (i) to the binding sites of the components and, (ii) to the index that selects the component's function from those available. Once these mutations have been performed, new shapes for each component are derived as described in Section 3 and shown in Fig. 4.

3.5 Selection Scheme

A conventional, q-tournament selection scheme is adopted; one of the advantages being that it does not require a global fitness comparison of all individuals in the population. From the population, a group of q individuals is randomly chosen (where q is the *tournament size*). The fittest individual from the tournament group will be selected and placed in a pool for recombination. The process is repeated until the required number of individuals has been attained. Experimentation suggests that for this application, a 9-tournament scheme is most likely to provide best performance for both maximum and average fitness over 20 runs.

3.6 Crossover Operator

An important benefit of an implicit context representation is that recombination supports meaningful variation filtering, i.e. the effects of inappropriate variation events are suppressed, whilst promoting meaningful change, leading to fitter solutions. For the implicit context representation of CGP described here, a conventional 2-point crossover was used to exchange components available to the two individuals. This is simply implemented as each component available to each individual is held in a sequential list.

4 Experimentation and Results

The performance of the implicit context representation version of CGP was compared with conventional CGP using the even-3 parity problem. This Boolean function outputs a one if an even number of its inputs are one, otherwise it outputs zero. The primitive function set used to evolve a solution to even-3 parity was {AND, OR, NAND, NOR}. It is well known that evolving a correct even-3 parity function is difficult using this function set [19].

To measure the difficulty of evolving these functions the minimum computational effort measure described by Koza [19] was employed. This calculates the minimum

Table 1. Parameters for both conventional and implicit context representation CGP

Parameter	Value
Problem	Even-3 parity
Population size	25
Number of generations	10000
Number of runs	100
Levels back	1
Available functions	AND, OR, NAND, NOR
Function mutation rate	2.0%-4.0%[*]
Binding site mutation rate	2.0%-4.0%[*]
Crossover rate	60%
q-tournament	9
Mutation rate	4.0%-10.0%[*]

([*]depending on network configuration)

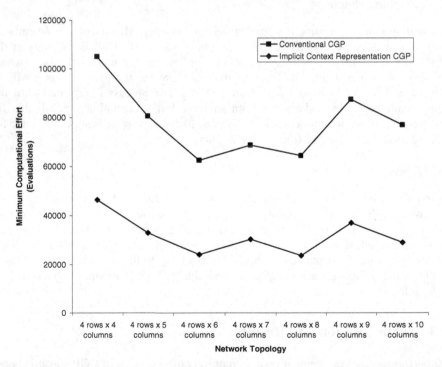

Fig. 6. Comparison of performance of conventional and implicit context representation CGP

number of genotype evaluations required to give a 0.99 probability of success in an evolutionary run. The performance of the implicit context representation of CGP was compared with that of conventional CGP over 100 evolutionary runs for a range of network topologies from 4 rows and 4 columns to 4 rows and 10 columns.

Common parameters for both conventional and implicit context representation CGP are listed in Table 1.

Results for 100 runs of both conventional and implicit context representation CGP on the even-3 parity problem, over a range of Cartesian configurations are shown in Fig. 6. The implicit context representation version of CGP can be seen to outperform the conventional form over all network topologies.

5 Conclusions

The work described here is intended to demonstrate that positional independence is an important feature in evolutionary computation and that when implemented in Cartesian genetic programming, leads to better performance by supporting constructive recombination. It is accepted that the performance benefits reported in Section 4 are probably outweighed by the additional processing required to form the network. However, more demanding problems are being investigated which will make this an acceptable overhead.

The principle of self-organising networks is being investigated further with respect to the optimum topology for the particular problem in hand and the mechanism by with the network is formed. These, in combination with more conventional parameters such as mutation and crossover rates have a fundamental effect on the performance of the algorithm.

References

1. J. F. Miller and P. Thomson, Cartesian Genetic Programming, In R. Poli, W. Banzhaf, W. B. Langdon, J. F. Miller, P. Nordin, T. C. Fogarty, (eds.), Third European Conference on Genetic Programming. Lecture Notes in Computer Science, Vol. 1802, 121-132, 2000.
2. J. F. Miller, D. Job, and V. K. Vasilev: Principles in the evolutionary design of digital circuits—Part I. Genetic Programming and Evolvable Machines, Vol. 1, 2000, 7–36.
3. M. A. Lones and A. M. Tyrrell: Enzyme genetic programming. Proc. 2001 Congress on Evolutionary Computation, J.-H. Kim, B.-T. Zhang, G. Fogel, and I. Kuscu (eds.), IEEE Press. Vol. 2, 2001, 1183–1190.
4. M. A. Lones and A. M. Tyrrell: Crossover and Bloat in the Functionality Model of Enzyme Genetic Programming. Proc. Congress on Evolutionary Computation 2002 (CEC2002), 2002, 986-992.
5. M. A. Lones and A. M. Tyrrell: Biomimetic Representation with Enzyme Genetic Programming. Journal of Genetic Programming and Evolvable Machines. Vol.3 No.2, 2002, 193-217.
6. M. A. Lones: Enzyme Genetic Programming. PhD Thesis, University of York, UK, 2003.
7. M. A. Lones and A. M. Tyrrell: Modeling biological evolvability: implicit context and variation filtering in enzyme generic programming. BioSystems, 2004.

8. J. R. Levenick, Inserting introns improves genetic algorithm success rate: Taking a cue from biology, In R. K. Belew and L. B. Booker (eds.), Proceedings of the Fourth International Conference on Genetic Algorithms, 123-127. Morgan Kaufmann, 1991.

9. S. Wu and R. K. Lindsay. Empirical studies of the genetic algorithm with non-coding segments. Evolutionary Computation, Vol. 3, 1995, 121-148.

10. W. Banzhaf, P. Nordin, R. E. Keller, and F. D. Francone. Geneticprogramming: An introduction. Morgan Kaufmann, San Francisco, 1998.

11. P. Nordin., A compiling genetic programming system that directly manipulates the machine code, In Kenneth E. Kinnear, Jr., editor, Advances in Genetic Programming, chapter 14, pp. 311.331. MIT Press, 1994.

12. P. W. Smith and K. Harries, Code growth, explicitly defined introns, and alternative selection schemes, Evolutionary Computation, Vol. 6, No. 4, 339-360, 1998.

13. R. Poli, Evolution of graph-like programs with parallel distributed genetic programming, In T. Bäck (ed.), Genetic Algorithms: Proceedings of the Seventh International Conference (ICGA96), 346-353. Morgan Kaufmann, 1996.

14. R. Rosenberg, Simulation of Genetic Populations with Biochemical Properties, PhD thesis, 1967.

15. J. Schaffer and A. Morishima, An adaptive crossover distribution mechanism for genetic algorithms, In Proceedings of the Second International Conference on Genetic Algorithms and their Applications, 1987.

16. D. E. Goldberg, K. Deb, H. Kargupta, and H. George, Rapid accurate optimization of difficult problems using fast messy genetic algorithms., In S. Forrest, editor, Proceedings of The Fifth International Conference On Genetic Algorithms. Morgan Kaufmann, 1993.

17. G. R. Harik. Learning gene linkage to efficiently solve problems of bounded difficulty using genetic algorithms. PhD thesis, University of Michigan, 1997.

18. S. Luke, S. Hamahashi, and H. Kitano, Genetic. Programming, In Wolfgang Banzhaf et al., editors, Proceedings of the Genetic and Evolutionary Computation Conference (GECCO'99). Morgan Kaufmann, 1999.

19. J. R. Koza, Genetic Programming: On the Programming of Computers by Means of Natural Selection. Cambridge, MIT Press, 1992.

Author Index

Lecture Notes in Computer Science

For information about Vols. 1–3816

please contact your bookseller or Springer

Vol. 3925: A. Valmari (Ed.), Model Checking Software. X, 307 pages. 2006.

Vol. 3924: P. Sestoft (Ed.), Programming Languages and Systems. XII, 343 pages. 2006.

Vol. 3923: A. Mycroft, A. Zeller (Eds.), Compiler Construction. XV, 277 pages. 2006.

Vol. 3922: L. Baresi, R. Heckel (Eds.), Fundamental Approaches to Software Engineering. XIII, 427 pages. 2006.

Vol. 3921: L. Aceto, A. Ingólfsdóttir (Eds.), Foundations of Software Science and Computational Structures. XV, 447 pages. 2006.

Vol. 3920: H. Hermanns, J. Palsberg (Eds.), Tools and Algorithms for the Construction and Analysis of Systems. XIV, 506 pages. 2006.

Vol. 3916: J. Li, Q. Yang, A.-H. Tan (Eds.), Data Mining for Biomedical Applications. VIII, 155 pages. 2006. (Sublibrary LNBI).

Vol. 3905: P. Collet, M. Tomassini, M. Ebner, S. Gustafson, A. Ekárt (Eds.), Genetic Programming. XI, 361 pages. 2006.

Vol. 3904: M. Baldoni, U. Endriss, A. Omicini, P. Torroni (Eds.), Declarative Agent Languages and Technologies III. XII, 245 pages. 2006. (Sublibrary LNAI).

Vol. 3903: K. Chen, R. Deng, X. Lai, J. Zhou (Eds.), Information Security Practice and Experience. XIV, 392 pages. 2006.

Vol. 3901: P.M. Hill (Ed.), Logic Based Program Synthesis and Transformation. X, 179 pages. 2006.

Vol. 3899: S. Frintrop, VOCUS: A Visual Attention System for Object Detection and Goal-Directed Search. XIV, 216 pages. 2006. (Sublibrary LNAI).

Vol. 3896: Y. Ioannidis, M.H. Scholl, J.W. Schmidt, F. Matthes, M. Hatzopoulos, K. Boehm, A. Kemper, T. Grust, C. Boehm (Eds.), Advances in Database Technology - EDBT 2006. XIV, 1208 pages. 2006.

Vol. 3895: O. Goldreich, A.L. Rosenberg, A.L. Selman (Eds.), Theoretical Computer Science. XII, 399 pages. 2006.

Vol. 3894: W. Grass, B. Sick, K. Waldschmidt (Eds.), Architecture of Computing Systems - ARCS 2006. XII, 496 pages. 2006.

Vol. 3890: S.G. Thompson, R. Ghanea-Hercock (Eds.), Defence Applications of Multi-Agent Systems. XII, 141 pages. 2006. (Sublibrary LNAI).

Vol. 3889: J. Rosca, D. Erdogmus, J.C. Príncipe, S. Haykin (Eds.), Independent Component Analysis and Blind Signal Separation. XXI, 980 pages. 2006.

Vol. 3888: D. Draheim, G. Weber (Eds.), Trends in Enterprise Application Architecture. IX, 145 pages. 2006.

Vol. 3887: J.R. Correa, A. Hevia, M. Kiwi (Eds.), LATIN 2006: Theoretical Informatics. XVI, 814 pages. 2006.

Vol. 3886: E.G. Bremer, J. Hakenberg, E.-H.(S.) Han, D. Berrar, W. Dubitzky (Eds.), Knowledge Discovery in Life Science Literature. XIV, 147 pages. 2006. (Sublibrary LNBI).

Vol. 3885: V. Torra, Y. Narukawa, A. Valls, J. Domingo-Ferrer (Eds.), Modeling Decisions for Artificial Intelligence. XII, 374 pages. 2006. (Sublibrary LNAI).

Vol. 3884: B. Durand, W. Thomas (Eds.), STACS 2006. XIV, 714 pages. 2006.

Vol. 3881: S. Gibet, N. Courty, J.-F. Kamp (Eds.), Gesture in Human-Computer Interaction and Simulation. XIII, 344 pages. 2006. (Sublibrary LNAI).

Vol. 3880: A. Rashid, M. Aksit (Eds.), Transactions on Aspect-Oriented Software Development I. IX, 335 pages. 2006.

Vol. 3879: T. Erlebach, G. Persinao (Eds.), Approximation and Online Algorithms. X, 349 pages. 2006.

Vol. 3878: A. Gelbukh (Ed.), Computational Linguistics and Intelligent Text Processing. XVII, 589 pages. 2006.

Vol. 3877: M. Detyniecki, J.M. Jose, A. Nürnberger, C. J. '. van Rijsbergen (Eds.), Adaptive Multimedia Retrieval: User, Context, and Feedback. XI, 279 pages. 2006.

Vol. 3876: S. Halevi, T. Rabin (Eds.), Theory of Cryptography. XI, 617 pages. 2006.

Vol. 3875: S. Ur, E. Bin, Y. Wolfsthal (Eds.), Haifa Verification Conference. X, 265 pages. 2006.

Vol. 3874: R. Missaoui, J. Schmidt (Eds.), Formal Concept Analysis. X, 309 pages. 2006. (Sublibrary LNAI).

Vol. 3873: L. Maicher, J. Park (Eds.), Charting the Topic Maps Research and Applications Landscape. VIII, 281 pages. 2006. (Sublibrary LNAI).

Vol. 3872: H. Bunke, A. L. Spitz (Eds.), Document Analysis Systems VII. XIII, 630 pages. 2006.

Vol. 3870: S. Spaccapietra, P. Atzeni, W.W. Chu, T. Catarci, K.P. Sycara (Eds.), Journal on Data Semantics V. XIII, 237 pages. 2006.

Vol. 3869: S. Renals, S. Bengio (Eds.), Machine Learning for Multimodal Interaction. XIII, 490 pages. 2006.

Vol. 3868: K. Römer, H. Karl, F. Mattern (Eds.), Wireless Sensor Networks. XI, 342 pages. 2006.

Vol. 3866: T. Dimitrakos, F. Martinelli, P.Y.A. Ryan, S. Schneider (Eds.), Formal Aspects in Security and Trust. X, 259 pages. 2006.

Vol. 3865: W. Shen, K.-M. Chao, Z. Lin, J.-P.A. Barthès (Eds.), Computer Supported Cooperative Work in Design II. XII, 359 pages. 2006.

Vol. 3863: M. Kohlhase (Ed.), Mathematical Knowledge Management. XI, 405 pages. 2006. (Sublibrary LNAI).

Vol. 3862: R.H. Bordini, M. Dastani, J. Dix, A.E.F. Seghrouchni (Eds.), Programming Multi-Agent Systems. XIV, 267 pages. 2006. (Sublibrary LNAI).

Vol. 3861: J. Dix, S.J. Hegner (Eds.), Foundations of Information and Knowledge Systems. X, 331 pages. 2006.

Vol. 3860: D. Pointcheval (Ed.), Topics in Cryptology – CT-RSA 2006. XI, 365 pages. 2006.

Vol. 3858: A. Valdes, D. Zamboni (Eds.), Recent Advances in Intrusion Detection. X, 351 pages. 2006.

Vol. 3857: M.P.C. Fossorier, H. Imai, S. Lin, A. Poli (Eds.), Applied Algebra, Algebraic Algorithms and Error-Correcting Codes. XI, 350 pages. 2006.

Vol. 3855: E. A. Emerson, K.S. Namjoshi (Eds.), Verification, Model Checking, and Abstract Interpretation. XI, 443 pages. 2005.

Vol. 3854: I. Stavrakakis, M. Smirnov (Eds.), Autonomic Communication. XIII, 303 pages. 2006.

Vol. 3853: A.J. Ijspeert, T. Masuzawa, S. Kusumoto (Eds.), Biologically Inspired Approaches to Advanced Information Technology. XIV, 388 pages. 2006.

Vol. 3852: P.J. Narayanan, S.K. Nayar, H.-Y. Shum (Eds.), Computer Vision – ACCV 2006, Part II. XXXI, 977 pages. 2006.

Vol. 3851: P.J. Narayanan, S.K. Nayar, H.-Y. Shum (Eds.), Computer Vision – ACCV 2006, Part I. XXXI, 973 pages. 2006.

Vol. 3850: R. Freund, G. Păun, G. Rozenberg, A. Salomaa (Eds.), Membrane Computing. IX, 371 pages. 2006.

Vol. 3849: I. Bloch, A. Petrosino, A.G.B. Tettamanzi (Eds.), Fuzzy Logic and Applications. XIV, 438 pages. 2006. (Sublibrary LNAI).

Vol. 3848: J.-F. Boulicaut, L. De Raedt, H. Mannila (Eds.), Constraint-Based Mining and Inductive Databases. X, 401 pages. 2006. (Sublibrary LNAI).

Vol. 3847: K.P. Jantke, A. Lunzer, N. Spyratos, Y. Tanaka (Eds.), Federation over the Web. X, 215 pages. 2006. (Sublibrary LNAI).

Vol. 3846: H. J. van den Herik, Y. Björnsson, N.S. Netanyahu (Eds.), Computers and Games. XIV, 333 pages. 2006.

Vol. 3845: J. Farré, I. Litovsky, S. Schmitz (Eds.), Implementation and Application of Automata. XIII, 360 pages. 2006.

Vol. 3844: J.-M. Bruel (Ed.), Satellite Events at the MoDELS 2005 Conference. XIII, 360 pages. 2006.

Vol. 3843: P. Healy, N.S. Nikolov (Eds.), Graph Drawing. XVII, 536 pages. 2006.

Vol. 3842: H.T. Shen, J. Li, M. Li, J. Ni, W. Wang (Eds.), Advanced Web and Network Technologies, and Applications. XXVII, 1057 pages. 2006.

Vol. 3841: X. Zhou, J. Li, H.T. Shen, M. Kitsuregawa, Y. Zhang (Eds.), Frontiers of WWW Research and Development - APWeb 2006. XXIV, 1223 pages. 2006.

Vol. 3840: M. Li, B. Boehm, L.J. Osterweil (Eds.), Unifying the Software Process Spectrum. XVI, 522 pages. 2006.

Vol. 3839: J.-C. Filliâtre, C. Paulin-Mohring, B. Werner (Eds.), Types for Proofs and Programs. VIII, 275 pages. 2006.

Vol. 3838: A. Middeldorp, V. van Oostrom, F. van Raamsdonk, R. de Vrijer (Eds.), Processes, Terms and Cycles: Steps on the Road to Infinity. XVIII, 639 pages. 2005.

Vol. 3837: K. Cho, P. Jacquet (Eds.), Technologies for Advanced Heterogeneous Networks. IX, 307 pages. 2005.

Vol. 3836: J.-M. Pierson (Ed.), Data Management in Grids. X, 143 pages. 2006.

Vol. 3835: G. Sutcliffe, A. Voronkov (Eds.), Logic for Programming, Artificial Intelligence, and Reasoning. XIV, 744 pages. 2005. (Sublibrary LNAI).

Vol. 3834: D.G. Feitelson, E. Frachtenberg, L. Rudolph, U. Schwiegelshohn (Eds.), Job Scheduling Strategies for Parallel Processing. VIII, 283 pages. 2005.

Vol. 3833: K.-J. Li, C. Vangenot (Eds.), Web and Wireless Geographical Information Systems. XI, 309 pages. 2005.

Vol. 3832: D. Zhang, A.K. Jain (Eds.), Advances in Biometrics. XX, 796 pages. 2005.

Vol. 3831: J. Wiedermann, G. Tel, J. Pokorný, M. Bieliková, J. Štuller (Eds.), SOFSEM 2006: Theory and Practice of Computer Science. XV, 576 pages. 2006.

Vol. 3830: D. Weyns, H. V.D. Parunak, F. Michel (Eds.), Environments for Multi-Agent Systems II. VIII, 291 pages. 2006. (Sublibrary LNAI).

Vol. 3829: P. Pettersson, W. Yi (Eds.), Formal Modeling and Analysis of Timed Systems. IX, 305 pages. 2005.

Vol. 3828: X. Deng, Y. Ye (Eds.), Internet and Network Economics. XVII, 1106 pages. 2005.

Vol. 3827: X. Deng, D.-Z. Du (Eds.), Algorithms and Computation. XX, 1190 pages. 2005.

Vol. 3826: B. Benatallah, F. Casati, P. Traverso (Eds.), Service-Oriented Computing - ICSOC 2005. XVIII, 597 pages. 2005.

Vol. 3824: L.T. Yang, M. Amamiya, Z. Liu, M. Guo, F.J. Rammig (Eds.), Embedded and Ubiquitous Computing – EUC 2005. XXIII, 1204 pages. 2005.

Vol. 3823: T. Enokido, L. Yan, B. Xiao, D. Kim, Y. Dai, L.T. Yang (Eds.), Embedded and Ubiquitous Computing – EUC 2005 Workshops. XXXII, 1317 pages. 2005.

Vol. 3822: D. Feng, D. Lin, M. Yung (Eds.), Information Security and Cryptology. XII, 420 pages. 2005.

Vol. 3821: R. Ramanujam, S. Sen (Eds.), FSTTCS 2005: Foundations of Software Technology and Theoretical Computer Science. XIV, 566 pages. 2005.

Vol. 3820: L.T. Yang, X.-s. Zhou, W. Zhao, Z. Wu, Y. Zhu, M. Lin (Eds.), Embedded Software and Systems. XXVIII, 779 pages. 2005.

Vol. 3819: P. Van Hentenryck (Ed.), Practical Aspects of Declarative Languages. X, 231 pages. 2005.

Vol. 3818: S. Grumbach, L. Sui, V. Vianu (Eds.), Advances in Computer Science – ASIAN 2005. XIII, 294 pages. 2005.

Vol. 3817: M. Faundez-Zanuy, L. Janer, A. Esposito, A. Satue-Villar, J. Roure, V. Espinosa-Duro (Eds.), Nonlinear Analyses and Algorithms for Speech Processing. XII, 380 pages. 2006. (Sublibrary LNAI).